The First World War
and
International Politics

The First World War
and
International Politics

David Stevenson

CLARENDON PRESS · OXFORD

This book has been printed digitally and produced in a standard design
in order to ensure its continuing availability

OXFORD
UNIVERSITY PRESS

Great Clarendon Street, Oxford OX2 6DP

Oxford University Press is a department of the University of Oxford.
It furthers the University's objective of excellence in research, scholarship,
and education by publishing worldwide in

Oxford New York

Athens Auckland Bangkok Bogotá Buenos Aires Cape Town
Chennai Dar es Salaam Delhi Florence Hong Kong Istanbul Karachi
Kolkata Kuala Lumpur Madrid Melbourne Mexico City Mumbai Nairobi
Paris São Paulo Shanghai Singapore Taipei Tokyo Toronto Warsaw
with associated companies in Berlin Ibadan

Oxford is a registered trade mark of Oxford University Press
in the UK and in certain other countries

Published in the United States
by Oxford University Press Inc., New York

© David Stephenson 1988

The moral rights of the author have been asserted
Database right Oxford University Press (maker)

Reprinted 2001

ISBN 0-19-820281-4

PREFACE

THE First World War was a disaster whose repercussions on the Western world continue to be felt. Without it the Tsarist Government in Russia might well have fallen anyway, but it is unlikely that Lenin and the Bolsheviks would have been the ultimate beneficiaries. Nor, without it, would the European inflation of the 1920s and the worldwide depression of the 1930s have been so severe. Without it, also, it is improbable that either Hitler or Mussolini would have come to office. As far as such things can be said with certainty, the First World War was an essential precondition for the Second.

But for the generation that experienced it, the war was first and foremost a colossal human tragedy. It claimed some eight million dead, and left many times that number of permanent physical and psychological scars. Yet this was a man-made catastrophe, not a natural one. The daily toll of slaughter and bereavement may appear remote from the world of statesmen and their advisers that fills the following pages; but the war took the course it did because of deliberate decisions. Its mainspring was political, and even this apparently most frustrating and intractable of conflicts conformed with Clausewitz's dictum that 'war . . . is a true political instrument, a continuation of political activity by other means'.[1]

The purpose of this book is simple. It is not a history of military operations, nor of the mobilization of economy and society in the belligerent States, nor an evocation of the effects of war on individual men and women. Rather, it seeks to explain why Governments decided to resort to violence in pursuit of their political objectives; why the conflict that resulted expanded from its European origins to become a global one; why it failed to be ended by compromise; and why the peace settlement that resulted took the form it did. My largest debt in such a work of synthesis has naturally been to other writers, and this, I trust, is acknowledged in the notes and *bibliography. But I have also* incurred other obligations, which it is a pleasure to take the opportunity to record. My thanks go to the staffs of the libraries and archives where I have

worked, and especially to those of the British Library of
Political and Economic Science, the Institute of Historical
Research, and the British Museum; to Mrs Karen Partridge,
for an excellent job of typing; to my former colleagues and
students at Downing College, Cambridge and to my present
ones in the Department of International History at the London
School of Economics and Political Science, on whom many of
the arguments that follow have been tried out in embryo; to
Mrs Sylvia Platt for the copy-editing; to Mrs Ann Hall, for
compiling the index; and to Mr Ivon Asquith and Mr Robert
Faber, who have been notably long-suffering editors at Oxford
University Press. To all of them my gratitude; responsibility
for the failings that remain here is naturally mine alone.

DAVID STEVENSON

London School of Economics and Political Science

PREFACE TO THE PAPERBACK EDITION

Opportunity has been taken of the appearance of the book in
paperback to correct some misprints in the hardback edition.
The text has not otherwise been changed. On economic war
aims, the reader is referred to the fundamental research of
G.-H. Soutou in his recently published *L'Or et le sang: les buts de
guerre économiques de la Première Guerre mondiale* (Paris, 1989).
Summaries and commentaries in English may be found in the
reviews of this book by D. Stevenson in *English Historical Review*
CV/417 (1990), 981–3 and by H.F.A. Strachan in *Historical
Journal* 33/3 (1990), 761–3.

DAVID STEVENSON

London School of Economics and Political Science
January 1991

CONTENTS

Note. Suggestions for further reading on the topics considered may be found in the notes. Russian dates have been given according to the Western European (Gregorian) calendar unless otherwise stated. For proper names in Chinese and in other foreign languages I have followed no consistent usage, and have adopted the spelling that seemed to me most familiar.

ABBREVIATIONS

ACFR	Advisory Council on Foreign Relations (Japan)
AHR	*American Historical Review*
AJPH	*Australian Journal of Politics and History*
ANI	Italian Nationalist Association
BJIS	*British Journal of International Studies*
CEH	*Central European History*
CGT	General Confederation of Labour (France)
CHD	Council of the Heads of Delegations (Peace Conference)
CJH	*Canadian Journal of History*
CNC	Czechoslovak National Council
CUP	Committee of Union and Progress (Turkey)
DDP	German Democratic Party
DH	*Diplomatic History*
EEQ	*East European Quarterly*
EHQ	*European History Quarterly*
EHR	*English Historical Review*
FRUS	*Papers Relating to the Foreign Relations of the United States* (see Bibliography)
GWU	*Geschichte in Wissenschaft und Unterricht*
H	*History*
HJ	*Historical Journal*
HLRO	House of Lords Record Office, London
IHR	*International History Review*
IRSH	*International Review of Social History*
ISB	International Socialist Bureau
JAH	*Journal of American History*
JAfr.H	*Journal of African History*
JAS	*Journal of American Studies*
JCEA	*Journal of Central European Affairs*
JCH	*Journal of Contemporary History*
JMH	*Journal of Modern History*
LG Papers	Lloyd George Papers, HLRO
MES	*Middle Eastern Studies*
MVHR	*Mississippi Valley Historical Review*
OHL	German Army High Command

PAH	*Proceedings in American History*
PAPS	*Proceedings of the American Philosophical Society*
P&P	*Past and Present*
PHR	*Pacific Historical Review*
PRO	Public Record Office, London
PSI	Italian Socialist Party
PSQ	*Political Science Quarterly*
RHMC	*Revue d'histoire moderne et contemporaine*
RIS	*Review of International Studies*
S&G	Scherer, A., and Grünewald, J. (eds.), *L'Allemagne et les problèmes de la paix pendant la Première Guerre Mondiale* (4 vols., Paris, 1966–78)
SFIO	French Socialist Party
Sl. EER	*Slavonic and East European Review*
SPD	German Social Democratic Party
SR	*Slavic Review*
SS	*Soviet Studies*
TAPS	*Transactions of the American Philosophical Society*
USPD	German Independent Social Democratic Party

LIST OF MAPS

Introduction

THE war of 1914–18 was the first general war, involving all the Great Powers of the day, to be fought out in the modern, industrialized world. It came at a moment of mounting cultural, economic, and political instability in the Western countries: an instability it dramatically increased. The inter-war years, in consequence, were a period of extreme disorder in international economic and political relations, as well as in the domestic histories of the leading States. Only in the 1950s did a new equilibrium emerge, later in its turn to come under strain. By contrast, the century that followed the Vienna peace settlement of 1814–15 was interrupted by a series of short and limited wars between 1854 and 1878, but witnessed two periods of nearly forty years of European peace. The absence of war never meant the absence of tension, and, as after 1945, there were moments, such as the middle 1880s, of a heightened sense of danger and acceleration in the arms race. Until the growing turbulence that set in after approximately 1905, however, these periodic upward fluctuations eventually subsided, and for the established Powers of the northern hemisphere the posthumous reputation of the later nineteenth century as a golden twilight of prosperity and peace was generally well deserved.

This had been achieved within an international political system that was subject only to a minimum of concerted management by the Powers. As ever, in the absence of a single preponderant State—or a supranational organization with independent coercive authority—sovereignty rested with individual Governments, varyingly endowed with the capacity for using force in furtherance of their ends. No Government controlled the actions of all the others, or could be sure of their intentions. All Governments, in consequence, lived in an environment of suspicion, insecurity, and danger, in which national foreign and defence policies were the inadequate

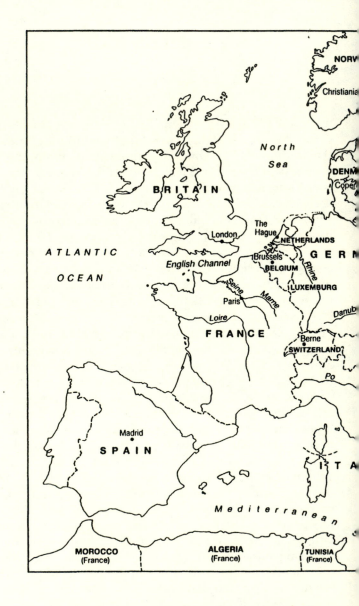

Map 1. Europe in 1914

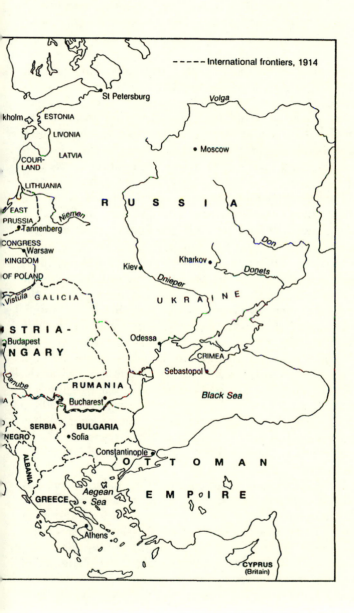

----- International frontiers, 1914

St Petersburg

Volga

kholm

ESTONIA

LIVONIA

LATVIA

COUR-
LAND

LITHUANIA

EAST
PRUSSIA

Niemen

Tannenberg

CONGRESS
Warsaw

KINGDOM

OF POLAND

Vistula GALICIA

STRIA-

NGARY

Budapest

Danube

A

RUMANIA

Bucharest

SERBIA BULGARIA

NEGRO

Sofia

ALBANIA

Constantinople

GREECE

Aegean
Sea

Athens

R U S S I A

Moscow

Kharkov

Kiev

Dnieper

Don

Donets

U K R A I N E

Odessa

CRIMEA

Sebastopol

Black Sea

O T T O M A N

E M P I R E

CYPRUS
(Britain)

means available to establish order, predictability, and safety. The principal nineteenth-century peacekeeping instrument, the Concert of Europe, did little to soften the harshness of these conditions.

The Concert had no permanent machinery, no founding document (unless Article IV of the 1815 Quadruple Alliance Treaty be so considered), no ringing declaration of principles. It consisted rather of a habit of mind, a willingness by the European Great Powers to discuss matters of common concern in *ad hoc* conferences of their Ambassadors in one or other capital, or (normally only after a war) in congresses of their Heads of Government and Foreign Ministers. The emergent flanking Powers of Japan and the United States were not habitual members of the system. The Concert could coerce small States, such as Montenegro in the Scutari crisis of 1913. When it addressed the interests of a Great Power, it might break up in disagreement, as over Schleswig-Holstein in 1864, or register a *fait accompli*, as did the London Conference on the Turkish Straits in 1871. If it antagonized a Power, as the Algeçiras Conference did Germany in 1906, that Power might avoid resorting to it again. Nor were Powers obliged so to resort. The stormy decade of the 1860s was littered with abortive conference proposals; and in the years before the First World War the system was again in decay. After Algeçiras the London Conference on the Balkans in 1912–13 was the last before hostilities broke out. In the Bosnia dispute of 1908–9 Germany and Austria-Hungary refused a conference, and they refused again in July 1914. In short, the Concert could be effective only when other considerations were already impelling the Powers towards restraint.[1]

Other forms of international co-operation failed to remedy the Concert's deficiencies. Between 1815 and 1914 over 450 private international organizations were founded, and over thirty inter-Governmental ones. But the latter dealt with technical questions, notably transport and communications, rather than political issues. Similarly, the Paris Congress of 1856 and the Hague Peace Conferences of 1899 and 1907 established a body of agreed restraints on the conduct of land and naval warfare, but made little effort to circumscribe the prior right of initiating hostilities. By 1914 peace societies, generally supported by the socialist and labour movements, were long-established in the Anglo-Saxon countries and much of continental Europe. But their efforts, which were concentrated on promoting arbitration, had also made little inroad on national sovereignty. Of the nearly 200 arbitration treaties in force by 1914, nearly all made reservations for matters affecting national interest and honour. The participants in the First Hague Peace Conference agreed to have recourse in serious disputes to mediation by friendly Powers 'as far as circumstances allow', and considered it their 'duty' to remind each other of the newly created Court of Arbitration machinery if such disputes threatened. But in practice, the Powers resorted to arbitration, as to the older mechanism of the Concert, only when it suited them for other reasons.[2]

International peace, therefore, continued to depend on the inducements at the national level for Governments to go to war being outweighed by the deterrents to such a course. This in turn depended heavily on the ambiguous operation of the balance of power. By the end of the eighteenth century there had emerged five States which (with the marginal addition of Italy in 1861 and the conversion of Prussia into Germany) remained the European Great Powers in 1914. Between them there applied conditions that had hitherto existed only in the much narrower confines of Renaissance Italy or Classical Greece. None had the potential for hegemony enjoyed by the Soviet Union after 1945. All, in consequence, were concerned by gains or losses in the strength of any one. And all were engaged in constant communication with and surveillance of each other through their diplomatic and intelligence services. By 1914 this European power balance was in transition to becoming global. Most of the independent States of Africa and Asia had been eliminated through the extension of European colonial rule into the underdeveloped world. Others—Persia, the Ottoman Empire, China—remained nominally sovereign, but were divided into unofficial spheres of influence. Even Japan, through its proximity to Russia and its 1902 alliance with Britain, was being drawn into the ceaseless competition and realignment of the European Powers. Only the United States and Latin America could still observe the manoeuvrings in the Old World with comparative indifference.

In theory, the balance of power might operate to inhibit war. Indeed, there seemed a parallel between the free pursuit of national interest in the diplomatic sphere and that of individual interest in the economic.[3] Both, paradoxically, could serve the maximum collective gain. If a State was growing too strong, others would combine to stop it from using piecemeal and localized wars as a ladder to hegemony. In such circumstances, resort to force might cease to be a rational act at all. Bismarck, after his localized victories over Austria in 1866 and France in 1870, had been threatened in the 1875 'War in Sight' crisis with British and Russian opposition to further conquests at French expense. At the 1878 Congress of Berlin Russia had been forced to relinquish much of the enhanced influence in the Balkans that it had hoped to gain from its victory in the war of 1877–8 with Turkey. Both these reassertions of the balance had been attained without hostilities. But the process might be far more destructive. Rather than encouraging peaceful mutual deterrence, a balance of power might lead *both* sides to favour their chances in a trial of strength, and indefinitely prolong such a trial once it had begun. In the 1870s and 1880s European peace rested not on a balance but on a complex system of alignments that eventually bound all the Powers, except for France, directly or indirectly to Bismarck's Germany. Between 1891 and 1907, however, this was replaced by an unstable bipolarity between opposing coalitions. In these circumstances, far from being the agent of the general good, the balance of power might be the engine of catastrophe.

In many ways—the identity of the Great Powers, the weakness of supranational restrictions on their sovereignty—the international system had altered little since 1815. In others it had changed profoundly. By the early twentieth century Britain had lost its former manufacturing, naval, and colonial monopoly, and the modern pattern had emerged of a world divided between a metropolis of rival industrial nations and a periphery of impoverished food and raw-material suppliers. The prosperity of the leading Powers had become unprecedentedly interdependent, and for some their imports of commodities had become essential to national survival. International trade may have risen in value from one-thirtieth to one-third of world production between 1800 and 1913. Trade dependence was greatest in Europe, which, including Russia, accounted for perhaps 65 per cent of all world imports and 59 per cent of all exports by the latter date. Britain imported two-thirds of the calorific value of its food. Almost equally striking evidence of interdependence was the growth of foreign investment, which rose perhaps elevenfold between 1855 and 1900, and doubled again by 1914.[4] But the international economic system, like the political one, exhibited a minimum of co-operation and concerted management, and indeed of State interference of any kind. Tariffs had risen since the 1870s, but by comparison with the inter-war years were modest, and there were few non-tariff barriers to trade. Controls on the movement of capital and labour across frontiers were still rare. And since the 1890s the leading currencies had become fixed in price and convertible in relation to each other through the general adoption of the gold standard.

This Eden could persist only while disruptive forces in the international economy remained small. The international gold standard, like other fixed-parity regimes, could function smoothly only while relatively gentle balance-of-payments adjustments were required. Its harmonious operation depended heavily on Britain's traditional pre-eminence as a trading nation and overseas lender, and this was fading. And with the growth of political tension in the pre-war decade, the continental European central banks further undermined the system by stockpiling strategic gold reserves.[5] The informal arrangements that regulated the world economy were increasingly vulnerable even before the outbreak of a life-and-death political struggle between the Powers. Nor did either growing interdependence or the open international economic system inhibit such a struggle from taking place. One of the publishing successes of the pre-war years, Norman Angell's *The Great Illusion*, argued, indeed, that trading and financial interdependence had made wars irrational if the material losses were balanced against the likely gains. But the British Admiralty, for example, seems to have been impressed more strongly by the evidence that the economic disruption caused by war would hurt Germany more than Britain.[6] And the operational planners in the German General Staff considered not that war should be abandoned as an instrument of policy, but that it was now more imperative than ever to decide it by immediate, overwhelming blows.[7] If war once began, moreover, and the open world economy fragmented, the rich and vulnerable European border regions such as the Upper Silesian coalfield and the iron-ore basin of Lorraine were likely to become the prizes in a scramble to establish autarkic economic zones.

No more than the balance of power, then, did the rise of the international economy necessarily guarantee peace. Nor did democratization. The nineteenth century was an era of expanding cities, in which millions of urban dwellers for the first time raised themselves above bare subsistence and, increasingly, became literate. In this society the cruder methods of coercion traditionally employed in peasant Europe were less appropriate. Governments responded in part through more subtle methods of repression and of managing opinion; in part through conceding a wider franchise, civil liberties, and greater parliamentary control over the executive agencies of State. Among the Great Powers in 1914, however, the legislative assemblies in Germany, Austria-Hungary, Russia, and Japan still lacked the authority to remove Ministers with whose policies they disagreed. In Britain, France, the USA and, for practical purposes, Italy, democratic control over the executive had been established, but even here official accountability was weakest over defence and foreign affairs. On balance, anyway, public and parliamentary influence was often aggressive. In most Great Powers the appeal of the peace movement and the liberal and socialist Left was at least equalled by that of patriotic pressure groups and the conservative Right. Before 1848 many European rulers had feared that war—or, at least, defeat in war—would unleash revolution at home. But the limited conflicts of the mid-nineteenth century suggested that success abroad could consolidate governmental authority. Despite the experience of the Russian Empire after its defeat by Japan in 1904–5, war was not excluded for the leaders of the Great Powers in 1914 by fears for domestic political stability.

In the middle decades of the nineteenth century industrialization had ushered in a military revolution. The machine gun and the breech-loading rifle replaced the muzzle-loading musket; and the cannon gave way to breech-loading, steel-barrelled artillery delivering high-explosive shells. At sea, the new guns were installed on steam-driven, steel-hulled battleships. But this was only the beginning of continuous and rapid further evolution in both land and naval technology. And armaments could now be mass-produced at a moment when railways allowed the Powers to deploy far larger armies than before and the electric telegraph alleviated problems of command and control. After Bismarck's victories in 1866 and 1870 the continental European Powers and the Japanese moved towards the Prussian system of universal liability to military service and its combination of a short-service standing army with a trained reserve that could be rapidly mobilized if the need arose. They similarly followed the model of a specially selected and trained General Staff engaged in continuous war planning and intelligence surveillance of potential enemies. Britain and the United States also adopted General Staffs, if not conscription, after the turn of the century.[8]

Bismarck's victories suggested that the devastating power of the new technology, so far from making war unmanageable, had lent it new effectiveness as an instrument of policy. But there was a twofold price to pay. A future European war would be fought with mass conscript armies and would open with complex mobilizations that could be disrupted by strategically placed groups of workers. The task of maintaining not simply cowed acquiescence in but positive consensus in support of Government policy acquired additional urgency. And the General Staffs, with their independent sources of intelligence and their need to make political assumptions in their planning, endangered civilian control over foreign affairs. In Germany, above all, after 1883 the Chief of the General Staff had the right of direct access to the Emperor independent of the civil Government, and liaison between military requirements and diplomacy depended on the ruler's uncertain abilities.[9] This was symptomatic of a more general increase in the complexity of decision-making as Governments grew larger, more professional, and more elaborately subdivided. Within the Foreign Ministries themselves, where the dispatches handled annually by the British Foreign Office, for example, rose from

6,000 to 111,000 between 1821 and 1905, the vast increase in business required increasing delegation from Ministers to their professional advisers.[10] Both the proliferation of agencies concerned with foreign policy and the more intricate internal structure of those agencies caused the responsibility for decision to be diffused.

Given that none of the Governments of the Powers were unconditionally pacifist, war in certain circumstances might appear to all of them a rational act. Yet in reality such rationality could be absent from compromise, collective decisions, which did not necessarily represent either the interests of the Government as a whole or those of the governed. And in an international system whose inherent tendencies to anarchy had been little bridled by the nineteenth-century developments in co-operation, individual Governments could pursue policies of apparent rationality that were fatal to the interests of the community of States as a whole.[11] The developments of the later nineteenth century—economic interdependence, democratization, the military revolution, the global extension of the balance of power—might none the less have strengthened the deterrents to a resort to force. In practice, none did so unambiguously, and after 1900 their effectiveness as inhibitions was in decline. The eclipse of the Concert of Europe was both cause and symptom of a general increase in insecurity to which alliances, strategic planning, and ultimately the war aims discussed in the following chapters were all attempts to respond. Once the brink of hostilities had been crossed, however, the same new forces of economic growth, democratization, and global interdependence magnified the scale of the disaster. It is the passage of that brink that the first chapter will examine.

1

The Outbreak of the Conflict

JULY–AUGUST 1914

(i) *The Balkan Precipitant*

In the gentlemanly statecraft of 1914, the resort to force was still preceded by a declaration of war.[1] Among the avalanche of declarations between 28 July and 12 August four stand out. That of Austria-Hungary on Serbia on 28 July initiated a local, Balkan conflict; those of Germany on France and Russia on 1 and 3 August a continental European one; and that of Britain on Germany on 4 August brought into the European balance the resources of a global Power. At stake in both the Balkan and the European conflicts was whether Austria-Hungary's internal divisions and external isolation would allow it to survive. And ostensibly Vienna gave the impetus to local war. On 28 June the heir to the Austrian throne, Franz Ferdinand, was assassinated with his wife at Sarajevo, the capital of the Habsburg province of Bosnia. On 23 July an Austro-Hungarian ultimatum accused the neighbouring kingdom of Serbia of having sheltered organizations aiming to deprive the Habsburg Monarchy of territory (and of Bosnia in particular) by terrorism and subversion. Serbian officials, it alleged, had helped the Sarajevo conspirators cross the frontier, and had provided them with weapons. The subversive organizations must be suppressed, and the conniving officials punished. Two days later a Serbian reply accepted almost all the Austrian demands. But for Habsburg representatives to participate in a judicial inquiry into those implicated in the conspiracy, it protested, would violate the Serbian constitution and criminal law. Nominally on this ground Austria-Hungary declared war on 28 July, and on the following day bombarded the Serbian capital, Belgrade.

Gavrilo Princip and the other assassins, although themselves Habsburg subjects, had indeed formulated their plans in

Serbia. A major in the Serbian army, Tankosić, had supplied their bombs and pistols and arranged the border crossing. Tankosić belonged to the Black Hand, a secret organization aiming to unify all Serbs, including those in Bosnia, and headed by the chief of Serbian military intelligence, Apis. But the Serbian Prime Minister, Pašić, was a political opponent of Apis and the Black Hand, and when he learned armed men had crossed the frontier he sent a veiled warning to the Austrians via his Minister in Vienna, which apparently failed to register. The Central Committee of the Black Hand itself sent a message, perhaps later rescinded, to hold the conspirators back. But Princip and most of his associates were not members of the organization, and they continued to act independently of it when it came to the test. It seems, therefore, that neither the Serbian Government nor the High Command was directly responsible for the assassination, and that neither intended to provoke war.[2] In Vienna, this was of small concern. On 7 July the Austro-Hungarian Joint Council of Ministers agreed, with one dissentient, that 'such stringent demands must be addressed to Serbia, that will make a refusal almost certain, so that the road to a radical solution by means of a military action should be opened'.[3] The ultimatum was merely a pretext for employing force. This was because the Sarajevo tragedy arose from the Monarchy's crisis of authority in Bosnia, and this crisis seemed a microcosm of the Habsburg predicament as a whole.

Austria-Hungary had administered Bosnia since 1878, and annexed it, causing a prolonged international crisis, in 1908. After the annexation a loosely organized group of secret societies, the Young Bosnians, turned to assassination as a means of touching off a revolutionary movement that would attain their goal of an independent federation uniting the South Slavs. From this milieu the Sarajevo conspirators came. But Bosnian unrest was only one, particularly sanguinary, manifestation of Austria-Hungary's central political problem. Few nineteenth-century developments seemed more inexorable than the advance of the Eastern European nationalities towards unity and independence at the Habsburg and Ottoman Empires' expense. And, unlike Germany or Russia, Austria-Hungary lacked a core or dominant nationality that could still provide a basis for Great-Power status even if the periphery were lost. Since 1867 the Monarchy had been divided constitutionally between the Kingdom of Hungary and the fringe of northern and western territories known usually (if strictly inaccurately) as 'Austria'. Neither the Magyars in Hungary nor the Germans in Austria comprised a numerical majority. But in Hungary the parliamentary franchise, outside the province of Croatia, included only 6.5 per cent of the population, and the special constitutional privileges of the Magyar-dominated Government in Budapest debarred the Vienna authorities from attempting to reduce the hostility of the Monarchy's neighbours by improving the treatment of the Hungarian South Slavs and Rumanians. Within the Austrian territories the Vienna Parliament, or Reichsrat, was elected by manhood suffrage, but the national rivalries within it obstructed any stable majority and in July 1914 it was in suspension and administration was being conducted by emergency decree. All of this made it natural for the Monarchy's leaders to construct a domino theory of its politics, and to fear the South Slav problem would culminate in an even worse catastrophe than the loss in 1859–66 of its territories in Italy and its privileged position in Germany.[4]

But only small minorities within Austria-Hungary desired complete national independence and the Monarchy's dissolution. The civil service and the polyglot Habsburg army remained loyal. Not internal problems but external ones made the South Slav problem seem insuperable without recourse to war. As the result of a long succession of foreign-policy reverses, Austria-Hungary by 1914 faced both an emerging irredentist coalition among its neighbours and near-total isolation among the Great Powers. Between 1885 and 1895 Serbia had been the Monarchy's ally, bound to negotiate no treaty without its prior agreement, and dependent on it for 80 to 90 per cent of its export earnings. This favourable position crumbled after a 1903 *coup d'état* brought the Karageorgević dynasty to the Serbian throne. In 1904 Serbia placed a large munitions contract not with the Austrian firm of Skoda but with its French rival, Schneider-Creusot; the Austrians retaliated in 1906 by closing their frontier to Serbian goods. But in the ensuing 'pig war' the Serbs successfully diversified away from

Austria-Hungary as a market for their livestock, only to be forced to acquiesce under the threat of invasion in the annexation of Bosnia and Herzegovina in the crisis of 1908–9.

It was therefore an antagonized and economically and politically independent Serbia that in 1912–13 doubled its territory and population at the expense of Turkey and Bulgaria in the First and Second Balkan Wars. The Ottoman Empire, hitherto a southern counterbalance to the Balkan States, was expelled almost completely from Europe. Bulgaria, which had no irredentist claims on Habsburg territory, was defeated in 1913 by Serbia and Rumania, both of which potentially did. Although Rumania had secretly been allied to Germany and Austria-Hungary since 1883, public opinion in Bucharest was increasingly preoccupied with discrimination against the Rumanian inhabitants of Hungary, where discussions between local representatives and the Budapest Government broke down in February 1914.[5] The Rumanians were also visibly improving relations with the Russian Tsar, who visited Constantza in June. And in the same spring Serbia and its neighbour, Montenegro, agreed to negotiate a union.

Even more threatening than the nascent coalition of Serbia, Montenegro, and Rumania, was Austria-Hungary's broader European isolation. This arose partly from the revival of an old antagonism with Italy, another nominal ally whose relations with the Habsburgs were clouded by the question of the Italians under Austrian rule and by rivalry for influence in the Adriatic. But the greatest danger to the Monarchy lay in its competition in the Balkans with St Petersburg.[6] A period of Austro-Russian coexistence had been inaugurated by an 1897 agreement to freeze the Balkan status quo, but this was already breaking down by the time of the Bosnian crisis. In March 1909 Russia participated in a joint note from the Powers to Serbia, requiring Belgrade to recognize the Bosnian annexation without receiving any compensation. The Tsar was threatened with the alternative of a German-supported Austrian invasion of Serbia that his armies were in no condition to challenge. Relations between Vienna and St Petersburg never resumed their former cordiality, and after 1909 Russian diplomats in the Balkans attempted to construct a grouping of the independent States that would counteract Austrian influence.[7] Although the

Balkan League, which fought the First Balkan War in 1912, proved to be anti-Turkish rather than anti-Habsburg, the Austrians had cause to fear that another such league, with Russian backing, might be formed against themselves.[8]

Austria-Hungary was also isolated because of more general European divisions. Its defensive alliance with Berlin, dating from 1879, could not be relied on to assure German diplomatic support. And Russia's alliance with France in 1891-4 and its entente with Britain in 1907 made it harder to balance off the Tsar against the Western European capitals. The 'Central Powers' (as Germany and Austria-Hungary were already known) lost confidence in a Concert-of-Europe machinery that apparently contained an inbuilt majority against them. At the London Conference of 1912-13 Britain and Germany temporarily co-operated in localizing the First Balkan War, but the Austrians so resented this that after the summer of 1913 the Germans felt obliged to give priority to reassuring Vienna of their support.[9] The Austro-Hungarian Foreign Minister, Berchtold, came to office in 1912 with a preference for the Concert over unilateral methods, but grew exasperated with its frustrations and delays. Ultimata sent to Serbia and Greece in October 1913 and March 1914, requiring them to evacuate the newly-formed State of Albania, and dispatched without consulting the potentially unsympathetic Powers, proved a speedier and more successful method of achieving Austrian goals. By the autumn of 1913 Berchtold believed that diplomatic victories over Serbia had gained little, that reconciliation was impossible, and that only war could resolve the conflict with Belgrade to Austria's satisfaction.[10]

By the time that Princip fired his bullets, then, the rulers of the Habsburg Monarchy were persuaded that they faced the imminent creation of an irredentist coalition on their Balkan frontiers, which they could not appease by domestic reform in Hungary, which might attack them as Turkey had been attacked, and which would enjoy support from Russia and probably at least tolerance from Britain, Italy, and France. Peaceful methods of fending off this coalition—through the Concert of Europe, economic influence, or diplomatic exploitation of Balkan rivalries—had failed. Against this background, the assassination not only excited pain and outrage but also removed a man—Franz Ferdinand—who had generally urged restraint during the crises of the Balkan Wars and whom many of the Monarchy's leaders saw as the last chance of peaceful internal reform.[11] And Sarajevo, with the odium that it brought on Serbia, was seen immediately as a suitable pretext for preventive war.

Whether the pretext would be seized on depended on the signals transmitted to Vienna from Berlin. Among the Emperor Franz Josef's advisers, Conrad von Hötzendorff, the Chief of the General Staff, had for many years advocated war with Serbia and did so again now. So did most of the Foreign Ministry officials. But the Hungarian Prime Minister, Tisza, a forceful personality with a constitutional right to consultation over foreign policy, insisted that war would lead to Russian intervention, and be a 'fateful error'. Berchtold and the Emperor themselves wished to act, but only after ascertaining Germany's attitude. This balance of forces was reflected in the mission of Count Hoyos to Berlin on 5 July. Hoyos, Berchtold's *Chef de Cabinet* at the Foreign Ministry and himself a hawk, brought a letter from Franz Josef and a memorandum from Berchtold. Both documents strongly hinted at but did not explicitly advocate using force.[12]

Hoyos's mission elicited the German 'blank cheque' that tipped the balance in Vienna. On the afternoon of 5 July the German Emperor, Wilhelm II, advised the Austrian Ambassador to 'march into Serbia', and that if war with Russia followed Vienna could count on Germany's support. On the following day the German Chancellor, Bethmann Hollweg, urged 'immediate action' against Serbia, and promised German backing for whatever was decided.[13] The Austro-Hungarian Joint Council of Ministers, except for Tisza, now decided to impose demands that it intended to be refused. Tisza was won round in the following week, probably because the alliance might be endangered if the Monarchy hesitated after receiving such emphatic assurances. It was agreed, however, because of his concern to mollify the Russians and to avoid incorporating more South Slavs in Hungary, to confine Habsburg territorial demands on Serbia to small frontier rectifications. Serbia would instead be weakened indirectly, through annexations by its Balkan neighbours.[14] The Austro-Hungarian leaders were now committed to a local victory that would shore up their domestic authority and dismember a small but provocative rival. The larger dangers of Russian intervention and escalation into European war received, except from Tisza, negligible thought.[15]

(ii) *Continental Escalation*

From this point on the Germans used their influence in Vienna to hasten delivery first of the ultimatum and then of the declaration of war, and to undermine attempts at mediation.[16] From 5–6 to at least 28 July German policy was unambiguously in favour of a local, Balkan war. And between 31 July and 3 August Germany initiated a continental war against Russia and France. On 30 July Tsar Nicholas II ordered his armies to be mobilized against the two Central Powers: a step he understood was grave but that was still distinct from opening hostilities. On the 31st the Berlin Government required Russia to cease mobilizing within twelve hours; as this was disregarded, it declared war on the following day. If Russia ventured to the brink, Germany crossed it. And France had not yet mobilized when on 31 July it was given eighteen hours to promise its neutrality in a Russo-German conflict. It it did so promise, the German Ambassador in Paris had been instructed to demand the occupation of two border fortresses for the duration of hostilities. But on 1 August the French Prime Minister replied that in the event of such hostilities 'France would act in accordance with her interests',[17] and two days later, fabricating allegations that French troops had crossed its borders and French aircraft had bombed its soil, Germany declared war. Russia's general mobilization and France's refusal to repudiate its alliance with the Tsar served as the occasions for a Balkan conflagration to become a European one.

There is little evidence that the exigencies of maintaining domestic authority dictated the German Government's decisions. The leading theme of internal German politics was the effort by successive Chancellors to win approval for legislation and direct taxes from the elected lower House of the Imperial Parliament, the Reichstag, while maintaining the principle that Governments were chosen by the Emperor. Since the 1912 elections the largest Reichstag party (though not with a majority) were the Socialists, or SPD, whose programme included constitutional democratization. But the SPD's success if anything made Bethmann Hollweg's task of parliamentary management easier, by reducing his dependence on the xenophobic and vociferously critical right-wing parties in the Reichstag.[18] And so far from seeing in war an antidote to socialism, Bethmann remarked privately in June 1914 that it would be 'bound to benefit the SPD, just because it was the party of peace. The power it stood to gain might even suffice to topple a few thrones.'[19]

The influence of domestic politics on German decision-making in July was strong, but exercised at one remove. A tradition of pursuing foreign successes in order to alleviate domestic difficulties bore much of the responsibility for the Empire's external predicament in 1914. Victorious wars had helped Bismarck overcome domestic opposition to his goal of unifying Germany on terms that would preserve the Prussian Monarchy's authority. His successors had launched a naval building programme against Britain in 1897–8 and challenged France in the second Moroccan crisis of 1911 in the hope of consolidating domestic support for the imperial regime. Both decisions had exacerbated Germany's main external problem. This, like Austria-Hungary's, was diplomatic isolation, but in the European rather than the Balkan arena, and its dangers were intensified by an accelerating arms race.

For most of the nineteenth century, France, rather than Germany, had been most liable to encirclement among the Powers. To the first fixed point of continental tension—the smouldering Austro-Russian conflict in the Balkans—the war of 1870 had added a second, between France and Germany in the west. Franco-German animosity was fuelled by the dispute over the annexed French provinces of Alsace-Lorraine and by periodic crises, most notably in 1875 and 1887. But Bismarck's system of alliances—with Austria-Hungary in 1879, with Austria-Hungary and Russia in the Three Emperors' League of 1881, with Austria-Hungary and Italy in the Triple Alliance of 1882, and with Russia again in the Reinsurance Treaty of 1887—had deprived France of a Great-Power partner and given the newly founded German Empire ·the most complete external security it had known. The first breach in the system was the Franco-Russian defensive alliance and military convention of 1891–4. For France, this was a precaution against renewed German attack; and the Russians also were sufficiently suspicious of Berlin to wish to deter such action. Economic conflicts and nationalist public opinion were beginning to undermine the old conservative solidarity between the Romanov and Hohenzollern dynasties. But at this stage Russo-German disagreement at official level remained largely indirect, arising from resentment in St Petersburg at what was deemed to be German support of Austria-Hungary in the Balkan crises of 1875–8 and 1885–7.[20] The danger to the Germans was further diminished by the prominence of African and Far Eastern questions in international politics from 1890 to 1905. During these years the most dangerous confrontations were not between the Austro-German and Franco-Russian alliances, but set France, Germany, and Russia individually against Britain. Only in 1904–7 did there emerge a more inflexible pattern of alignments in which Germany, rather than France or Britain, was exposed.

Germany's underlying industrial and demographic growth was part of the reason for this development. But in addition Bismarck before his fall in 1890 had believed—and to some extent convinced his neighbours—that Germany was a satiated State, preferring to hold securely its existing gains rather than to risk upheaval by pursuing more. After 1897 German policy was in the hands of men—Bülow as Foreign Minister and later Chancellor, Tirpitz as Navy Minister, and the Kaiser himself—for whom the status quo did not suffice. Ostentatious claims to influence in China, Africa, and the Ottoman Empire were one result. So was the construction of a navy designed for diplomatic leverage and possible eventual force against the British. So, finally, were attempts to realign the Powers. An unprecedented opportunity for this latter appeared to be presented by Russia's defeat at Japanese hands in 1904–5 and the ensuing revolution, which temporarily nullified the Tsar's military power. This was the gravest disruption of the

European equilibrium since 1870. It marked the onset of a time of turbulence in international politics that was not to be assuaged for twenty, even fifty, years. Bülow's Government tried to profit from it by negotiating an alliance with the Russians.[21] In the spring of 1905 it also challenged France's efforts to establish hegemony in Morocco, and obliged the French to accept an international conference. But neither blandishments in the east nor pressure in the west achieved what had been hoped for. By 1907 the Franco-Russian alliance had emerged intact, and had been supplemented by ententes between each of its members and Britain.

Britain's April 1904 colonial agreement—the Entente Cordiale—with France began as one of several measures taken to eliminate points of friction along the frontiers of the British Empire. It contained a pledge of 'diplomatic support' for France's aspirations in Morocco, but British backing for France in the 1905–6 Moroccan crisis had deeper foundations than this. Commercial rivalry, disputes in southern Africa, and Tirpitz's naval programme had gradually persuaded British politicians and officials that Germany was a dangerous, bullying force. The Moroccan war scare suggested that it also menaced Britain's traditional objective of preventing any one continental State from dominating Western Europe. Under Sir Edward Grey, Foreign Secretary after December 1905, the Entente evolved into a habit of diplomatic co-operation, supported by military and later by naval conversations. In this way the French were encouraged to maintain their independence of Germany without Britain's being committed to their defence. And the 1907 entente with Russia—demarcating spheres of influence in Central Asia—was intended from the start to help contain Germany in Europe as well as to relieve the British of what they feared would be the impossible task of securing India militarily against Russian invasion.[22] A third, Anglo-German, antagonism now joined the older Austro-Russian and Franco-German ones. Finally, the unreliability of Italy (which had secretly agreed with France in 1902 to remain neutral even in the event of a 'provoked' French attack on the Triple Alliance) completed Germany's and Austria-Hungary's isolation.

Between 1904 and 1907 there emerged a pattern of European alignments that would survive until 1917. There resulted the

first of the two great upward movements on the fever chart of
international tension before the First World War. The second
came in and after 1911, as the consequence of a chain of
Mediterranean upheavals touched off by the second Moroccan,
or Agadir, crisis in that year. Italy's conquest of Libya and the
Aegean islands from Turkey in 1911-12 led on to the Balkan
Wars, and these were followed by the Russo-German Liman
von Sanders crisis in the winter of 1913-14. With the demise of
the Ottoman and Habsburg Empires possibly drawing near, all
the continental Powers turned to the time-honoured methods of
assuring their security by strengthening their alliances and
their military might. On the diplomatic plane, German efforts
to split the French-Russian-British grouping confronted the
determination of the Entente Powers to remain aligned.
Bethmann Hollweg became Chancellor in 1909 with, according to his private secretary, Riezler, 'to split up the coalition
directed against us' as his primary foreign aim.[23] In negotiations with London in 1909-12 he attempted to exchange a
limitation on the two sides' navies for a British commitment to
neutrality in a continental war. Neither materialized, and the
Anglo-German détente that emerged in 1912-14 rested on
lesser agreements: over the British and German shares in a
hypothetical partition of the Portuguese colonies, and the
demarcation of economic interests in the Ottoman Empire. In
the winter of 1912-13 the two Governments co-operated at the
London Conference on the Balkans, but by 1914 both were
again concerting their Balkan policies with the other members
of their respective diplomatic alignments.[24]

Bethmann's 1910-12 détente with Russia had already
broken down. By 1914 a deep-seated Russo-German antagonism was coming into being, feeding not only on Germany's
intermittent support for Austria-Hungary in the Balkans but
also on its growing economic presence and political influence in
Turkey. The Turkish Straits had become a zone of Russian
vital interest, through which grain exports were shipped in payment for the machinery imported in the reverse direction for
the developing industries of the Ukraine. As long as Russia was
too weak to seize the Straits itself, its policy was to uphold
Turkey's independence from rival Powers. The crisis caused
by the appointment in November 1913 of the German General
Liman von Sanders to command the first Ottoman Army Corps

in Constantinople ended in a compromise, but reinforced Russian fears that this policy was under challenge.[25]

In spite of Bethmann's efforts, the European power group-ings were becoming more cohesive in the pre-war years. Poincaré, who as Prime Minister and then as President of the Republic was the moving spirit behind French foreign policy in 1912–14, opposed the 'interpenetration' of the two alignments, and tightened the bonds with London and St Petersburg. Britain and France approved contingency plans for co-operation in a war on land (1911) and at sea (1913), and undertook in an exchange of letters in November 1912 to con-sult each other and take these plans into consideration in the event of peace being threatened. In 1912–13 the French and Russian General Staffs agreed that if war broke out Russia would accelerate its planned attack on Germany's eastern borders, with the aid of new strategic railways financed by French loans. After the Liman von Sanders crisis the Russian Foreign Minister, Sazonov, wanted to turn the Triple Entente into a defensive alliance, although he had to content himself with an arrangement in May 1914 for Anglo-Russian naval discussions.[26] And this diplomatic impasse—between Bethmann and Poincaré, Sazonov, and Grey—was accom-panied by a continental arms race. Military laws were passed in 1912 and 1913 to raise the German standing army's peacetime strength from 624,000 to nearly 800,000. The 1913 French Law extended the term of service from two to three years. And the Russian 'great programme' of 1913–14 was designed to expand the Tsarist army by 500,000 to over two million by 1917.

None of this necessarily indicated an intention to initiate war. It could be interpreted as a deterrent and an insurance policy, meant to dissuade the enemy from aggression and to defeat him only if dissuasion failed. But it must be seen in the context of the two sides' war plans, whose nature has been well described by Edward Spears:

To understand the problem of mobilizing a modern continental army, it is important to realize that the whole process is a race against time. If the mobilization is delayed or slow the enemy will be able to advance with a fully equipped army against an unprepared one, which would be disastrous. . . . [The] prearranged plan is therefore obviously of vital importance. . . . Each unit, once complete and fully equipped, must be ready to proceed on a given day at the appointed hour to a pre-arranged destination in a train awaiting it, which in its turn must move according to a carefully prepared railway scheme. . . . Improvization, when dealing with nearly three million men and the movements of 4,278 trains, as the French had to do, is out of the question.[27]

The 1914 war plans bore the imprint of the nineteenth-century military revolution. They betrayed a general expectation that the next war would be decided in the opening campaigns, and that victory would go to the side that struck first. The plans of Germany, France, Austria-Hungary, and Russia all envisaged an offensive at the earliest possible opportunity, and therefore generated powerful incentives for pre-emptive action that made the July crisis all the harder to contain. They also created, at least in Germany, a body of opinion that opposed a peaceful outcome. Schlieffen, the Chief of the German General Staff from 1891 to 1905, had envisaged that by invading Holland and Belgium the German armies could outflank the French defences on the Franco-German border and take Paris in a matter of weeks before being redeployed to face the slowly mobilizing Russians. His successor, the younger Moltke, preferred to respect Dutch neutrality, but needed in consequence to take the Belgian railway junction at Liège by surprise attack at the very outset of hostilities if the German right flank's westward movement was to proceed on schedule. In 1913 planning for the alternative of an opening offensive against Russia was discontinued, and the Schlieffen–Moltke strategy became Germany's only contingency arrangement for conducting a continental war. Yet Schlieffen himself had considered it a risky venture, and in 1914 it entailed taking the offensive against a French army almost equal to Germany's in size. And German military intelligence was accurately apprised of how with every year the Russian armaments build-up and new strategic railways added to the potential speed and strength of an enemy offensive in the east.

Germany's encirclement, and the erosion of the safety margin required by the Schlieffen Plan, reinforced the commitment to Austria-Hungary that culminated in the 1914 decisions to approve a Balkan war, and, in certain circumstances, to fight a European one as well. The 1879 alliance contained no German obligation to support Austrian aggression against Serbia, and Bismarck had withheld his backing from such a course. But during the Bosnian crisis, in January 1909, Moltke informed Conrad that if Austria grew impatient with Serbian provocation and invaded, Germany would regard Russian intervention as obliging it to mobilize and go to war with both Russia and, presumably, France. This was approved by Bülow, as Chancellor, and the Kaiser, who noted that if France failed to promise clearly its neutrality Germany must take the lead and force it into hostilities.[28] Bülow, like Bismarck, believed that if the Habsburg Monarchy broke up and its Roman Catholic German population were united with Germany, they would tip the Reichstag balance of power decisively away from the pro-Government parties.[29] In addition, by 1909, Austria-Hungary for all its weaknesses was Germany's last reliable Great-Power ally. And a Moltke–Conrad agreement in March of the same year provided for an Austrian offensive against Russia that was expected to be crucial in enabling Germany to win a two-front war.

The Germans were therefore bound to feel alarmed by the growing challenge to Austria-Hungary's survival. Their response in July 1914 required the formation of a consensus among their divided leaders. In Vienna, St Petersburg, and London the outlines of policy in the crisis were decided in the relevant Council of Ministers or Cabinet on 7 July, 24 July, and 2 August. In Berlin, foreign policy emanated from three or four spasmodically co-ordinated sources: the Kaiser and his *entourage*;[30] the civilian Government, including Bethmann Hollweg and his Foreign Minister, Jagow; the General Staff; and the Navy Ministry under Tirpitz. Given Moltke's constitutional and Tirpitz's *de facto* right of independent access to the Kaiser, responsibility for liaison rested not with a Cabinet system but with the inconsistent and mercurial Emperor.

At the height of the international tension arising from the First Balkan War, on 8 December 1912, Wilhelm had met in the so-called 'War Council' with his naval and military advisers. Tirpitz considered that for another eighteen months the navy would be unready for a European conflict. In July

1914 he would probably still have considered it unready, if his opinion had been ascertained.[31] Moltke, however, alarmed by Russian rearmament, was the leading advocate of a preventive continental war. In December 1912 he wanted one as soon as possible. At the end of May or early in June 1914 he told Jagow that at present Germany could still defeat its enemies, but that it might no longer be able to do so after two to three more years and the Government should therefore seek a chance to launch hostilities while a chance of victory remained. But Moltke, like Conrad in Vienna, could prevail only when other elements of the leadership rallied to this point of view. At the time when the blank cheque was given to the Austrians he was anyway absent from Berlin, and the General Staff was informed only retrospectively.[32]

Wilhelm undoubtedly sympathized with Moltke's views. In March 1914 he wrote to his Ambassador in St Petersburg that he was sure that Russia was preparing to go to war when the military balance had moved in its favour, and he based his policy accordingly. On 21 June he told the banker, Max Warburg, that Russia's armaments and strategic railways were directed towards a great war that could start in 1916, and it might be best for Germany to strike first.[33] The Emperor's asides and explosive marginalia, however, were designed in part to meet the need of an insecure and unstable ruler to posture as a strong man. At the December 1912 War Council he urged that Austria-Hungary should 'deal energetically' with Serbia, even if this embroiled Germany in war with Russia, France, and Britain. Yet if this appeared a call for immediate European war, the Council's practical results were limited to an expansion of the 1913 army estimates and half-hearted attempts to prepare the economy and public opinion against possible hostilities. The evidence so far uncovered suggests that these measures are best viewed as precautions similar to those being taken by all the European Powers, and that the Council did not lay down a timetable for war to be initiated in eighteen months' time. More significant as a precursor of the 1914 crisis was the Kaiser's advice to Conrad at Leipzig on 18 October 1913 that Austria-Hungary should invade Serbia and that he did *not* expect other Powers to intervene. With Berchtold at Schönbrunn eight days later, and apparently also in his last meeting with Franz Ferdinand in June 1914, the Kaiser again pressed for war with Serbia, and again supposed that Russia would remain quiescent.[34] For Wilhelm, Sarajevo was an outrage to monarchy in general and the death of a man who, if in a curious way, had been a friend. It strengthened his determination for a local war with Serbia, yet in his crucial conference with the Austro-Hungarian Ambassador on 5 July he said that Germany would back Vienna if Russia intervened but that the Tsarist Government was 'unprepared for war, and would think twice before it appealed to arms'.[35]

The Kaiser is best seen, therefore, as seeking a localized attack on Serbia rather than a preventive war with Russia and France. But, having given the blank cheque, he absented himself on a Baltic cruise until 28 July. In previous crises—Agadir, for instance—when tension mounted he had backed away from war. True to form, on his return he belatedly concluded that Serbia's reply to Austria-Hungary's ultimatum was a 'capitulation of the most humiliating kind', and proposed that the Habsburg army should confine itself to occupying Belgrade, located immediately across the frontier, as a surety until Austria's demands had been satisfied. In forwarding this 'Halt in Belgrade' proposal to Vienna, however, Bethmann Hollweg neither indicated that his sovereign was behind it nor reported Wilhelm's view that 'every cause for war falls to the ground'. On the contrary, Bethmann's tortuous phrasing suggested his concern was as much to create favourable conditions for a European war as to prevent one from breaking out. Wilhelm's last-minute effort to prevent the local war from escalating was undermined by his own Chancellor.[36]

This leads to the final element in the German decision-making equation. Bethmann had been absent from the December 1912 War Council, but was later briefed about it and took steps to implement most of its recommendations. He acknowledged that Austria must be supported if attacked by Russia 'in the course of securing her vital interests' against Serbia, and although more resistant than the Kaiser to glamorous illusions about warfare, he was willing to accept a European conflict under certain conditions.[37] In particular, he attributed more importance than did Moltke to keeping Britain neutral, and was more optimistic that this could be achieved.

Warning the Austrians in February 1913 against attacking
Serbia now, he suggested that to wait might be to see British
policy reorientated and a 'possibility—if only a remote
one—that we may be able to wage the conflict under conditions
much more favourable to us'.[38] It is true that the Chancellor's
assessment of the British fluctuated, and the news in June 1914
that Britain had agreed to naval conversations with the
Russians suggested that efforts to detach London from the
Entente were failing. None the less, the German Foreign
Ministry still doubted the strength of Britain's commitment to
France, and Bethmann's behaviour in the July crisis is
inexplicable unless he had persuaded himself that there was
still a chance of keeping Britain out.[39] About Russia he was
also in uncertainty, doubting in June 1914 'that Russia is
planning an early war against us', yet also fearing its growing
military strength and the influence of chauvinist Panslav
opinion on its rulers.[40]

The Chancellor's response to these uncertainties was a two-
way bet. He may have been pitchforked into the blank-cheque
policy by his impulsive sovereign, who did not consult him
before giving the fateful assurances on the afternoon of 5 July.
But Bethmann not only confirmed the promise of support to
Austria-Hungary on the following day; he also persisted in the
established course on 28 July when Wilhelm himself wavered.
To have rebuffed the Hoyos mission, he feared, would have
driven Vienna into the Western Powers' arms. After 6 July
Bethmann certainly desired a local, Balkan conflict, but
beyond this the evidence of his secretary's diary suggests at
times a preference for a crisis ending in a continental war, at
times one for a limited Austrian victory over Serbia that would
humiliate Russia and sever it diplomatically from Britain and
France. The German leaders handled the opening stages of the
crisis in a manner calculated to keep the impending Balkan
showdown localized, and Jagow and his Foreign Ministry
officials hoped and expected that this strategy would succeed.
But the Chancellor himself was more fatalistic. Even before
Austria-Hungary's ultimatum, he believed that if Russia
mobilized Germany could no longer negotiate but must strike
at once. It is therefore wrong to say the crisis slipped out of his
control. On the contrary, he had never been in control, in that

he was not fully master of the German Government and the denouement would depend on Russian decisions. Perhaps for this reason, he saw 'a Fate, greater than human power, hanging over Europe and our people'. But he knew and accepted that continental war was a possible outcome.[41] Bethmann has accurately been likened to a motorist embarking on a risky overtaking manoeuvre, who, seeing traffic in the oncoming lane, does not drop back but hurtles on towards catastrophe. And, eventually, on 1 and 3 August, he approved the declarations of war upon Russia and France.

Once it became evident that Russia was likely to retaliate and that the localization strategy was crumbling, Bethmann's main concern became not to avert a continental war but to fight it in favourable conditions. In particular, to throw the onus of responsibility on the Russians was essential to influence the SPD at home and Sir Edward Grey in London. Contacts with the Socialists after 25 July suggested that they would join in defending Germany against attack by the reactionary Tsarist regime, but had reservations about a war unleashed through Austrian aggression against Serbia.[42] Bethmann gave the appearance of co-operating with British efforts to mediate in the crisis, and on 23 July informed the Kaiser that 'it was impossible that England would enter the fray'.[43] On the 29th he offered to annex no territory from Belgium or from metropolitan France (though not the French Empire) if Britain would remain neutral. But on the same day Grey warned that Britain would quickly be forced to take sides if an Austro-Russian war developed into a Franco-German one. Only now did Bethmann follow the Kaiser in attempting, on 30 July, to confine the Austrians to a Halt in Belgrade, but within hours he abandoned the effort.[44] By this stage the growing evidence of Russian military preparations had panicked the Kaiser into believing he must mobilize; Moltke, thus fortified, pressed for immediate general mobilization and war, and undermined Bethmann's restraining efforts in Vienna by encouraging the Austrians to mobilize as soon as possible against Russia as well as Serbia. This was an act of military insubordination; and another indication of the independence of the General Staff is that it appears that only on 31 July was Bethmann told of Moltke's need to open hostilities by a surprise attack on

Liège.[45] German mobilization, and German mobilization alone, required an immediate passage of the frontiers and was effectively synonymous with war. But Bethmann and the Kaiser understood the outlines of the Schlieffen Plan, and acknowledged the need to implement it. Not to mobilize, and to allow the French and Russians to deploy their forces, would make the plan inoperable and leave no alternative but diplomatic humiliation. Given Bethmann's prior determination to use force if Russia mobilized, from the moment the Tsar ordered general mobilization on 30 July the fate of the long European peace was sealed. But because Bethmann held off German mobilization until news of the Russian initiative came through, he succeeded in his goals of appearing provoked and could command support from the SPD.

(iii) *The Response of the Entente*

German policy in the July crisis was therefore a compromise between the advocates of local and those of continental war. Either outcome, for Bethmann and presumably the General Staff, was preferable to the status quo. How the balance would fall depended on the Entente response to the blank-cheque policy. If the Central Powers threw down the gauntlet, their enemies were not obliged to pick it up. War resulted from both sides' preference to fight rather than back down.

The crucial Russian decisions in the July crisis were to support the Serbs, and to do so by ordering first partial and then general mobilization.[46] There was no formal Russian guarantee of Serbia or treaty of alliance, and the ambiguity of Russia's commitment helps explain the hopes in Vienna and Berlin that the crisis could be localized. The Russians had backed away from war on Serbia's behalf in 1909, and failed to support the Serbs in October 1913 against the Austrian ultimatum requiring their evacuation of Albania. But precisely the memory of the past stiffened the Russians' resolve not to be humiliated again. In addition to their sentimental ties to Serbia—the historic bonds of kinship, religion, and language— they valued it as a military distraction on Austria-Hungary's southern frontier. It would also be the nucleus of any alliance system built up in the Balkans as an advance guard for Russia's interests at the Straits.[47] In the emergency Council of Ministers held, after Austria-Hungary's ultimatum, on 24 July, Sazonov spoke of Russia's prestige and credibility in the Balkans and its 'historic mission' to uphold its Slav brothers' independence. He and the other Ministers who spoke agreed that further concessions to Germany would bring not peace, but fresh demands, and honour and national interest dictated that it was time to stand fast. The Premier, Goremykin, concluded that firmness was more likely than conciliation to secure peace, but that if need be Russia should accept war. Serbia was informed that evening that Russia could not 'remain indifferent' to its fate, and this possibly emboldened it to reject Point Six of the Austrian ultimatum and give Vienna the necessary pretext for force. The Council of Ministers also agreed that if the Tsar saw fit Russia should back up its diplomacy by partial mobilization against Austria-Hungary. On the following day Nicholas approved his Ministers' recommendations, and Russia was now committed to a deterrent policy of assurances to Serbia combined with the possibility of military measures.[48]

From now on decision rested with a more restricted circle: Sazonov, the Tsar, and Nicholas's military advisers, of whom the most important were his uncle, the Grand Duke Nicholas, the War Minister, Sukhomlinov, and the Chief of Staff, Janushkevich. In November 1912 Goremykin's predecessor, Kokovtsov, had co-operated with Sazonov in opposing partial mobilization during the First Balkan War. In the Liman von Sanders crisis, by which time Sazonov favoured applying pressure by seizing Turkish ports, Kokovtsov again opposed escalation. But by July 1914 he had been replaced by the less effective Goremykin, and the Tsar was left alone when Sazonov and the military recommended raising the stakes.[49] Having earlier cleared partial mobilization—that is, against Austria-Hungary alone—with the Council of Ministers and Janushkevich, Sazonov advised after Vienna declared war on Serbia that the measure should be implemented, and on 29 July the order was signed. This was accompanied, however, by assurances of willingness to compromise and that no attack was planned on Germany or even Austria-Hungary unless 'Russia's Balkan interests were threatened'.[50]

At this point the disastrous consequences of deficient civil–military liaison became apparent. Sazonov may have been led on by misleading assurances from Jagow to the French and British Ambassadors in Berlin that Russian mobilization against the Austrians alone need not entail German mobilization. In reality Moltke's letter to Conrad in January 1909 did pledge German mobilization in such circumstances, and therefore war with Russia and France. On 29 July Moltke spelled this out in a memorandum to Bethmann, and a crest-fallen Jagow had to admit that even partial mobilization would make European war unavoidable.[51] Co-ordination was also lacking on the Russian side. In March 1913 the military authorities had been authorized to take preliminary measures on their own initiative in time of crisis; from 26 July, and apparently without consulting Sazonov, they accordingly made preparations opposite Germany as well as Austria-Hungary. Hence Moltke intervened not only to correct Jagow but also because he feared that Russia in effect was secretly mobilizing; and overwhelming pressures were created for the Germans to resolve the situation before the prospects for the Schlieffen Plan had been fatally compromised. The inexperienced Janushkevich also failed to warn Sazonov that there were no plans for partial mobilization and that if it were attempted it would prejudice the arrangements for general mobilization, should this be needed later on. Having been attracted by the option of a middle road, Sazonov was belatedly informed that the real choice was general mobilization against both Central Powers or nothing at all.[52]

On the evening of 29 July the news of the bombardment of Belgrade and a warning from Germany against even partial mobilization persuaded Sazonov that 'war is probably inevitable'. He agreed with Sukhomlinov and Janushkevich that 'in view of the small probability of avoiding war with Germany it was indispensable to prepare for it in every way in good time, and therefore the risk could not be accepted of delaying a general mobilization later by effecting a partial mobilization now'.[53] Avoiding defeat in war thus took priority over avoiding war itself, although only after agonized discussions did the Tsar consent to sign the general mobilization decree. Russian decision-making in July was more truly a tragedy of miscalculation than in Germany, a policy of deterrence that failed to deter. Yet it too rested on assumptions that war was possible without domestic breakdown, and that it could be waged with a reasonable prospect of success. Russia was more vulnerable to social upheaval than any other Power. Its socialists were more estranged from the existing order than those elsewhere in Europe, and a strike wave among the industrial workforce reached a crescendo with a general stoppage in St Petersburg in July 1914. But the majority of the press and the elected Chamber, the Duma, wanted the Government to support the Serbs. Hence Sazonov, ironically, could warn the Tsar that 'unless he yielded to the popular demand and unsheathed the sword on Serbia's behalf, he would run the risk of revolution and the loss of his throne'.[54] Reports from the provinces concluded that mobilization would not be resisted and that the majority of the population could be relied on, and for a while this appraisal was vindicated by events.[55]

Russian policy also rested on a military judgement. In the Bosnian crisis the then Minister of War had opposed even defensive operations against the Central Powers. But by 1914 the armed forces had recovered from defeat by the Japanese, and the army had recently adopted an offensive war plan. Privately, Sukhomlinov and Grigorovich, the Navy Minister, doubted their readiness to fight Germany, but both recommended 'firmness' in the Council of Ministers on 24 July.[56]

These recommendations were bound to depend heavily on assumptions about Russia's ally. French policy in the crisis was likely to be mainly that of Poincaré, as President of the Republic, given the inexperience and nervous instability of Viviani, the Premier and Foreign Minister.[57] Both men were in St Petersburg on a State visit from 20 to 23 July, and they agreed with Sazonov to warn Austria-Hungary against threatening Serbian independence, although they appear not to have discussed the partial mobilization scheme. The Vienna Government deliberately withheld its ultimatum until Poincaré and Viviani had left the Russian capital, and until the two men returned to Paris on the 29th they were at sea and largely out of radio contact. In the interim the French Ambassador in Russia, Paléologue, advised in favour of firmness, and told

Sazonov that France 'placed herself unreservedly on Russia's side'. He also failed to alert his Government promptly that Russian mobilization was impending, and although Viviani warned the Russians on the 30th to take no action that would give Germany a pretext to mobilize, by then it was too late. How independently the Ambassador acted is one of the unsolved mysteries of 1914, but for the Russians in the hour of decision Paléologue's was the voice of France, and it spoke with more authority because of his supposed long-standing friendship with Poincaré. Partly because of the dislocation of French decision-making, the Russians were given grounds for thinking they had received their own version of a blank cheque.[58]

Once Russian mobilization had been ordered, French freedom of action relentlessly narrowed. In the first instance the crisis was transferred to Western Europe by the Schlieffen Plan, with its assumption that war with Russia inevitably meant war with France as well. But this assumption rested on the prior existence of the Franco-Russian alliance, and the stake perceived by each of the alliance partners in the other's continuing independence. Immediately after Germany declared war on Russia Poincaré confirmed to the Russian Ambassador that France would meet its treaty obligations, although parliamentary consent could be obtained more easily if Berlin took the initiative in opening hostilities.[59] This preference Germany duly satisfied.

The French authorities, considered Poincaré in retrospect, had a duty to urge moderation in St Petersburg, but also one not to endanger an alliance whose 'break-up . . . would leave us in isolation and at the mercy of our rivals'. They were bound 'to do our utmost to prevent a conflict, to do our utmost in order that, should it burst forth in spite of us, we should be prepared'.[60] The French upheld the alliance at the cost of war in part because they believed there were good prospects of victory. Their General Staff, relatively cautious in the Agadir crisis, had advised in September 1912 that in a war with the Central Powers caused by Austrian intervention in the Balkans, the Triple Entente 'would have the best chances of success'. In 1913 it had adopted a recklessly offensive war plan, Plan XVII.[61] Ultimately, however, the French civilian leaders rather than the military determined policy. They placed a premium on securing domestic consensus and British support. Because of this, they had in 1912 vetoed plans for a preemptive offensive into Belgium, and on 30 July 1914 the Government decided to hold its troops ten kilometres behind the frontier, despite the risk to France's border deposits of iron ore. It again overrode military opinion by deciding to suspend the pre-war plans for the arrest of potential left-wing opponents of mobilization, who were listed in the so-called *Carnet B*. This appearance of passivity and non-provocation (given that Paléologue's conduct remained secret) united French opinion with surprising ease. The majority of the Socialist Party, or SFIO, already accepted the legitimacy of national self-defence against attack from the more authoritarian neighbour across the Rhine. The main trade-union federation, the CGT, was committed to disrupting mobilization by a general strike, but its anti-militarism was a superficial covering for the visceral nationalism of much of its rank and file, and it followed the SFIO's lead. Jaurès, the Socialist leader, who was assassinated on 31 July, accepted that the Government was sincerely seeking peace, and if he had lived it is doubtful that the movement's attitude would have differed. By the time of his funeral on 4 August Germany's declaration of war had supervened, and the CGT leader, Jouhaux, took the lead in pledging support for the war effort.[62]

The French Government's other source of uncertainty lay in London. In the first days after the Austrian ultimatum British policy centred on Grey's attempts to mediate. Once these efforts failed, the decision on whether to intervene rested ultimately with Parliament but in practice would depend heavily on the recommendations of the Liberal Cabinet. As late as 1 August Grey was obliged to tell the French Ambassador that France must make up its own mind about whether to take sides in a Russo-German war, without being able to count on any British assistance; and that the Cabinet had decided in any event against sending an expeditionary force to the continent.[63] But on Sunday 2 August the Cabinet agreed to inform Paris that the Royal Navy would prevent German attacks on the French coast or French shipping via the Channel or the North

Sea. It also agreed to oppose by force any 'substantial violation' of Belgian neutrality. On the following day Grey defended the Cabinet's policy in the Commons, and on 4 August, following Germany's failure to respond to a British ultimatum to withdraw its troops from Belgium immediately, Britain declared war. Only two members of the Cabinet resigned.

Neither of the decisions of 2 August was prompted by a sense of legal commitment. The November 1912 exchange of letters with Paris made clear that Britain and France were obliged only to 'discuss' common action, in the event of either being threatened by an unprovoked attack or there being a danger to the general peace. Unlike the French army, however, the French navy assumed in its war plans that the contingency agreements with its British counterpart would take effect. Although it had alternative battle orders ready if necessary, its strength was concentrated in the Mediterranean, and it had left the Channel coast exposed in the expectation that this would be a British area of responsibility. Even if the Cabinet was not obliged to come to France's aid, therefore, Grey was able to persuade it that it was in Britain's interest to do so. But as the Germans were willing to keep out of the Channel in return for British neutrality, the promise of naval protection to the French could not alone bring Britain into the conflict.[64]

The guarantee of Belgium, by contrast, seems adequate in its own right to explain British intervention. Keeping the Low Countries and the coastline opposite the Thames estuary out of the control of a continental Power had for centuries been a mainstay of English security policy. The guarantee of Belgian independence, integrity, and neutrality in the 1839 Treaty of London embodied a long-standing national interest. To uphold it against Germany's unprovoked attack was also to defend the rights of small nations and the rule of law, and to demonstrate that aggression would not pay. For these reasons, the Belgian issue mattered for both the Left and Right of British political opinion and played a major part in uniting that opinion in favour of war. But in reality the British Cabinet acknowledged no binding obligation to defend Belgium against all comers. It would act only against a 'substantial' violation, and not necessarily against a minor incursion onto Belgian soil. And on 29 July it resolved that it was 'doubtful' whether one signatory was bound to uphold the 1839 Treaty if others failed to do so. The decision would be 'rather . . . of policy than legal obligation'.[65] Britain went to war against specifically a *German* violation of Belgium, and there would probably have been no Cabinet or Commons majority for resistance to a similar act by France. The outcome of the Franco-German struggle was not a matter of indifference, and the Prime Minister, Asquith, himself noted on 2 August that 'It is against British interests that France should be wiped out as a Great Power'.[66]

That German domination of Western Europe would threaten British security had long been accepted by the General Staff and by Grey and his senior officials, as well as by the leaders of the Unionist opposition. But in the early stages of the crisis Grey continued his semi-detached policy of refusal to commit himself in the event of war either to neutrality, or to intervention on the Franco-Russian side. He hoped that Britain and Germany could jointly exercise restraint, and was the more embittered when evidence accumulated that German co-operation with his mediation proposals had been tactical only and that in reality Berlin had escalated rather than defused the Balkan crisis. His hardening views were demonstrated in his warning on 29 July, without Cabinet authorization, that although Britain would stay out of an Austro-Russian conflict, in a Franco-German one it was likely rapidly to intervene. For as long as possible within the Cabinet itself, however, he held his hand. There was no clear-cut division among Ministers between a neutralist and an interventionist faction. The majority of the Cabinet were uncommitted, a diminutive minority opposed intervention in any circumstances, and a larger minority (including Grey and Asquith) accepted from the start that Britain should go to war rather than see France defeated. On 2 August, after Germany's declaration of war on Russia and its ultimatum to France, Grey pressed for an immediate decision over the Channel and Belgium. He threatened to resign, and the Prime Minister made his solidarity clear. Asquith also read out a promise from the Unionist leaders of 'unhesitating support' for measures to assist Russia and France. For the Cabinet to persevere in favouring neutrality would therefore split the Government and the Liberal Party and probably only delay an intervention that a Unionist or coalition ministry would carry through anyway against a background of perilous national recrimination. And the obvious leader of a neutralist revolt—the Chancellor of the Exchequer, Lloyd George—had been persuaded since the Agadir crisis that Britain could not allow Germany to overwhelm France. For Lloyd George and for other waverers, Belgium served as an invaluable pretext for a decision that personal, party, and national interest all appeared to dictate.[67]

Britain's decision for intervention also rested, if implicitly, on a comparison of the likely costs with those of remaining neutral. These latter were likely to be high. Even if France and Russia won, Britain would be isolated and in probable confrontation with its old colonial antagonists, with the German counterbalance to their power now removed. The intractable problem of defending India against Russia would return to the fore. Anglo-Russian relations in Persia were acutely strained on the eve of the July crisis, and during it Sazonov warned that Britain had to choose 'between giving Russia our active support or renouncing her friendship. If we fail her now we cannot hope to maintain that friendly co-operation with her in Asia that is of such vital importance to us.'[68] This weighed with the Foreign Office hierarchy and with Grey, although the Cabinet was presumably more impressed by the danger of neutrality leading to a *German* victory. Second, as Grey put it to the Commons, 'if we are engaged in war, we shall suffer but little more than we shall suffer even if we stand aside'. Foreign trade would anyway be disrupted, and there would be hardship and disturbances at home; indeed, a run on the Bank of England and the paralysis of the marine insurance market had already begun. Since 1910 Britain had experienced an unprecedented wave of national strikes in essential industries such as the railways, the docks, and coal, and by July 1914 Ulster's resistance to the Government's Irish Home Rule Bill had brought Ireland to the brink of civil war. The Cabinet did not go to war to escape its domestic difficulties, but its decision was facilitated by the lugubrious expectation of civil unrest whatever happened and by Asquith's sense of a near-providential release from his dilemma over Home Rule.[69] Finally, the Cabinet had reason to suppose it would be fighting a primarily naval and colonial, limited-liability war. When it deliberated on 2 August, the previous day's decision not to commit the British Expeditionary Force to the continent still stood, and only on 5–6 August did a sub-committee of interventionist Ministers in the War Council decide to send the BEF after all. In the short war that was expected British losses would fall mainly on the regular forces, and Grey knew of the optimism of British naval planners that if the initial blow to business confidence could be surmounted Britain's blockade would create far worse civilian hardship in Germany than would be suffered at home.[70] In short, the British government went to war for reasons of calculated national interest, although it was able to unite opinion behind it because it appeared also to be committed to an altruistic cause.

A general precondition for the outbreak of the First World War was the failure of resistance to belligerency within the Great Powers. This was not only a failure to prevent the war, but in large measure a failure even to try. In Britain Asquith's skilful political management, and the incursion of the Belgian issue, marginalized Cabinet and backbench Liberal opposition to a balance-of-power war. On the continent almost all the Socialist parties of the Second International disregarded its resolutions against voting military credits and participating in bourgeois Governments.[71] But the International had no power to coerce its members, and no strength greater than the sum of its parts. Socialist support was unevenly distributed, and the strongest parties—those in France and Germany—were also among the most integrated in their societies and the most tempered in their internationalist convictions by patriotic loyalty. Although the International's resolutions—most comprehensively the Stuttgart Congress resolution of 1907—had condemned war as a product of the capitalist system, it had failed to agree on concerted action to prevent war, pending the eventual abolition of capitalism itself. In particular, the crucial German party and trade unions had opposed an international general strike on the grounds that it would be a futile gesture that would cause their organizations to be suppressed, and in so far as the strength of the movement in Germany caused more disruption there than elsewhere, Germany's war effort would disproportionately suffer. Hence the Stuttgart and later resolutions left each national movement to decide its policy; but as this meant the Germans would probably do nothing the French movement, if it attempted direct action on its own, would similarly inflict unilateral damage on the French war effort.

Such considerations mattered because Marx and Engels, so far from being pacifists, had judged wars in the capitalist international order by their implications for the advance of socialism. From such a standpoint, the French party could support a war against the Kaiser as the Austrians and Germans could support one against the Tsar. And in practice the French and German Socialist leaders accepted a distinction, foreign to Marx and Engels, between an aggressive imperialist war and a legitimate one of self-defence. This latter, partly because of the presentational skills of Bethmann Hollweg and the Viviani Government, was what 1914 seemed to be. Finally, the Socialists faced a problem of timing. In 1911–12 a succession of crises had been peacefully surmounted, and although an emergency congress had been held at Basle in November 1912, during the First Balkan War, events had seemed to vindicate the German leaders' fears of over-hasty action. The relaxation of Franco-German tension in 1913 lent support to the theorists in the movement who held that international capitalism was evolving in a way that made armed conflict obsolete. In 1914, caught in the dilemma of whether to risk premature commitment or to delay, the leaders of the European parties met in an extraordinary session of the International Socialist Bureau at Brussels on 29 July. They deferred a decision on strike action to a special congress scheduled for 9 August. But by that date hostilities had begun and the French and German Socialists had rallied behind their Governments.

In a broad sense it is true that the First World War resulted from an international system based on sovereign States. Yet that same system had permitted Great-Power peace for over a generation, and such conceptual generalities fail to explain why the 1914 crisis ended differently from its predecessors and this particular war began at this particular time. All the leaders of the Powers were prepared in certain circumstances to use violence to defend their interests. But by 1914 those of Austria-

Hungary and Germany were reaching the conclusion that peaceful solutions to their problems of Balkan and European encirclement were exhausted, and that local and if necessary continental preventive war was preferable to the status quo. Conversely, the Russians were prepared to fight in order to prevent a local victory by the Central Powers, and the French and British in order to prevent a continental one. Technical considerations of mobilization planning hastened the decisions in Berlin and St Petersburg to escalate the crisis. But the decision to resort to war was at bottom a political one. War was seen as a potentially effective instrument of policy because of the advice of Treasuries, Interior Ministries, and General Staffs that it would be fierce, but short, and that its damage to domestic economic and political stability could be contained. In addition, whereas France over Morocco in 1905 and Russia over Bosnia in 1909 had backed down in part because of military advice that there was no reasonable likelihood of victory, by 1914 both Powers were more confident in their assessment, at the same time as Moltke and Conrad urged that victory was still possible if the opportunity for it was seized now. A more genuine balance of power indeed existed than in previous years, but it was an unstable balance that permitted both camps the delusion that rapid victory was obtainable rather than the correct perception that *neither* could achieve it at an acceptable cost. In reality the escalation of the conflict was only just beginning. As the war turned out to be none of the things that were predicted for it, so the fragile domestic coalitions that crystallized at its outset were subjected to an unimagined test.

2

The Expansion of the Conflict
AUGUST 1914–APRIL 1917

(i) *Japan and the Ottoman Empire*

The war of 1914 originated in a sequence of decisions that seemed rational to the Governments that made them yet in their cumulative effects brought no belligerent what it sought. States went to war on the assumptions that its international ramifications could be limited, its domestic repercussions managed, and that military operations would yield a rapid and decisive result that could be translated into a corresponding political gain. In the event, the opening offensives brought not victory, but frustration or disaster: to the French, in Lorraine and the Ardennes; to the Austrians, in Serbia and Galicia; to the Russians, at Tannenberg; and to the Germans, on the Marne. Nor were the succeeding counter-offensives more conclusive. From now on, the outstanding feature of the conflict was stalemate. From Switzerland to Flanders there formed an unbroken line of trenches that the attacks of neither side displaced by more than a few miles for the next three and a half years. In Eastern Europe large tracts of territory did change hands, and smaller belligerents were overrun; but Germany, Austria-Hungary, and Russia remained in the field. Stalemate on land was matched by stalemate at sea, where the expected clash of battlefleets failed to materialize and neither the Allied blockade nor German submarine warfare had rapid results. And stalemate in battle was paralleled by stalemate on the home fronts and in the diplomacy that intermittently continued across the barbed wire. Neither side could end the war by military operations. But neither could end it by inducing a collapse in enemy morale and revolution behind the lines. Nor could either end it by negotiation and compromise on its political objectives, or war aims.[1]

The war, therefore, went on. And as it did so, it subverted the internationally agreed conventions built up in the nineteenth century to place some limits on the brutality of modern conflict. It also diminished Europe's power and prestige in the world outside. War between the European States automatically entailed hostilities between their colonies, and in 1914 campaigning extended from Africa to the South Seas. In this sense the war was a world war from the start, but so also had been earlier European conflicts since the sixteenth century. By 1917 fighting was confined largely to Europe and the Middle East, but the war had become a world war in a second, and more novel, way: through the entry of the most powerful independent States in the remainder of the globe.

It is tempting to regard this global extension as a by-product of the central impasse. The belligerents tried to break the deadlock by ever more massive frontal assaults; but they also used more circuitous means. Hence the rival British surface and German submarine blockades at sea, both in violation of the maritime law of war. Hence also a competitive search for allies. But the decisions for intervention after the July crisis were not primarily accomplished by belligerent diplomacy. True, the more vulnerable neutrals needed to consider not just which side could offer more but also which was more likely to win, and even, whichever won, whether States that had remained aloof would suffer. But with the partial exception of the Greeks the new entrants came in through independent decisions and processes of bargaining in which they, rather than the belligerents, held the stronger hand. Underlying the broadening of the conflict was a decentralization of the balance of power away from the historic European circle and in favour of interlopers from outside.

These points are evidenced in the events preceding Japan's declaration of war on Germany on 23 August 1914.[2] The declaration gave as its principal ground 'the general interests contemplated in the agreement of alliance' between Japan and Britain. But no more than the European Powers was Japan brought in by the letter of an international undertaking. The 1902 alliance had been expanded on its renewals in 1905 and 1911 to require Japan to assist the British if they had to defend their Asian possessions because of an unprovoked attack by another Power. Grey avoided invoking it when on 7 August he asked the Japanese to declare war on Germany for the strictly limited purpose of allowing their warships to protect British shipping against enemy commerce raiders in the Western Pacific. Even this degree of intervention he requested only because of a brief and unfounded fear by the Admiralty that it would be too stretched to deal with the German Far Eastern squadron. But the Japanese replied that they wished to justify their entry under the alliance, and to destroy all German forces in East Asia. Grey, taken aback, tried to withdraw his appeal, and on 17 August he issued a unilateral declaration that attempted unsuccessfully to restrict Japanese operations to China and its offshore waters. But he had lost the diplomatic initiative. And the American Government, disabled by President Wilson's absence from Washington as a result of the death of his first wife, considered attempting to neutralize the Pacific region, but eventually accepted assurances from the Japanese that they sought no 'territorial or selfish advantage in China' and would restore to the Chinese the German leasehold territory there.[3]

Invited simply to escort British shipping in the Orient, the Japanese had by the end of 1914 used the British alliance as a pretext to occupy the Germans' leased territory in the Chinese province of Shantung and their Caroline, Mariana, and Marshall island chains in the North Pacific. One motive for their intervention was therefore to overrun at little cost and risk Germany's possessions in the Far East. There was also a lingering resentment in Tokyo against Germany, which had joined France and Russia in forcing Japan to relinquish some of the gains it had made in the 1894–5 Sino-Japanese War. The Foreign Minister, Kato, deployed these arguments in the decisive meeting on 8 August between the Okuma Cabinet and the group of veteran statesmen and associates of the Emperor known as the genro, who allowed their reservations about intervention to be overborne. Japan, considered Kato, stood to benefit from the elimination of a German naval threat; he thought Britain certain to be on the winning side, and even if it were not Japan would lose little. Two other considerations appear to have weighed on his mind. One was the opportunity to overcome resistance in the Diet, or Parliament, to Government proposals for higher armaments spending. The second was China. As Ambassador in London in January 1913 Kato had suggested to Grey that 'at the psychological moment' Japan would negotiate with the Chinese to extend its railway leases in the northern province of Manchuria. Such a moment had now arrived, and on 22 August Grey indicated that he assumed Japan's compensation for its war effort would take this form. Immediately after Japanese entry work began on what would become notorious as the Twenty-One Demands.[4]

Japan was able, by a well-calculated intervention, to gain impressively in a region where Britain and the other belligerents were strategially over-extended. The Ottoman Empire was much more vulnerable to European naval and military force. And despite the Young Turk revolution that had begun in 1908 it had progressed little down the trail towards internal modernization and external independence that the Japanese had blazed a generation before. The foreign creditors represented on the Ottoman Public Debt Administration controlled much of its public finance, and the system of the Capitulations further limited its sovereignty. These exempted foreign nationals from certain taxes and from the jurisdiction of the Turkish courts, as well as requiring the Powers' consent for changes in customs duties. None the less, the Ottoman Government was a nationalist regime, and it antagonized both groups of belligerents when in September 1914 it unilaterally abrogated the Capitulations and raised its tariffs. German diplomacy facilitated the secret alliance that the Empire made with Berlin on 2 August 1914 and its intervention on the Central Powers' side at the end of October, but both actions resulted primarily from a power struggle among the Turks themselves.[5]

A *coup d'état* in 1913 had replaced a short-lived liberal regime by a more authoritarian Government under the control of the Young Turks, or members of the Committee of Union and Progress. Power rested partly with the Cabinet, headed by the Grand Vizier, Said Halim, but ultimately with the CUP leaders, several of whom were also Ministers. The most influential members of the Government were the triumvirate of Enver Pasha, Djemal Pasha, and Talat Pasha, who held respectively the portfolios for War, the Navy, and the Interior. Enver, a former military attaché in Berlin and an admirer of the Germans' martial qualities, expected the Central Powers to win and favoured alignment with them, but needed support from his more detached and calculating colleagues. And on the eve of war the Turks were moving closer to the Entente. Talat appears in May 1914 to have proposed an alliance to the Russians, and Djemal in July to have suggested military co-operation against Greece to the French, although in neither case with success. Virtually all the army command positions were held by Turks, and Liman von Sanders, at the head of the German military mission, bewailed his lack of influence. Both Jagow and Moltke, and the Ambassador in Constantinople, Wangenheim, considered a Turkish alliance would bind them to a military liability.[6]

The initiative for change came from the Ottoman side, and as a direct result of the July crisis. On 22 July Enver urgently requested Wangenheim for an alliance, saying that Turkey needed the support of one or other camp and the majority of the CUP did not want to depend on Russia and deemed the Central Powers militarily stronger. Djemal, for example, had concluded that Britain and France would not protect Turkey at the cost of good relations with St Petersburg. Characteristically, most Ministers, apart from the Grand Vizier and the triumvirate, were not consulted. In Berlin the Kaiser insisted on the approach being taken up, and Wangenheim was authorized to sign. The treaty explicitly required the Turks to assist Germany if the latter's own commitments obliged it to support Austria-Hungary in a war caused by Russian interference in an Austro-Serb conflict. But Britain's entry, a contingency not contemplated in the treaty, at once made intervention a much riskier act. The Turkish Cabinet wished to remedy its empire's military unpreparedness, and on 4 August it proclaimed neutrality. Only a second conspiracy, from which even the Grand Vizier was excluded, would finally commit the country to the Central Powers.[7]

By the time that this occurred it was evident that the Allies could not satisfy Turkish desires. Both the British and the Russian military hoped to avoid, at least initially, a Holy War with Constantinople that might unsettle the Moslems of British India and distract forces away from Europe. The Turks were also willing to talk. They wanted the return of the Aegean islands lost to Greece in the Balkan Wars, and Anglo-French protection against Russian interference or attack. The Russians, paradoxically, were willing to give most, but their partners withheld support both from taking territory from Greece and from abolishing the Capitulations. The Entente offered to guarantee Turkey in return for strict neutrality, but the Turks feared this would enable Russia to import through the Straits all it needed to become dangerously strong. After the Capitulations were denounced relations worsened rapidly, and on 27 September Turkey closed the Straits to shipping.[8]

The Central Powers could offer greater diplomatic satisfaction, as well as military aid. At the beginning of August the Government in London decided to withhold delivery of a battleship and a cruiser that had been under construction for Turkey in Britain. The Germans seized this opportune moment to order two of their cruisers in the Mediterranean, the *Goeben* and the *Breslau*, to make for the Dardanelles. In return for admitting the cruisers to its territorial waters Constantinople was promised informally on 6 August that if Germany won the war it would support Turkish frontier gains from Russia and the abolition of the Capitulations, as well as, if Greece intervened against Turkey, the restoration of the Aegean islands. The Turkish Government avoided an immediate confrontation with the Allies[9] by announcing it had 'bought' the *Goeben* and *Breslau*, but the two ships retained their German crews and their commander, Admiral Souchon, became Commander-in-Chief of the Turkish navy. By October the Germans had won the diplomatic bidding match, and the Turks were navally and militarily better equipped. But the sensible course would still have been to wait, and a majority of the Cabinet favoured this in a meeting on the 25th. The Germans prevailed at this moment only because of a successful *fait accompli* by their sympathizers.

War was triggered when on 29 October naval forces under Souchon shelled Odessa and attacked Russian shipping in the Black Sea. Enver and the Admiral had already agreed on the operation in September, but the Grand Vizier and the Cabinet majority had at that stage successfully insisted that the order should be countermanded. In renewing authorization on 21 October Enver therefore acted covertly with Talat and Djemal, arguing that Turkey was now sufficiently prepared, that the Central Powers were scoring impressive victories over Russia in Poland, and that unless the Ottoman Empire joined them they would not help it to survive. When the news of Souchon's raid reached Constantinople the Grand Vizier threatened to resign, but a 17 : 10 majority on the Committee of Union and Progress favoured intervention, and the Cabinet dissentients were prevailed upon to stay. On 2 November Russia declared war, swiftly followed by the other Allies.[10] Turkish entry therefore rested partly on Enver's impetuous confidence that the Central Powers would win—a judgement repeatedly challenged by the Finance Minister, Djavid Bey. But it also rested on the historic enmity with Russia, and the fear that neutrality on the Allies' terms might leave Turkey at the mercy of the Tsar. Neutrality was a flimsy shield against the storms outside, and there was no risk-free course.

(ii) *Italy and the Balkans*

Similarities are apparent in the circumstances of Italy's declaration of war on Austria-Hungary on 23 May 1915. Like the Turks, the Italians feared that even neutrality was dangerous; like them they miscalculated, if not about the winning side, at least about the cost and duration of achieving victory. As against this, although Austro-Italian hostility was almost as old as that between Russia and the Turks, Rome and Vienna were partners with Germany in the Triple Alliance, which had been renewed in December 1912. And Italy was a liberal, parliamentary State, in which in the spring of 1915 the majority of the Chamber of Deputies supported the neutrality adopted in the previous year. As a preliminary, the reasons for this neutrality must be examined.

Italian decision-making in July 1914 was concentrated in the hands of the Foreign Minister, San Giuliano.[11] The Prime Minister, Salandra, had been in office with a fragile parliamentary base only since March, and he delegated the management of the crisis to his more experienced subordinate. Italian public opinion, as manifested in the press, welcomed the neutrality decree of 3 August, but until then was divided: nationalist

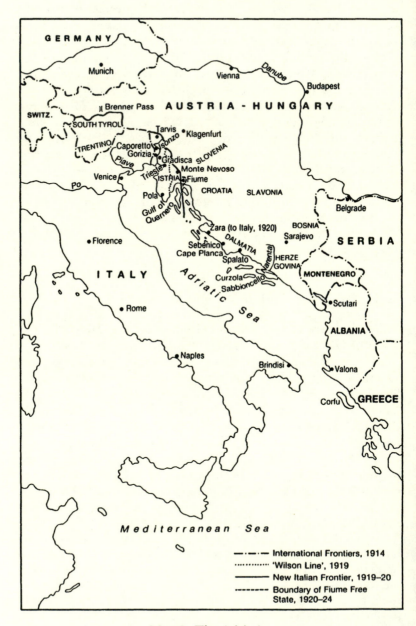

MAP 2. The Adriatic

and clerical opinion wished to join the Central Powers, while the moderate Left sympathized with the Entente. The Triple Alliance itself was a defensive arrangement that bound Italy at most to benevolent neutrality in the circumstances of 1914. San Giuliano told his partners that Italy might join them none the less if conditions became more favourable, but for the moment such conditions failed to apply.

Probably the most important reason for this was British entry into the war. For Italy, with its exposed coastal railways and cities and its dependence on imported coal and wheat, Britain's drift into the Franco-Russian camp had already lessened the Triple Alliance's attractions. In July 1914 the Chief of Naval Staff warned that in a war with Britain he could guarantee neither the loyalty of the seaboard towns nor communications with the colonies. Second, the 1902 Prinetti–Barrère agreement had bound Italy to neutrality in the event of 'direct or indirect aggression' against France by one or more Powers, although it is doubtful if this greatly influenced the Italian leaders. Third, and conversely, the Foreign Ministry and the General Staff had traditionally supported the German alliance for the security connection with the strongest army on the continent. Yet Salandra, for one, feared that Italian independence would be jeopardized in a German-dominated Europe, and the German army could not do the immediate damage to a neutral Italy that the Royal Navy could to a belligerent one. Finally, the attachment to Berlin was offset by the awkwardness of alliance with Vienna. The Triple Alliance was a fairweather system, preferable to confrontation when there was little chance of war with Austria-Hungary and Germany being won. But with the advent of a general European conflict, this last premiss ceased to hold.[12]

San Giuliano had attempted to improve relations with the Austrians. But in a dispatch on 14 July he ruminated that within a few years Italy's best interests might lie in leaving the alliance, and he blamed Vienna for a grave increase in tension in the previous months.[13] The oldest source of friction was *Italia irredenta*: the approximately 800,000 Italian-speakers under Habsburg rule, mostly in the Trentino, the Isonzo basin, and round Trieste. In August 1913 the 'Hohenlohe decrees' revived the issue by debarring Italian nationals from public employment in the latter city. Although the decrees were later modified, there were nationalist demonstrations on both sides of the border in May 1914. But at inter-governmental level irredentism mattered less than rivalry in the Adriatic. Since the turn of the century the two Powers had engaged in a naval race, frontier fortification-building, and competition for political influence. In 1913 both had welcomed the formation of an independent Albania, strategically located at the Adriatic entrance, but they supported different parties there and by 1914 their earlier agreement on the subject had broken down. Article VII of the Triple Alliance had provided that if either side altered the Balkan, Adriatic, or Aegean status quo by 'a temporary or permanent occupation' it would agree beforehand with the other on 'reciprocal compensation'. But in practice Austria's annexation of Bosnia in 1908 had been accompanied neither by consultation satisfactory to the Italian Government nor by compensation acceptable to Italian public opinion. During the Balkan Wars San Giuliano had acted promptly, and twice warned the Austrians against unilaterally using force against Serbia. In the July crisis Berchtold, with German approval, decided to ignore Article VII and present Italy with a *fait accompli*, rather than risk demands for prior compensation or attempts to sabotage his policy by indiscretions to St Petersburg.[14]

Salandra and San Giuliano therefore considered that Article VII had been violated and that anyway they were under no alliance obligation to assist an act of aggression against Serbia that would further strengthen Austria in the Adriatic. Yet they also suggested to Germany that Italy might still join the Central Powers in return for compensation, and this, they made clear on 27 July, meant the Trentino. The Germans pressed Berchtold to offer concessions, but the furthest he would go was to accept merely the principle of compensation, and not necessarily in Austria-Hungary itself, if Italy came in. San Giuliano replied that compensation must be unconditional, and the Government now decided to remain neutral.[15] Joining the Central Powers had never been more than a remote possibility, held out before Britain's attitude became clear. And the Italian civilian leaders (if not the military) believed that intervention on either side would impose a strain for which neither the armed forces, nor the economy, nor Italian social cohesion were well prepared. The Libyan war of 1911–12 had pushed the Government into deficit and shifted the Socialist Party (the PSI) to the left. In 'Red Week', in June 1914, nationwide demonstrations against the punishment of a soldier who had tried to murder his commander in the Libyan war developed into a local seizure of power in Emilia that 10,000 troops were employed to put down.[16] Yet despite—and partly because of—Italy's domestic fragility, Salandra's Government on 26 April 1915 signed the secret Treaty of London, which bound it to end neutrality within a month and join the Allies. To account for this requires consideration of the Italian expansionism manifested in the Treaty; the diplomacy that led up to the breach with the Central Powers; and the political crisis in which the Government imposed its will on a reluctant Parliament and people.

The Italians presented their negotiating demands in London on 4 March 1915. In return for joining the Allies they wanted to annex the bay of Valona; Trentino and the South Tyrol up to the Brenner Pass; Trieste, Gorizia, and Gradisca; and Istria as far as the Quarnero. This much San Giuliano had already considered necessary before his death in October 1914. His successor, Sonnino, added more. Thus, the Italian March programme also demanded Dalmatia, as far south as the river Narenta; the offshore islands; and the Sabbioncello peninsula. The coastline to the south could be divided between Serbia, Montenegro, Albania, and Greece, on condition that almost all of it was neutralized. By comparison with the Adriatic, colonial expansion had a low priority. The Treaty of London promised Italy 'equitable compensation' in Africa if Britain and France enlarged their colonies there at Germany's expense, as well as 'a just share' of the Turkish Mediterranean coast adjacent to Adalia if the Ottoman Empire were partitioned. But what mattered for Salandra was to seize on a historic possibility of completing the nineteenth-century work of unification, of acquiring European 'frontiers on land and sea no longer open to annexation, and of raising Italy, in reality, to the status of a Great Power'.[17]

The Italian programme appeared particularly blatant because of its heavy reliance on annexation rather than the buffer-state conceptions characteristic of other Powers' war aims. It entailed annexing not only *Italia irredenta* but also a quarter of a million German-speakers in the South Tyrol and, even in the whittled-down terms of the eventual Treaty of London, some 700,000 Slavs. Italy would acquire, indeed, more Slavs and Germans than Italians. These demands had some historical and cultural inspiration—the Roman and Venetian presence on the east coast of the Adriatic, and the survival of a beleaguered Italian minority in the cities there—but the primary motivation was strategic. Taking the South Tyrol up to the Brenner would eliminate a southward-pointing salient and establish a military frontier on the Alpine watershed. In the Adriatic, Italy's eastern coast lacked a suitable naval base between Venice and Brindisi: for five hundred miles it ran parallel to the archipelagos and inlets of the opposing shore. Italian security, felt Salandra, required 'complete domination' of both coasts, and the denial of naval facilities to Serbia and Montenegro. The Italian leaders had no intention of permitting a new Adriatic threat from the South Slavs. They envisaged that a weakened Habsburg Monarchy would continue to control Croatia and the port of Fiume. It would not be worth fighting, noted Sonnino, if the old vulnerability to Austria became a new vulnerability to a young and vigorous 'Yugoslav League'. Russia, he feared, would become the dominant Eastern Mediterranean naval Power, and seek an Adriatic base from its Serbian ally.[18]

Italy's decision for the Allies would depend on its assessment of their military prospects, and on their ability to outbid the Central Powers in endorsing its territorial claims. The halting on the Marne of Germany's offensive into France had 'a more or less decisive influence' on Salandra, and now that there was a prospect of the Central Powers being defeated he and Sonnino pressed ahead during the winter with military preparations. After the General Staff had advised that these would be ready in mid-April, they opened the bidding in London. There was room for optimism in the early spring of 1915 that the military stalemate was coming to an end.[19] The Allies were preparing an attempt to force the Dardanelles, whose outlying forts were bombarded on 26 February. This, coupled with Russian successes against the Austrians in Galicia, opened the prospect of a landslide of Balkan adhesions to the Allied cause, which might finish off the Habsburgs before Sonnino could negotiate his terms. The Italians, aware of their military shortcomings, intended not to enter until others had broken the back of enemy resistance, but not to delay until their aid had lost its bargaining value. They now impaled themselves upon the first horn of this dilemma by allowing themselves to be precipitated into action to escape the second.

The British Cabinet reluctantly concluded on 24 March that Italy's 'very sweeping' claims must receive Britain's 'general consent'. This reflected Grey's over-optimistic assessment of Italy's military capacities, and the likelihood that its entry would bring in the Balkan States. The French Government similarly suppressed its reservations about Italy's demands.[20] Sazonov agreed that the Italians should get Valona and the Brenner, and both he and the Serbian Government under Pašić were willing to abandon the Roman Catholic Slovenes of Istria to Italian rule. They withheld support from the protests of the leaders in exile of the Habsburg Monarchy's South Slavs, who constituted themselves in May 1915 as the Yugoslav Committee. But the sticking point came over Dalmatia, which Sazonov and Pašić wished to see incorporated into Serbia, without its coast being neutralized. Perhaps because of hints that Russia was in contact with Vienna over a separate peace, the Italians moderated their demands. The Russian offensive in Galicia had meanwhile ground to a halt, and Sazonov was under pressure from his General Staff, as well as London and Paris, to bring in Italy as rapidly as possible. The eventual compromise promised Italy the Dalmatian coast from Zara to Cape Planca, as well as the Curzolari islands. South of Cape Planca the Great Powers would decide the future of the coast, including Sabbioncello, and presumably assign it to Serbia, although almost all of it would be neutralized. On this basis the London Treaty was signed.[21]

After the battle of the Marne only imminent German victory would have induced Italy to join the Central Powers, but the choice between continuing neutrality and adherence to the Allies remained open for much longer. In December 1914 Austro-Italian negotiations began in Vienna over what compensation Italy would receive under Article VII of the Triple Alliance for Austrian gains in the Balkans. These proceeded in parallel with Italy's exchanges with the Allies in London, and throughout them Germany urged concessions on the Austrians, especially after the former German Chancellor, Bülow, became Ambassador in Rome in December 1914. But the Austrians stonewalled, meeting Italian demands for the Trentino and Trieste by refusing to concede any Habsburg possessions. When Sonnino presented his 4 March programme to the Allies, no Austro-Hungarian territory was on offer at all. Five days later, however, after a tense discussion in the Joint Council of Ministers, the new Austro-Hungarian Foreign Minister, Burián, agreed in principle to surrender Habsburg soil. Sonnino responded by claiming 'immediate execution': that any transfer should take place now, rather than after the war. He also, on 10 April, raised his demands to something comparable with the Allies' promises: the Trentino, Gradisca, and Gorizia; the Curzolari archipelago; and an independent Trieste. Burián offered only part of the Trentino and nothing elsewhere, and he refused immediate execution. Sonnino therefore closed with the Allies, and Italy denounced the Triple Alliance on 4 May.

The Italians had repeatedly expanded their requirements as the Austrians made concessions. This suggested they were negotiating in bad faith; and, as the demand for immediate execution showed, they assumed Vienna to be doing the same. Salandra and Sonnino agreed that if their sweeping 10 April proposals were accepted they would have to renounce war for the present, but they hardly thought acceptance likely. After March, at the latest, their principal motive for continuing was to win time for military preparations and for the discussions in London. The deliberations of the Austrian Government also make it difficult to see in the negotiations a genuine lost opportunity for preserving peace. The Vienna leaders overestimated their military vulnerability on the Alpine frontier, and feared an Italian–Rumanian irredentist coalition. But Tisza considered that yielding in the Trentino would lead simply to further exactions, as well as to Rumanian demands on Hungary. The Emperor, similarly, at first objected to concessions on principle, and when Berchtold reluctantly proposed in January to abandon the Trentino Tisza was able to secure the Foreign Minister's resignation. Berchtold's successor, Burián, was

Tisza's nominee and agreed with him on many things, although he had a mind of his own. Tougher and more self-confident than Berchtold, he agreed to discuss cessions as a way of buying time, and intended to avoid commitment. Conrad, Stürgkh, and Tisza, as well probably as the Germans, also envisaged that promises extracted now under duress might be reneged on after the war. In short, there is little evidence of significant alteration in the Austrian position until the Italian political crisis of 'Radiant May' 1915. This final stage must now be examined.[22]

'Radiant May' began with a further offer from the Central Powers. On the 9th Bülow and the Reichstag deputy, Erzberger, who was visiting Rome on an ostensibly unofficial mission, badgered the Austrian Ambassador, Macchio, into signing a fresh list of concessions, which was published in *La Stampa*. Italy was offered the Italian-speaking areas of the Trentino and the Tyrol; the west bank of the Isonzo; Valona; an Italian university, a free port, and municipal autonomy for Trieste; and there were also vaguer promises to consider Italian claims to Gorizia and the Adriatic islands. The Germans added an undertaking that Austro-Italian commissions would at once begin delimiting the new frontier, and offered the Kaiser's personal guarantee of Italy's possession of the territories in question. But this still fell short of immediate execution, and Macchio signed without authority from his government, which considered he had gone too far. Burián confirmed to his Ambassador, however, that he was prepared to cede immediately the Trentino, the west bank of the Isonzo, and a special status for Trieste. This is probably the most accurate measure of what was really on offer. It included most of *Italia irredenta*; and so it was for strategic frontiers on the Brenner and in the Adriatic that Salandra and Sonnino now proposed to open hostilities, if they could carry the country with them.[23]

Both men came from the smaller and more conservative section of the liberal parliamentary grouping that had supplied the personnel of Italian Cabinets since unification. The Government had come to office on the sufferance of Giolitti, the dominating figure among the centrist and left-wing liberals; and for Salandra, a proud and chilly southerner, this was a difficult position to endure. But Parliament was rarely in session between July 1914 and the eventual denouement. Salandra and Sonnino decided policy in the negotiations with the belligerents, and of the two the Premier took the more forceful role. If the General Staff had been consulted, it would have objected that the proposed Dalmatian gains would be defenceless against a hostile Slav State, although the navy supported the Government's demands. Within the Cabinet, Martini, the Minister of Colonies, belonged to the inner group, but the other Ministers discussed the course of policy in depth only at the beginning of May, and by then their freedom of decision had been heavily compromised.[24] As for public opinion generally, Sonnino privately admitted in December 1914 that a majority of Parliament and the Italian people opposed entering the war. But he considered that the Government should ride roughshod over this if need be; and Salandra took a similar view.[25] On 12 April the Prime Minister asked his Prefects to report on the public mood. Their replies suggested a prevalence of neutralist feeling, but also much indifference and a likelihood of 'calm resignation' in Rome in the event of hostilities. This suggested that resistance to an interventionist coup from above would be slight.[26] Indeed, Salandra, Sonnino, and Martini believed that a short, victorious war could consolidate the monarchy and unify the nation, and feared that not to seize the opportunity for unification and expansion would intensify the revolutionary danger at home.[27]

Support for war with Austria came originally mainly from the moderate Left. In the autumn of 1914 the interventionists were strengthened by the Italian Nationalist Association, or ANI, and a breakaway faction from the revolutionary wing of the PSI under the leadership of Benito Mussolini. But their appeal was far outweighed by that of the anti-interventionist forces. Given that Italy faced no invasion by a more reactionary enemy as France and Germany had done in 1914, the PSI and the main trade-union organization had every reason to favour continuing neutrality. Benedict XV, who became Pope in September 1914, was also neutralist, both for humanitarian reasons and in order to preserve the Habsburg Monarchy, whose Government was the least equivocally Catholic among those of the Great Powers. Finally, the most strategically located group of anti-interventionists were Giolitti's supporters in

Parliament. Whereas some Giolittians were truly neutralist, however, others were essentially loyalists to the former Premier; and Giolitti himself, who had authorized the Libyan war, differed from the Government over the expediency rather than the principle of intervention. His so-called *parecchio* letter, published on 2 February, regarded war as a misfortune, to be embarked on only when national honour and vital interests were at stake. But at present '*parecchio*', or 'much', could be obtained without it. This allowed the neutralists, perhaps mistakenly, to see Giolitti as their champion. But henceforth intervention offered Salandra a chance to break up the parliamentary base of a politician he detested, and to consolidate his own ministry's support.[28]

'Radiant May' consisted of a Cabinet crisis at the centre and interventionist demonstrations, often violent, outside. On 9 May Giolitti arrived in Rome, before the reassembly of Parliament scheduled for the 20th. Although the Treaty of London was officially secret, its existence was widely known. Technically, it required no parliamentary ratification, but Salandra would need approval from the Chamber for emergency powers. After Giolitti's arrival, well over 300 Deputies (out of approximately 500) sent him telegrams or letters or deposited visiting cards as a gesture of support. The final Bülow–Macchio peace offer was published at the same time. Whatever the feeling of the country as a whole, the interventionists were the stronger on the streets of Rome. They abused Giolitti and his followers, and tried to storm the Parliament building. But it was Giolitti's lack at the crucial moment of the political killer instinct that undid the neutralist cause. Meeting the King and Salandra on 9–10 May he urged that a ministry resting on the Chamber neutralists should accept the Bülow–Macchio proposal. He excluded himself as the head of such a ministry, on the grounds that he could be called pro-Austrian; but he was willing to let Salandra carry on with his backing. War, however, he thought the majority of the population opposed. It would end in revolution and defeat. Salandra, who estimated his own support as being no more than 150 votes, decided to resign. But Giolitti would not form a ministry himself, and recommended two other politicians, both of whom were interventionists and both of whom refused to serve. The King recalled Salandra and rejected his resignation; on 17 May Giolitti left Rome. On the 20th the Chamber voted emergency powers by 407 : 74, and three days later Italy declared war.[29]

The neutralist forces had collapsed with breathtaking speed. But support for Giolitti, as manifested by the visiting cards, was not necessarily opposition to intervention, and once he had bowed out his followers were freer to follow their own inclinations. Given that the neutrality debate had been largely about expediency, when it had become clear that a ministry accepting the *parecchio* was not a real alternative a closing of the ranks could occur. Even the PSI, though voting against Salandra, stopped short of sabotaging the war effort. Giolitti had sought power less for himself than for a Government committed to the *parecchio*. But only the threat of war had pushed the Central Powers as far as they had gone; and he himself acknowledged that his 2 February letter had ruled him out as one who could credibly step up the pressure. Hence he sought a substitute leader to do the deed. But Salandra refused to jettison the London programme in order to continue as Prime Minister on Giolitti's sufferance, and the neutralist option ran into the sands.

A final irony remained. Events soon showed that May 1915 was a highly inopportune moment to choose to join the Allies. The Cabinet was aware that the Russians were in retreat in Poland and that the recent Anglo-French landings had failed to win control of the Dardanelles. But it chose to honour a treaty negotiated on the basis of a more optimistic military prognosis. The Chief of the General Staff promised a short, victorious operation, and no preparations were made for a winter campaign.[30] In the event, the Austro-Italian front almost at once became a trench stalemate analogous to those in France and at the Dardanelles. The Italians in *Italia irredenta* who were eventually united with the mother country were almost equalled in number by those other Italians who paid for Radiant May with their lives.

Until this point the Balkan peninsula had remained incongruously calm. In spite of intense diplomatic activity, Serbia and Montenegro, which had entered the war at the outset, were still the only belligerents. The 1913 settlement after the Balkan Wars largely determined the region's international politics.

Serbia, Rumania, and Greece had all emerged victorious, even if they had further territorial aspirations; Bulgaria and Turkey were defeated and dissatisfied. Avoiding initial commitment, the Balkan Governments waited to see what the rival coalitions would promise and which was the more likely to be able to deliver. Once stalemate set in, they could exact a high price.

Bulgaria had the greatest immediate, if not ultimate, success. Its policy was determined in broad outline by King Ferdinand and executed by the Prime Minister, Radoslavov. Both men had sentimental attachments to Germany, although this was of limited influence on their decisions. Public opinion was traditionally Russophile, but in August 1914 the Government took powers to prorogue the National Assembly and control the press. The joint protest of the opposition leaders when Bulgaria mobilized in September 1915 was without effect.[31]

If Germany and Austria always operated at an advantage in Sofia this was not only because of the domestic political balance but also because they were better placed to satisfy the Bulgarian Government's desires. This, with the aid of Germany's shattering victories over Russia in the 1915 Polish campaign, largely determined events. In 1913 Bulgaria had lost the southern Dobrudja to Rumania, Kavalla to Greece, and, above all, most of Macedonia, including both the 'uncontested zone' and the more northerly 'contested zone', to Serbia. Skilfully exploiting the offers from the Allies, Radoslavov in June 1915 won from the Central Powers an unconditional promise of both the uncontested and contested zones in return simply for continuing neutrality. At the end of July, by which time the Russians had become much less dangerous and discussions with the Allies were approaching deadlock, Ferdinand decided to negotiate in earnest with Berlin and Vienna. Agreements signed on 6 September conceded most of his demands. An alliance treaty guaranteed Bulgaria against unprovoked attack. An accompanying convention promised the uncontested and contested zones and further territory to the north. If Greece or Rumania joined the enemy Bulgaria would regain from them its losses of 1913. Finally, a separate agreement with Turkey transferred to Bulgaria an area on both banks of the Maritsa river that allowed it uninterrupted possession of the Burgos–

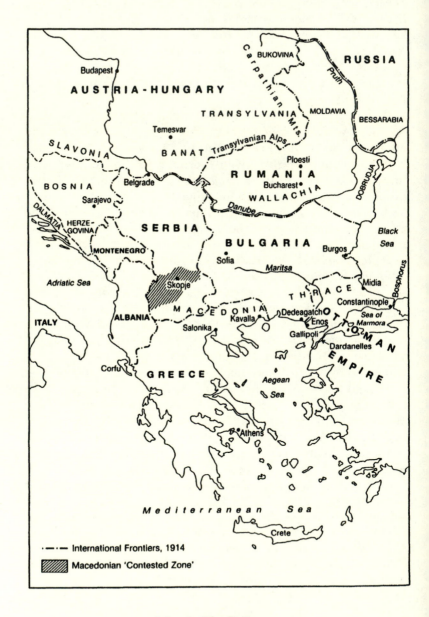

MAP 3. The Balkans

Dedeagatch railway. Between them, these understandings were analogous in Bulgaria's approach to war to the Treaty of London in Italy's.

Allied diplomacy in Bulgaria was hampered by disunity among the Governments concerned and by repeated military setbacks. Its main effect was to raise the price Ferdinand could exact from the Central Powers.[32] It was easy for the Allies to promise Turkish territory, but beyond this Bulgaria had pretensions on two States—Greece and Rumania—that they wanted to win over, and on a third—Serbia—that was already on their side. The Greeks, from their position of neutrality, naturally refused concessions. Pašić, at moments of maximum Serbian military danger, was willing to talk, but feared that the Serbian Parliament and military might disavow him. Compensating him at Austria-Hungary's expense became more difficult after the Treaty of London gave priority in Dalmatia to Italy's claims. On 29 May the Allies offered Bulgaria territory from Turkey, most of the uncontested zone in Macedonia (on condition Serbia obtained Bosnia-Herzegovina and an outlet to the Adriatic), and Allied assistance in obtaining Kavalla in return for Greek gains in Asia Minor. This cut no ice in Sofia, and Pašić warned that he could yield no Serbian territory. The Allies' next *démarche*, in August, therefore promised that in return for concessions to Bulgaria Serbia would acquire Bosnia-Herzegovina, wide access to the Adriatic, and Slavonia, if this latter were in Allied hands at the end of the war. In reply, the Serbs offered to give up part of the uncontested zone, but with so many qualifications that the Allies considered their conditions unfulfilled. Apart from a personal and unofficial commitment given by Grey, therefore, Serbian expansion to the Adriatic remained excluded from Allied war aims.[33] The question, anyway, now became hypothetical. Bulgaria mobilized on 21 September; with Germany and Austria-Hungary it overran Serbia by the end of the year, and Montenegro by January 1916. The Allies declared war on Bulgaria, and landed French and British forces at Salonika, but failed to move them inland. For the moment, diplomacy had no further role.

Rumania's course to war was in many ways a mirror image of the Bulgarian one.[34] Its appetite was concentrated on Hungary.

And although its calculations ended in military catastrophe in the short term, they paid off handsomely in the long. Its 1883 alliance with Berlin and Vienna had been renewed in 1913, but had never been disclosed to Parliament, and was therefore of doubtful constitutionality. On the eve of war the alliance was outweighed in importance by the growing agitation on behalf of the two and a half million Rumanians under Magyar rule in Transylvania. King Carol's constitutional power was less then Ferdinand's in Sofia, and control of policy therefore rested with the Prime Minister, Bratianu, whose Liberal Party held commanding majorities in both Houses of Parliament. Like Radoslavov, Bratianu bided his time, but he was a Francophile with a Paris education who hoped for and expected Allied victory. In a Crown Council on 3 August 1914 Carol pleaded unavailingly that Rumania should join the Central Powers. Of the others present, including Bratianu and representatives of all the political parties, all but one favoured neutrality, on the grounds that the *casus foederis* of the alliance had not been met, that they should take account of public opinion and the Transylvanian question, and that they should wait upon events. The news of Italy's declaration of neutrality strengthened a consensus that was already clear.[35]

In October Carol died and was replaced by Ferdinand, a more self-effacing ruler with a Queen who was sympathetic to the Allies. This left the Central Powers with few negotiating assets. Transylvania, unlike the Trentino, was in the Hungarian portion of the Habsburg Monarchy, and therefore even harder for Burián and Tisza to renounce. In June 1915, under the impact of Italian belligerency and German pressure, Austria-Hungary made its maximum bid. In return for joining the Central Powers Bucharest would obtain Bessarabia (from Russia) and the Bukovina (which was in the Austrian part of the Monarchy and contained only a quarter of a million Rumanians). Even the Bukovina was subsequently withdrawn. The Central Powers would have to rely on their military might to deter Rumania from joining their enemies.

Bratianu used his negotiations with the Austrians as a lever in dealing with the Allies. A secret Russo-Rumanian agreement of 2 October 1914 secured him, in return for benevolent neutrality, Russian recognition of Rumania's right to occupy the Rumanian-majority areas of Transylvania and the Bukovina at the moment of its choosing. Encouraged, like the Italians, by the Allies' transient successes in the spring of 1915, Bratianu offered on 3 May to intervene in exchange for Transylvania, the Bukovina up to the river Pruth, and the Banat of Temesvar. Giving Rumania this latter would bring it to the gates of Belgrade, and although Bratianu agreed not to fortify the river bank opposite the city, it entailed yet a further sacrifice of Serbian aspirations. Bratianu's conditions would also deprive Russia of a strategic frontier in the Bukovina and transfer a large Ruthene (i.e. Ukrainian) population from Habsburg to Rumanian rule. But their military débâcle in Poland, combined with British and French intercessions, persuaded the Russians to accept in principle. Bratianu himself, however, now feared that he was backing a losing horse. On 20 August the Allies confined themselves to an oral statement accepting his territorial claims, on the understanding that Rumania would join them when the military position improved.

With the territorial issue settled, the negotiations leading up to the alliance and military convention signed at Bucharest on 17 August 1916 turned on strategy and the quantity of Allied aid. In the war of 1877–8 Rumania had intervened against Turkey, only to lose southern Bessarabia to the Tsar. In addition to his uncertainties about Allied military prospects, Bratianu therefore distrusted Russian good faith. In June–July 1916, however, the Brusilov offensive—named after the Tsarist General who commanded it—inflicted disaster on the Habsburg army and brought Russian troops into the northern Bukovina, the very area Sazonov had pledged so reluctantly the year before. By the time Bratianu committed himself to war, in August, the offensive had faltered. But further hesitation, he apparently believed, would jeopardize the attainment of his aims: the Allies were losing patience, and Russia and Austria-Hungary might conclude a separate peace. Even a defeat like Piedmont's at the battle of Novara in 1849, he told a Crown Council on the 26th, could still advance Rumania's claims.[36] He was unaware that France and Russia had secretly agreed to decide on the main issues at the eventual peace conference

before admitting Rumania to the negotiations, and had resolved
that 'the annexations promised to Rumania will be effective
only as the general situation permits'.[37] Rumanian intervention,
then, was a desperate throw, although more than a simple miscalculation. By January 1917 the army had been driven back
and more than half the country was under German and Austrian
occupation. Yet eventually this would prove indeed to be a
Novara of a sort. With the exception of the squalid circumstances of Greece's entry into the war, however, South-Eastern
Europe now became a military and diplomatic backwater until
September 1918.[38] Far greater events were about to unfold
than a replay of the Balkan Wars.

(iii) *The USA*

The United States and the United States alone could through
intervention break the European stalemate that was the central
element in the war. It could afford to disregard the preliminary
question of which side was the more likely to win, as it could
bestow victory on either. In fact the American authorities—
President and Congress—made two decisions in the spring of
1917. They broke off diplomatic relations with Germany on
3 February; and they declared war on 6 April. Only the first of
these directly answered Germany's resumption on 1 February
of unrestricted submarine warfare against the Allies. This
resumption violated the '*Sussex* pledge' given by Berlin to
Washington on 4 May 1916, at least in the American interpretation of that pledge. But for President Wilson, breaking off
relations was by no means a commitment to declaring war. His
decision for the latter came afterwards, and for much broader
reasons, foremost among which was his desire to restructure
international politics between the industrialized Powers and his
acceptance that Germany's defeat was essential to that end.
The U-boat crisis was a pre-condition but not a sufficient cause
of American entry. It is therefore necessary to consider why the
American Government challenged German unrestricted submarine warfare; why the German Government defied that
challenge; why Wilson advanced from breaking off relations to
recommending war; and why he carried for the declaration the

support of Congress and American opinion that he considered indispensable.

Wilson's initial decision for neutrality was a matter of course, and supported right across the spectrum of opinion. It echoed the sentiments of American leaders since President Washington's Farewell Address in 1796: that trade with Europe was welcome, but its rivalries were no American concern and political commitments there should be shunned. The Monroe Doctrine, asserted by successive administrations since 1823, balanced American non-intervention in the Old World with a warning to the Europeans against extending their 'system' into the New. For most of the nineteenth century the United States enjoyed free, or nearly free, security against external threat. Satisfactory relations with the British and the debilities of the Latin American Republics obviated the need for large armed forces and balance-of-power diplomacy. But the emergence of the ironclad battleship opened a chink in the Atlantic Ocean barrier. By 1914 the Americans had responded by acquiring the third largest navy in the world and by adopting a policy of preventive intervention in the Caribbean and Central America in order to debar European intrusions. The annexation of Hawaii and the Philippines in 1898 created a new security concern, and a war of words and of competition for influence began to develop with the Japanese in East Asia.

Other developments beneath the surface made it dangerous to predict that even in Europe the United States would stay aloof when normal times were next replaced by exceptional ones. Many of the eastern business and professional élite from which government officials were disproportionately recruited had travelled to or been educated in Europe, and had personal contacts there. The United States had become a net exporter of manufactures, and foreign trade, although smaller as a percentage of output than in Western Europe, was needed to maintain high utilization of capacity. Although on balance still a capital importer, by 1914 the USA was also a substantial foreign investor. And there was a new preoccupation with national security. The General Board was created in 1900 as an advisory naval general staff, and plans were made for possible operations against Japan and Germany. Several leaders of the Republican Party, including the former President, Theodore

Roosevelt, and the Republican Senate leader, Henry Cabot Lodge, identified a German security threat. But in 1914 the Republicans supported Wilson, a Democrat, in the neutrality decision.[39]

American neutrality differed in its implications from any other because of American potential to supply commodities, manufactures, and loans. Once the European war became a struggle between munitions industries the United States came to hold the economic balance, and American neutrality was bound to be asymmetrical. The Allies had the finance to pay for purchases in America, and the naval mastery and merchant shipping needed to transport those purchases. The Central Powers did not. American decisions either to permit or to prohibit sales and credit to belligerents must objectively aid one or other side. A further asymmetry arose from the differing British and German capacities to mount a surface naval blockade. Even rigorous adherence to the rights and duties of a neutral under international law, therefore, might fail to deflect charges of partisanship. And on certain of the questions that confronted Wilson, international law was elastic or ambiguous, or drawn up without regard to the technological conditions of twentieth-century naval warfare. In the absence of a legal automatic pilot, he was guided by his sense of American national interest and of international morality and, to a lesser extent, of domestic political exigencies. The upshot was that the operation of American neutrality became highly favourable to the Allies, and the moderates in Berlin were undermined.[40]

American policy over trade and loans may be examined before considering the rival British and German blockades. Wilson had a Gladstonian faith in the civilizing virtues of international trade, and accepted that government had a duty to promote it. The initial decision to allow unlimited exports, including armaments, to belligerents was straightforward. But once it became evident that the Allies were the overwhelming beneficiaries, bills were introduced in Congress, with German–American backing, in favour of an arms embargo. This idea, thought the President, was 'a foolish one, as it would restrict our plants', and he successfully resisted it.[41] At least this was consistent: unlike his policy towards belligerent loans. In October 1914, again primarily for export promotion, the administration permitted the granting of commercial credits, while continuing to prohibit bond issues by belligerent Governments. In September 1915, however, the British were permitted to make precisely such an issue. In giving authorization Wilson followed the recommendation of his personal confidant, House; of his Secretary of State since June 1915, Lansing; and of his Treasury Secretary, McAdoo. All three were sympathetic to the Allies, but McAdoo emphasized most strongly the economic dimension: 'To maintain our prosperity we must finance it. Otherwise it may stop, and that would be disastrous.'[42] In fact the bond issue was a failure. But between 1914 and 1916 American trade with the Allies quadrupled in value; that with the Central Powers fell to one hundreth of the pre-war figure.[43] A large trade surplus was made possible because America became a major creditor of the Allies. For the Germans, whether this had economic motives or was caused by political sympathy for their enemies might well appear secondary.

This was the backdrop to the controversy over the law of war. As hopes of rapid victory faded, both sides sought out new ways of striking at their adversaries. The United States, as the strongest remaining neutral, could either condone violations of international law or resist them on behalf of its own citizens' prerogatives and such sense of international community as remained. The existing rules of naval warfare, as modified by the 1856 Declaration of Paris and the 1907 Second Hague Peace Conference, permitted a close (i.e. inshore) blockade of enemy coasts and the capture of enemy merchant vessels. Neutral merchantmen could travel to belligerent ports, but were subject to 'visit and search' on the high seas, and the confiscation of potential military supplies, or contraband. The 1909 Declaration of London had attempted to limit the power of blockade and narrow the definition of contraband, but the British never ratified it, and in 1914 they promised to respect it only with such extensive 'modifications and additions' as to deprive their theoretical adherence of much meaning. Under the cover of their legal right of reprisal, in March 1915 they took advantage of the first unrestricted U-boat campaign in order to attempt the total suppression of German trade. Neutral as well as enemy harbours were blockaded; neutral shipping was intercepted outside territorial waters and taken into port to be searched; and by this stage contraband had been defined in practice as including food.[44]

This was an unprecedented interference with neutral shipping, and obscured the cardinal distinction between combatants and civilians. It violated—and was understood in London to violate—not only the Declaration of London but also the older body of Anglo-American prize law. From the end of 1915, moreover, the British opened mail on the neutral ships that they detained, and in July 1916 they published a 'black list' of neutral, including American, firms that were suspected of trading with the Central Powers and with whom British subjects were forbidden to deal. Yet as the British measures took shape, in the first months of the war, Wilson confined himself to piecemeal representations over individual cases. Under pressure from mounting domestic agitation he made more generalized protests in December 1914 and March and August 1915, but these were cautiously worded and stopped short of threats. The British took some care to limit the damage to American interests, notably through their 1915 intervention to support the cotton price. In essence, however, although aware that a confrontation with Washington could spell disaster for their war effort, they were able both to tighten the blockade as much as they felt necessary and to avoid damaging reprisals from Wilson. This was in part because whatever the blockade might do to German civilians, it threatened only American property, not American lives. The issue could be postponed, once a protest had been made. In addition, Wilson felt that to confront both sides simultaneously would be 'folly',[45] and during the year of submarine crises with the Germans from May 1915 to May 1916 he kept the conflict with the British below danger level. Only afterwards did his indignation against London reach its peak, and in September 1916 Congress voted him discretion to deny access for British shipping to American ports. But from the outset he was determined not to let the issue force him into war as he supposed President Madison had been in 1812, given that both he and his advisers believed that hostilities with the Allies would conflict radically with American national interest.[46] Hence, although supposing he was still observing neutral conduct, he connived at the destruction of a major part of pre-war international law.

It is true that the Allied blockade had at least some claim to represent an adaptation of the law of war to modern conditions. It was orderly, from the neutral point of view humane, and 'effective' in the sense legally required: not a mere proclamation of warning, but a procedure comprehensively enforced. A submarine, by contrast, was highly vulnerable once it surfaced, and could take on board neither contraband nor crews. It could only sink its victims. If it followed 'cruiser rules' it would surface, and allow the passengers and seamen time to get into the boats. Under 'unrestricted' warfare it could torpedo without warning, and in practice it was often difficult to distinguish neutral from belligerent vessels. Nor could the U-boats mount an 'effective' blockade. In October 1914 Germany had only twenty-one available, twelve of them obsolescent. The first unrestricted campaign, which began on 18 February 1915, was therefore intended less to destroy shipping physically than to frighten neutral merchantmen out of British home waters.[47] Wilson's response was immediately much firmer than over the British blockade. On 10 February he warned that Germany would be held to 'strict accountability', and that steps would be taken to safeguard American lives and property on the high seas. The sinking in March of a British liner, the *Falaba*, with the loss of an American passenger, showed the danger of staking national prestige on the right of citizens to travel on belligerent ships. But Wilson was probably inclining to this course even before another British liner, the *Lusitania*, was torpedoed on 4 May. This time 1,201 people, including 124 Americans, died.

The *Lusitania* crisis committed American policy unambiguously against unrestricted submarine warfare, and resolved a struggle for influence among Wilson's advisers. The crucial speeches and diplomatic documents of his Presidency were essentially his unaided work. But he consulted the State Department and the relevant Cabinet officers over legal and financial technicalities, and, on occasion, tried out his ideas on his friend and confidant Colonel House. House had no official position, and owed his closeness to the President mainly to his skills as a sympathetic listener. His influence was greater over mediation and war aims than the submarine question, but he believed that a German victory would endanger American security, and he advised in favour of firmness. Lansing, the Counsellor at the State Department, held similar views, and was at odds with the Secretary of State, Bryan, whose near-pacifist and strongly non-interventionist views isolated him from most of Wilson's Cabinet.[48] Over the *Lusitania*, Bryan reluctantly agreed that there should be a protest, but he wanted to accompany this by a simultaneous protest against the British blockade, and to warn American citizens against travelling on belligerent ships. Wilson's first *Lusitania* note, however, on 13 May, called on the German Government to repudiate the sinking, make immediate reparation, and take steps to prevent a recurrence. This was to advance from protests to demands, and to reject the alternative of acquiescence. And a second note, sent on 13 June in response to an unapologetic German reply, asserted the rights of American merchant ships and passengers in the war zone, and sought assurances that even belligerent merchantment would be treated in accordance with cruiser rules. Bryan now resigned, and in the same month Lansing replaced him.[49]

In an ill-timed speech at Philadelphia on 10 May Wilson had declared that 'there is such a thing as a man being too proud to fight'. Although not meant with reference to the *Lusitania*, it provoked a flood of letters to the White House warning against submission.[50] But hardly any voices in the public debate favoured belligerency. 'I wish', Wilson wrote to Bryan, 'that I saw a way to carry out the double wish of our people, to maintain a firm front in respect of what we demand from Germany and yet do nothing that might by any possibility involve us in the war.' A show of resolution now, he hoped, would make it easier to surmount the issue without resort to force. It offered a middle way between belligerency and humiliation. But to warn Americans against travelling on belligerent vessels would, he thought, be 'both weak and futile. To show this sort of weak yielding to threat and danger would only make matters worse.' Britain's 'violation of neutral rights' differed in kind from Germany's 'violation of the rights of humanity'. Anxious not to force the issue with both sides simultaneously, he insisted that Germany must respect American rights regardless of British behaviour. Finally, he feared that a display of weakness would impair America's larger 'influence for good'. A letter from House that Wilson read out to his Cabinet asserted that the United States's actions in this crisis would determine its influence on the peace settlement.[51]

After the *Lusitania* Wilson and the bulk of American opinion were set on the course that led eventually to the breaking of relations with Germany. But the American position took its final form only after a year of intermittent further confrontation. In August yet another British liner, the *Arabic*, was torpedoed without warning, and again Americans died. The German Ambassador in Washington, Bernstorff, judged the situation so serious that he exceeded his instructions. He handed over to be published the two '*Arabic* pledges' of 1 September and 6 October 1915, the first agreeing to follow cruiser rules for liners (if not freighters), the second repudiating the *Arabic* sinking and offering an indemnity. He was reproved by his superiors, but not disowned. The second development of this period was a short-lived Congressional revolt. In January and February 1916 resolutions were introduced into the Senate and the House of Representatives respectively to prohibit travel by Americans on belligerent ships and to warn them against travel on armed merchant vessels. Wilson, nettled, set out his position in a letter on 24 February to the Chairman of the Senate Foreign Relations Committee, Senator Stone. For him to accept any abridgement of American rights in violation of the law of war, he warned, would be a 'humiliation', and would lead to others, so that 'the whole fine fabric of international law would crumble under our hands piece by piece'. This was enough to get the offending resolutions shelved, at the cost of still more firmly barring the door against retreat. But Wilson enjoyed, at least in public, support from Congress and from the press in the next crisis, when the French Channel steamer, the *Sussex*, was torpedoed on 24 March.[52]

Little is known of the President's thinking after this event. But on 18 April he called on Germany to apply immediately cruiser rules against merchantment as well as liners (thus going beyond the *Arabic* pledge), or diplomatic relations would be cut off. The Germans' '*Sussex* pledge' on 4 May replied that they had instructed their submarines accordingly, but warned that if the United States could not obtain British compliance with international law they would resume their freedom of action. Another American note four days later denied that the new policy should be contingent on successful negotiations with London. 'Responsibility in such matters', Wilson inserted in the draft, 'is single, not joint; absolute, not relative.'[53] Still less than Britain's ultimatum over Belgium in 1914, however, can the American commitment be explained by simple reference to international law, whose guidance was anyway uncertain. Though willing to use the rule of law in justification, Wilson allowed economic interest (over loans) and national dignity and humanitarian feeling (over the submarines) to sway his judgement. The *Sussex* pledge was the coping stone on a structure of American neutrality that aggrieved the Allies in many details but on the major issues operated heavily against the Central Powers. This was evident in the prodigious flow of American goods and credit, and in the differing treatments of the British policy of starving German civilians and the German policy of drowning Allied and American ones. The cumulative effect was viewed with a very jaundiced eye in Berlin, where the fate of the *Sussex* pledge had now to be resolved.

The U-boats' unexpected early successes against British warships encouraged the German navy to experiment with the submarine as a commerce-raiding weapon. Bethmann Hollweg had reservations from the start: not, or so he professed, on legal or humanitarian grounds, but because of the likely damage to Germany's relations with the neutrals. In practice his policy, mirroring Grey's, became to seek the maximum that was possible short of a confrontation with Wilson.[54] The navy, conversely, questioned whether American threats would ever be implemented, and whether American intervention would matter anyway. It was supported by a 'U-boat movement' of academics, business pressure groups, and right-wing political parties similar to the coalition that lobbied for draconian German war aims.[55] For Bethmann's critics in the Reichstag the agitation was an opportunity, irrespective of the merits of the issue, to strike at his most vulnerable point. And the advantages given to the Allies by American neutrality made it difficult for the Chancellor to contend that great sacrifices to prevent American intervention would be justified.

None the less, divisions among Bethmann's enemies allowed him to keep the upper hand down to the summer of 1916. The Kaiser was advised on naval questions by the Chief of the Naval Staff, the Navy Minister, and the Chief of the Naval Cabinet. The latter, von Müller, generally supported Bethmann on the submarine issue. The Chiefs of the Naval Staff in the first part of the war (Pohl and Bachmann) and the Navy Minister (Tirpitz), were fierce advocates of U-boat warfare; but Holtzendorff, who replaced Bachmann in the summer of 1915, and Capelle, who replaced Tirpitz in March 1916, were more tractable. And for most of 1915 Tirpitz lacked support from Falkenhayn, who in September 1914 had taken over from Moltke as Chief of the General Staff and was the army's leading spokesman. The conflicting arguments were presented in a succession of Crown Councils, generally followed by executive orders favouring Bethmann being agreed between the Chancellor and Wilhelm. Thus in June 1915 Bethmann secured secret orders for liners and merchant ships to be respected; and all U-boat action in the Channel and the Western Approaches was suspended after the *Arabic* pledge.[56]

These successes were fragile. Falkenhayn supported Bethmann in the *Lusitania* crisis less because he feared American entry than because of the danger of antagonizing Italy and the Balkan neutrals. By the end of the year, however, the Italians had been stalemated, and Bulgaria had joined the Central Powers. In his so-called 'Christmas Memorial' Falkenhayn came out in favour of a submarine offensive in order to break Britain's will. Spring was always the season in which the U-boat advocates pressed hardest, at the beginning of the long months during which the British Isles depended on wheat shipped from the southern hemisphere until their own harvest was gathered. But Bethmann continued to resist. Unrestricted submarine warfare, he maintained, would lead inevitably to American belligerency, bringing volunteers, naval support, moral encouragement, and unlimited financial assistance to Germany's enemies, and allowing them to tighten the blockade. In short, it would lose Germany the war. Conversely, he doubted whether Britain could be starved into defeat in a matter of months, as the navy claimed. To attempt it would be an irresponsible *Vabanquespiel*—a break-the-bank game—with national survival. Instead, he won approval in the spring of 1916 for a compromise course: an 'intensified' submarine offensive that would dispense with cruiser rules against armed enemy merchantment. After the *Sussex* crisis, however, even this was suspended, all the German leaders being temporarily agreed that preventing the Americans from breaking off relations should have first priority.[57]

In the longer term, however, whereas the U-boat lobby promised rapid victory, Bethmann could offer only a continuing battle of attrition, in which the Allies seemed likely gradually to gain the upper hand. His position was also fatally weakened when in August 1916 Falkenhayn was replaced as Chief of the General Staff by Hindenburg, with Ludendorff, Hindenburg's indispensable and more intelligent and forceful adjutant, becoming First Quartermaster-General. In any confrontation between Bethmann and Hindenburg the latter's enormous reputation as the supposed architect of Germany's victories on the Eastern Front would make it very difficult for the Kaiser to remove him. Wilhelm's arbitrating role and Bethmann's Reichstag support were alike enfeebled. Although unrestricted submarine warfare was supported by the Conservatives and National Liberals on the right, Bethmann had been able to defeat them in the Reichstag budget committee in March 1916 with support from the SPD, the Progressives, and Erzberger of the Catholic Centre Party. But the balance in the Centre Party now altered, and in October Erzberger acquiesced in a resolution by its Reichstag deputies that a decision on the U-boat question must be 'supported basically by the conclusion of the Supreme Command'. Initially Hindenburg and Ludendorff preferred to wait until the fresh Balkan emergency caused by Rumanian intervention had been contained. But by the autumn, with the Central Powers' forces advancing on Bucharest, the pieces were falling into place.[58]

Bethmann had one more argument for postponing a showdown that he was now bound to lose: the possibility of American mediation. Wilson's intercession, he envisaged, might begin conversations that the Allies would be unable to break off, and in which the Central Powers, because of the territory they had overrun, would enjoy a negotiating edge.

Bernstorff encouraged him in the further hope that if the Allies appeared responsible for American mediation having failed, it would be possible to launch the submarine campaign without Wilson retaliating. Hindenburg and Ludendorff were willing to wait until the possibility had been explored. But even after Wilson's victory in the November Presidential elections, Bernstorff reported a succession of postponements in the administration's mediation plans. A peace note launched by the Central Powers on 12 December was promptly and vehemently rejected by the Allies, and this reduced the prospects of success for Wilson's own note when it eventually followed on the 18th. [59] With its failure the last alternative path appeared to have been closed, and if a U-boat offensive was to be launched in the spring of 1917 the decision could wait no longer.

In late December Hindenburg and Ludendorff agreed that an unrestricted campaign must begin at the end of January 1917; when Bethmann remonstrated Hindenburg threatened to make the dispute public. A memorandum presented to the Chancellor by Holtzendorff on 5 January estimated that the British could be starved out in five months if they were attacked without warning, before they could accumulate shipping and supplies. Holtzendorff reached an agreement with the Kaiser before the final Pless conference on 9 January, and Bethmann no longer resisted strongly. Indeed, he had resolved to stay in office, believing that resigning would be futile, and would damage public consensus. In the final weeks, however, there was a flurry of diplomacy. House, unaware of what was impending, twice suggested to Bernstorff that Wilson would be willing to attempt confidential mediation to initiate a peace conference, and invited Germany to state its terms. On the first occasion Bethmann ordered his Ambassador to be dilatory. On the second he did send a list of conditions; but these arrived simultaneously with the news that Germany was repudiating the *Sussex* pledge. Because of the navy's desire for surprise, it was only on 31 January that the American Government was told that all shipping, including neutral vessels, in the waters round the British Isles, France, and Italy would be liable to be sunk without warning from the following day.[60]

Bethmann had the sense in January of reliving July 1914: once again the military were hurrying everything, inhibiting last-minute attempts at compromise before they had time to mature. In reality, there is little evidence that Germany had an opportunity to pursue unrestricted submarine warfare while avoiding hostilities with the USA. The belligerents were too far separated for American mediation to be likely to succeed, and Wilson and House, unbeknown to Bethmann, had secretly endorsed the Allies' major territorial aims. There was, however, a missed opportunity of another kind. The Holtzendorff memorandum accurately assessed British food stocks and the likely tonnage losses, but it underestimated the ability of the British to tolerate such losses, and in the summer of 1917 a record wheat harvest and the introduction of the convoy system allowed them to survive. And the benefits of the American entry to the Allies were all, and more than, Bethmann had foreseen. Yet in October 1916 the Germans had resumed submarine warfare in accordance with cruiser rules and were already sinking British merchant ships much faster than they could be replaced. Lifting the restrictions brought the monthly sinkings up from 400,000 to 600,000 tons.[61] But by waiting, the Germans could still have done enormous damage, and they would have been speedily rewarded by the fall of the Tsar in Russia and an Anglo-French financial crisis. By February 1917 the end of Allied purchasing capacity was only weeks away, and it is improbable that Wilson would have responded as did Franklin Roosevelt, who baled out the British with Lend-Lease aid in the analogous foreign-exchange crisis of 1940–1. The Holtzendorff memorandum, however, considered Allied financial difficulties unlikely to bring results 'within a determinable period'.[62] As for the Russian Revolution, Bethmann and the German High Command had foreseen the possibility, but neither could predict the timing.[63] To gamble on it seemed even more hazardous than to trust in Holtzendorff's calculations. The fact remains that Bethmann, as the responsible political authority, was wiser in his judgement than the military and naval chiefs, and yet he felt obliged to concede. This was symptomatic of the deeper ailments of Imperial Germany: the lack of constitutional subordination of the High Command, and the exaggerated respect held for it in the larger world outside the governmental corridors. But the decision was now taken, and the initiative

passed back from Berlin to Washington. It remained to be seen
how Washington would respond.

Wilson hesitated even over breaking off relations, but after
listening to the advocacy of Lansing, House, and the majority
of his Cabinet he went ahead. Between 3 February and his war
message to Congress on 2 April, three main developments
occurred. The first was the submarine campaign. The British
liner *Laconia* went down on 25 February; American ships
followed, with heavy casualties. American cargo vessels refused
to put to sea, commerce along the eastern seaboard was
disrupted, and there were food riots in the coastal cities. On
26 February Wilson asked Congress for powers to arm American merchantmen. The House voted 403 : 14 in favour, and
although a filibuster prevented approval from being given in
the Senate, the President judged he had the authority to
proceed. The second development was the Zimmermann
telegram. Zimmermann had replaced Jagow as German
Foreign Minister in December 1916. In January he authorized
his diplomatic representative in Mexico to propose an alliance
if Germany and the United States went to war. Mexico was to
be offered the territory it had lost in 1848 in Texas, New
Mexico, and Arizona, and was to be encouraged to invite
Japan to join the new combination. British naval intelligence
intercepted and decrypted the telegram, which was passed over
to the American authorities and published by Wilson on
1 March. The President himself was deeply angered; and the
hostility felt towards Germany by American public opinion
diffused outwards from its previous centre in the north-east.
The third development was the abdication of the Tsar on
15 March. Meeting the Cabinet five days later, Wilson said that
if American belligerency would 'hasten and fix' democratization
in Russia and Germany this would be an additional justification for it, although insufficient alone. He found the Cabinet
unanimously in favour of entering the war and assisting the
Alies, and on the following day, 21 March, he decided to
reconvene Congress early. Presumably his mind was now
made up.[64]
Why did Wilson recommend war? In his address on 2 April
he mentioned the submarine controversy, the Zimmermann

telegram, German spying and sabotage in the United States, and the revolution in Petrograd. He also urged belligerency rather than continuing 'armed neutrality'. To arm American shipping was inadequate: prudence dictated seeking out the U-boats and destroying them as soon as they were detected. And armed neutrality would give ' America neither the effectiveness of a belligerent nor its rights. Wilson had already given the Allies easier financial treatment since February, and he now additionally proposed half a million conscripts, expansion of the navy, and Government loans and supplies. These would be greater sacrifices than under armed neutrality; but they would be outweighed by participation in the peace conference, and the most memorable portion of the War Message set out the principles on which America would attend. Its quarrel was not with the German people, but with autocracy, which was a menace to world peace. It sought neither territory nor indemnities for itself, but would be fighting a war for democracy and the rights of great and small nations alike.[65]

The President seriously considered the alternatives. It would be a 'crime', he told his advisers in February, to go to war if this prevented America from being able to help reconstruct Europe afterwards. 'White civilization', he feared, would be weakened relative to the yellow race. If he deemed it necessary, he would do nothing, and disregard accusations of weakness and cowardice.[66] His decision was a difficult and lonely one, over which he consulted little until the end. For this reason, its motives remain obscure. But essential to an understanding of it are Wilson's long-maturing ambition to remodel the international order, and his equivocal relation to the Allies.

By calling for belligerency rather than armed neutrality the President was committing the United States to support for the Allied war effort. His advisers—House, Lansing, McAdoo—believed an Allied victory was in America's strategic interest;[67] and there were powerful economic considerations. The U-boats' primary target was Britain's wheat trade with the southern hemisphere, but if they succeeded in their objectives they would destroy American commerce with the Allies. The great wartime boom would end, and the credits extended by American citizens might never be repaid. Yet it is difficult to show that such preoccupations influenced Wilson himself, and national security arguments also rarely appear in his private correspondence or public statements. Until the *Lusitania* crisis he rejected House's pleas for urgent rearmament. In July 1915 he at length asked his Army and Navy secretaries to draw up plans for military 'preparedness', although leaving unclear the contingencies it was designed to meet. Indeed, he seems to have envisaged the naval programme approved by Congress in 1916 as a means of leverage against Britain rather than Germany.[68] The only security consideration he mentioned in the final crisis was the danger from the yellow peril, and this as an argument against belligerency. In the economic sphere there is further evidence that Wilson divided his sympathies more evenly than did his advisers, and that he was willing to apply pressure to the Allies. When the British Government tried to sell short-term Treasury bills in the United States, the Federal Reserve Board on 27 November 1916 advised the member banks of the Federal Reserve System against buying foreign securities of the kind. They should generally be more cautious, and lend below the legal limit. The Board was worried about tight credit and inflationary pressures. But Wilson, when consulted, approved the action also on the grounds that at present relations with London were more strained than those with Berlin.[69] The President, in fact, appears to have failed to appreciate the seriousness of the Allies' position. They successfully concealed the gravity of their shortages of foreign exchange, shipping, and manpower until after American entry, and then turned out to need far more generous aid than he had originally envisaged. But in the spring of 1917 German victory—with the attendant loss of American loans and the broader threat to democracy and the balance of power—was not perceived in Washington as being imminent. Rather, American belligerency might at relatively small expense permit a marginal Allied victory in conditions that would suit American purposes, and give Wilson maximum influence on the peace settlement.[70] And by entering formally as an 'Associated' rather than an 'Allied' Government, the United States preserved the option of negotiating separately with the enemy.

This leads back to the argument of the War Message that belligerency would enhance American influence on the peace settlement, and to Wilson's emerging grand design for a new international order. This was a more compelling reason for intervention than any narrower sense of American security and economic interest, and certainly more compelling than any affinity or solidarity with the Western Europeans. The President's thinking on the subject had crystallized during successive mediation efforts since the outbreak of war, and it was here that House's influence was greatest. In May–July 1914 the Colonel had already been in Europe, seeking arms limitation between the Powers and co-operation between them in safeguarding loans to the 'waste places of the earth'. In August the American Government offered its services as an intermediary, although without success. And in February–May 1915 House was in Europe on another unofficial mission, meeting the British, French, and German leaders in an attempt to discover their peace terms. As early as August 1914 Wilson had envisaged a post-war association of nations that would punish violations of territorial integrity. His desire to influence the peace settlement had encouraged his firmness over the *Lusitania*.[71] And on 24 August 1915 Lansing suggested that if the United States broke off relations with Germany over the submarine issue and Germany declared war, the American Government could later urge leniency on the Allies in the peace negotiations and regain Germany's goodwill. This letter, Wilson replied, 'runs along very much the same lines as my own thought'.[72]

This approach—of influence on the settlement through co-operation with the Allies—achieved a first expression in the House–Grey Memorandum.[73] In September 1915 Grey, who had cultivated House during the latter's most recent visit to Europe, wrote to him to suggest that Wilson should propose a League of Nations, whose members would combine against a Power that broke a treaty, violated the laws of war, or refused to settle a dispute by peaceful means. 'Personally', he added, he hoped that at the peace France would regain Alsace-Lorraine, Belgium recover its integrity, and Russia win an outlet to the sea. House, with Wilson's approval, replied that the United States would be willing after the war to belong to such a League. And on a third visit to Europe in the following spring the Colonel reached agreement with the British Foreign

Secretary on the House–Grey memorandum of 22 February
1916. This stated that House had favoured as peace terms the
restoration of Belgian independence, the transfer of Alsace-
Lorraine to France (with compensation for Germany outside
Europe), and a sea outlet for Russia. It proposed that at a
moment France and Britain deemed opportune Wilson would
call a peace conference, and if Germany refused to attend the
United States would 'probably' declare war. If Germany did
attend, but the conference failed to secure terms favourable to
the Allies because Berlin was 'unreasonable', the United
States, again, would intervene. Wilson qualified this latter
contingency with a second 'probably', but otherwise approved
the document. The ball was now in the Allies' court.

The memorandum showed a striking lack of realism about
American domestic politics. Its 'probablies' acknowledged
Congress's constitutional prerogatives, but Wilson still went
further than was wise without consulting Cabinet or Congressional opinion, and committed himself only just after
the Congressional revolt that he had quelled by the letter to
Senator Stone. It is extremely unlikely that the United States
could have gone to war in the circumstances envisaged in the
memorandum, which Wilson sanctioned, presumably, in a
momentary lapse of judgement caused partly by his regard for
his friend. It was fortunate for him that the Allies failed to take
it up. House had informed the French Government of the
memorandum, but the French were reluctant to pursue it
unless their allies broached it, and the British, expecting
French hostility, remained silent. Grey probably wished to take
things further, but he deferred to the opposition of the British
naval and military advisers. And Asquith doubted that Wilson
had the domestic political authority to implement the proposal.
In May House urged Grey to act on the memorandum at once,
but the British again failed to respond, preferring to gamble
that the forthcoming Somme offensive would improve their
military prospects. The House–Grey memorandum was
therefore a dead end, although one element of it entered the
administration's public policy. On 27 May 1916 Wilson spoke
to the main American pro-League pressure group, the League
to Enforce Peace. He declared his willingness to join a
universal association of States, to be set up after the conflict in

order to uphold free passage on the seas and to prevent wars begun contrary to treaty and without warning. In the ensuing Presidential election campaign American membership of the League was supported by both Wilson and his Republican challenger.

In its muddled way, the House–Grey memorandum marked a high point of American sympathy for the Allies, and gave approval for their most important war aims. Its rejection, the suspension of the submarine controversy after the *Sussex* pledge, and the disputes with the British over blacklisting and neutral mails made Wilson more equidistant between the two sides. He had little sentimental attachment to the Allies, and repeatedly infuriated them by his assertions that the rights and wrongs of the origins of the war were no American concern. After his re-election early in November he prepared a new and more even-handed initiative. But on 12 December the Central Powers anticipated him by issuing a separate invitation to the Allies to enter peace talks. Wilson now had to move rapidly, before Allied rejection of the Central Powers' initiative ruined the prospects for his own scheme, and his peace note went off to the belligerents on the 18th. Formally, it was not a mediation proposal but an invitation to both sides to state their war aims in concrete detail rather than in generalities. Its unlucky timing aroused unjustified Allied suspicions that it had been concerted with their enemies. Actually, in contrast with the House–Grey memorandum, there had been prior consultation with neither side. The new initiative was a desperate attempt to forestall the danger of a resurgence of the submarine controversy forcing the United States into co-belligerency with the Allies. It was preceded by financial pressure on them through the Federal Reserve Board's warning on 27 November 1916. When Lansing (intending to sabotage the peace note) let slip in a press conference that the United States was coming to the 'verge of war', he was severely reprimanded by Wilson. But the President admitted to House that his principal motivation had been fear that a new submarine crisis would force his hand.[74]

As an attempt to restore peace and avert a confrontation with the Germans the note failed. As an attempt to elicit information about war aims it had more success. The Allies' reply on 10 January set out their objectives more fully than had any previous statement.[75] The Germans' public reply on 26 December refused to state terms, although, as has been seen, Bethmann secretly communicated conditions on 31 January. Wilson's 'Peace without Victory' speech to the Senate on 22 January 1917 commented on these developments, and for the first time committed the United States not only to the League of Nations but also to more specific peace proposals. In drafting the speech Wilson moved back to closer sympathy with the Allies, whose reply to his note had been more definite. Although 'not quite sure' about Alsace-Lorraine, he and House privately agreed that Belgium and Serbia should be restored, and the Turkish Empire cease to exist. In public, the speech supported a 'united, independent, and autonomous Poland': a provision House and Wilson supposed would be uncontroversial but that in fact deeply angered the German leaders. The United States, according to the speech, would join the League of Nations only on condition that the post-war settlement thus guaranteed was a 'peace without victory', with no resentful loser: a peace based on democratic liberties for all peoples, on transfers of territory made only with the inhabitants' consent, on the freedom of the seas, and on limits on armaments. This marked a further large elaboration of Wilson's conception of the post-war order.[76] But there was an implicit contradiction between these goals and peace without victory as a means of achieving them, and this was impressed on the President in the final stage.

On 19 March, finding that Wilson believed U-boat attacks on American shipping were insufficient to justify declaring war, Lansing urged that war would come anyway and that America should take the initiative, not only to encourage the democrats in Germany and Russia and because the Allies represented the cause of democracy against autocracy, but also to gain more influence on the eventual peace. House, on Lansing's prompting, wrote in similar vein.[77] So the argument was put; and it appeared in the War Message as an explanation of why armed neutrality was insufficient. Wilson still had doubts. He told the journalist Frank Cobb that belligerency would mean an attempt to reconstruct a peacetime civilization with war standards, and at the end of it no peacetime standards might be left. None the less, he confessed to House, he saw no alternative.[78]

The assumption of the analysis thus far has been that American belligerency depended on Wilson's decision. Certainly he was not driven into war by irresistible pressure from Congress and outside. He had the necessary moral courage to advise against hostilities with Germany, and if he had chosen to acquiesce in unrestricted U-boat warfare he could probably have commanded sufficient Congressional support. In the 1916 election campaign he had allowed his party to campaign strongly on the accusation that a Republican victory would be more likely to draw American in. Only after the breaking of diplomatic relations did elements in Congress and the press begin to advocate war, but both in majority remained uncommitted.

Yet when Wilson made his choice he was able to carry overwhelming Congressional majorities with him.[79] The traditional foreign-policy alignment on Capitol Hill had altered during the neutrality period, and the Democrats had tended to become more interventionist than their opponents. Of the fifty-four Representatives who voted against the War Resolution, only eighteen were Democrats, as against thirty-five Republicans. But the Resolution was anyway approved by large majorities in both parties. Among the American regions, bipartisan consensus was strongest in the north-east. The eastern Republican leaders had become more sceptical about the League of Nations, and Roosevelt and Cabot Lodge condemned the Peace without Victory speech; but they regarded Germany as a threat to American security and a violator of international law, and they approved of American intervention. The Republican opponents of entry came overwhelmingly from the Middle West, with its large German-American vote, its interior location, and its Progressive distrust of war as capitalist-inspired. The rebel Democrats tended similarly to be agrarian Progressives, mainly from the West and South. Two things help explain the failure of the Democratic Party, whose support lay mainly away from the eastern seaboard, to oppose the war more strongly. The first was the threat to the West and South implicit in the Zimmermann telegram; the second was Wilson's example. The President had twice led the party to victory, after a generation of defeats. He had also given an idealistic justification for belligerency, and in the final crisis he waited not only for his own misgivings to resolve themselves but also for public acceptance of intervention to mature. On 30 March his Cabinet correctly advised him that the country would now endorse a declaration of war.[80]

Since the turn of the century portions of educated American opinion had seen Germany as a potential danger to the western hemisphere. In 1915 an alarmist literature warned of a possible German invasion of the United States itself. Much of American society was benefiting from the unprecedented prosperity created by the Allied war trade. Finally, the submarine attacks produced genuine anger and shock. All these reasons help explain why a national consensus could form in support of intervention, and why a majority in Congress rallied to the President's call. But Wilson's personal initiative was indispensable. And for the President security and economic considerations in a narrow sense were not determinant. Even after the violation of the *Sussex* pledge he would have confined himself to armed neutrality had it not been for the extra leverage belligerency would lend to American efforts to create a new international order at the peace settlement. He helped the Allies in the interests of a higher design with which he might later have to dragoon them into compliance.

Wilson went to war with negligible advance strategic planning and with little effort to assess the balance of military strength. He could afford to do so because of his geographical remoteness and because American adherence in itself made the difference between victory and defeat. However, a military calculation of sorts was implicit in the War Message: the United States would make a primarily naval and economic contribution that would give it disproportionate influence at the peace conference for a small toll in lives. The other interventionist Governments—except the Japanese—were weaker, and were closer to the conflict's epicentre. Their strategic calculations were accordingly more difficult and complex. Wilson resembled Sonnino and Bratianu in having decided in advance what he wanted from the war. Yet American goals were a product of more enlightened self-interest, both vaguer and more ambitious, than those of the other recruits to the Allied cause, and were likely sooner or later to conflict with them.

After the entry of the USA most of the remaining independent States, from Latin America to China and Siam, followed suit. That the war had become global testified to the existence of a global balance of power. War in Europe created a vacuum in Asia, which the Japanese moved to fill. In such a world Turkey, Italy, and even House and Lansing in Washington feared that neutrality offered little protection. After the invasion of Belgium, no one was safe. But the world was also becoming a single entity in more subtle ways. The nineteenth-century transport and communications revolution had helped to unify the North Atlantic basin by ties of trade and sentiment. The Wilson administration's peace programme recognized this, as well as reflecting American national interest. But at the same time the opposing war aims of the Allies and the Central Powers were tearing Western unity apart; and to these war aims we must now turn.

3

War Aims

AUGUST 1914–APRIL 1917

(i) *The Central Powers*

It is time to probe more deeply the fundamental conflict into which the peripheral Powers were drawn. Despite escalating levels of violence, that conflict's central feature was a military, political, and diplomatic impasse. Deadlock in military operations and the steadfastness of the political truces formed on the home fronts were complemented by a deepening incompatibility between the opposing coalitions' war aims. Although the sacrifices that the war exacted were immensely greater than had been foreseen, the sacrifices entailed in compromise were still thought to exceed the price of fighting on. More precisely, Governments became entangled in a web of incremental commitment. The practical choice they faced was whether to launch the next offensive, or spurn the latest peace offer, in the knowledge that a few more weeks or months of effort might yield breakthrough and redeem the losses so far borne. And war deadened the sensibilities. It was easier to forfeit the second than the first 50,000 lives, especially if to do so might bring victory and not to do so would make certain that the casualties so far suffered were in vain. Only afterwards, with hindsight, could a later generation weigh the fruits of victory against their cumulative cost, and find them wanting.

The political goals of victory were referred to at the time as *Kriegsziele, buts de guerre*, war aims. They are inherently difficult to define. The Governments of the period were already complex bureaucracies, imperfectly co-ordinated and internally compartmentalized. Government 'policy' is at its most elusive when, as with war aims, it consists of speeches, cabinet resolutions, and instructions to Ambassadors: not of actions, but of intentions and of words. War aims also are inevitably conditional, predicated on the assumption of a victory that may materialize only partially, if at all. Most simply, they are the terms—economic, territorial, military—that Governments hope to incorporate in a peace treaty, although negotiable war aims must be distinguished from absolute ones, to be abandoned only in the event of utter defeat. Crucially at issue in the First World War, however, was not only the content of the peace treaty but also with whom it would be made. For either coalition to split its enemies by signing with one or more of them a separate peace would in itself accomplish an essential goal.

Public statements about war aims referred in coded language to 'sureties' and 'safeguards': to reliable 'guarantees'. This defensive tone was necessary to preserve domestic political truces that rested on the postulate that hostilities had been started by the other side. In reality, to distinguish offensive from defensive war aims obscures the issue. All the belligerents attempted to ensure their own security and independence by encroaching on those of their enemies. War aims, like the pre-war alliances, were responses to the decline of the Concert of Europe and the growing international insecurity since the turn of the century. But the pre-war generation was also one of imperialist expansion into the underdeveloped world, and this continued, simultaneously with the pursuit of new objectives within Europe, after war broke out. The war aims of 1914 to 1918 can be seen in one sense as the climax of the overseas expansion that preceded and accompanied them: as if the Powers had absorbed the vacant places outside Europe and turned to rend themselves. But imperialism within Europe rarely took a naked, annexationist form. It heeded the pervasive nineteenth-century trends of growing national consciousness and economic interdependence. Spurious arguments of national self-determination could justify severing a territory's connection with the existing sovereign Power and making it dependent on another through alliance treaties and economic ties. Governments characteristically pursued their intra-European objectives—strategic, economic, sentimental—less through annexation than via indirect control. And in this they foreshadowed future forms of domination rather than reverting to the past.

These generalizations will be tested first by reference to the Central Powers. The initial phase of German policy coincided with the European war of movement down to November–December 1914. During these weeks Serbia beat off two Austrian attacks, and an Austrian invasion of Russian Poland ended in disaster. The Russians' invasion of East Prussia was repelled at Tannenberg and the Masurian Lakes, but at the end of the campaigning season they held most of their own Polish territories and of the Austrian provinces of Eastern Galicia and the Bukovina. In France, the Germans advanced to the eastern approaches of Paris before being held in the second week of September at the battle of the Marne. Between the subsequent battle of the Aisne and the first battle of Ypres in October–November the trench stalemate on the Western Front took form. It left Germany in possession of almost all of Belgium and the French industrial regions of the Nord and Lorraine. As against this, Britain had swept the German navy and German trade and shipping from the high seas, and Germany's colonies, except East Africa and the Cameroons, were in Allied hands. During this first phase the German leaders evolved two approaches to the war-aims question that would dominate their thinking from now on. The first was embodied in Bethmann Hollweg's 'September Programme', and the second in a conversation on 18 November between the Chancellor and Falkenhayn, Moltke's successor as Chief of the General Staff after the failure on the Marne.

Bethmann's programme of 9 September 1914 defined 'the general aim of the war' as 'security for the German Reich in west and east for all imaginable time. For this purpose France must be so weakened as to make her revival as a Great Power impossible for all time. Russia must be thrust back as far as possible from the German eastern frontier, and her domination over the non-Russian vassal peoples broken.' He proposed a 'central European customs association', embracing continental Western Europe, Poland, Scandinavia, and the Central Powers, which would 'stabilize Germany's economic dominance over Central Europe'. According to his 'provisional notes' for a western peace settlement, Germany would annex all of Luxemburg, as well as Liège and Antwerp from Belgium,

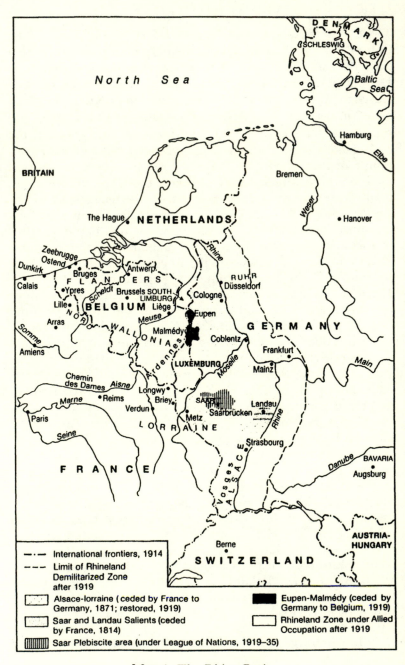

with a corridor from the latter city to the German frontier. France would lose the Longwy-Briey iron ore field, the western Vosges, and possibly the Dunkirk-Boulogne coastal strip. Beyond these small, though strategic, annexations, a crippling war indemnity would prevent France from rearming for fifteen to twenty years, and a commercial treaty would make the country 'economically dependent on Germany'. As for Belgium, it 'must be reduced to a vassal State, must allow us to occupy any militarily important ports, must place her coast at our disposal in military respects, must become economically a German province', thus giving 'the advantages of annexation without its inescapable domestic political disadvantages'. Finally, there would be a 'continuous Central African colonial empire'.[1]

Although approved by Bethmann, the Programme was largely Riezler's work, drafted after a series of discussions between the military and civilian leaders since the end of August. Bethmann supported annexing Longwy-Briey and, possibly, a corridor to Antwerp, on advice respectively from steel-industry spokesmen and from Tirpitz. Rathenau, director of the AEG electrical concern and now head of the Raw Materials Department in the War Ministry, favoured the customs association scheme. But whereas Rathenau had envisaged that the association would supplement a peace of reconciliation with France, the Programme instead reflected Riezler's conception of it as a means of indirect control. The Belgian 'vassal State' also derived from Riezler's ideas. The *Mittelafrika* notion of a belt of Central African territory originated with the Colonial Secretary, Solf, who intended to acquire it from Belgium, France, and Portugal rather than Britain. Indeed, the Programme said nothing about war aims against Britain, and nothing in detail about Russia. Even against France it was a provisional first draft, and the Chancellor seems never again, for example, to have considered annexing the Channel ports. The Programme represented Bethmann's and Riezler's views rather than those of the Government as a whole, and was a guide of temporary significance to their maximum aims.[2]

By the time of Bethmann's conversation with Falkenhayn on 18 November, however, it was clear that hope of rapid victory must be abandoned, and a very different emphasis was given to the statements of the German leaders. Germany could win an

'acceptable peace', said Falkenhayn, only by isolating the main
enemy, Britain, and by making generous separate treaties with
Russia and France, indeed, without annexations from France
at all. Bethmann agreed that only a separate peace with Russia
could make possible a decisive victory in Western Europe.
With the Kaiser's backing, feelers therefore went out to
Petrograd via Andersen, a Danish shipowner and confidant
of the Danish King, at the end of the year.[3] And in a speech
to a delegation of industrialists on 6 December, Bethmann expressed the hope that a separate peace with Russia would be
followed by a treaty that would incorporate France in a 'central
European customs union' and impose a heavy indemnity, but
take little or no French territory.[4] German policy, in other
words, was schizophrenic: both expansionist and yet willing to
moderate its expansionism in order to split the enemy.

How closely did these aspirations resemble pre-war policy?
In the July crisis itself there had been little consideration of war
aims. In 1912 Rathenau had discussed a Central European
customs union with Bethmann, but in January 1914 the
Government had still seen no cause for a fundamental change
in tariff policy.[5] The idea of gains from France, Portugal, and
Belgium in Central Africa, however, had certainly motivated
Germany in the Agadir crisis and the pre-war *rapprochement*
with Britain. In the east the Kaiser had in 1892 and on 31 July
1914 envisaged separating Poland from Russia in the event of
war, and in 1905–6 he considered annexing Russia's Baltic
provinces.[6] Finally, in his bid for British neutrality on 29 July
Bethmann had promised to renounce annexations from
Belgium and France in Europe only if Britain remained out of
the war.[7] Much of the September Programme therefore had
pre-war antecedents, even though in general these were vague
and ill-defined. And the new goal added in November
exhibited much clearer continuity with the pre-war years.
Bethmann continued to pursue the disruption of the European
alignments established in 1904–7: through diplomacy before
the war, through total victory in its first few weeks, and now
through an admixture of diplomacy with force.

This modified programme contained deep contradictions.
A separate peace that would break up the enemy coalition was
possible only if France or Russia would allow their partners to

be defeated in detail and permit the balance of power, which safeguarded their own independence against Germany, to be destroyed. Bethmann was now prepared to jettison elements of the September Programme in order to achieve this end. But that, if the Allies attached as high a price to maintaining their unity as Germany did to smashing it, would not suffice. Second, Bethmann had by the end of the year come closer to Tirpitz's and Falkenhayn's view that Britain, not Russia, was Germany's most dangerous foe. But only indirect pressure— weakening or detaching Britain's continental allies, acquiring naval bases on the Belgian coast and if possible overseas— could be applied against London. The goal of security against Britain therefore conflicted with that of reconciliation with France, on whom harsh terms could more easily be imposed. A Europe united under German leadership against Britain would be held together by coercion rather than consent.

In the war on land the Central Powers generally held the initiative until the summer of 1916. The French army's offensives on the Western Front in 1915 were insignificant in their results, and numbing in their cost. The trench impasse was reproduced in Southern Europe after Italy's intervention, and again during the abortive Allied campaign at Gallipoli. Between May and September 1915, in the meantime, Germany and Austria-Hungary conquered most of Russian Poland, together with the Baltic provinces of Courland and Lithuania. In October and November, with Bulgarian assistance, they overran Serbia. But although driven back hundreds of miles and deprived of their allies in the Balkans, the Russians refused a separate peace. From February 1916 onwards, therefore, a very different kind of warfare was pursued in the battle of Verdun, designed, in Falkenhayn's merciless conception, to 'bleed to death' the French army and drive the French people beyond 'breaking point'.[8] But once again no separate peace materialized, and when the Russian Brusilov offensive opened in June and the Anglo-French one on the Somme in July, a new and much less favourable conjuncture for the Central Powers had arrived.

In the west, for most of 1915, German planners could elaborate on the September Programme without facing complicating

decisions about a possible separate peace. Against France,
Longwy-Briey remained the primary goal. In Belgium, replying
on 31 December 1914 to a request by Bethmann for plans for
indirect control, the Foreign and Interior Ministries envisaged
a disarmed 'tributary State', whose foreign policy would be
in German hands and whose legislation would be subject to
German veto: its coasts and fortresses would be available for
German occupation, it would enter monetary and customs
union with Germany, and the two countries' railway systems
would be linked 'as completely as possible'. In October 1915
the Kaiser approved the Navy's claim to occupy indefinitely
the Ostend–Zeebrugge–Bruges triangle. The German occupation authorities, meanwhile, tried to loosen the authority of
the traditionally French-speaking royal administration over the
Flemings of northern Belgium. In 1915 they introduced Flemish
instruction into the region's primary schools; in 1916 they
opened a Flemish university; and early in 1917 they established
a consultative Council of Flanders.[9]

In the spring and summer of 1916, however, these objectives
had to be weighed against the possibility of a negotiated
settlement. During June, at the height of the Verdun
campaign, the German Minister in Switzerland reported with
misleading optimism on the prospects that French politicians
with whom he was in contact would make a separate peace.
Jagow replied that Germany would be willing to restore to
France all of its territory except Longwy-Briey and a protective
glacis round the iron-ore basin, but it could cede only small
frontier districts of Alsace-Lorraine, and would demand a large
war indemnity. French economic subjection and diplomatic
isolation might still be an alternative to the September-
Programme goals. But if France fought on in alliance with
Britain, Jagow warned, its 'complete overthrow' would be
required.[10] War aims towards Belgium were similarly
illuminated when Count Törring, on behalf of Germany, met
Professor Waxweiler, on behalf of the exiled King Albert, in
the winter of 1915–16. Albert showed willingness to move
towards diplomatic alignment with the Central Powers, but he
had not consulted his Cabinet and the conversations had little
chance of succeeding even before Germany communicated its
final terms. These required a disarmed Belgium to come under

German military protection, and to grant occupation and transit rights, a coastal naval base, and a German majority shareholding in the Belgian railways, as well as, if possible, a closer customs union. If Belgium resisted a 'leaning' towards Germany in international politics, even more would be necessary. Unsurprisingly,' at the end of the Törring–Waxweiler conversations the two sides remained far apart. [11]

At first, Bethmann and Jagow were ready to concede much more in order to win a separate peace in the east. Via Andersen and other channels in the early months of 1915 they intimated their willingness to talk, suggesting that they would require of Russia only a favourable trade treaty and small frontier gains. [12] From discussions within the German Government emerged the secret project for a Polish 'frontier strip': a band of territory on the northern and western fringes of Russian Poland would be annexed, and settled with German colonists, the existing Polish and Jewish population being bought out and moved to the Russian zone. A meeting of Prussian Ministers in July approved the plan in principle, and Bethmann himself gave it veiled support in conversations with Reichstag deputies and the Austrians during the year. Chilling though it appeared, the 'frontier strip' was intended as a moderate policy, that would entice Russia into a separate agreement. But this, both in public and in private, the Tsarist Government refused. In July Bethmann warned the Russians that they risked losing Poland for good. [13] Just as in France and Belgium in 1914, so now in Poland German territorial occupation became the stimulus by which German appetites were swelled.

Before 1914 the three eastern Empires had had a common interest in maintaining the partition of Poland between them. Once they came to blows, however, they found themselves in competition for Polish nationalist favours. Russia opened the bidding in August 1914 with a promise to unite the Poles under Tsarist sovereignty. Poland also became the most divisive territorial issue within the Austro-German alliance. Burián, when he became Austro-Hungarian Foreign Minister in March 1915, feared that an independent Poland or one under exclusively German influence would jeopardize the loyalty of the Habsburgs' own eight million Polish subjects. But to partition Russian Poland would also create a source of permanent unrest within Austria-Hungary and Germany. In August he therefore proposed to Bethmann the 'Austrian solution' to the question: unification of Russian Poland with the Austrian Poles of Galicia in an autonomous kingdom under Habsburg sovereignty. The Chancellor was evasive, fearing that this would swamp the influence of the German-speakers in Austria-Hungary; but privately he and Jagow decided that the Austrian solution, on certain conditions, was preferable to bringing millions of Jews and Poles under Germany's own rule.[14]

At this point the Polish question became entangled with a revival of the German project for a Central European customs union, or *Mitteleuropa*. After approving the September Programme, Bethmann charged his deputy, Delbrück, with overseeing inter-departmental discussions. In October 1914 and the spring of 1915 Delbrück reported back that *Mitteleuropa* was encountering opposition on the grounds that broader access to European markets would be outweighed by increased discrimination against German trade elsewhere. Hence no consensus had emerged.[15] But in August Falkenhayn, soon supported by the Kaiser, advocated a long-term defensive alliance between the Central Powers, with economic and cultural objectives as well as military ones. And while the politicians in Berlin deliberated, the lines of trenches and the Allied blockade appeared to be turning *Mitteleuropa* into reality as a military and economic unit. The conquest of Serbia, moreover, enabled continuous overland contact between Berlin, Vienna, and Constantinople. At this apposite moment the Reichstag deputy Friedrich Naumann's book *Mitteleuropa* made its appearance, and became the greatest German publishing success since Bismarck's memoirs.[16] At governmental level, however, the concept re-entered policy as one element in a package answer to the Polish question. Meeting Burián in Berlin in November, Bethmann cautiously supported the Austrian solution in Poland if no separate peace were obtainable with Russia, on the conditions of a frontier strip and of German economic interests being safeguarded. But he also proposed a long-term Austro-German mutual territorial guarantee, and a thirty-year economic agreement that would provide for reciprocal tariff preference and eventual customs union. Greater German influence over Austria-Hungary itself would therefore neutralize the risks entailed in Habsburg custody of the Poles.[17]

Neither the Austrian solution in Poland nor the *Mitteleuropa* project, however, would see the light of day. *Mitteleuropa* was an elusive concept, more important in German unofficial agitation and the demonology of Allied propaganda than in German Government policy. But Rathenau and the Prussian departmental planners hoped to create a zone of industrial predominance that would place Germany's economic potential on a par with the supposed emergent 'world Powers' of the United States, the British Empire, and Tsarist Russia.[18] In Austria-Hungary, however, few except the German-speakers desired closer association with Berlin, and even the latter shared the Government's anxiety to preserve its independence. Stürgkh wished to postpone negotiations, and Tisza was more emphatically opposed. The Austro-Hungarian reply to Bethmann on 24 November agreed to discuss renewing the alliance, to military staff conversations, and to tariff negotiations. Progress then halted until the Austrian and Hungarian halves of the Monarchy had renegotiated the ten-yearly economic agreement between them, in 1917. Tariff reductions agreed between Germany and Austria-Hungary at Salzburg in the following autumn were all that were accomplished before the end of the war.[19]

As for the Austro-Polish scheme, the German leaders soon thought better of Bethmann's provisional acceptance. An Austria-Hungary that absorbed too many Slavs, they feared, would expand disproportionately relative to Germany and become an unreliable ally. In April 1916 Bethmann proposed instead an autonomous Poland with military and economic ties to Germany on the Belgian model. Burián's resistance was broken when the Brusilov offensive smashed through the Habsburg armies and again forced Germany to come to their aid. This made it difficult to portray an Austrian Poland as an effective defensive barrier. Facing in addition an Italian offensive in the south and imminent intervention by Rumania, Burián consented to the Vienna Agreements of August 1916. Germany and Austria-Hungary would publicly commit themselves to establish an independent constitutional monarchy in

Russian Poland after the war. It would have no independent
foreign policy, Germany would command its armies, and its
railways would fall under the Central Powers' control. Both
Germany and Austria-Hungary would annex territory from it,
and its border with Russia would be pushed as far as possible to
the east.[20] A reorientation of German policy towards Lithuania
and Courland paralleled the Vienna Agreements. In June 1915
Bethmann still considered that acquisition of the Baltic region,
with its German urban and landowning minorities, would
unacceptably compromise all chance of future good relations
with the Tsar. But by September it was under German
occupation, and the Kaiser approved a Jagow memorandum
proposing an autonomous duchy under a German prince,
linked to the Reich by military and customs agreements and a
common railway system. In April 1916 Bethmann publicly
promised not to return the region to Russia, thus opening the
way for a further extension of the Belgian formula for indirect
control.[21]

The Vienna Agreements brought Germany and Austria-
Hungary to the brink of an irreparable rupture with the Tsar.
A separate peace would anyway now entail returning territory
for which thousands of their soldiers had died. But given the
failure at Verdun to detach France from the Allies, the quest
for such a peace continued. Between March and May 1916 the
Ruhr industrialist, Stinnes, and the German and Japanese
Ministers in Stockholm discussed, among other things, a
Russian–German–Japanese alliance. The Japanese Govern-
ment terminated this curious episode by disavowing its own
representative. Later in the year the Germans attempted to
make contact with the Russian parliamentary opposition.[22]
Pressure from a new quarter was required before the Central
Powers would issue the proclamation envisaged at Vienna. In
August Hindenburg and Ludendorff took over from Falkenhayn.
They believed a proclamation would attract Polish volunteers
into their depleted armies, and saw little prospect of a Russian
separate peace. Bethmann accepted there were military
arguments for going ahead, and considered the proclamation
might create a valuable *fait accompli* for future peace
negotiations: on balance, he expected it not to deter the
Russians from a separate understanding. On 5 November

Germany and Austria-Hungary duly proclaimed the future Polish kingdom. The number of Polish volunteers that resulted was derisory. None the less, wrote Bethmann afterwards, this was the one act of his Chancellorship by which in future peace talks Germany would be bound. The die, it seemed, was cast.[23]

Not only in Poland did the war aims of the Central Powers come into conflict. Bulgaria's objectives, however, had largely been defined in the agreements of August–September 1915.[24] The Turks, by contrast, won a string of negotiating victories that modified the German–Ottoman alliance in their favour. A German–Turkish treaty in September 1916 bound both sides to make no peace against the other's consent while territory belonging to either remained in enemy hands. This made it harder for the Allies to pursue a separate peace with Turkey; but it also made it harder for Germany to split off Russia by offering it the Ottoman territory conquered by the Tsarist armies in the Caucasus campaigns. The Turks generally succeeded in protecting their independence against German encroachment, and were an additional obstacle to Bethmann's hopes of dividing his enemies.[25]

Austria-Hungary's war aims were a further impediment. Against Italy these were modest, although the Vienna leaders decided to claim frontier rectifications. From Russia the Austrians were determined to regain the territory they had lost, and in Poland they hoped to achieve more. Their other main field of ambition lay in the Balkans. In a meeting of the Joint Council of Ministers on 7 January 1916 Burián wished to reduce Serbia to less than half its present population, and to annex the Montenegro coastline in order to acquire a common frontier with a Habsburg 'protectorate' in Albania. As in 1914, Tisza opposed annexing what would be left of Serbia, but Conrad, Stürgkh, and Burián disagreed, and Burián reported to the Germans that in the majority view Serbia should 'disappear', unless its survival would help secure a separate peace with the Tsar.[26] Like the Germans, the Austrians were torn between imperialist objectives and a diplomatic solution that would relieve the strain of war. But for them also the conquest of enemy territory led on almost automatically to pretensions for that territory to remain permanently under direct or indirect control.

The diplomacy of each Central Power rested on an internal political balance. Radoslavov in Bulgaria and Talat and Enver in Turkey were liable to challenge from domestic rivals whose allegiance lay with the Allies. In Austria-Hungary, by contrast, the different nationalities and parties at first supported the war with surprising unity, serious disaffection being confined to the Serbs, Czechs, and Ruthenes. Until 1917 the Austrian Reichsrat remained suspended, and the main constraints on Burián came from his Government colleagues. Stürgkh believed his domestic reform plans necessitated a 'good peace', and Conrad wanted extensive Balkan annexations; but there was much support for Tisza's view that an Austrian 'solution' in Poland would upset the domestic political equilibrium. Burián himself favoured expansion in Poland and the Balkans, though not to the extent of sharing Conrad's views.[27]

In Germany, during the first two years of war the *Kriegsziel-mehrheit* (or 'War-aims majority') of annexationist parties in the Reichstag and the *Kriegszielbewegung* (or 'War-aims movement') of annexationist pressure groups were confronted by the SPD as the chief, if lukewarm, exponent of restraint. The most effective lobbyist among the patriotic pressure groups was the Pan-German League. Its *Memorandum on German War Aims*, of 28 August 1914, resembled the September Programme in its demands on Belgium, but wanted much larger annexations from Russia and France. The Government tried to stop the memorandum from being distributed, but similar views about the extent of territory to be annexed were held by industrialists such as Stinnes, Thyssen, and Krupp, and by politicians such as Erzberger of the Catholic Centre Party and Stresemann of the National Liberals. The Pan-Germans played a crucial part in instigating the annexationist Petition of the Six Economic Associations, of 20 May 1915, and the Petition of the Intellectuals, of 8 July. The Economic Associations included both the leading organizations of industrial employers (the Central Association of German Industrialists and the Industrialists' League), as well as the main agricultural lobbyist, the Agrarian League. Opposing 'a premature peace with any of

Germany's enemies', they called, among other things, for annexation of the French northern coalfield and territory for peasant settlement in Russia's Baltic provinces. The Petition of the Intellectuals called notably for 'the most ruthless humiliation of England' through an indemnity and the acquisition of overseas naval bases. Its 1,347 signatories included 352 university professors; a rival, anti-annexationist, petition gained only 141 names.[28]

There now existed a formidable unofficial movement in favour of sweeping annexations and opposed to a compromise peace. It enjoyed widespread sympathy among the German Princes represented in the Bundesrat, or Upper Chamber of the Federal Parliament, and among the Conservatives, Free Conservatives, and National Liberals in the Reichstag. A majority of the pivotal Catholic Centre also wanted extensive economic and territorial gains. The Progressive DDP was more moderate, but it too supported the 9 December 1915 declaration of the non-Socialist parties that in the eventual peace negotiations 'Germany's military, economic, financial, and political interests must be permanently guaranteed to their full extent and by all means, including the necessary territorial acquisitions'.[29] The SPD, conversely, had in 1914 voted war credits and an Enabling Act, but had received little, beyond freedom from suppression, in return. The party began to fragment into a small annexationist Right, a moderate Centre, and a Left that was itself divided but opposed supporting unconditionally what it considered an imperialist war. Although the SPD leadership consistently opposed annexations, notably in Belgium, a group of eighteen deputies who had voted against war credits formed a breakaway parliamentary group in March 1916.[30] As in other European countries, then, once the initial political truce began to fray, opinion over war aims polarized essentially on Left–Right lines. Some of the leaders of the Right, indeed, openly acknowledged that they wanted gains abroad in part because these would consolidate the status quo at home.[31]

Bethmann's own pronouncements were increasingly annexationist, but deliberately ambiguous. He regretted that his doubts about German military prospects were not more widely shared, and wished to keep a free hand for possible peace negotiations, but ambiguity was also necessary to maintain the political truce. 'To preserve the unity of the nation', he wrote, 'no policy other than that of the diagonal could be pursued.'[32] His Government consulted unofficial opinion—for example, the industrialists over *Mitteleuropa* and Longwy-Briey—but was not at its dictation and discarded its most extreme proposals. None the less, the Reichstag's attitude severely handicapped him in his disputes *within* the Government with the naval and military authorities over U-boat warfare and war aims. Never a popular or charismatic figure, his position in the repeated bureaucratic confrontations of these years rested heavily on the Kaiser's support, but after the outbreak of war Wilhelm's political interventions became still more inconsistent and erratic, and his backing depended largely on Bethmann's ability to fight for himself. Although from a conventional Prussian administrative background, the Chancellor posed self-consciously as a humane, philosophizing statesman, who pondered the moral responsibilities of decision. Yet characteristically at times of crisis—in July 1914, over the Polish proclamation, or the unrestricted submarine campaign—he opted for a two-way bet, favourable or at least acceptable in either outcome, and therefore relieving him from pressing unequivocally for one or other course. His private opinions over such questions as the future of Belgium and the Polish frontier strip appear close to those of the Pan-Germans, and when he resisted annexationist arguments this was on grounds of realism—Germany's predicament in a war against a coalition of superior long-term strength—rather than moral principle. In some ways, even so, he grew in office, becoming disillusioned with the chauvinism of official Germany and drawing closer in spirit to the SPD. The enigma of his ultimate motivation remains.

Bethmann's differences with Falkenhayn arose in good measure from a clash of temperaments. Sarcastic, ruthless, and self-confident, Falkenhayn none the less had a sounder and more flexible political judgement than Hindenburg and Ludendorff, his rivals and successors. He agreed with Bethmann on the priority of splitting the enemy, even at the sacrifice of territorial gains. But in August 1916 Hindenburg and Ludendorff were brought in with the Chancellor's support,

Bethmann hoping that Hindenburg's authority as the victor of Tannenberg would help to legitimate the compromise peace needed to divide the Allies.[33] The Kaiser, fearing the creation of a new power centre whose authority would eclipse his own, saw more clearly. Hindenburg and Ludendorff, like Tirpitz earlier, exploited their connections with the extremism of unofficial opinion and the Reichstag parties. Until their appointment Bethmann won the crucial battles over foreign policy; afterwards, he almost invariably lost.

The external and internal influences on German policy are evident in the circumstances of the Central Powers' Peace Note of 12 December 1916. Since the Allied offensive had opened in the summer the military balance seemed to have moved in favour of the enemy, and Bethmann was anxious about declining German and Austro-Hungarian morale. He also needed an alternative to the hazards of unrestricted submarine warfare. Having previously rejected American mediation, by August he was willing to accept it as a means of getting the belligerents to the negotiating table, but he grew tired of waiting for an initiative from an American President whom he considered indecisive and anyway prejudiced in favour of the other side.[34]

The Chancellor had meanwhile given thought to an open peace offer by the Central Powers. This might reassure the German Left that the war was a defensive one, and strengthen pressure for negotiation from Allied public opinion. Hence his enthusiasm when Burián made a similar proposal to him on 18 October at Pless. Burián wanted the Central Powers to make their war aims public. Austria-Hungary, he said, would want frontier rectifications from Italy and Rumania and a protectorate over Albania, although it would allow a much truncated Serbia and Montenegro to survive as nominally independent States, Serbia being economically linked to Austria-Hungary. Bethmann, however, opposed specifying war aims, saying that the Allies could use this as a pretext to refuse negotiations, and that if negotiations did result it would be harmful to have stated conditions in advance. In mid-November he and Burián reached the compromise that the Central Powers would declare their willingness to bring detailed terms to the conference table. Bulgarian and Turkish consent was also secured.[35] Although the coalition drew up no common programme of objectives, the Austrians evidently favoured greater sacrifices in Western Europe than the Germans were prepared to make, and it was as well for the diplomatic solidarity of the Central Powers that no peace conference materialized.

The Peace Note also necessitated bargaining within the German Government. In the Prussian Council of Ministers on 27 October, Bethmann suggested that part of the Briey basin could be annexed in exchange for returning parts of Alsace-Lorraine; that there should be an exchange of colonies with France; that Belgium should cede Liège and promise to stay out of economic 'boycotts' of Germany; and that Russia should cede parts of Lithuania and Courland and recognize an independent Poland. Germany should seek economic concessions and a favourable trade treaty, and be willing to abandon its Far Eastern possessions in return for a consolidated Central African Empire. To Hindenburg and Ludendorff on 4 November he proposed essentially the same terms, although in more ruthless language and specifying that if 'guarantees' could not be negotiated with Belgium Germany must annex Liège and a strip of territory to protect the Ruhr. Hindenburg and Ludendorff's reply was harsher on every point: they opposed any territorial cession whatever to France, required Luxemburg to be annexed, and insisted that the Belgian and Polish economies must be subordinated to Germany's and their railways placed under German control. They also wanted to annex a new frontier strip on Poland's eastern border, in addition to the one already envisaged in the west. Although Bethmann's own proposals had been more moderate than those of September 1914, he accepted all the High Command's modifications, except their demand for a Belgian indemnity. The outcome of the policy process therefore differed significantly from his initial ideas.[36]

The timing of the Central Powers' Peace Note was determined largely by the victory in Rumania, where Bucharest fell on 6 December. Bethmann and Burián agreed with Hindenburg and Ludendorff that the note should not appear as a sign of weakness, and it therefore had a bellicose tone that marred it as an appeal to Allied public opinion. The Central Powers offered unspecified conditions that 'would aim to secure the existence, honour, and free development of their peoples', and form the basis of a lasting peace. Bethmann thought rejection likely, but hoped to impress the enemy public, and perhaps find a way to launch unrestricted submarine warfare without a confrontation with Wilson. Whether the Allies accepted negotiations (in which Germany's conquests would give it the advantage) or whether they rejected them, sending the note seemed better than taking no action at all.[37]

In the event the Allies' reception of the Peace Note was unanimously hostile, and culminated in a vehement collective reply. The Kaiser was infuriated, and the advocates in Germany of compromise were gravely weakened. On 23 December Hindenburg hardened his conditions and demanded new annexations from Russia, Belgium, and France. With his support, the navy demanded the Courland and Belgian coasts and the Ostend–Zeebrugge–Bruges triangle, as well as a world-wide chain of naval bases. Solf renewed his *Mittelafrika* proposals. If Bethmann had moderated his position since the September Programme, the military, naval, and colonial authorities had if anything grown more extreme. But the Chancellor took his stand on the conditions agreed with the High Command in November. Even Longwy-Briey, he said, might have to be surrendered if this would split the enemy coalition or if it was the sole obstacle to a general peace. And in the last round of discussions with the Americans in January 1917 Bethmann forwarded a summary of the November conditions as representative of his peace terms.[38]

To talk of 'German war aims' therefore evades the question of who ruled in Berlin. Splendidly efficient in many ways, the German Government was a shambles at the top. Germany could undoubtedly force the other Central Powers to negotiate if it judged the moment opportune. But who, in such conditions, would settle Germany's own demands? Under Hindenburg the General Staff intervened repeatedly in the political sphere, and usually got its way; while the Kaiser became less willing and competent than ever to impose a consistent line. But in any case even the more moderate German leaders were too far removed from their Allied counterparts to make possible either a general or a separate peace. For Bethmann's determination to divide the enemy coalition was matched by the Allies' determination to maintain it, and to make territorial and economic impositions of their own. These Allied objectives must now be analysed in their turn.

(ii) *The Allies*

Among the Allies as among the Central Powers public war aims were distinct from confidential ones; new objectives within Europe accompanied long-established extra-European imperialist drives; and indirect control of European territory was preferred to outright annexation. No one Ally, however, was as dominant as was Germany on the other side. Britain, France, and Russia were comparable in strength; Italy and Japan had local monopolies of force in the Adriatic and the Far East. And each Ally hoped to profit from the war in order to stake out positions against its own partners, as well as against its enemies. Russia and Japan formulated their objectives early, in the winter of 1914–15. At the same time Italy elaborated the demands that it presented in the negotiations leading to the Treaty of London. Britain and France, by contrast, attempted to define their central goals in Europe only in the summer and autumn of 1916; and only in France did this debate reach a conclusion. Hardly had it done so than the Russian Revolution and American belligerency forced all the Allies into a painful reassessment. Attention will now be given to the aims of Britain, France, and Russia against Germany and Austria-Hungary, and to Allied goals in the Near and Far East. The Allies' response to the peace notes of December 1916 will be used to illustrate the coalition's unwieldy diplomatic machinery in action.

It was difficult, noted the Secretary of State for India, Edwin Montagu, with the studied irony peculiar to British official debate, to find 'some convincing argument for not annexing all the territories in the world'.[39] But the Liberal Government took a united Parliament and country into war, and maintained that unity in the trials that followed, only because it could present the conflict both as necessary to the traditional strategic interests of the British Empire and as a humanitarian crusade for a more peaceful and democratic world order. British policy combined uncertainty and even altruism within Europe with *Realpolitik* outside.

Probably the most viscerally desired of British objectives was Germany's permanent elimination as a naval threat. In March 1915 the Liberal Ministers responsible for the Admiralty and the War Office agreed with the Unionist leader, Bonar Law, that the German navy must be destroyed: a position reiterated by the First Sea Lord in October 1916.[40] Intimately linked with this was the fate of Germany's colonies. By February 1916 all of these, except for East Africa, had fallen into Allied, mainly British Empire, hands. The Admiralty considered that the colonies, with their wireless stations and their harbours for commerce-raiding submarines and cruisers, were too dangerous to British imperial communications to be returned. Ministers also feared that an immense German 'black army' could menace neighbouring possessions. And the British Government's hands were partly tied by the Dominions. The territories in the South Pacific were occupied by Australians and New Zealanders anxious about the seizure of Germany's North Pacific islands by Japan. German South-West Africa was overrun by a South African Government that suppressed a Boer rebellion against it in October–November 1914 and whose domestic position the British needed to sustain. But elsewhere London could more easily make concessions to the other Allies. Provisional administrative boundaries for Togoland were agreed with France in August 1914. A similar arrangement in February 1916 gave France control over nine-tenths of the Cameroons. And in February 1917 Britain secretly promised to support Japanese claims at the peace conference to the German North Pacific islands and to Germany's rights in Shantung, in return for naval assistance and Japanese backing for British Empire claims in the South Pacific. Strategic interests, and the need to accommodate the Dominions and the Allies, gradually committed Britain to destroying Germany as a colonial as well as a naval Power.[41]

The German challenge to pre-war British interests had also been economic. After 1914 the protectionist lobby in the House of Commons expanded, and in the business community the free-trading Manchester Chamber of Commerce turned in favour of tariffs. In January 1916 the President of the Board of Trade told Parliament that after the war Germany must be prevented from reconstructing its commercial position. At the inter-Allied Paris Economic Conference in June, Britain approved a battery of measures designed to strengthen the Allies in the future against their enemies. The Government also decided in principle to use tariffs in order to enable British manufacturers to produce goods that had previously been imported from Germany, and the Imperial War Cabinet of British and Dominion leaders agreed in 1917 to bring the Empire closer to self-sufficiency in commodities and strategic industries. The British were circumspect, however, about a common external tariff for the Empire that might raise domestic food prices and estrange the other Allies and the USA. And the Board of Trade in January 1917 doubted whether the 'permanent crushing' of German industry and commerce was either practicable or in Britain's long-term interest. It advised that any reparations claims on Germany should be predominantly in kind (rather than cash), and that little of the cost of the war could be thus recovered. British economic war aims contained a strain of caution, and anyway, apart from the Paris Economic Conference, remained at the level of resolutions of principle and departmental recommendations. [42]

In Europe, returning Belgium to its pre-war status was reaffirmed as an objective in Asquith's Guildhall speech of 9 December 1914, which set the tone for Government war-aims statements for the next two years. [43] In the 'Declaration of Sainte Adresse' on 14 February 1916 Britain, France, and Russia pledged themselves to continue fighting until Belgium had been compensated for the physical damage it had suffered and its economic and political independence had been regained. Belgium's strategic importance, indeed, as an invasion corridor into France and as a U-boat base, had been underlined since August 1914. But to return to the pre-war status quo there would be to revive arrangements that had already failed under the test. Starting from this premiss, in the summer of 1916 the Belgian Government-in-exile called for a new Anglo-French guarantee, suggested that it should take over control of navigation in the Scheldt estuary from the Dutch, and broached the possibility of a union with Luxemburg. The last of these proposals enjoyed some sympathy in British official circles, but on all three Grey resisted being bound. British objectives in the Low Countries remained defensive and restorative, encapsulating a larger British uncertainty about the European settlement as a whole.[44]

Until 1917 Ministers appear to have believed that detailed statements about war aims would be divisive, and would damage rather than strengthen public morale. The imprecision of official policy was mirrored by the lack of an unofficial debate on German lines. No British territory was under enemy occupation, and not even the most vociferous German annexationists had claims on the British Isles themselves. Yet despite this absence of an obvious defensive justification, the war effort was initially supported by both major parties, by a majority in the Labour Party, by the trade unions, and by the Unionist and Nationalist leaders in Ireland. When dissatisfaction set in, it expressed itself politically in attacks on a supposedly incompetent strategic direction of the war. Primarily because of such attacks Labour and the Unionists were brought into the Government in May 1915; and Lloyd George replaced Asquith as Prime Minister when a second coalition was formed in December of the following year. War aims, by contrast, became an important political issue only in 1917. There was no annexationist 'war-aims movement' on German, or even French, lines, in part because annexations were less evidently relevant to the security of the British Isles. Once Germany had been weakened as a naval and colonial rival, the need was to alter its behaviour: to punish it for violating international law and morality and to demonstrate that aggression did not pay. Similarly, although there was much acrimony between the civilian and military authorities, this was less over war aims than over strategy. Sir Douglas Haig and Sir William Robertson, who at the end of 1915 took over respectively as Commander-in-Chief on the Western Front and Chief of the Imperial General Staff, combined a single-minded commitment to the battle of attrition in France and Flanders with a surprising moderation about the war's political goals. Although their support from the Unionists and in the press made them potentially a formidable obstacle to a compromise peace, they left the civilians largely free to determine Britain's objectives.[45]

Governmental thinking on security in Europe rested not on acquiring territory for Britain but on denying it to Germany and keeping the Allied coalition in being. Under the 'Pact of London' of 5 September 1914 Britain, France, and Russia bound themselves to make no separate peace, and not to offer peace conditions without previous agreement with each of the other Allies.[46] From now on Grey saw maintaining and expanding the coalition as the Foreign Office's primary task.[47] Beyond this, Asquith's Guildhall speech expressed another major element in official thinking with its assertion that Germany must be defeated so that 'the military domination of Prussia' could be destroyed. Smashing 'Prussian militarism', in the parlance of the time, could be achieved through a decisive victory that would create the political and psychological upheaval necessary for Germany's behaviour to change. Asquith's Government reaffirmed its commitment to an unequivocal triumph and a dictated peace in the controversy provoked by the memorandum submitted to the Cabinet's War Committee in November 1916 by Lord Lansdowne. Lansdowne, a former Unionist Foreign Secretary and now Minister without Portfolio, called on the Government to consider at what point the Allies should content themselves with war aims, as he put it, of less than twenty shillings in the pound. 'Can we afford', he asked, given the more than 1.1 million British casualties to date, 'to go on paying the same sort of price for the same sort of gains?' Robertson, probably encouraged by Lloyd George, replied that only 'cranks, cowards, and philosophers' would think of peace before the enemy had been crushed. Grey considered peace would be premature for as long as the military and naval authorities thought Germany could be defeated and satisfactory terms imposed. In contrast to Lansdowne's balance-sheet approach, this amounted to a blank cheque for ruinous extravagance with the national resources. But it remained the prevalent official view.[48]

In August 1916 Asquith belatedly invited members of his Government to submit memoranda on possible British terms. This was stimulated partly by the sense that with the opening of the summer offensive the military initiative was now in the Allies' hands. In addition, Grey thought that the possibility of American mediation called for inter-Allied discussion, while Robertson, and probably Asquith, believed the French were closer to defining their objectives and might therefore possess a bargaining edge. In August, even before the Prime Minister's initiative, a memorandum was presented by Robertson and another by two members of the Foreign Office, Tyrrell and Paget. Further contributions followed in October from Balfour (at this stage First Lord of the Admiralty), Sir Henry Jackson (the First Sea Lord), and the Board of Trade. The latter, anxious not to ruin the German economy, and Robertson, who wanted Germany to remain strong enough to balance Russia and France, were the most restrained. Jackson pressed for Germany to lose its colonies and navy, but said little about Europe. Robertson, Balfour, and the Tyrrell–Paget memorandum agreed that Belgium must be restored and France regain Alsace-Lorraine. In the east Tyrrell and Paget came out boldly for an independent Poland enlarged at Germany's expense; Robertson and Balfour envisaged, at most, autonomy. Without a continuing common frontier in Poland, Balfour believed, Russia would cease to balance Germany in Europe, and would again threaten British India. Although Asquith's Cabinet never formally debated the memoranda, they suggested a general preference for only mild German territorial losses in Europe, in contrast to the destruction of German power overseas.[49]

Lloyd George's Prime Ministership ushered in more elaborate deliberations. The December 1916 Cabinet crisis removed from office not only Grey (who was replaced by Balfour) and Asquith, but also much of the Liberal leadership. Lloyd George's new creation, a small, supervisory War Cabinet, included the Unionist elder statesmen, Lords Curzon and Milner, both of whom could be expected to focus on the interests of the British Empire overseas rather than the security of the British Isles in Europe. This was also true of several members of the War Cabinet secretariat, such as Leo Amery

and Sir Mark Sykes, who helped to formulate the new
Premier's policy in the Middle East.

When the first Imperial War Conference met, in March–
April 1917, the War Cabinet became the Imperial War
Cabinet, through the addition of the Dominion Prime
Ministers. It appointed sub-committees on territorial and non-
territorial war aims under Curzon and Milner respectively.
Milner's report was discussed by the Cabinet but never
formally adopted; it considered the 1916 Paris Economic
Conference resolutions now inapplicable, and it followed the
cautious reparations policy of the Board of Trade. As for the
League of Nations, which the Allies had accepted in principle
in a note to Wilson on 10 January,[50] Milner adopted what
would henceforth be the normal British approach of seeking an
organization that would subordinate any decision for war to
prior consideration by a conference of the Powers. This, in
essence, was to strengthen the Concert of Europe machinery
that had failed in 1914. Curzon's territorial report said little
about Europe, beyond that Serbia and Belgium must be restored
and the Polish and Alsace-Lorraine questions settled in ways
that tried to meet the wishes of the local population and
the interests of a lasting peace. As the Committee doubted
whether Germany could be contained in Eastern Europe,
it recommended depriving it of all its colonies, and annexing
Palestine and Mesopotamia from the Turks in order to protect
the British Empire in the Middle East. The Imperial War
Cabinet accepted this 'as an indication of the objects to be
sought by the British representatives at the Peace Conference
and of their relative importance, rather than definite
instructions from which they were not intended in any
circumstances to depart'.[51] This guarded approval for the new
imperial priority reflected the division of Lloyd George's own
sympathies between the imperialists in the Cabinet and the
Dominions on the one hand and, on the other, the Foreign
Office's more Eurocentric concerns. The Prime Minister
wished not to be tied down, and to retain the option of
returning some enemy colonies if necessary for peace; he also
wanted to restore Polish 'freedom', to punish aggression, and
to promote democratization. 'If Germany had had a
democracy', he felt, 'we should not have had this trouble.'[52]

Unable to renounce the hope of violently remoulding the German psyche, or to compromise more than marginally on their maritime and imperial goals, the British remained far removed from a negotiated settlement with the Central Powers.

French war aims were similarly ill-defined before the winter of 1916–17. But French imperial objectives could never rival in importance those in Europe, especially when the German armies occupied the country's richest provinces and remained in striking distance of the capital city. In a nation legendary for political instability the German invasion created a 'sacred union', or political truce, but one based on the expectation of a short, victorious war, and the evidence that the struggle was defensive, unscrupulously provoked by the other side.[53] The truce was therefore fragile. Earlier French regimes had been destroyed by military defeat, and one, if largely unspoken, reason for French politicians to persevere was that failure might bring the Third Republic down.

The politics of war aims fell into a mould intermediate between those of Germany and Britain. As in London, civil–military conflict was over strategy rather than political objectives, and after an initially greater abdication French politicians by 1917 controlled their military more completely than did the British.[54] Unlike Britain, however, France had its own 'war-aims movement' of right-wing parties, business spokesmen, patriotic journalists, and pressure groups, which favoured annexations on the eastern frontier. This was smaller and less well co-ordinated than in Germany, and was balanced by the Socialists and CGT, whose leaders' authority over their rank and file depended partly on their being able to deny that France was fighting an imperialist war. There were Socialists in the Cabinet until September 1917, and they generally opposed annexationist demands.

The need to preserve the sacred union made French Governments cautious in formulating aims. And Delcassé, Foreign Minister until October 1915, appears to have shared Grey's fear that premature discussion might dangerously divide the Allies. The French, with their long experience of Germany as an uncomfortably powerful and aggressive neighbour, probably felt more deeply than any other Allied

Government that preserving the coalition was itself a vital war aim. Hence Delcassé and his successor Briand, Premier and Foreign Minister from October 1915 until March 1917, consistently urged upon their partners that reported enemy feelers and attempts at mediation should be disregarded, and that only decisive victory could bring lasting peace. France, like Britain, squarely opposed Bethmann's efforts to realign the Powers.[55]

The first major public statement of French aims came in a speech by Viviani to the Chamber in December 1914. France, he said, would require 'indemnities' to reconstruct its devastated areas, and would not make peace without regaining Alsace-Lorraine, restoring Belgian prosperity and independence, and breaking 'Prussian militarism'. Each point was ambiguous, and could be expanded if circumstances proved opportune.

The claim to Alsace-Lorraine was itself sufficient to prevent a compromise with Germany, which was never willing to cede more than a few Alsatian frontier districts even for a separate peace. It was not a claim on simple self-determination grounds. The allegiances of the Alsatians and Lorrainers were obscure, as most of them had voted before 1914 for deputies who favoured remaining within Germany, and partly for this reason the British and American Governments were always wary about unequivocally supporting the French position. The French Government revealed its own uncertainties by refusing Socialist proposals for a plebiscite. With their steel mills, iron ore, and phosphates, and their eastern frontier on the Rhine, the lost provinces could substantially increase French power. And if their boundary were defined as that of 1814 or 1790 rather than 1870 they would encroach on the Saar coalfield to the north. So closely did the provinces' economy intermesh with those of neighbouring regions that the unofficial and semi-official committees of civil servants and industrialists who examined eastern frontier questions in 1915–16 were quickly drawn on to making further claims on German soil.[56]

The Belgian objective was similarly elastic. A neutral Belgium had been created in the 1830s as a barrier to French expansion. It had shown itself to be a vulnerable northern flank. But French attempts to draw the Belgians into economic and strategic co-operation were frustrated by the latters' anxiety to safeguard their independence and preserve consensus between Flemings and Walloons. In October 1916 the Government-in-exile rejected French proposals for a customs union. The Briand Government, conversely, withheld approval from Belgian claims to Luxemburg; and Briand's influential *chef de cabinet*, Berthelot, wished to keep the option of claiming part or all of Luxemburg for France. Only under Briand's successor, Ribot, were the Belgians given reassurance that France had no annexationist ambitions, although French approval for Belgium's own claim was held in reserve as a possible quid pro quo for more general co-operation between Paris and Brussels.[57]

Viviani's third point concerned indemnity. French economic war aims, however, were concerned less with reparations than with trade, and their leading architect was Clémentel, who became Commerce Minister at the end of 1915. Clémentel wished to end France's dependence on Germany for strategic manufactures; he also feared that the devastation of the north and east would prevent the country from earning the foreign exchange it would need in the intense commercial competition that he expected to follow the war. He was concerned, too, that the enemy plans for *Mitteleuropa* were coming to fruition. In December 1915 Briand therefore proposed an inter-Allied conference to construct a rival 'economic bloc'. Meeting in Paris in June 1916, the Conference adopted a British proposal to deny the enemy most-favoured-nation treatment for a period after the war. But most of its resolutions were French-inspired. The Allies agreed to seek joint measures for reconstructing the devastated regions; undertook in the immediate post-war period to conserve their natural resources for themselves and prevent dumping by the Central Powers; and, in the longer term, to eliminate dependence on the enemy for all essential manufactures and raw materials. This apparent triumph of French diplomacy, however, proved to be stillborn. The Paris resolutions caused alarm in Germany and anger in the USA, but they meant nothing without more detailed follow-up agreements, and these never materialized. Indeed, Russia and Italy, fearing the loss of their former agricultural export markets in the Central Powers, never ratified even the Paris resolutions themselves.[58]

The final element in Viviani's December 1914 programme was breaking 'Prussian militarism'. But few French leaders shared the British hopes that democratizing Germany, even if feasible, would be an adequate security guarantee. Their preferred solution to the German question emerged only slowly, under a combination of internal and external influences. On the extreme Right of the French political spectrum the royalist *Action française* wanted German unity to end, and the *Ligue des patriotes* wanted the left bank of the Rhine to be annexed or turned into a French-dominated buffer state, but these opinions went well beyond the prevailing Ministerial view. Given the importance of the mineral wealth and metal-lurgical capacity located in the Franco-German borderlands, more significance attached to the views of the French steel and engineering industries represented in the *Comité des forges*, whose spokesmen were consulted by the interested Government departments and by Briand himself in 1915–16. The *Comité* eventually recommended that the peace treaty should include compulsory coal deliveries from Germany, and that France should annex, at the least, Alsace-Lorraine and the Saar. The primary external influence on policy towards Germany was the relationship with Russia, which until 1916 was more valuable than the British as an ally on land and was more willing to do business over European territory. In the winter of 1914–15 Nicholas II and Sazonov repeatedly expressed their sympathy for French expansion in the Rhineland, and in March 1915, in return for supporting Russian claims to Constantinople and the Straits, Britain and France obtained a pledge of Russian backing 'for the realization of plans which they may frame with reference to other regions of the Ottoman Empire *or elsewhere*'. The Quai d'Orsay treated this assurance as a blanket promise of support for eventual demands on Germany, and its very generality diminished the incentive to stake out more precise claims.[59]

In the summer of 1916 debate revived. Poincaré, as President, foresaw possible American mediation and an Austro-Hungarian collapse. Briand may have felt his Ministers' growing indi-vidual interest in war aims necessitated a collective line. Grey was reported in August to favour an 'immediate conversation' between the Allies. Above all, the Embassy in Petrograd warned repeatedly that unless Russia were promised gains on Germany's eastern frontier it might conclude a separate peace. It seemed urgent to consult with France's partners, and a gathering of Ministers on 7 October agreed to demand from them a free hand to settle the future of the left bank of the Rhine. Suggestions for a more detailed formulation came from two directions. The French General Staff wanted Germany to be broken up into nine independent States, but this was not pursued. Probably more influential was its recommendation in August that the left bank north of Alsace-Lorraine and the Saar should be occupied for a generation while Germany paid off an indemnity, and should be divided into small autonomous States in customs union with France. This demand—for a strategic frontier on the Rhine, and buffer States west of the river—reappeared in the second war-aims programme, drawn up by Jules Cambon, the Secretary-General of the Foreign Ministry, and his brother Paul, the Ambassador in London. The Cambons accepted that the German nation-State must survive, and relied on disarmament and territorial amputations to keep it in check. But for some Ministers the brothers went too far; for others only annexation of the left bank would suffice. Hence the 'Cambon letter', sent out to Paul on 12 January 1917 with the Cabinet's approval as a basis for discussion with the British, differed considerably from the original draft. It demanded Alsace-Lorraine with the frontier of 1790 (and therefore the southern portion of the Saar). Over the remainder of the left bank German sovereignty must end, and in deciding the region's future France must have 'the preponderant voice'. Again, therefore, the Cabinet united on the policy of the free hand.

By the time the letter was sent Balfour and Lloyd George had replaced Grey and Asquith, and Paul Cambon did not broach the subject until July. But Doumergue, the Minister of Colonies, took the letter with him on a mission to Petrograd in February 1917. Uncertain of his mandate, he telegraphed back to Paris for permission to conclude a more precise and ambitious accord· Alsace-Lorraine with 'at the very least' the 1790 frontier, including the whole of the Saar; the rest of the left bank being divided into nominally independent States, under French occupation until the peace treaty had been executed in full. Berthelot authorized Doumergue to sign, possibly without consulting Briand, and certainly without discussion by the Cabinet, which had just been divided over stipulations of exactly this kind. None the less, on 14 February letters were exchanged. The Russians demanded in return 'complete liberty' to fix their western frontiers with Germany and Austria-Hungary, and this Briand conceded on 8 March, believing this would cement the Russian alliance and that it was necessary in order to weaken the Central Powers. The understandings of 14 February and 8 March together constituted the 'Doumergue Agreement': an apparent climax of French ambition that in fact never represented the Briand Government's collective view. But Briand's successor, Ribot, still felt bound by it, and only events in Russia after the Tsar was overthrown made it effectively irrelevant.[60]

In Russia, as elsewhere, the war appeared at its outset to be defensive, and it had the usual effect of stilling troubled waters at home. The pre-war strike wave among the urban workforce dwindled away. The liberal and conservative parties in the Duma voted war credits with enthusiasm. Even the Social Democrats, who abstained, advised the working class to defend the homeland.[61] But political consensus was more precarious than in the West. After the 1905 Revolution the monarchy had conceded limited civil liberties and a Parliament with an unrepresentative franchise and severely restricted powers. To hold its sprawling, backward, multi-national territories together it still had ultimately to rule as an autocracy. But in so doing it antagonized many in the educated middle and upper classes whose collaboration was essential for political stability. The war exacerbated this dilemma by creating a divide between the nationalism of the Duma parties and the press and the growing desire of the Russian masses to end the burdens of the conflict at almost any price. It also heightened the alienation of patriotic opinion from a regime that was accused not only of incompetence but also of treason.

    In reality, loyalty to the alliance was the first and crucial element of Tsarist policy. The Government initiated the September 1914 Pact of London, and consistently rejected enemy feelers. The Empress Alexandra, despite her German origins, opposed a compromise. Nor is there evidence that Stürmer, Prime Minister during most of 1916 and deeply suspect to the French Embassy, made approaches to the Central Powers.[62] It was much less clear for Russia than for Britain and France, however, that Germany was the principal antagonist. Tsarist territorial claims against Vienna and Constantinople were at least as important as those against Berlin. In addition, the Russian military record was one of repeated defeats by Germany, and catastrophe in Poland in 1915, but of successes against both the Habsburgs and the Turks in Galicia and Armenia in 1916. This experience of initial optimism, disaster, and qualified recovery was paralleled in the evolution of Tsarist war aims.

Russia's principal objective against the Central Powers was unveiled in the proclamation of 14 August 1914 calling for the Polish people to be 'united under the sceptre of the Russian Emperor, . . . free in faith, language, and self-government'.[63] This was a commitment to incorporate Galicia from Austria-Hungary, as well as Posen and the Polish provinces of Germany, in a unified Polish buffer State under Tsarist sovereignty. Potentially it was as insuperable an obstacle to compromise in Eastern Europe as were Belgium and Alsace-Lorraine in the West. But it was only part of a more general development of Russian thinking in the winter of 1914–15. Although no programme was officially adopted, the ideas of the Tsar, of Sazonov, and of other Ministers moved on similar lines. Probably on 12 September 1914, Sazonov unveiled to the French and British Ambassadors his 'Thirteen Points'. Russia, he considered, should annex the Lower Niemen basin from Germany and eastern Galicia from Austria-Hungary, and take eastern Posen, southern Silesia, and western Galicia for Poland. France would gain Alsace-Lorraine, and more if it desired. The kingdom of Hanover, annexed by Prussia in 1866, would be restored. But otherwise Sazonov proposed not to interfere in Germany's internal affairs, weakening it rather by territorial losses, reparations, and keeping the French–Russian–British alliance in being. In a conversation with the French Ambassador on 21 November the Tsar expressed similar views. Although the Russian General Staff wished to annex from Germany the whole of East Prussia up to the mouth of the Vistula, they lacked support from their superiors, and Russian objectives rested on a combination of veiled expansion through buffer States with small, if significant, annexations.[64]

Sazonov's Thirteen Points elicited only an assurance of personal support from Delcassé, and no response from Grey. When the Eastern Front had stabilized after the débâcle in Poland Sazonov tried again, seeking from Briand in March 1916 a mutual acknowledgement of a free hand to settle the eastern and western borders of the Central Powers.[65] Only a year later, however, in the confusion of the Doumergue negotiations, was such an understanding reached, and by now it had little chance of being implemented. The Tsar reaffirmed the goal of Polish unity in an Order to his troops on Christmas Day 1916, but he privately acknowledged that the cost of conquering Posen from Germany would be too high.[66]

As in the Second World War, however, the Polish question concerned not only frontiers but also Poland's future political regime. In October–November 1914 the Council of Ministers agreed that Poland within its ethnic limits should have a special status within the Empire, but in the following March it also decided that the armed forces, foreign policy, transport, and finance would remain under Russian control. This was unacceptable even to the more conservative Polish politicians in Roman Dmowski's National Democratic Party; and in November 1915 Dmowski moved to Western Europe and began to favour Polish independence. In March 1916 a conference of Polish exiles voted unanimously to try to 'internationalize' the question by applying pressure on Russia via its allies.[67]

Until now France and Britain had respected the Tsarist Government's insistence that Poland was a domestic issue. But a contest had opened between the warring eastern monarchies to create a Polish buffer State at the other side's expense. The Poles' exasperation with Petrograd might lead them to volunteer *en masse* for military service with the enemy and to demand independence rather than mere autonomy. In the spring of 1916 Briand urged on the Russians that Britain and France should reassure the Poles by publicly endorsing the Tsar's promise of autonomy; this Sazonov rejected absolutely, warning that French persistence would threaten the alliance.

He did, however, arrange for the Foreign Ministry to draw up a constitutional charter, promising a Polish Parliament although keeping defence, foreign policy, railways, tariffs, and the currency in Russian hands. Even this went too far for Stürmer, who replaced Sazonov as Foreign Minister in July 1916, largely because of the latter's relative liberalism on the Polish issue. The Central Powers therefore got their blow in first, promising Polish independence in their declaration of 5 November. Dissatisfied with the feebleness of the Russian counter-declaration, Briand and Asquith unilaterally announced their 'entire solidarity' with Russian promises of 'restored unity' to the Poles. [68] With this Polish reunification had finally become an objective of the alliance as a whole, although one it lacked the military power to attain.

In committing themselves to Polish reunification Britain and France were once again treating Austria-Hungary primarily as a bait: its purpose to keep Russia in the war and to attract the neutrals. Hence the Treaties of London with Italy and of Bucharest with Rumania, and the offers made to Serbia in 1915, as part of the fruitless effort to woo Bulgaria. [69] The Western European Allies had cause for conflict with Austria-Hungary only in so far as the latter supported Germany. But to seek peace with Vienna would endanger alliance solidarity, and especially the bond with Petrograd. At the beginning of 1915 Paléologue proposed to Sazonov that Austria-Hungary should be offered a separate peace with mild territorial losses. Sazonov objected, and Delcassé secured a French Cabinet decision repudiating the Ambassador, who was instructed to avoid the topic in future. Grey also respected the Russian veto. The one definite feeler from Vienna in this period—a letter to the Tsar from Prince Hohenlohe in March 1915—convinced Sazonov that the Habsburgs were unwilling to accept Russian terms. [70] The possibility of an Austro-Hungarian separate peace therefore gathered dust until the very different circumstances of 1917.

Russia's most concrete demand on Austria-Hungary was the project for a Polish buffer State. In addition, a proclamation to the 'Peoples of Austria-Hungary' on 17 September 1914 promised more generally 'freedom and the realization of your national strivings'.[71] In his 'Thirteen Points', besides his plans for Poland and for Russian annexation of eastern Galicia, Sazonov envisaged that Serbia would acquire Bosnia-Herzegovina, part or all of Dalmatia, and northern Albania. But the decisive question concerned the Czechs. Even if the periphery were lost, the German, Magyar, and Czechoslovak core of Austria-Hungary would still constitute a bloc of over twenty-five million people with defensible frontiers and a sizeable industrial base. But if the Czechs and Slovaks also broke away, there would be little reason for the Austro-Magyar union to continue, and the Austrian Germans might drift into *Anschluss*, or union, with Germany. Before the war the Czech nationalists had favoured autonomy rather than independence, and the Russians still hesitated. The Thirteen Points envisaged a restructured tripartite monarchy of Austria, Hungary, and Bohemia, a proposal the Tsar confirmed in his conversation with the French Ambassador on 21 November 1914. In two memoranda in September and October 1916 the Czech expert in the Russian Foreign Ministry advocated an independent Czechoslovakia, but this never became official policy.[72]

Western policy was also guarded. The Italians adhered unswervingly to their Treaty of London demands, but beyond this wished the Habsburg monarchy to survive, and were unfriendly to the Czechs as well as to the Yugoslavs.[73] In Paris and London in 1915–16 the Czech National Committee, under Masaryk and Beneš, presented the case for independence, but won only Briand's personal sympathy. The war-aims memoranda circulated to the British Cabinet in 1916 displayed a variety of opinions on the subject, and neither under Asquith nor later in the Curzon Committee were these reconciled. In the French debate, Poincaré and Jules Cambon viewed the possibility of *Anschluss* with alarm, and the Cambon letter in its final form dropped earlier proposals for Austria-Hungary to be broken up. All of this diminishes the significance of the Allies' statement in their reply of 10 January 1917 to President Wilson's peace note that they favoured 'the liberation of the Czecho-Slovaks . . . from foreign domination'. In reality, within weeks of publishing this declaration Britain and France were again pursuing a separate peace that would keep the Habsburg Monarchy in being.[74]

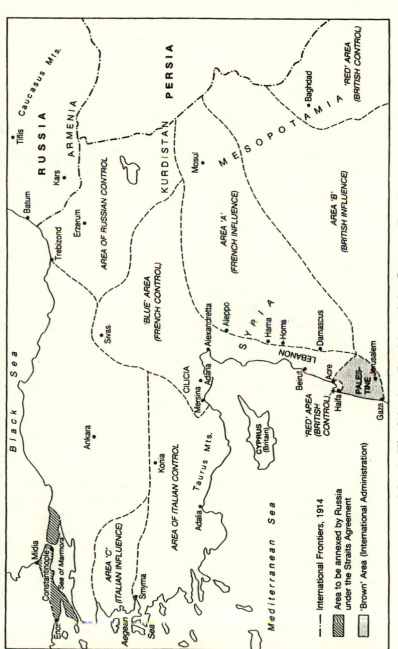

MAP 5. The Wartime Partition of the Ottoman Empire

The Ottoman Empire was another potential bait for consolidating loyalties to the coalition and for drawing in new
members. By 1914 Ottoman sovereignty over non-Turks was
virtually confined to the Empire's Arab and Armenian possessions. An Arab nationalist movement existed, especially
in Syria and the Lebanon, but it was far too weak to end
Turkish overlordship unaided. In the Arabian peninsula,
however, the ruler of the Najd, Ibn Saud, had achieved semi-
independence. And the Hejaz, which included the holy cities
of Mecca and Medina, was governed by the Sharif Hussein,
who in the spring of 1914 unsuccessfully sounded out the British
in Egypt for assistance against the attempts of the local
Ottoman representatives to reassert central authority. The
European Chancelleries had long identified their preferred
zones of control if Turkey-in-Asia should be partitioned. The
Bosphorus and Dardanelles, as has been seen, had become of
paramount importance to Russia. The economic and strategic
interests of the British centred on the Persian Gulf and on the
Suez Canal. Since 1892 they had administered the Sinai
peninsula, as well as Egypt itself, which they had occupied ten
years earlier, but by 1914 the General Staff in London doubted
whether the Sinai protected the Canal adequately. Finally, the
French concentrated their attention on their railways and
missionary activities in Syria and the Lebanon. Whereas on the
eve of war, however, none of the Entente Governments considered partition of the Ottoman Empire as being in their
immediate interest, by April 1917 inter-Allied arrangements
for a hypothetical distribution of the Ottoman spoils were
almost complete.[75]

The partition opened with an agreement directed at the
Empire's heart. On 26 September 1914 Sazonov told the French
and British Ambassadors that he wished to see the Straits
placed under an international authority with its own naval
force, and the Ottoman fortifications destroyed. After hostilities
began a commission of Russian naval, military, and diplomatic
experts recommended post-war occupation of the Gallipoli
peninsula and both sides of the Bosphorus, although not yet
Constantinople itself. It soon became clear that British opposition to such pretensions would be slight. On 2 November the
Cabinet agreed that 'henceforward Britain must finally

abandon the formula of "Ottoman integrity", whether in Europe or Asia';[76] Grey then informed Sazonov that 'a complete settlement of the Turkish question, including the Straits and Constantinople, in agreement with Russia' was inevitable; and George V told the Russian Ambassador that Constantinople 'must be yours'. Since the British had acquired an Eastern Mediterranean presence in Cyprus and Egypt the Straits had become less important to them, and they had accepted well before the war that they could tolerate alterations in the status quo. They strengthened their position by declaring protectorates over Egypt and Cyprus in November 1914. Grey probably also hoped, however, to distract the Russians from a flank attack via Persia that would endanger Britain's sphere of influence there.[77] Whatever the motive, his precipitate action weakened the Western Powers' ability to resist the much more drastic Russian requirements that were presented in the following spring.

The question came to a head when the British and French tried to clear the Straits by naval action, prior to the Gallipoli landings of April 1915. The Russians, unable to launch an amphibious assault themselves, objected violently when their allies negotiated for Greek military aid. A Commons statement by Grey on 25 February was misquoted in the Petrograd press as suggesting he would oppose Russian aspirations at the Straits, and this gave Sazonov the pretext to bring forward his demands. On 4 March he asked for French and British support for Russian annexation of Constantinople and European Turkey up to the Enos–Media line, including the entire western shore of the Straits, together with the Asiatic coastline of the Bosphorus. According to his memoirs, he presented the claim against his better judgement, under pressure from public opinion and the military. Certainly, annexation was supported by the more conservative members of the Council of Ministers, and there had been calls for action in the Duma. The fear of being pre-empted by the Western Allies or the Greeks, however, was the final precipitant.[78]

The French and British failed to co-ordinate their response. In London, in recognition of the historic departure that was being contemplated, Unionist representatives were brought into the Cabinet. Grey dwelt on the dangers to the alliance if

Russia were refused; and, given the lack of objection on strategic grounds by the service departments, the Cabinet concentrated on seeking a quid pro quo. On 12 March Britain acceded to Sazonov's programme, on condition that the war ended in victory and Britain and France achieved their own objectives in the Ottoman Empire and elsewhere. These had still to be worked out; but Arabia was to be under 'independent Mussulman dominion'. Britain also required free passage through the Straits for its merchant shipping, access to Constantinople as a free port, and that central Persia, which had remained neutral in the 1907 Anglo-Russian Central Asian agreement, should be incorporated in the southern, British sphere of influence. With some reservations over Persia, the Russians accepted these counter-claims.[79] In Paris, by contrast, Poincaré and Delcassé objected strongly to demands which they feared would make Russia a great Mediterranean naval Power. But British acquiescence left them isolated; and their Ambassador warned that Sazonov was threatening to resign and Germany had supposedly offered Constantinople and the Straits in return for a separate peace. Conversely, Sazonov had offered his reciprocal promise to support French and British ambitions in the Ottoman Empire and elsewhere, and the Tsar had made clear that 'elsewhere' could include the Rhineland. On 8 March France sent a qualified acceptance. It then made a counter-claim to the whole of Syria including part of Palestine, and to Alexandretta and Cilicia up to the Taurus mountains. This the Russians agreed to with one reservation over the Palestine Holy Places, and on 10 April a final French note confirmed the understanding. The 'Straits Agreement' was now in being.[80]

The next stage in the partition arose from the British search for allies. It was embodied in the 'McMahon–Hussein correspondence' of July 1915 to March 1916 between the British High Commissioner in Cairo and the Sharif of Mecca. On the outbreak of war with Turkey the British had offered Hussein a guarantee in return for his co-operation. They had also suggested that he might displace the Turkish Sultan as Caliph of the Sunni Moslems, the Caliphate being misunderstood in London as carrying spiritual authority only, whereas in Sunni dogma it also implied temporal authority over all members of the faith. Perhaps emboldened by this, on 14 July 1915 Hussein offered economic preference and a defensive alliance in return for British approval of an Arab Caliphate and British assistance in winning independence throughout the Arab-inhabited areas of Turkey-in-Asia, apart from Aden. The Sharif exercised authority over a small fraction of this area, and could field perhaps 3,000 tribesmen. His demands, however, had probably been expanded as a result of his contacts with the nationalist secret societies that had formed among the Arab officers serving in the Turkish armies in Syria. The reaction in Cairo was that these conditions were exorbitant, and the Foreign Office sent an equivocal reply.[81]

At this point, however, al-Faruqui, a member of the Arab officers' movement who had managed to cross the lines at Gallipoli, arrived in Egypt. The Syrian conspirators, he warned, had received offers from Germany and the Turks that met their demands in full. This set off a panic, extending up to Kitchener as Secretary of State for War, that the Arabs would go over to the enemy and Egypt be jeopardized. On 20 October Grey authorized McMahon to inform Hussein that an independent Arab State could include not only the Arabian peninsula but also the territory to the north. He made exceptions only for Mesopotamia, where Britain must have freedom of action in the area around the vilayet (or Ottoman administrative province) of Basra, and for the north-west, where France would have its claims.[82] All of this resulted from al-Faruqui's testimony, although there is no evidence on the German side that the offers he referred to had actually be made, and the alliance between the Sharif and the Syrian nationalists that the British supposed they were dealing with was in fact poorly co-ordinated and militarily feeble. Similar tactics to those earlier employed by Sazonov, however, were having similar effects.

The process culminated in the crucial letter sent on 24 October 1915 by McMahon to Hussein. As usual, this was phrased more grandiloquently and emphatically than the authorization from the Foreign Office, and its drafting was exceedingly careless. Britain, said McMahon, was 'prepared to recognize and support the independence of the Arabs in all the regions within the limits demanded by the Sharif of Mecca', but this excluded the districts of Mersina and Alexandretta, and Syria to the west of the districts of Damascus, Homs, Hama, and Aleppo, as well, more generally, as those regions where Britain could not act 'without detriment to the interests of her ally, France'. In the areas not covered by these exemptions, the independent Arab authorities would take advisers exclusively from Britain, and would accept 'special administrative arrangements' in the Mesopotamian vilayets of Baghdad and Basra. McMahon hoped that these assurances would lead on to an Anglo-Arab alliance, with 'the expulsion of the Turks from the Arab countries' as the immediate result. But he failed to tie up the letter's numerous loose ends. The Sharif accepted the exclusion of Adana and Mersina, but maintained his claim to the coastline of the Lebanon. He was promised further clarification of the French claims, but did not receive it before he took up arms. For McMahon, indeed, what mattered was to get the Arabs in, and the negotiations were 'largely a matter of words'.[83] Thus a conflict opened between French and Arab aspirations. McMahon also failed to stipulate that the territorial offer was conditional on an Arab revolt, although in a later letter he said the 'permanence and strength' of the agreement would depend on Arab military action. In the event, only in June 1916 did the preparations of a suspicious Ottoman Government belatedly drive the Sharif into a pre-emptive uprising. The Syrian nationalists gave no assistance, and by the end of the year the Arab Revolt depended for its survival on British military aid.

The possibility of an insurrection, however, made it necessary to settle with the French. A further storey rose upon the edifice of inter-Allied accords. On the British side, deficient control of policy gave undue influence to the pro-Arab enthusiasts in Cairo; on the French, the beneficiary was the colonialist pressure group, the *Comité de l'Asie française*. The *Comité*'s tendrils took in not only the Syrian lobby in the Chamber of Deputies, but also the most senior Foreign Ministry officials, including the former Consul-General in Beirut, François Georges-Picot. In February 1915 the *Comité* had abandoned its traditional policy of seeking French predominance in a unified Ottoman Empire in favour of demanding French control of Cilicia and 'integral Syria', from the Taurus to the Sinai, and therefore including Palestine. In the Straits negotiations, Delcassé secured Russian acquiescence in this claim. In October 1915, after sending his authorization to McMahon, Grey asked the French to send a delegate in order to reach agreement on the Syrian boundaries. Georges-Picot was selected for the mission.[84]

Picot drafted his own instructions, which Briand approved without amendment. He demanded the whole of Syria, including Palestine, and the oil-bearing vilayet of Mosul in northern Mesopotamia. The British negotiators, led in the final stage by Sir Mark Sykes, wished to protect their own imperial interests and to accommodate the Sharif by including as much as possible of Syria in the independent Arab zone. An understanding was reached provisionally in January 1916, and confirmed in an exchange of letters in May. It promised France 'direct or indirect administration or control' in a 'blue area' covering Cilicia and the Syrian and Lebanese coastal zone; a similar British 'red area' took in central and southern Mesopotamia and Acre and Haifa in Palestine. The 'brown area' in the rest of the Holy Land would come under an 'international administration'. The Jordanian and Syrian interior, including Damascus, Homs, Hama, and Aleppo, would be assigned to an independent Arab State or confederation, but would be divided into a northern area 'A' and a southern area 'B', in which France and Britain respectively would have the sole right to appoint advisers and would enjoy priority in applying for economic concessions and making loans.[85]

The Sykes–Picot agreement was an ingenious compromise. Picot acquired Alexandretta, and brought Mosul into area 'A', the British thinking it more important to have a French buffer between them and the Russians than to control the Mosul oil. The British gained a Mediterranean base at Haifa and recognition of their rights in Mesopotamia, as well as the appearance of extensive territory for the new Arab State. Grey supported the agreement, however, in the belief that its realization depended on an Arab Revolt that he still thought unlikely to occur; and the equilibrium of the compromise depended on a strained interpretation of the commitment given to Hussein. The British envisaged Arab 'independence' as meaning only freedom from the Turks; both they and the French expected zones 'A' and 'B' to become *de facto* spheres of influence. There was a further problem over the international regime intended for Palestine. McMahon's letter to Hussein of 24 October appears to have been intended to exclude Palestine from the Arab State, but its phrasing was neither explicit nor unambiguous, and led to prolonged controversy in the inter-war years. Although the Cairo authorities professed to see no inconsistency between the McMahon–Hussein correspondence and the Sykes–Picot agreement, the latter was withheld from the Sharif, who therefore began his revolt in ignorance of Britain's undertakings. [86]

While these dragon's teeth were being sown, Sykes and Picot went on to Petrograd for negotiations with the Russians. Since Turkey's entry into the war the Tsarist Government had intended to expand into Armenia, whose Christian population inhabited both sides of the border and therefore occupied a position analogous to that of the Poles. Russian military successes in the Caucasus and the brutal massacres of the Ottoman Armenians in 1915 maintained the prominence of the issue. In an exchange of notes on 26 April 1916 the Russians acknowledged the transfer of Western Armenia to the French 'blue area', but acquired in exchange a sphere of influence in Kurdistan and the right to annex Erzerum and Trebizond. A Russo-British agreement in September about commercial rights completed this northward extension of the partition. [87]

It remained to bring in Italy, which had been promised a share in the Adalia region under the Treaty of London. The Italians had been deliberately excluded from the Sykes–Picot negotiations, and Sonnino had to threaten to resign before he was informed of the contents of the agreement. In November 1916 the Italians defined their claims as embracing the entire southern third of the Anatolian peninsula. But Sonnino's priority remained the Adriatic. At the Saint-Jean-de-Maurienne conference, on 19 April 1917, he settled for a 'green zone' in the Smyrna and Konia regions, and a 'zone C' of influence further north. A formal agreement in London on 18 August confirmed Italian acceptance of the 1916 tripartite arrangements and the Saint-Jean-de-Maurienne compromise. [88] But by this point the whole structure of secret agreements was being rocked by the Russian Revolution and American entry into the war. One small sign of this was that the 18 August agreement was conditional on the assent of the Russan Provisional Government, and this was never given. The fall of the Tsar also left the British as the only Ally with much striking power in the Levant, and the new Lloyd George ministry was resolved to use it. In December 1916 the Cabinet decided to invade Palestine in the New Year. In March 1917 British forces took Baghdad. The Curzon Committee report, approved in principle by the Cabinet, wanted Palestine as well as Mesopotamia to remain 'under British control'. The partition of Turkey-in-Asia was now under attack not only from new outside forces but also from the traditional bureaucratic imperialism that had brought it into being.

The final sphere of Allied expansionist ambition was the Far East. Here also there existed a decaying empire, in China, where the Manchu dynasty had been overthrown in 1911–12. After 1916–17 the Republican authorities lost control over most of the provinces, and the chaotic 'warlord' period began. Unlike Austria-Hungary or Turkey, however, China was not, in the Western sense, a multi-national empire, and there was a different constellation of potential predators. During the war the only State with the power and inclination to carve out an exclusive zone of influence for itself was China's Asian neighbour, Japan. Before 1914 the United States and Britain had been committed in principle to upholding Chinese independence and integrity and the 'Open Door', or equal opportunity for foreign commerce, enterprise, and loans. In practice the European Powers, including Britain, had divided China south of the Great Wall into enclaves where their nationals had monopolies of railway construction and finance. Japan, because of its financial weakness and because of Chinese hostility, had failed to secure a single railway concession in this area, although the Americans and Europeans had been able to make loans in South Manchuria, where the Japanese considered they had special interests.[89] The outbreak of war, however, transformed the regional balance of power, and unexpectedly dealt the Japanese a winning hand. Their shipping and exports captured markets that other belligerents could no longer supply. Between 1912 and 1916 Japan's

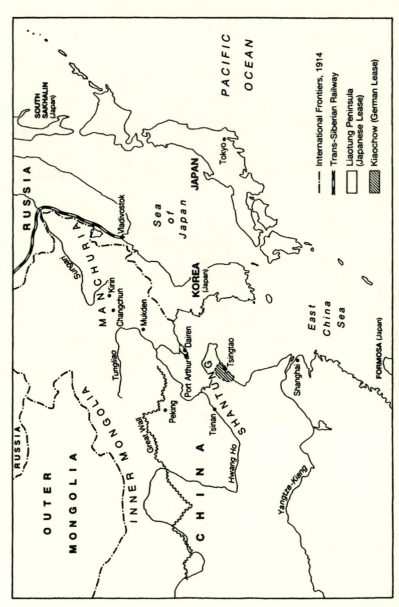

MAP 6. North-East Asia

exports doubled in value and it became a net international lender. The Royal Navy urgently required Japanese assistance; Russia needed Japanese munitions and loans. The United States, anyway uncertain in its Oriental diplomacy, was deprived of effective allies.

All of this presented an opportunity that helps account for Kato's eagerness to enter the war. Preparation of Japan's Twenty-One Demands on China extended from August to December 1914, against the background of the Shantung campaign. Eighty-three years of Germany's lease on the territory remained: it included, at Tsingtao, the finest harbour on the China coast, together with a railway towards Tsinan in the interior and a hinterland fifty miles in radius. As well as capturing Tsingtao itself, in November 1914, the Japanese occupied the whole of the railway. Their ultimatum to Germany had envisaged returning the lease to China, but the Okuma Government wished to acquire at least some of Germany's rights in Shantung before the war ended. A second area of Japanese concern was Eastern Inner Mongolia, whose importance as a buffer had grown since Outer Mongolia had declared its independence from China in 1911 and fallen increasingly under Russian influence. Third, Kato wished to extend the Japanese leases on the port of Dairen and the tip of the Liaotung peninsula, which were due to expire in 1923, and that on the Kirin–Changchun railway, which would run until 1934. In August 1914 Grey, anxious to divert Japanese expansion away from Britain's economic interests in the Yangtze basin, confided that he would support Japan's claim to an extension. But the Twenty-One Demands were shaped by broader forces than the Tokyo Foreign Ministry. Kato consulted the genro, among whom one, Inoue, was a lobbyist for the Government-owned Yawata steel works, a creditor of the Hanyehping Company, which owned the largest coal and iron deposits in China. In 1914 it seemed possible that the Chinese would nationalize the Hanyehping Company, although its ores were widely used by Japanese armaments manufacturers. The final influence on the Demands was a memorandum from Uchida, the head of the ultra-nationalist Black Dragon Society. Much of this memorandum was incorporated into Group V of the Demands, although, as will be seen, this was the section over which the Japanese Government was most prepared to compromise.

The Demands were presented, initially in secret, in Peking on 18 January 1915. They were divided into five Groups, of which the first required China to accept whatever Japan agreed with Germany about Shantung. Group II required the Port Arthur and Dairen leases and Japanese control over three southern Manchurian railways to be extended to ninety-nine years. Japan was to have a monopoly of advisers in Manchuria and Eastern Inner Mongolia, and a veto over loans by and railway concessions to other Powers. Group III provided for the Hanyehping Company to become a joint Sino-Japanese concern; Group IV forbade China to cede or lease any coastal territory to a foreign Power. Group V, officially 'wishes' rather than Demands, included notably a requirement for the Chinese central Government to employ Japanese advisers. The Demands, therefore, were another example of informal imperialism and indirect control: consolidating Japan's own spheres of influence in the north and in Shantung while weakening the position of the other Powers and reducing the rest of China in some ways to a Japanese protectorate.[90]

The Demands led to bilateral negotiations, in which the Chinese used delaying tactics until a Japanese ultimatum on 7 May insisted on their accepting a scaled-down version of the conditions, with the omission of Group V. The Chinese gave way, and treaties signed on 25 May brought the crisis to an end. The Japanese Government was supported by its domestic public opinion, and was successful in the elections to the Diet held in March. Given this, and the helplessness of the Chinese, it was primarily opposition from the Anglo-Saxon Powers that inhibited Kato from requiring more. This meant especially Britain. The Americans were preoccupied with the submarine question; moreover, Bryan inclined to conciliate the Japanese, although Wilson took a firmer line. A note by Bryan on 13 March protested against some of the Demands, but accepted there were 'special relations' between Japan and Shantung, southern Manchuria, and Eastern Inner Mongolia. After the Japanese ultimatum, Bryan warned on 11 May that the United States would recognize no Sino-Japanese agreement that infringed American treaty rights, Chinese independence and integrity, or the Open Door. But he failed to concert his representations with the other Powers; and Grey had already undertaken more effective unilateral action. The British Foreign Office had been infuriated by Japan's failure to consult or even inform it about the Demands, which violated the provision in the Anglo-Japanese alliance that Chinese independence and integrity should be respected. The British press and Parliament were also anti-Japanese. Grey warned that Japanese insistence on Group V might destroy the alliance, and that British support was unlikely in a Sino-Japanese war. The genro, impressed, attacked Kato at a crucial meeting with the Cabinet on 4 May, and it was decided to drop Group V from the ultimatum to Peking. Once this was done, Grey urged the Chinese to yield, advising that they too could expect no British support in a war. The outcome of the crisis showed, therefore, that a residual balance of power still operated in the Pacific. It also demonstrated the continuing predominance of the more cautious and internationalist elements in Tokyo.[91]

After May 1915 the first paroxysm of Japanese imperialism had passed. Kato left office in July, and his successors endeavoured to repair relations with the European Allies. Japan adhered to the September 1914 Pact of London in October 1915, and in July 1916 concluded a separate alliance with Russia. The Terauchi Government that came to office in October 1916 reorientated Japanese policy in a direction still more favourable to the Allies. It resolved to respect Chinese independence and integrity, and to continue the alignment with Britain, France, and Russia after the war.[92] In February and March 1917, as has been see, Japan's partners secretly promised to support its claims to Germany's rights in Shantung and the North Pacific islands. This was the new equilibrium in the Far East that the Russian Revolution and American belligerency challenged.

The German and American Peace Notes of December 1916 opened a propaganda battle for the sympathy of public opinion in the North Atlantic basin. Britain and France took the lead in formulating a response, and the British, after their altercations with Wilson during the summer, were happy to leave the drafting initiative to the Quai d'Orsay. There was little argument about the appropriate reply to Bethman Hollweg. Lloyd George told the Commons that the war must continue until the purposes for which it had been embarked on were fulfilled; Briand denounced the enemy note as a 'crude snare', designed to 'poison' Allied morale. The joint Allied reply to the Central Powers on 31 December closely followed the rancorous French initial draft. Its purpose was to close the door on further discussion, and it offered only vague generalities about Allied war aims.[93]

The French also proposed, however, to be similarly equivocal about the coalition's objectives in the reply to Wilson. And on this French and British views diverged. Berthelot, Briand's leading adviser in the episode, considered Wilson was unlikely to impose a munitions embargo, and wanted to give no details that might assist the President in attempting mediation. In London, reports drawn up on the Allies' economic dependence concluded that a total American embargo would paralyse their war effort, though only after some months. It was deemed politic to humour Wilson, although not to come completely to heel. The Cabinet therefore accepted the arguments of Lord Robert Cecil, Parliamentary Under-Secretary at the Foreign Office, that the Allies could win a propaganda victory by publishing a moderately detailed list of terms. An Anglo-French conference held from 26 to 28 December agreed to tack on Cecil's proposals as an additional paragraph to the original French draft, and the Allies published substantially this text as their reply to Wilson on 10 January 1917.[94]

If only for opportunist reasons, the Allied reply accepted the principle of a League of Nations. It also set out Allied war aims in unprecedented detail, and in a way the Central Powers had failed to do. Belgium, Serbia, and Montenegro were to be compensated and restored to their integrity and independence; France, Russia, and Rumania would be evacuated and receive 'just reparations'. The Italians, Slavs, and Rumanians should be freed from 'foreign domination'; the Turks expelled from Europe and their subject peoples liberated. Provinces and other territory formerly taken from the Allies against the inhabitants' will should be returned, and there should be international arrangements to safeguard land and sea frontiers against unjustified attack. These last, ill-concealed references to Alsace-Lorraine and France's eastern border were symptomatic of the document's Anglo-French provenance. British and French objectives in Europe and Asiatic Turkey were safely covered. Russian designs on Constantinople were mentioned only obliquely; but with French and British consent the Russians had already published the Straits Agreement in December 1916. Over Poland, France and Britain agreed to refer to the Tsar's recent Christmas proclamation.[95] Italian aspirations in the Adriatic, however, remained unmentioned. Finally, the specific reference to the 'Czecho-Slovaks' was inserted at the behest of Berthelot and Briand. But it would be wrong to see the Allies as committed by this action to destroy the Habsburg Monarchy;[96] wrong, probably, to think of any Allied Government as feeling irrevocably committed by the document at all. In the distinction used by Stalin in the Second World War, the note of 10 January constituted the 'algebra' of Allied war aims: the secret treaties were the practical arithmetic.

The drive to annex and to establish spheres of influence was not a purely German sickness. Once the relatively calm and stable order of the later nineteenth century atrophied, it diseased the international system as a whole. Governments on both sides scrambled to obtain some certainty and safety for themselves and for their peoples in an unpredictable and threatening world. Allied statesmen also struggled to uphold the existing international alignment against their enemies' attempts to sunder it, and to prolong it into a post-war future where the German stimulus that had created it would have been destroyed. It is tempting, when juxtaposing the public rhetoric and secret diplomacy of the Allies and the Central Powers, to follow Woodrow Wilson in equating the two; or to think of Orwell's farm animals gazing on their present and their former masters, unable to distinguish which was which. Right-wing political parties, patriotic pressure groups, elements of the business community, of the armed forces, and of the Government bureaucracy supported the imperialism of both sides. Yet not all the Allied rhetoric can be dismissed as a cloud of deceit. The central dynamic of the war—the struggle between Germany and its enemies in Europe—differed in kind from the conflicts on the periphery. A peace imposed by the Allied coalition of February 1917, in which the Western democracies were only one, and not necessarily the preponderant, element, would have been much harsher than the treaty that eventually emerged at Versailles. But submerged beneath the clash of rival imperialisms there was also an ideological contest between liberal and autocratic Powers, and this aspect of the struggle was now to be dramatically enhanced. Riots on the bread lines in the Russian capital and Congressional votes in Washington DC brought the opposing coalitions to the watershed of the war.

4

The Failure to Compromise
MARCH-NOVEMBER 1917

(i) *The Austrian Search for Peace*

In 1917 the earth trembled under the belligerents' feet. Thus
far the pre-existing balance of power and the European social
and political order had withstood the strains of conflict with
remarkable resilience. The battles on the Western Front grew
in length and cost and scale, but the geography of the Front
stayed virtually unchanged. The German Socialists continued
to vote war credits; the French Socialists and the British
Labour Party remained in the Paris and London Cabinets.
Britain and Germany remained divided over Belgium, the
German navy, and rival colonial claims; France and Germany
over the Rhineland and Alsace-Lorraine; Russia and the
Central Powers over Poland; Austria-Hungary and Italy over
the Adriatic and the Tyrol. Germany sought victory through a
separate peace that would shatter its encirclement; its
opponents were unanimous at least in their determination not
to be divided by the Central Powers. As a result of this multiple
impasse the haemorrhage of European manpower at a previously unimaginable rate went on.

The logjam now began to break. A new phase opened, of
radical shifts in the balance of power and breakdown in
consensus at home. Between the two Russian Revolutions of
March and November 1917,[1] the most sustained attempts to
end the war by compromise were made. These were also
months of ascendancy for the moderate Left, during which
there seemed a possibility of establishing liberal regimes from
the Rhineland to the Urals. After November this chance, if
such it was, disappeared. Both sides' war aims had been
modified, but insufficiently for the contradictions between
them to be resolved. When peace came, it would be based on
victory rather than on mutual renunciation, and it would be

made precarious from the start by the ideological conflict that the Bolshevik Revolution set in train. The tragedy of 1917 must be examined in the light of four main themes: the attempts by Austria-Hungary to promote a settlement; the challenge to domestic consensus after the overthrow of the Tsar; the secret contacts between the Western European belligerents in the autumn; and the global diplomatic impact of American entry into the war.

The first of the new imponderables injected into European politics was a change of leadership in Vienna. In November 1916 Franz Josef died. His successor, Karl, replaced the principal architects of the Monarchy's foreign policy. Conrad at the General Staff gave way to the more pliable Arz; Tisza resigned from the Hungarian Premiership in May 1917; Burián's successor as Foreign Minister was Count Czernin. Like Karl, Czernin was a nervous activist, alarmed at the Monarchy's predicament, and anxious to terminate a policy of drift. But confidence between the two men was limited. Czernin disliked German policy, and tried to alter it by pressure as well as negotiation. But he also ruled out a separate peace, despite his occasional willingness to hint at one. Karl's estrangement from Berlin went deeper. A dramatic German victory, he wrote to Czernin in May 1917, would mean Austria-Hungary's ruin. In the most prolonged of the 1917 peace contacts, the Sixte de Bourbon affair, he persisted in discussing a general settlement on conditions he knew to be unacceptable to his ally. This may not constitute willingness for a separate peace, but the distinction becomes fine.[2]

Czernin disclosed his peace terms at a Crown Council on 12 January. Although he still wished to modify the frontiers with Rumania, Serbia, and Montenegro, he stressed the defensive goal of preserving the Monarchy's existing possessions. In the following month he accordingly sent Count Mensdorff, the pre-war Ambassador in London, on a mission to Scandinavia, with instructions that Austria-Hungary sought a 'mediated' but not separate peace on the basis of territorial integrity and frontier rectifications. The British Government, inaccurately informed that Vienna *was* interested in a separate peace, sent Sir Francis Hopwood to Scandinavia, but he and Mensdorff never met. When Danish intermediaries tried instead to make contact between Hopwood and German, rather than Austrian diplomats, Balfour warned his envoy that Britain had 'no desire to negotiate with Germany'. If Czernin sought a general compromise peace, the British wanted only a separate, Austrian one.[3]

A second feeler, this time initiated by the Americans, underlined the point. On 8 February Wilson sent the British a message whose phrasing suggested that he hoped to arrange a general European settlement through an agreement with Vienna. Hence he wanted an assurance that the Allies' reply to him of 10 January 1917 did not commit them to the 'virtual dismemberment' of Austria-Hungary. Lloyd George at first replied that a separate peace with the Habsburg Monarchy would bring no advantage, especially if the Allies lost Italy as a consequence. But then he changed his mind, and said he was willing to accept an Austrian proposal, although even for a separate peace he was willing to guarantee continued Habsburg sovereignty only over Austria, Hungary, and Bohemia. Hence he remained loyal to the Allies' promises to the Habsburg Monarchy's neighbours, while Czernin rejected as wholly inadequate the soundings made by the American Ambassador in Vienna, and reiterated to the Americans that he would consider only a general and not a separate settlement.[4]

In contrast with these brief exchanges, the peace mediation attempted by Prince Sixte de Bourbon extended from December 1916 to the following June. Part of the reason for this was Sixte's unusual personal capacity to inspire trust. A member of the former French royal family, in 1916 he was serving with the Belgian army; his sister Zita was married to Karl, and Sixte therefore combined evident French patriotism with a personal connection with the Emperor. Like other intermediaries in 1917, he strung out the contact by exaggerating to each participant the other's favourable dispositions. But the decisive reason on the Austrian side for the longevity of the Sixte affair was that Karl kept Czernin largely uninformed about it, and handled it as an enterprise in personal diplomacy.[5] Soon after Karl's accession to the throne he sent a message via his mother-in-law to Sixte that he wished to make contact with the French Government. With French connivance, Sixte met the Emperor's confidant, Count Erdödy, in Switzerland. In the second half of March he went on for conversations in Vienna, having been advised beforehand that the French would require the full programme of the Cambon letter, including a neutralized left bank of the Rhine. He returned to Paris with a personal message, dated 24 March, from Karl, in which the Emperor agreed that Serbia should regain its sovereignty and have access to the Adriatic, provided it suppressed organizations that attempted subversion in Austria-Hungary. Karl had therefore much scaled down the Habsburgs' Balkan ambitions. And more dramatically, in Western Europe he accepted that Belgium should be restored, and promised to support 'by every means' France's 'just claims' to Alsace-Lorraine. Czernin, in a memorandum given to Sixte on 21 February, had also supported the restoration of Alsace-Lorraine, but had as usual excluded a separate peace. An accompanying personal note from Karl, however, had been more ambiguous on the latter, crucial point. And Czernin was not informed about the 24 March letter at all. As the French understood it when Sixte returned to Paris on the 31st, they were being offered not only support over Alsace-Lorraine but also an Austrian schism with Germany.[6]

Only now did the French Government, headed since mid-March by Alexandre Ribot, consult its allies. At Folkestone on 11 April Ribot briefed an enthusiastic Lloyd George. But the real problem lay with the Italians, whose claims had been neglected in the Franco-Austrian discussions. Sixte insisted, to protect Karl, that the 24 March letter should be kept from them, and Lloyd George and Ribot could therefore allude only generally to a possible peace with Austria when they met Sonnino on 19 April at Saint-Jean-de-Maurienne. Probably it made little difference. Sonnino held firm to the Treaty of London. He warned of possible revolution if the Italian Government compromised. Lloyd George's addition of Smyrna to the Italian zone in Asia Minor failed to move him. The meeting agreed that to pursue a separate peace with Austria-Hungary would be inopportune and would endanger Allied unity. Simultaneously, evidence that the Austrians were concerting with Germany their diplomacy towards Russia persuaded the French authorities that Karl was not sincerely seeking a separate peace. Sixte still managed to prolong the affair for a few more weeks. He visited Vienna for a second time in May, and brought back conflicting documents that again suggested Karl was less hostile than Czernin to a separate understanding. The Austrians also professed to have received a feeler from the Italians hinting that the latter would be satisfied with no more than the Trentino. The basis for this appears to have been a mysterious approach, purportedly from the Italian General Staff, to the German Legation in Berne. Certainly it did not come from the Italian Government. At an inter-Allied conference in Paris on 25 July Ribot at last showed Sonnino all the correspondence concerning the Sixte affair, but the Italian attitude was unchanged.[7]

By the final stages the main reason that Paris and Vienna persisted was probably to sow dissension in the other camp. Both the British and French were impatient with Sonnino; Karl's antipathy towards the Germans was stronger still. But this infused greater ambiguity into the two sides' signals rather than reversing the underlying alignment. The Sixte initiative failed partly because of Austria's refusal to cede to Italy anything more than the Trentino, which had already been on offer before May 1915. Both Karl and Czernin were contemptuous of the Italian war effort. But the initiative also failed because of the continuing solidity of the alliances. Under the impact of their worsening military situation France and Britain appeared to be altering their policy towards Vienna from partition to a search for separate peace. But they had never had a direct quarrel with Austria-Hungary anyway. Rather, the Habsburgs' loyalty to Germany had drawn the Western European Allies into a series of commitments to the Dual Monarchy's neighbours. By 1917, however, Serbia and Rumania had been defeated and Italy's armies stalemated. Lloyd George, though not Ribot, came to believe that a separate peace with Austria-Hungary, even if Italy and the Balkan Allies were lost, would be a strategic gain.[8] But he was not prepared to strike a unilateral bargain over Sonnino's head. And Karl, despite the equivocation in his messages, probably lacked the domestic political authority to abandon the German alliance. The possibility of a separate peace remained hypothetical, and Britain and France remained free to give more far-reaching undertakings to the Austro-Hungarian subject nationalities when circumstances altered in the following year.

The Sixte affair took place against the background of a further reassessment by the Central Powers of their war aims. The impetus for this came from Czernin and from the German High Command under Hindenburg and Ludendorff, OHL. Czernin hoped to moderate Germany's objectives, OHL to make them more ambitious, but both had an interest in tying Bethmann down. The Chancellor, conversely, wanted flexibility and vagueness, so that he could seize on any opportunity to divide the Allies. In circumstances of great uncertainty a series of high-level conferences argued out the issue. The initial successes of the submarine campaign suggested that splitting the enemy might after all be unnecessary; although even Hindenburg and Ludendorff felt anxiety about the impending synchronized Allied spring offensives. In the event, the Russian Revolution reduced these largely to a campaign in the west, in the shape of a British attack at Arras and an ill-fated French offensive under General Nivelle on the Chemin des Dames. But the fall of the Tsar also revived the possibility of a separate peace with Russia, and by May it was beginning to appear unlikely that the U-boats could cripple British resistance before American power was brought to bear.

Czernin began his diplomatic offensive when he met Bethmann in Vienna on 16–17 March. Austria-Hungary, he said, was 'at the end of her strength', critically short of raw materials, manpower, and food; and the Central Powers must agree on the terms of an acceptable general peace. But he also urged a principle of equivalence between German and Austrian gains. If Germany contented itself with a return to the 1914 status quo, Austria-Hungary must recover the territory it had lost. And if Germany made acquisitions, so should the Habsburgs, preferably in Rumania, which should be partitioned and its largest and richest portion brought under their control. Czernin was not, in fact, trying simply to attain a general peace before the Dual Monarchy suffered disaster. He hoped also to reorientate the Central Powers' objectives in a direction more favourable to Habsburg interests. But this implied renunciation in the west, which Bethmann resisted at the Vienna meeting. Germany, the Chancellor insisted, must be free to trade its French and Belgian conquests in order to regain its colonies, and it must keep the Longwy-Briey iron-ore field indefinitely, in exchange for the cession of only small portions of Alsace-Lorraine. Despite this, in a second meeting with the German civilian leaders, this time in Berlin on 26–27 March, Czernin obtained some satisfaction in a joint statement. The two Governments agreed that the 1914 status quo was the minimum that was acceptable, but if the war ended more favourably Germany would expand mainly on its eastern frontier, and Austria-Hungary in Rumania. Bethmann, subdued, seemed willing to accept a railway and customs union as the principal safeguard of Germany's interests in Belgium, although he held to his previous position over Longwy-Briey and Alsace-Lorraine.[9]

Czernin wanted Rumania not only for its wheat and oil, but also as a pawn in a larger game. When the Austrian and German Emperors met at Homburg on 3 April he proposed that in exchange for predominance in Rumania Austria-Hungary would be willing to allow German control over the whole of the projected independent Poland, including Galicia, but that Germany should cede the whole of Alsace-Lorraine. But with this over-ingenious proposal he went too far.[10] The Germans' own intelligence sources had made clear to them that he was exaggerating Austria-Hungary's predicament. There was indeed a food shortage in the Austrian half of the Monarchy at the beginning of 1917, but this was partly because surpluses were withheld by the Hungarian half, and the situation later improved. When the Parliament of the Austrian half, the Reichsrat, was convened in May, the subject peoples had hardened in their attitude. The representatives of the Poles and Ruthenes called for independence and union with their brothers outside the Monarchy's borders, while the Czechs and the South Slavs wished to convert it into a federation. The danger of *social* revolution, however, was relatively small,[11] although it was on this that Czernin concentrated in an apocalyptic memorandum delivered to the German Emperor on 12 April. In order to preserve their dynasties, he insisted, Germany and Austria-Hungary must take the initiative in restoring peace, even on unsatisfactory terms, before they had to undergo another winter of war. Nor did he confine himself to diplomatic channels. Karl gave a copy of the memorandum to Erzberger, and Czernin issued an unofficial statement appearing to support the opposition to annexations and indemnities that was being voiced in the Reichstag by the SPD.[12]

Bethmann, however, was also under pressure from a contrasting quarter. Hindenburg, arguing that the Russian Revolution had brought the end of the war closer, wanted Germany to decide on its objectives in peace negotiations before proceeding to discussion with the other Central Powers. The Chancellor, as usual, wished to be free to negotiate with whichever enemy seemed most willing, and resisted being committed to inflexible aims. But the Kaiser threw his weight onto OHL's side, and the German leaders duly conferred at Kreuznach on 23 April. Bethmann, Zimmermann, Hindenburg, and Ludendorff initialled the resulting document. It was formidable. Germany would annex Courland and Lithuania, and other parts of the Baltic provinces if possible, as well as extensive areas of Poland, in the rest of which it would enjoy economic, military, and political predominance. Belgium would remain under military control until it was ready for an alliance with Germany, which would have transit and occupation rights and manage its railways, and must possess Liège and the Flanders coast for at least a century. Germany would also annex Luxemburg and Longwy-Briey and cede only fragments of Alsace-Lorraine to France. Supplementary documents from the Naval Staff and the Colonial Secretary added the usual demands for a global chain of naval bases and a consolidated Central African empire.[13]

Bethmann wrote into the Foreign Ministry record that he had accepted the Kreuznach Programme on the explicit understanding that it was attainable only if Germany could dictate peace: a contingency he thought very remote indeed. It would be 'laughable' to resign over 'fantasies', and the quest for a separate agreement would go on. All the same, Kreuznach represented Wilhelm's views, as well as those of OHL, whose influence on German diplomacy would from this point forward be continuous.[14] In the west it resembled the heady aspirations of the September Programme and the agreements of November 1916; in the east it ran counter to the pressing need for agreement with the new authorities in Russia. It was based on confidence that total victory could still be won, and in his reply on 11 May to Czernin's 12 April memorandum Bethmann rebutted the Austrian Foreign Minister's despondency about the military prospects. As for the danger of revolution, he contended, this would be serious only if the Central Powers submitted. No doubt these were good debating points.[15] But the Chancellor was not fighting for a free hand relative to OHL simply in order to abandon it to Czernin. And at the same time as the Germans hardened their position the Austrian peace offensive was suspended. At a second Kreuznach conference, on 17–18 May, the two Powers came to a revised understanding about war aims. Nothing was said about the west, which in itself favoured Germany. In the east, Austria-Hungary would preserve its full territorial integrity, and what was left of Serbia, Montenegro, and Albania would become its economic, military, and political dependencies. Almost all of occupied Rumania would come within its sphere of influence, although Germany would have the preponderant share in owning and exploiting the oilfields, railways, and Danube shipping lines. The former Russian Poland would be under exclusively German influence, and Courland and Lithuania would be tightly 'attached' to Germany. But Czernin was broadly satisfied, and called off his attempts to cultivate the Reichstag opposition. Tension between Vienna and Berlin subsided, and the first phase in the Austrian search for peace was at an end.[16]

Improvements in Austria-Hungary's domestic, especially its economic, situation, facilitated compromise. But the Austrians also confronted a dilemma. Karl kept the Germans in ignorance of the Sixte affair, and his conduct in it is difficult to account for unless he had at least considered reaching a separate understanding with the Allies. But such a course, considered Czernin afterwards, would have led to German intervention and a civil war that would have destroyed the Monarchy.[17] It would certainly have divided both Karl's Ministers and his subjects and tested to the limits the dynasty's authority. But the Allies, when sounded, had given little encouragement to such a step, and had even remained loyal to the despised Italians. Although Karl kept a channel to the enemy open, the emphasis of his policy anyway lay in supporting Czernin's efforts to expedite a general peace by softening up the Germans. But the weaknesses of this strategy were almost equally severe. Czernin saw Paris as the most receptive enemy capital, whereas Germany's diplomatic efforts during 1917 were concentrated first on Petrograd and then on London. Even Bethmann was unwilling to let Vienna take the lead in defining the Central Powers' conditions, and Bethmann's control over the more intransigent forces in Berlin was weakening. If Germany, as the stronger partner, insisted on its western war aims, Austria-Hungary would have either to acquiesce and continue fighting or make peace in defiance of its ally. But the latter course was effectively excluded, and the free hand offered in the Balkans at the second Kreuznach conference—anyway qualified by major sacrifices to Germany in Rumania—was little compensation for the fading prospects of a general settlement. Such a settlement would stay out of reach unless Austrian action in the Central Powers' camp was matched by changes in the Allies' attitude. And in the spring and summer of 1917 sufficient change was unforthcoming. It is time to consider why, in spite of the repercussions of the Russian Revolution, this was so.

(ii) *The February Revolution and the Powers*

The Russian February Revolution began when the Petrograd garrison refused to fire on rioting strikers and food demonstrators in the city, and culminated in the abdication of Nicholas II. Such authority as remained was divided between the Provisional Government under Prince Lvov, composed initially mainly of Liberal deputies from the Duma, and the Petrograd Soviet of workers' and soldiers' deputies. The reluctant revolutionaries of the Duma opposition had detested the old regime because of its incompetence and its supposed sympathy for Germany. For this reason much opinion outside Russia, especially in Paris, greeted the February Revolution with wishful thinking that it might revitalize the Russian war effort along the lines of the French precedent of 1792.[18] The Petrograd Soviet, by contrast, voiced the demands of the Russian masses for peace, if a way to peace could be found. Until the last weeks before the Bolsheviks seized power, however, a majority on the Soviet was held by the more moderate Russian socialists, from the Menshevik and Socialist Revolutionary parties. They supported the war on the condition that its objectives were modified. Thus the All-Russian Conference of Soviets on 11 April pledged backing for the Provisional Government and the war effort, but appealed to the peoples of the world to press their rulers to give up conquests, annexations, and indemnities, and invited the Government to negotiate with the Allies towards this goal.[19]

The 'Petrograd formula'—a peace without annexations or indemnities, based on national self-determination—had yet to be accepted by the Lvov Cabinet. Indeed, the new Foreign Minister, Miliukov, reassured the Allies that Russia would respect its international undertakings, and he publicly re-affirmed the claim to the Straits. This was challenged by Kerensky, the one holder of a Cabinet post who was also a member of the Soviet, and a Government declaration on 9 April tried unconvincingly to reconcile the differing points of view. It denied that Russia sought to dominate other nations or seize their national possessions; but it stood by the country's obligations to the Allies. When the Soviet pressed for this to be forwarded to Russia's partners Miliukov agreed to send it only with a covering note expressing confidence that at the peace the Allies would establish the 'guarantees and sanctions' needed to prevent another war in the future. This enraged the Soviet, and led to demonstrations in the Petrograd streets. When the Government was broadened early in May to take in representatives from the Soviet Miliukov's residual annexationism therefore isolated him in the Cabinet, and he was obliged to resign.[20]

The new alliance of liberals, Mensheviks, and Socialist Revolutionaries was threatened from the start by Lenin's return from exile in mid-April and his manoeuvring of the Bolsheviks into uncompromising opposition to the war effort. The war, and the failure of the moderate Left to extricate

Russia from it, further diminished the slim chances of a liberal regime being implanted in the Tsar's former domains. Even after May, the Provisional Government's aims were not purely defensive. Miliukov's successor, Tereshchenko, may have hankered after some continuing control of Constantinople and gains from Turkey in Armenia.[21] The Government had also bound itself by a declaration of 29 March in favour of an independent Poland in 'free military alliance' with Russia, embracing the areas of Polish majority population in the German, Austrian, and Russian Empires. A joint French–British–Italian declaration of 14 April expressed solidarity with this pledge. This new promise of independence was certainly a gesture towards national self-determination, although Russia's traditional security interest in Poland was not entirely jettisoned. But it was also a commitment to conquering territory in the Prussian military heartland at a moment when the faltering Russian armies had long since been expelled even from their own part of Poland. In these circumstances, the Western Allies carefully avoided making their commitment one that would apply irrespective of the military performance of the Russians themselves.[22] But neither the Provisional Government nor the Soviet was committed to peace at any price; and both repudiated a separate ceasefire. Yet if the new regime was to survive at home it needed to end the war on any terms it could obtain.

Russia's position had become comparable to that of Austria-Hungary in the other camp: intense war-weariness, willingness to reduce its own war aims (more seriously in the Russian than the Austrian case) and to press revision on its partners, but ultimate shrinking from unilateral action. None of the Russian peace contacts with the Central Powers in March–June 1917 were as significant as the Sixte affair. But they demonstrated Germany's continuing unwillingness to relent sufficiently on its war aims for a separate peace to become a serious proposition. Hence the Berlin leaders jeopardized their last remaining chance of victory after American entry and the Allies' containment of the submarine challenge.

In a speech by Bethmann on 29 March and an inspired press statement on 15 April the Germans deliberately avoided disavowing annexations, but disclosed their willingness for an 'honourable' settlement.[23] This was tested in the Erzberger–Kolyschko conversations. Kolyschko was a Russian official with an uncertain mandate from Petrograd. In March and April Erzberger, with Bethmann's approval, twice met him in Stockholm. They agreed on a draft armistice and on peace conditions that would restore Russia's 1914 border, though with extensive 'frontier corrections' and a plebiscite (which Erzberger expected to favour the Central Powers) in Poland. But as so often in 1917, this agreement was possible only because neither intermediary accurately represented his Government. Some of the Ministers in Petrograd tolerated Kolyschko's activities; others condemned him as a German agent. Zimmermann reprimanded Erzberger for having exceeded his instructions, which were only to listen. Ludendorff was furious at not having been consulted, and objected that Erzberger had conceded too much. On 29 April the Foreign Ministry and OHL agreed a new draft armistice. It provided unambiguously for an independent Poland and for German 'frontier rectifications' towards Courland and Lithuania. And the Kreuznach agreement with Austria-Hungary in May went further still. The basis for agreement had collapsed even before Kolyschko refused a proposed third meeting.[24]

Two further contacts met a similar fate. Early in May there were conversations at the front between the German military authorities and the Russian General Dragomirow. Bethmann approved the handing over on the 14th of a new set of conditions: Russian grain and oil deliveries; an independent Poland 'leaning towards' the Central Powers; Courland and Lithuania bound economically, militarily, and politically to Germany. When the German Commander-in-Chief on the Russian Front appealed by radio for a separate peace, Kerensky unsurprisingly responded with an absolute refusal. The final peace initiative was the Grimm–Hoffmann affair. When Grimm, a Swiss socialist, visited Russia in April, Ministers of the Provisional Government asked him to obtain an authoritative statement of Germany's conditions. Hoffmann, the Swiss Foreign Minister, secured conditions from Zimmermann that resembled those communicated on 14 May. He telegraphed the terms to Grimm, but the Provisional

Government intercepted the message and expelled Grimm as a German agent, while Hoffman was obliged to resign.[25] At least at first, the Russians seem to have been divided in their views. But by June it was evident to them that a separate peace would mean renouncing Courland, Lithuania, and Poland. Although they were committed to an independent Poland, they envisaged one that would remain an ally and in their own rather than the enemy sphere. They abandoned their feelers to the Central Powers, and switched to the alternative approach of a military offensive at the front combined with a diplomatic offensive against the war aims of their allies. They did so at a moment when the long developing crisis on the European domestic front at last came to a head.

In the spring of 1917 the diplomatic deadlock between the opposing coalitions remained stubbornly in place. Nor were military developments, in what was becoming a broken-backed war, able to break the stalemate. The third element in the deadly equilibrium of 1914–17, however, was the primacy within each belligerent of political forces committed to victory at almost any cost. True, although the Governments in Vienna and Petrograd had not renounced all hopes of expansion they would now be willing to accept the 1914 status quo as the price of a general peace. And elsewhere the advocates of a negotiated settlement without annexations were everywhere gaining strength. But they failed, both in Germany and in the Western Allied capitals, to advance enough to break the stalemate at the third, domestic political level.

Events in Germany culminated in the July 1917 political crisis in which Bethmann Hollweg was removed and a new majority in the Reichstag passed the so-called Peace Resolution. Behind this lay a social crisis from which all the belligerents suffered to a greater or lesser degree. Its deepest cause was the spectacle of continuing unprecedented slaughter to little visible gain and with no foreseeable end. But it became acute as a result of the bitter 'turnip winter' of 1916–17. In Germany, as in Russia, an overloaded railway system was unable to distribute food and coal efficiently as well as meet military needs. In mid-April the bread ration was cut, and over 200,000 went on strike in Berlin alone. More strikes followed, directed not only against economic hardship but also in favour of democratization and a non-annexationist peace. In April there was formed the breakaway Independent Social Democratic Party, or USPD. Its leaders opposed annexations, and were willing to vote against war credits. As a result the SPD now had to shift its ground in order to retain control over its following. On 19 April it came out in favour of a peace without annexations and indemnities.[26]

Bethmann responded to these developments with a gesture towards democratic reform. Much of the German federal administration was linked with that of Prussia, the largest and the dominant member-State, of which Wilhelm was King and Bethmann was Minister President. The 'Easter Message', which Bethmann prevailed on the Kaiser to issue at the beginning of April, pledged to end after the war the unrepresentative Prussian three-class franchise, although it avoided an explicit commitment to equal suffrage. Even so, it earned the Chancellor more opprobrium from OHL, which objected to democratization in its own right and considered the Message a dangerous signal of weakness to the Allies.[27] Bethmann was therefore caught in a growing polarization between OHL and its supporters on the one hand and the movement for constitutional reform and a compromise peace on the other. As in the submarine controversy, Erzberger and the Centre Party held the balance, and on 6 July Erzberger triggered off the crisis with a speech in the Reichstag Main Committee that expressed dark pessimism about the military prospects and called for a resolution opposing annexations. Erzberger's disclosures of confidential information had a sensational effect. He believed the submarine campaign was proving indecisive and that Germany had lost the gamble undertaken in January. His contacts with the Vienna leaders had impressed on him the gravity of Austria-Hungary's plight. And he foresaw that if no move was made towards the SPD they would vote against war credits. A suitable resolution, on the other hand, might allay Socialist and Austrian frustration, while improving the chances for the Papal mediation Erzberger knew to be projected. A new Reichstag majority of National Liberals, Centre, Progressives, and SPD came into being. The four parties called for franchise reform in Prussia and a democratization of the federal Government; and on 19 July the Centre, Progressives, and SPD voted through the Peace Resolution by a 212 : 126 majority.[28]

The Resolution was far from being an unambiguous endorsement of the Petrograd formula. It called for a 'peace of understanding', and declared that 'forced territorial acquisitions and political, economic, or financial oppressions are irreconcilable with such a peace'. It warned that while the enemy continued to threaten Germany and its partners with conquest and coercion the German people would fight on. It condemned annexationism and plans for continuing economic warfare on either side, but its wording would allow indirect expansion through nominally independent buffer States. On the day after the Resolution Erzberger wrote to the new Chancellor, Michaelis, recommending that Lithuania should be an independent Duchy with the Kaiser as its Duke, in customs union with Germany. Alsace-Lorraine should become autonomous, but remain under German sovereignty; even Longwy-Briey might be obtainable within the Resolution as part of a suitable exchange. This helps explain why the USPD, who favoured a plebiscite in Alsace-Lorraine, voted against the Resolution. Erzberger had joined Czernin and the Russian moderate Socialists in the camp of those who had abandoned hope of outright military victory but still cherished the alternative, little more realistic, hope that they could cut their losses and yet expand their country's influence through a general compromise.[29]

Erzberger had probably not originally intended to remove Bethmann, but he changed his mind when the latter opposed the Resolution on the grounds that it would give an impression of weakness to the enemy. Erzberger supposed that Bethmann's predecessor, Bülow, might be better able to act on the Resolution and face down OHL. But Bülow was unacceptable to the Kaiser, and Erzberger ended up by seeking to replace Bethmann without having an alternative candidate. Hindenburg and Ludendorff perceived an opportunity to eliminate a man they now found impossible to work with, and, knowing of Erzberger's opposition to Bethmann, they threatened to resign if the Chancellor did not go. The absence of a Reichstag majority made it harder for Bethmann to resist, and for Wilhelm to oppose what he resented as military dictation. To this extent Bethmann's resignation on 13 July was due to a paradoxical co-operation between conflicting forces. But the Reichstag parties had no say in the choice of his successor, Michaelis, an obscure Prussian civil servant who was previously unknown to the Kaiser but was acceptable to the High Command. Michaelis turned out not to be a puppet of OHL, but he was more conservative than Bethmann in both domestic and foreign affairs.[30]

This was demonstrated by his handling of the Peace Resolution, which he accepted 'as I understand it', but with a warning that he would not allow the Reichstag to narrow his constitutional prerogatives. 'My interpretation', he wrote to the Crown Prince, 'has removed the greatest danger from the notorious Resolution. One can, after all, now make any peace that one likes under its terms.'[31] The Resolution had negligible effects on the policy of the German Government, and failed to impress the Allies. In the following year it was shown to be flexible enough to accommodate the draconian Treaty of Brest-Litovsk. Neither through peace contacts with the German leaders nor through an upsurge of protest from below did the Russian Revolution succeed in moderating German aims.

In the meantime the new authorities in Petrograd tried to create the conditions for a general peace by diminishing the war aims of their allies. They acted partly at inter-Governmental level and partly by sponsoring an attempt to revive the Socialist International through a conference of neutral and belligerent Socialist parties at Stockholm. At inter-Governmental level the Provisional Government's compromise declaration of 9 April was forwarded to the Allies on 1 May. The British replied that they were willing to review their international agreements; the French, although defending 'reparatory indemnities' and guarantees against new enemy provocations, were also prepared to talk. On this unpromising basis a new circular from Tereshchenko on 13 June informed his partners that Russia sought a general, non-imperialist peace, and proposed a conference to revise the coalition's war aims. He received no reply, and at the end of July he himself suggested that the conference should be postponed.[32] For by

this time the Provisional Government had unsuccessfully
played its military card. Hoping to increase its persuasiveness
in the Allied capitals, on 1 July it launched the so-called
Kerensky offensive. This was quickly halted, and during the
remainder of the month there was an enemy counter-offensive
and an attempted Bolshevik insurrection in Petrograd. Land
seizures in the countryside reached their height, and the
fighting power of the largely peasant army further declined.

Tereshchenko correctly suspected that the Western European
Allies had written Russia off. A committee under Curzon
reported to the British Cabinet on 14 May that Russia would
probably stay in the war, but its military performance would
not improve. Ribot, meanwhile, sent his Socialist Minister of
Armaments, Thomas, on a special mission to Petrograd.
Thomas, enthusiastic, reported that by agreeing to renegotiate
their war aims the Allies might stimulate a new Russian effort,
but Ribot replied that he was against any inter-Allied
conference to revise war aims, and he later evaded
commitment over Tereshchenko's conference proposal.[33] After
the Kerensky offensive failed Tereshchenko's last remaining
means of leverage at inter-Governmental level was to threaten
a separate peace, and from this he refrained. Pressure through
more traditional channels had therefore had little effect.

The more formidable challenge presented by the Russian
revolutionaries to the Allies was the attempted Stockholm
Conference. Since the breakdown of its international solidarity
in 1914 the Socialist movement had divided into three broad
ideological groupings. The patriotic Right supported the
national war efforts (though not necessarily annexations),
voted war credits, and sometimes entered coalition Governments. It included a majority of the SPD, the SFIO, and the
Labour Party, as well as of the British, French, and German
trade-union leaders. By 1917 the Centre, or 'minority',
presented it with a serious challenge. The SFIO 'minority'
mustered nearly half the vote at Party congresses; their
German counterparts split off as the USPD. Most of the PSI in
Italy and the Mensheviks and Socialist Revolutionaries in
Russia were also in the Centre camp, although its British
representation, concentrated in the Independent Labour Party
and the Union of Democratic Control, was weaker. In general

the Centre, though acting by constitutional means, refused to vote war credits and supported trying to restore peace by reviving the Second International. It opposed annexations and favoured national self-determination, both the USPD and the French 'minority' being willing, for example, to accept a plebiscite in Alsace-Lorraine. Finally, the revolutionary Left, represented by Lenin in Russia and by much smaller groups elsewhere, wished to transform the conflict into an international class war, and to build up a new summit organization separate from the Second International. Elements of the Left and Centre from both belligerent camps joined neutral socialists at two conferences in Switzerland, at Zimmerwald in September 1915 and Kienthal in April 1916. The Zimmerwald Conference denounced the Right and set up a permanent International Socialist Commission in rivalry with the International Socialist Bureau (or ISB), the executive of the Second International. The Kienthal Conference attacked the Centre as well.

The Stockholm proposal originated with the Centre. Most of the Right eventually rallied to it, but it was condemned by Lenin and the revolutionaries. Support from the Right came only because an idea started by the ISB was taken up by the Russian Socialists who by the end of May dominated not only the Petrograd Soviet but also the Provisional Government. On 22 April, Huysmans, the Secretary of the ISB, sent out invitations to an international socialist conference. A preparatory committee of Dutch and Scandinavian Socialists was set up in Stockholm. On 15 May the Petrograd Soviet issued a parallel, but separate, appeal. Liaison between the two led to the formation of a Russian–Dutch–Scandinavian Committee, which issued a joint invitation on 11 July. No conference, however, ensued. The only gathering in Stockholm to bring together socialists from the opposing camps during 1917 was a third Zimmerwaldian assembly, which took place in September. Between May and July delegations from Austria-Hungary, Germany (SPD and USPD), Russia, the United States, and Belgium separately visited the Dutch–Scandinavian organizers in the city, but no British, French, or Italian socialists came.[34]

Responsibility for the stillbirth of the Stockholm Conference therefore lay primarily with the Allies. In Berlin and Vienna it caused little dispute. Czernin was willing to give socialist mediation a chance to end the war; Bethmann, though unenthusiastic, thought that allowing the SPD to attend would help maintain its support for the war effort. Concerned that the SPD should not appear to be Government agents, he allowed the USPD to go as well.[35] On the opposite side, there was least heart-searching in Washington. Wilson considered discussions between the socialists were 'likely to make a deal of mischief', and his Government took the lead in denying to the small, Centrist American party passports for the conference called on 11 July.[36] This had few repercussions on the American home front. But it relieved the much greater difficulties of the Government in Britain, France, and Italy. In all three countries Stockholm occasioned a trial of strength between the opponents and supporters of official policy. And in all three countries, as in Germany in July 1917, the opposition won at best cosmetic concessions.

In Italy the equivalent of the socialist Right elsewhere was the small reformist socialist party led by Bissolati, who had a seat in the Boselli coalition Government that replaced Salandra's ministry in June 1916. The PSI, which was much larger, continued to support immediate peace negotiations, and sent strong delegations to Zimmerwald and Kienthal. It was therefore unsurprising that Sonnino opposed granting passports for Stockholm. The more serious question was whether governmental authority could be maintained. By October 1917 the Italian army had lost over 200,000 dead and advanced only half the twenty-five miles from the border to Trieste. Real industrial wages were 27 per cent less than in 1913. The opponents of Italian intervention now resurfaced. In August 1917 the Pope's Peace Note[37] called for an end to the 'useless struggle' and for a negotiated solution to the Austro-Italian territorial dispute. In a speech in Cuneo in the same month Giolitti called for 'profound changes in the conduct of foreign policy' after the war. Also in August a delegation from the Petrograd Soviet arrived in Turin, an example almost as outstanding as Petrograd itself of the swollen cities that had sucked in workers to giant armaments plants and overcrowded housing. There was a large anti-war demonstration, and a week later three days of insurrection cost nearly fifty lives. The final characteristic of the Italian malaise was a crisis in military morale. When Austrian and German forces attacked at Caporetto on 24 October resistance collapsed, and they advanced seventy miles before the front was stabilized along the river Piave. But the shock of defeat arrested the disintegration of 1917. The Boselli coalition was replaced by a rather more effective one under Orlando. The clergy, some Socialists, and, if more guardedly, Giolitti, urged the duty of resistance. In 1918 civilian food supply and conditions at the front were modestly improved and several Left-wing leaders brought to trial. Neither Austrian concessions nor defeat and revolution in Italy would end the struggle between the two Powers.[38]

In some ways France followed a similar course. In the war industries of the Paris basin there existed, if in less extreme conditions, the same raw and speedily expanded workforce as in Petrograd and Turin. In May and June 1917 there occurred the biggest strikes since the outbreak of war and, as elsewhere, the strikers used pacifist and revolutionary slogans as well as presenting more straightforwardly economic demands. In the same months the surveys by the authorities revealed a trough of deep depression in civilian morale. And early June also saw the climax of an army mutiny that had gathered momentum since the troops were flung unavailingly against the Chemin des Dames in April. The crisis had analogies with Caporetto, and the new Commander-in-Chief, Pétain, overcame it by providing better material conditions for the soldiers and long months of largely defensive fighting. The Clemenceau ministry, which came to office in November, took action against those suspected of defeatism, foremost among them being the pre-war leader of the Radical Party, Caillaux. Clemenceau also ended a period of ministerial instability in the Chamber of Deputies, and demonstrated that France was governable without Socialist participation in the Cabinet. This, however, was still unproven when the Stockholm issue exploded in the critical months of May and June.[39]

Because of the SFIO's support for the war effort, there was more of a domestic consensus to defend than in Italy. The party executive overrode the *minoritaires*, and refused the first invitation from the ISB. But by the time a special National Council of the party met on 27–29 May the Petrograd Soviet had launched its parallel appeal. And two previously patriotic Socialist deputies, Cachin and Moutet, returned from a mission to Petrograd filled with revolutionary ardour and supplied with knowledge of the Doumergue agreement. The National Council voted to accept the Stockholm invitation, and a delegation went to Ribot to ask for the secret treaties to be annulled.

The resulting parliamentary debates from 1 to 6 June tested the Government's attitude to Stockholm and to the war aims adopted under Briand. Although Ribot wavered over passports for the Conference, his Ministers and the Right-wing parties in the Chamber emphatically opposed them. So, decisively, did Pétain, who refused to answer for discipline in the army if the Socialists went to Stockholm. As for war aims, the Dumont resolution of 5 June, passed in the Chamber by 467 : 52 and approved not only by the Government but also by nearly half the Socialist Deputies, declared that France was fighting for 'the liberation of invaded territories, the return of Alsace-Lorraine, . . . and the just reparation of damages'. Although opposed to 'conquering and subjugating foreign populations', it desired the overthrow of 'Prussian militarism', and 'lasting guarantees of peace and independence for both large and small nations in an organization . . . of the League of Nations'. This was almost as ambiguous as the Reichstag Peace Resolution. In the preceding debates Ribot gave the impression of disapproving of the Doumergue agreement (though not the Cambon letter) while not explicitly disavowing it. In the more congenial atmosphere of a secret session of the Senate, however, he affirmed that by 'Alsace-Lorraine' his Government understood the frontier of 1790, and that a neutral and autonomous buffer State between France and Germany would be not a 'conquest' but a 'protective measure'. This was the programme of the Cambon letter in all but name. No more than for Erzberger did repudiating annexations mean repudiating more indirect control. In Paris as in Berlin the opposition failed to win a real, rather than a superficial, renunciation of expansionist war aims.[40]

In Britain the symptoms of the Russian disease were milder. Voting in the Commons suggested that support for the Stockholm Conference and the Petrograd formula was confined to twenty or thirty MPs. Mutiny broke out at the Étaples base in the rear of the murderous Third Ypres offensive, but there was no breakdown of military morale on the French or Italian scale. In Ireland there was a tidal movement of opinion away from the Home Rule party towards the intransigent nationalism of Sinn Féin, but this, apart from increasing the importance of good relations with America, had few implications for the Lloyd George Government's war aims. East of the Irish Sea the biggest challenge to consensus was the declining authority of regular trade-union officials over the shop-steward movement in the engineering and munitions industries. But in general the danger of revolution was less than on the Continent, and Ministers could handle the Stockholm issue with greater assurance.[41]

Like the SFIO, the Labour Party Executive Committee declined the first ISB appeal. After the Petrograd Soviet's invitation, however, the Cabinet itself decided that British representatives could attend, both for the favourable propaganda effect in Russia and to prevent a Russo-German tête-à-tête with no more reliable socialists being present. Given the attitude of the Labour leaders, however, only the British equivalent of the *minoritaires* wished to attend the Conference, most notable of whom was Ramsay MacDonald. But the Russian–Dutch–Scandinavian invitation of 11 July opened a second phase in the British debate. The eminently respectable Arthur Henderson, Leader of the Parliamentary Labour Party and a member of the War Cabinet, had visited Russia and returned with his ideas transformed, to some extent like Cachin and Moutet. Without consulting the Cabinet, he advised in favour of attending Stockholm, and a special Labour Party Conference on 10 August confirmed this. But the Cabinet had meanwhile decided to refuse passports, and accepted Henderson's resignation. Both sides had therefore reversed their positions. Henderson had exasperated his colleagues, who felt he had misled them. But the Cabinet also noted the unanimous opposition to Stockholm from Britain's allies, and especially Wilson. Even in Russia, the Soviet had declined in influence, and Kerensky, who had replaced Lvov as Premier, was reported to be hostile to the Conference, although his Government could not openly admit it.[42]

Whereas the SFIO left the French Government in September 1917, largely because of the Stockholm and war-aims issues,

Labour Ministers continued to serve in the Lloyd George coalition. But Henderson himself had been persuaded by his trip to Russia of the need for an effective left-wing party that could head off the danger of a British revolution more successfully than the Provisional Government was meeting the Bolshevik challenge. After August 1917 the Labour Party underwent changes in its organization and its programme that were designed to enable it to compete for office in its own right after the war rather than in alliance with the Liberals. Among these was the Programme of War Aims adopted on 28 December 1917, and predominantly drafted by MacDonald. But this, although it condemned annexationism and gave extensive functions to the League of Nations, was a programme of reformist objectives to be attained through victory rather than a blueprint for a compromise peace.[43] In Western Europe, unlike Eastern Europe, the bloodletting would not be halted by insurrection from below. But nor would it be halted by secret negotiations between the belligerent Governments, for reasons that must now be considered.

(iii) *The Papal Peace Note and the Impasse in the West*

On 16 August the Vatican published a peace note from Pope Benedict XV. It had already been forwarded confidentially to the belligerents. Quite apart from the obvious, humanitarian concern, the Vatican needed to terminate a conflict that had set Catholic against Catholic and endangered its authority over its congregations. The Pope also had a special interest in the survival of Austria-Hungary, and perhaps for this reason he consulted in advance only one of the two sides. Within the Central Powers, however, he concentrated on an understanding with Germany, with the paradoxical result that Karl, Czernin, and the Austro-Hungarian press disapproved of the note when it appeared.[44]

In June Pacelli, the Papal Nuncio in Munich, visited the Kaiser, who urged the Vatican to act, and Bethmann, who said that Alsace-Lorraine need not prevent a peace of understanding, but Belgium could not regain full independence if this made France and Britain predominant there. Both this and a later conversation between Pacelli and Zimmermann seem to have been fed into the drafting of the Papal appeal.[45] The Pope's note proposed simultaneous disarmament by agreement; international arbitration backed by sanctions; freedom of the seas; and generally that each side should pay its own war expenses. France should be evacuated, Germany regain its colonies, Belgium's full independence be guaranteed 'against any Power whatsoever', and the Franco-German and Austro-Italian territorial disputes settled in a conciliatory manner that heeded, as far as possible, the aspirations of the populations concerned. The note said little about Eastern Europe, though it expressed sympathy for Poland. Otherwise this was more or less a peace without annexations and indemnities, as incompatible with the war aims of the Western European Allies as with those of OHL.[46]

The response of the Central Powers waited on the outcome of a new round of consultations over war aims, necessitated by Michaelis's appointment. Inexperienced in external questions, the new Chancellor normally backed the judgement of Richard von Kühlmann, who in August succeeded Zimmermann as Foreign Minister. Like Bethmann-Hollweg, Kühlmann intended to resist OHL encroachments on civilian authority, and saw a rift in the opposing coalition as Germany's means of salvation, although he conceived of London rather than Petrograd as the weak link in the Allied chain. But he also inherited Bethmann's unenviable middle position between Ludendorff and Czernin. On 1 August the Austrian Foreign Minister renewed his earlier offer to abandon Galicia to a German-dominated Poland if Germany would cede part of Alsace-Lorraine. But in a third Kreuznach meeting eight days later Michaelis agreed with OHL on an even more extensive war-aims programme than the 23 April one. In particular, a new German ally was envisaged in the shape of a nominally independent Ukraine. No more than Bethmann, however, did Michaelis consider himself absolutely bound to the military position. Meeting Czernin again on 14–15 August, he said that Germany might not have to annex even Longwy-Briey, although it must have continuing access to its ore. But he could make no important cessions in Alsace-Lorraine. The cycle of conversations first completed on 26 March, 23 April, and 17–18 May had repeated itself. Once again the offer of Galicia had failed to tempt the Germans into moderating their demands sufficiently for an accord with France. And Kühlmann and Michaelis agreed at first on a dilatory handling of the Papal Peace Note that would prevent their being drawn into premature negotiations.[47]

Early in September two developments persuaded the Germans to launch a diplomatic offensive after all. These were the British response to the Pope's note, and the Armand–Revertera conversations. In June the French General Staff had learned that Count Revertera, a highly placed figure at the Austrian court, wished to meet a French military intelligence officer, Armand. Painlevé, the War Minister, won the consent of Ribot and Lloyd George, and on 7 and 22 August two meetings followed in Switzerland. The main significance of these conversations lay in the remarkable 'terms' communicated by Armand and their galvanic effect on the diplomacy of the Central Powers. He offered Austria-Hungary sovereignty over Silesia and Bavaria and a reunited Poland with its borders of 1792, in return for a separate peace and the cession to Italy of the Trentino and Trieste, or at least the latter's elevation into a free port. But whom did Armand represent? Ribot and Lloyd George had approved the contact on condition that he listened without attempting to negotiate. Painlevé, however, had authorized the Silesia and Poland offers in general terms, although feeling afterwards that Armand had been too categorical. Painlevé's appeared to be a rising political star, and he briefly served as French Prime Minister in September–November 1917. German agents in Switzerland had received a stream of reports that if this happened he would be ready for a compromise peace. So when at the end of August Czernin proposed to the Germans that he should meet Painlevé, Kühlmann was startled, and rushed to Vienna. He considered the affair a clever and dangerous bid to drive a wedge between the Central Powers. Nor could he let Czernin take the lead in representing Germany in general negotiations. It was time for Berlin to launch an initiative of its own.[48]

At the same time as Kühlmann gained a motive to act, Britain's response to Benedict XV gave him an occasion. Neither the French, nor the Italian, nor the American Government wished to follow up the Vatican initiative.[49] But when

Lloyd George's Cabinet met on 20 August the coalition's unity splintered. The British Government had been much chastened during the year, and the Cabinet felt in retrospect that the 10 January Allied reply to Wilson had appeared 'imperialistic and grasping'. It agreed to tell the Pope that the Central Powers had not spelled out their objectives on the earlier occasion and it was for them to speak first now. This was evidently to leave the door ajar, especially given the phrasing of a confidential telegram from the Foreign Secretary to the British representative at the Vatican, de Salis. Even over Belgium, this observed, singling out Britain's primary concern, the enemy had failed to demonstrate any intention to restore the country's sovereignty or repair the damage to it. Ribot, without seeing the contents of the message, and to his subsequent regret, asked to be associated with it. And de Salis actually handed the document over rather than obeying his instructions to communicate its contents orally.[50] The American President's reply to the Pope, published unilaterally on 27 August, meanwhile condemned the idea of returning to the pre-war status quo and came close to summoning the German people to overthrow their rulers. But at the same time as this terminated the public diplomacy over the Pope's initiative the Vatican forwarded to Kühlmann the de Salis message.[51] During September 1917, while the British and German soldiers caught up in Haig's Third Ypres offensive butchered each other in the Flanders mud, the attempts to end the war by compromise reached their culmination.

Both the French and British Governments now received feelers from Berlin: the French through the Briand-Lancken affair, which will be discussed below, and the British in response to the de Salis overture. For Kühlmann, it was the contact with London that mattered. In a memorandum of 3 September, approved by Michaelis, he urged that Germany should counter the Armand–Revertera conversations by trying to divide Britain and France. An 'ocean of hate' separated Berlin from Paris, and nothing important could be given in Alsace-Lorraine, but if Britain was reassured over Belgium it might press its ally to yield. Before Germany could satisfy the British on the issue, however, the Allies must promise to restore all of Germany's pre-war territories, including its colonies. This, although Kühlmann was willing to negotiate over it, conflicted with another fundamental British aim.[52]

At the Bellevue Crown Council on 11 September, Kühlmann's proposed *démarche* briefly won approval from the Kaiser and OHL. Michaelis believed the navy's objective of permanent control of the Flanders coast to be of questionable value and unobtainable short of complete British defeat. But he agreed with Hindenburg and Ludendorff that Liège and military guarantees in inland Belgium could be abandoned only after many years, when such close economic ties had been created that it would be impossible for Belgium to go to war with Germany. As he expected compromise over Belgium to make possible a settlement in which Germany would regain its colonies and advance its power in Eastern Europe, he could convincingly deny having a peace of 'renunciation' in mind. The navy was isolated, and the Kaiser, though sympathetic to its pleas, told Kühlmann after the conference that he had a free hand to get a peace before Christmas. Actually this was authority only to drop the demand for coastal naval bases. None the less, Kühlmann went ahead, selecting as an intermediary Villalobar, the Spanish diplomatic representative in the Low Countries. Villalobar referred to the Spanish Foreign Minister, who eventually conveyed to the British Ambassador in Madrid the bald information that 'a very exalted personage' in Germany wished to make 'a communication relative to peace'.[53]

Kühlmann's message therefore arrived in London in a less authoritative and explicit form than he had intended, and it said nothing about Belgium. But Balfour correctly divined its author, and felt that simply to ignore it might discourage British opinion and strengthen the Pan-Germans in Berlin. He also felt, however, that any answer must spell out that Britain could not engage in even the most non-committal conservations without informing its partners. On this crucial principle the Cabinet again wavered. On 24 September it decided to reconsider after Lloyd George had spoken to Painlevé, now French Prime Minister, at Boulogne on the following day. But several Ministers, including Lloyd George, wanted to delay communicating with the remaining Allies until Germany's proposals were known. If Russia, especially, dropped out of the war, Lloyd George considered it should pay the penalty in territorial losses. Conversely,

Milner objected that Germany would leave the war more powerful than it had entered if Britain gave it a free hand in the east. And Balfour feared that Russia would drop out all the faster if it learned its partners were discussing terms behind its back. Could Britain tolerate German hegemony in Eastern Europe or not? For the moment the Cabinet waited on the conversation at Boulogne.[54]

Painlevé and Lloyd George also had to consider the second, Briand–Lancken, feeler. Lancken was the head of the Political Department of the German occupation administration in Brussels. In April he had been authorized to sound out French politicians and officials with token cessions in Alsace-Lorraine. He also made contact with the Prime Minister of the Belgian Government-in-exile, de Broqueville. But his interest focused on Briand, who was now out of office and trimming his sails to the new, conciliatory winds. Having agreed in principle to meet Lancken in Switzerland, Briand was assured by de Broqueville that Germany was in good faith and it might be possible to regain the lost provinces. He approached the new Painlevé ministry that was formed on 13 September, in which Ribot continued at the Quai d'Orsay. The Foreign Minister considered Lancken's approach a 'snare', but Painlevé himself was willing to approve a meeting if the Allies agreed. Neither the French nor the British Government, therefore, any longer objected to the principle of talking, unless this meant divisive separate conversations.

From here on the affair was clouded by personal rivalry between Briand and Ribot and by acts of bad faith on the part of the two men. Asked to prepare a basis for consultation with the Allies, Briand presented a letter on 20 September that specified there could be no separate agreement, but omitted the claims of France's partners from its proposed peace terms. Ribot then sent a circular to his Ambassadors, in which he distanced himself from Briand, and gave the impression that the latter had wished to proceed without consulting the Allies. This elicited predictably hostile responses from the Allied capitals, and on the 23rd Briand was told the meeting could not take place. Painlevé himself had now lost his enthusiasm, not because of confidence in French military prospects—he expected these to worsen—but because he feared for French

civilian morale if the offer were genuine. At Boulogne he told
Lloyd George that he doubted 'whether France would continue
fighting if it were offered both nine-tenths of Alsace-Lorraine
and the whole of Belgium'.[55]

Painlevé overestimated German willingness to compromise.
In reality Berlin was offering minimal concessions in Alsace-
Lorraine and Belgium in return for a free hand in the east.
Michaelis's main advance on earlier thinking was his willing-
ness to renounce annexation—though not indirect control—of
Longwy-Briey. The opening to France was anyway subsidiary:
before Lancken's fruitless visit to Switzerland he was told that
Germany could 'offer little' and he should play for time while
the Villalobar feeler was pursued.[56] Kühlmann supposed that a
declared readiness for compromise could prompt the ousting of
Lloyd George by Balfour and Asquith, whom he wrongly
judged to be more emollient.[57] He also reasoned that the
British could compel the French to make peace, whereas the
French could not compel the British, and the two could be
driven apart over Alsace-Lorraine. Certainly, France needed
British loans and shipping, and Haig's armies continued to
attack while the morale of Pétain's forces was being healed.
And the French Government was uneasy about Anglo-American
evasion of an unequivocal and public pledge to restore the lost
provinces. But Allied solidarity was more robust than Kühlmann
hoped, and the possibility of a compromise peace now abruptly
receded.

After returning from Boulogne, Lloyd George told his
Cabinet of Painlevé's surmise that the Lancken feeler was
genuine. Lloyd George doubted more than ever that the
Western Allies should continue fighting simply in order to
prevent German aggrandizement in Russia, but his colleagues
now disapproved more strongly of a compromise at Petrograd's
expense. On 6 October Balfour at last convened the Allied
Ambassadors, and told them of the German approach. It was
agreed to tell the Germans that Britain would be willing to
receive any communication about peace, and discuss it with its
partners. There was no reply. In the Reichstag on 9 October
Kühlmann warned that Germany would never concede Alsace-
Lorraine to France; two days later Lloyd George declared that
'however long this war may last, this country intends to stand

by . . . France until she redeems her oppressed children from the degradation of a foreign yoke'. A fortnight later the Austrians suspended the Armand–Revertera conversations on the grounds that the French conditions were too severe and that the Monarchy's position had improved. All three main channels of communications were thus closed.[58]

October 1917 was a turning point in the diplomatic history of the war. The Bolshevik Revolution opened a new round of confidential feelers and public statements, but the conflict would be ended not by compromise but by military triumph and dictated treaties. The ascendancy of the moderate, Centrist Left was also a transient bloom. The technical problems of conversations via unofficial intermediaries were only a subsidiary reason for this outcome. Sixte and de Broqueville tried to break the barriers by over-representing the goodwill on the two sides. Spanish diplomacy did rather the reverse. The Vatican harmed its chances of success by pursuing prior agreement only with one Power. But the very profusion of these contacts, and their unremitting failure, reinforces the conclusion that no simple solution was waiting to drop off the bough. The divisions to be overcome were real and deep. German willingness to compromise went little beyond the Flanders ports and border concessions in Alsace. Kühlmann and Michaelis's greater flexibility made few inroads on the stark demands of OHL, inspired by Ludendorff's belief that struggle was the natural law of nations and Germany must be economically and territorially prepared for a further instalment.[59] Conversely, the Allied Governments continued to believe that a compromise with Germany would be only a truce, with little possibility of lasting. Not even in Russia before November 1917 did unconditional advocates of peace hold the reins of power. Whether to equip Germany for new wars in the future or as a war to end war, the struggle would go on.

(iv) *The Impact of American Entry*

One last factor must be added in. Although crucial in the longer term, American belligerency at first neither destroyed the resistance of the Central Powers nor radically altered Allied war aims. It reinforced the European stalemate, and only later undermined it. In the summer of 1917 Czernin, Erzberger, and Bethmann Hollweg concluded that the submarine campaign had failed to bring decision. But by the autumn developments in Russia made clear that all was not yet lost. Ludendorff, predictably, advised in September that the outlook for the Central Powers was better than for their enemies. Michaelis thought that Germany could survive another winter, and although he hoped for peace before Christmas he was unwilling to concede much to obtain it.[60] The Americans entered the war with neither the advance strategic planning nor the trained manpower and equipment needed for an effective military contribution on land. With only 80,000 men in France by October 1917 they remained a potential menace rather than an actual one.[61]

At the same time, American aid allowed the Allies to survive the disasters of the spring, but to do little more. This was in part because it was deliberately rationed. US Treasury loans saved the Allied Governments from financial calamity, but were neither as generous as the latter wished, nor unconditional. The American Government also limited the number of warships it committed against the U-boats, and refused to transfer merchant ships to European waters from more profitable routes elsewhere. The shipping shortage held down grain and steel deliveries to disappointing levels.[62] But the psychological importance of American assistance was immense. Lloyd George, at least in retrospect, gave it as a reason for hanging on in September 1917. And in the same month Ribot telegraphed to his Ambassador in Washington that 'until the United States has made the decisive effort it is preparing, we shall not be in a favourable position to negotiate'.[63]

If American entry failed to tip the military balance, would Wilson join the Russian Revolutionaries and the Western European radicals and socialists in their efforts to revise his partners' war aims? The answer, broadly, was no, although he stayed out of the 1914 Pact of London and remained an 'Associated Power' rather than an Ally. He warned the British Cabinet in August that the American public felt themselves to be arbiters rather than being bound to one or other side. He replied to the Papal Peace Note without consulting the Western Europeans, and his answer condemned as 'inexpedient' any plans for 'punitive damages, the dismemberment of empires, the establishment of selfish and exclusive economic leagues'. Immediately afterwards he proposed to House that they should ascertain the Allies' likely peace conditions, 'in order that we may formulate our own position for or against them and begin to gather the influence we can use . . .'. House responded by setting up the Inquiry, a commission formed mainly of academics, which gathered information about the issues in dispute. As for the 'influence' available to Wilson, he had already written in July that although the French and British Governments did not share American views, 'when the war is over we can force them to our way of thinking because by that time they will, among other things, be financially in our hands'.[64] But although Wilson was anxious to preserve his diplomatic independence, he was playing a waiting game. The moment for applying pressure would be when the war was won, and he vetoed an announcement proposed by McAdoo that the granting of American loans would depend partly on their being used to accomplish American war aims. When Balfour visited Washington in April 1917, he brought details of many of the secret treaties, including Sykes–Picot and the April 1915 Treaty of London. House and Wilson disliked the arrangements for partitioning Turkey, but took no immediate action. Indeed, they took the lead in withholding passports for the Stockholm Conference, and Wilson's notes to the Provisional Government and the Vatican ruled out a peace based on the pre-war status quo.[65] Wilson was pursuing the strategy recommended by Lansing before intervention: to defeat Germany in co-operation with the Allies, but then to exploit the dependence of the latter in order to carry through his grand design for reform of the international order. A peace following the defeat of Germany, with the destruction of its military power and its autocratic regime, would differ greatly from a compromise negotiated before American strength had been applied. But in the meantime he held back from a confrontation over war aims with his partners that might endanger victory by disrupting Allied unity. So far from being a subjection of the Allies to American views, therefore, what happened during 1917 was a more complex readjustment of their war aims to a multiplicity of new developments, of which Wilson's belligerency was only one. This adjustment—by Italy, France, Japan, and Britain—will now be examined.

In Italy little changed until after Caporetto, despite the conflict between the Treaty of London and the growing force of Yugoslav nationalism. In July 1917 Trumbić, representing the leaders in exile of the South Slavs of the Habsburg Monarchy, signed with Pašić the Declaration of Corfu. This supported an independent State under the existing Serbian Karageorgević dynasty that would incorporate the Austro-Hungarian Croats and Slovenes as well as all the Serbs. Sonnino, meanwhile, observed silence about the Treaty of London in his dealings with the Americans, but reassured himself that Britain and France remained committed to it. This Balfour confirmed in a letter to Wilson in January 1918.[66]

Readjustment by the French went further. While not forgetting the goals adopted by the Briand Government, in their day-to-day diplomacy they concentrated on more modest aims. In the summer of 1917 Ribot felt obliged to launch a campaign of propaganda and Ambassadorial lobbying in Washington on behalf of the claim even to the Alsace-Lorraine of 1870, let alone anything more, but the Americans remained non-committal. Ribot's hopes that Wilson would participate in an inter-Allied economic conference similar to that of June 1916 were also disappointed. Instead, beginning in August, he and Painlevé supported Clémentel's efforts to win Anglo-American backing for a system of permanent inter-Allied controls over international trade in a dozen key commodities. This, believed the Commerce Minister, might frighten the Germans into negotiating, and would assure France's needs in food and raw materials during the difficult reconstruction period that was expected to follow the war. Finally, the scheme could force delinquent Governments to accept arbitration in future international disputes. None of these arguments won British or American approval for the plan. Whereas in the spring France had gained the Tsar's support for a military frontier on the Rhine, by the autumn of 1917 it was dependent on two maritime Powers that had given no such assurances and were traditionally wary of commitments on the European mainland. Nor could it humour Wilson by genuflexions to the League of Nations. When Ribot raised the subject in Washington, Wilson deprecated discussion of it as 'premature'. No more than Sonnino, however, had the French genuinely been converted to Wilsonian principles, and they too were biding their time.[67]

In the Far East America's declaration of war against Germany was followed by that of China in August 1917. This made urgent the reconciliation of Japanese and American views attempted in the Lansing–Ishii agreement in November, as the intervention question accelerated China's descent into anarchy. The Chinese central Government controlled only precariously the provincial military Governors, who in northern China constituted a faction known as the tuchuns. In the spring of 1917 conflict was developing between them and the Kuomintang, or nationalist party, which held a majority in the Peking Parliament. In this conflict the Prime Minister, Tuan Chi-jui, tended to co-operate with the tuchuns, whereas the President, Li Yuan-hung, had Kuomintang support. The Tuan Government favoured declaring war on Germany as a means of winning Allied loans and financial concessions that would aid it in the internal struggle. In May Tuan was dismissed by Li, but he later re-entered Peking with a military force and the backing of the tuchuns: Li resigned, and most of the Kuomintang leaders fled southwards to establish a rival Government at Canton. Tuan's declaration of war on Germany was therefore primarily a domestic political move.[68]

Until the spring of 1917 the Japanese Government had opposed Chinese belligerency, but once its secret agreements with the Allies had assured it of their support over Shantung at the peace conference, its attitude changed. Conversely, the American Government wished the Chinese not to go beyond breaking off relations with Germany. On 4 June the State Department advised Peking that war entry mattered less than the survival of a united and responsible Chinese central Government. The Japanese, incensed, delivered a memorandum asserting their 'paramount' interests in China, a pretension that Wilson and Lansing refused to acknowledge.[69] China had long been a source of Japanese–American friction, and the European Powers' preoccupation with events elsewhere brought Tokyo and Washington into a starker, more bilateral confrontation than before. During the period of American neutrality they competed in making loans to China, and each navy considered the possibility of war against the other. But there were powerful reasons for restraint. After April 1917 the Americans concentrated their fleet in the Atlantic. But they also imposed a general embargo on steel exports, which temporarily checked the growth of Japanese shipbuilding. The Terauchi Government was advised by its naval staff that it would lose a war with the Americans, and it was anyway committed in principle to respecting China's independence and integrity and building up Japanese economic influence there in co-operation with the United States and other Powers. Wilson, too, was prepared to compromise. He foresaw little danger of Japan attacking American possessions 'at any early time after peace is declared'. House and Lansing both thought concessions should be made to the needs of Japan's expanding population and economy. Following on Bryan's note of 13 March 1915 during the Twenty-One Demands affair, Lansing had in January 1917 secretly reassured the Japanese Ambassador of American respect for Japan's 'special interests' in Manchuria.[70]

Lansing, with Wilson's backing, conducted two months of negotiations in Washington in September–November 1917 with a Japanese Delegation headed by Ishii. Ishii had been instructed that Japan would allow no other Power to establish a position of influence in China that endangered its own 'special and vital' political and security interests there. Foreign contracts in areas such as southern Manchuria and eastern Inner Mongolia should be subject to its veto. Lansing, however, wanted an agreement that would reaffirm the two Powers' commitment to Chinese integrity and the Open Door. Indeed, Wilson wanted to abolish all spheres of influence in China, but to this the Japanese refused to agree. Ishii would accept a new declaration of principle only if Japan's special interests were mentioned, and on this basis the Lansing–Ishii agreement was concluded on 2 November 1917.

According to the key provision of the agreement, 'the United States recognizes that Japan has special interests in China, particularly in the part to which her possessions are contiguous', but 'the territorial sovereignty of China . . . remains unimpaired'. After the war the two signatories disagreed publicly over what this meant. Lansing maintained that he had recognized Japan's economic interests, its leases, and its railway concessions, but not a special political influence in the regions concerned. This Ishii rejected. Lansing assured the Chinese Minister in Washington that the formula was merely a truism, but the Peking Government was not a party to the agreement, and denied being bound. The Japanese considered they had won a diplomatic victory, and in the following months they enlarged their administrative powers in Shantung and enhanced their influence on the Peking Government through the so-called Nishihara loans. It is difficult not to see the agreement as an American retreat, possibly caused by information reaching Lansing about the danger of a German–Japanese alliance. This was qualified, however, by an intention to return to the subject after the war when America might have a stronger bargaining position. As in Europe, the administration played a waiting game.[71]

A Japanese–American confrontation would have imposed harsh decisions in London. The British were anxious for the Washington negotiations to succeed, and urged patience on Ishii. But in July Balfour had assured House that public opinion would force the British Government to aid America if the latter were attacked by Tokyo.[72] There was mutual sympathy in the Anglo-American relationship, but also rivalry and growing British dependence. Lloyd George, like Ribot, felt obliged to endorse the principle of a League of Nations, despite the scepticism about the project felt in his Cabinet. But Wilson, whose ideas on the subject were still unformulated, resisted an exchange of views, and the British eventually set up their own committee under Lord Phillimore, which presented detailed proposals in 1918.[73] In the economic power balance, Britain's larger merchant navy counted for less than did American financial strength. The June 1916 Paris resolutions were being criticized in the Cabinet as a mistake, and by the end of the year British economic war aims, like French, centred on post-war controls over international commodity trade [74] Like the other belligerents, moreover, the British had to try to reconcile their territorial ambitions with the support for national self-determination emanating from Washington, Petrograd, and the domestic Left. The outstanding example of such an attempted reconciliation was the Balfour Declaration of 2 November 1917.

The Declaration was embodied in a letter from Balfour to Lord Rothschild, who was asked to convey it to the Zionist Federation. The Cabinet had approved it, and it was intended to be published. It stated that 'His Majesty's Government view with favour the establishment in Palestine of a national home for the Jewish people, and will use their best endeavours to facilitate the attainment of this object, it being clearly understood that nothing shall be done which may prejudice the civil and religious rights of the existing non-Jewish communities in Palestine, or the rights and status enjoyed by Jews in any other country'.[75] This was issued on the eve of a British offensive that culminated in December with the capture of Jerusalem. At the same time as announcing the intention of creating a Jewish national home, the British therefore acquired the power on the ground to do it. The Declaration arose from the strategic importance of Palestine to the British Empire, and from the propaganda importance of Zionist support for the British war effort; but the second mattered more. The genuine sympathy felt by Balfour and Lloyd George for Zionist aspirations would have counted little, had not these and British interests been perceived to coincide.

Palestine's greatest strategic importance lay in its proximity to the Suez Canal. By 1915 it was also being thought of as a Mediterranean terminus for a railway to the Persian Gulf. In January 1915 Herbert Samuel, President of the Local Government Board, suggested that it should be annexed, and the Jews allowed to immigrate freely until they could attain self-government. Grey and Asquith were slow to give support to this, and the Sykes–Picot agreement placed most of Palestine in an internationally administered 'brown zone'. But Lloyd George's Government authorized a series of offensives into the Holy Land, and accepted the Curzon Committee's recommendation that it should come under British control. This was partly caused by fears that in future a German-dominated *Mitteleuropa* from Hamburg to Baghdad would permanently menace the British Empire. And in a war that might well end in stalemate, it was tempting to occupy for bargaining purposes anything that might be available. The change of government had strengthened Unionist and imperialist representation in the War Cabinet and its newly created secretariat; and Lloyd George himself regretted the Sykes–Picot agreement and wanted British predominance in Palestine.[76]

None of this suffices to account for British espousal of the Zionist cause. Such espousal lent a figleaf of self-determination to British claims in the Holy Land, given that the Zionist leaders in the West preferred British to international control. In the spring of 1917 Lloyd George probably saw the Zionists as a means of outmanœuvering the French, but the Cabinet's eventual decision was moved by much broader considerations. The relatively small and assimilated Jewish communities of nineteenth-century Western Europe had been transformed by emigration from Russia in the thirty years before 1914. In England the Jewish population rose from 60,000 to 300,000; in the USA it rose from under 250,000 to about three million. In Palestine itself it grew from about 35,000 to 85,000, but was still massively outnumbered by 600,000 Arabs. The Zionist organization, which had lobbied since 1897 for a home for Jewish settlement in Palestine under international guarantee, had to contend not only with this but also with indifference among the Jews of the Diaspora. But between 1913 and 1921 the enrolled membership of the movement rose from 130,000 to 778,000. By 1917 the Zionists were a dynamic and expanding force among the Jews of the United States and revolutionary Russia, both of which countries the British Government badly needed to influence and in which, apart from propaganda, it had few means of influence to hand. For British politicians and officials, who frequently combined mild anti-semitism with an inflated estimate of international Jewry's lobbying power, the arguments for a gesture to the Zionists therefore went beyond Palestine's local importance. In addition, as in the earlier competition for Arab sympathy, the British feared being outbid by the enemy. In 1914 the Zionist headquarters were in Berlin, and the organization's principal leaders came from Germany and Austria-Hungary Although it was officially neutral, a mass deportation of Jews from western Russia by the Tsarist

armies at the outbreak of hostilities gave it little encouragement
to support the Allies. In reality the Germans were too concerned for their relationship with the Turks to try to commit
the latter to the Zionist programme. But the possibility that
they might do so helped to accelerate events.[77]

From the beginning of the war the most effective Zionist
lobbyist in Britain, Chaim Weizmann, had perceived a
common interest between British goals in Palestine and Zionist
aspirations. But at first his patient establishment of contact
with politicians such as Balfour and Lloyd George had little
effect. The Zionist breakthrough came in the six months
between December 1916 and the following June. The advent of
the Lloyd George Government was a first important step.
From January 1917 Sir Mark Sykes, now with the Cabinet
secretariat, began meeting unofficially the British Zionist
leaders. The Foreign Office, still loyal to the Sykes–Picot
agreement, was not informed. The second development was a
minor revolution in the British Jewish community, many
of whose more established leaders feared that the creation
of a Jewish entity elsewhere would foster anti-semitism and
attacks on their civil rights in the United Kingdom. In May
1917 the Conjoint Foreign Committee, which represented the
two principal lay Jewish organizations, the Anglo-Jewish
Association and the Board of Deputies of British Jews,
published an anti-Zionist statement in *The Times*. But in the
following month a vote in the Board of Deputies condemned
the statement, and a change in the Board's leadership made it
more favourable to Zionist goals. Even after this, however,
Montagu, the Secretary of State for India, fought a Cabinet
rearguard action on the assimilationists' behalf.[78]

A further obstacle was the attitude of Britain's allies. But on
4 June 1917 a letter from Jules Cambon to another Zionist
leader, Sokolow, avowed the French Government's sympathy
for Jewish colonization and 'the renaissance of Jewish
nationality' in Palestine, under Allied protection. Without this
prior 'Cambon Declaration', motivated probably by fear of
losing Zionist allegiance entirely to Germany or Britain,
Balfour's could not have been made. As for Russia, the British
Ambassador there reported in April that there was little
Zionism among the Russian Jews and that the matter was best

avoided, but his Foreign Office superiors eventually came to a
contrary view. In the United States the pivotal figure was the
Supreme Court Justice and Chairman of the Provisional
Executive for General Zionist Affairs, Brandeis. After war was
declared on Germany the American Zionists lauched a
campaign of propaganda for a national home; in May Brandeis
told Balfour that he favoured a British protectorate, and
Wilson, who appears to have been genuinely converted to the
Zionist ideal, told Brandeis he had reached the same
conclusion.[79]

Because the United States never went to war with Turkey
Wilson held back from public commitment, but his attitude
helped to tip the balance in the final Cabinet debates. In June,
after the Cambon Declaration and the upheaval in the Board of
Deputies, Balfour took up a suggestion from Weizmann that
the British Zionists should draft a declaration. The result, with
minor Foreign Office amendments, went before the Cabinet in
August. But it emerged as the Balfour Declaration only much
revised, and after weeks of debate. Montagu, alleging it would
encourage anti-semitism, led the attack. A first approach to
Wilson in September indicated that he favoured only a
declaration of sympathy. But the fear of losing the Zionists to
Germany brought the subject back on to the Cabinet's agenda,
and a second, more urgent approach was made to Wilson in
October, now with a draft text. This time the President
approved, although still not publicly binding himself.
Consultations with the British non-Zionist Jews revealed that
they shared many Zionist aspirations, and that Zionist support
was growing fast. In the final discussions Balfour stressed the
value of the Declaration for propaganda in Russia and the
USA, the danger of Germany capturing the Zionist movement,
and the sympathy of Wilson and the French. The Declaration's
advocates denied it would encourage anti-semitism outside
Palestine, and contended that the Holy Land had the economic
potential to support a far larger population than at present.
These arguments finally prevailed.[80]

Weizmann and the British Zionists undoubtedly intended
that Palestine should become a Jewish State, though judging it
prudent to request only a 'national home'. Lloyd George and
Balfour seem to have supposed that a Jewish State would

eventually result, but the Declaration immediately committed them to much less than this, and after 1923 the British Government denied having intended to foster the emergence of a State from the new entity. The final draft, unlike the original Zionist submission to the Cabinet, reserved the rights of the Palestinian Arabs. None the less, Balfour at least was aware that the Declaration's proponents had championed a form of self-determination in which some nations were more equal than others. This, he considered, the 'absolutely exceptional' nature of the Jewish case justified.[81]

There was also ground, if infirm ground, for saying that Britain's Arab protégés had washed their hands of Palestine. In May 1917 Sykes and Picot met Hussein in Jeddah and informed him, in what detail is uncertain, of the Sykes–Picot accord. Hussein agreed to co-operate with France in Syria and Britain in Mesopotamia 'to the fullest extent', probably because he received a misleading impression that neither territory would be under direct European control. Palestine was not a principal theme of the discussions, and an assessment of Hussein's attitude towards it depends on the unresolved question of whether he had accepted Sykes–Picot itself. But after the Balfour Declaration he received a new British Government assurance, in the 'Hogarth Message' of 4 January 1918. This provided for a 'return of the Jews' to Palestine as far as was compatible with the political and economic freedom of the existing inhabitants. Hussein accepted with the proviso that the matter might need to be reconsidered after the war. As the Message referred to the Palestinian Arabs' 'political' rights, however, which the Balfour Declaration had not, the British were again laying themselves open to charges of irresponsibility and contradictory promises in the Middle East.[82]

The final significance of the Declaration was as another barrier to compromise. Support in London for negotiations with the Turks came from the General Staff, which opposed distractions from the Western Front, and the Foreign Office. Lloyd George himself, however, loathed the Ottomans and preferred operations on the periphery to further slaughter in France and Flanders. After British forces were defeated at Gaza in March 1917, however, the Cabinet became more favourable to conversations, and the French and Americans were also sympathetic. None of the ensuing feelers got very far. In June Henry Morgenthau, the former American Ambassador in Constantinople, arrived in Europe with Wilson's approval and in the hope of unofficially meeting Turkish representatives. Weizmann met him at Gibraltar and dissuaded him from travelling farther. Meanwhile the Foreign Office allowed Aubrey Herbert, a gentleman of independent means, to sound out Turkish contacts in Switzerland, and learned that Talat might be willing to depose Enver and make peace if the Allies would accept greater devolution and spheres of influence within Turkey rather than partition. At the inter-Allied London Conference in August the British did indeed propose that the envisaged annexations should become spheres of influence, but the French and Italians stood by Sykes–Picot and Saint-Jean-de-Maurienne. On the Turkish side, Talat in June 1917 proposed to the other Central Powers that the Allies should be offered a non-annexationist general peace. But the chances of a separate agreement with Constantinople were small, and the Balfour Declaration further diminished them.[83]

This brings the discussion back to the persistence of alliance ties and of territorial and economic war aims as obstacles to restoring peace. The Russian Revolution, American belligerency, and the growing power and militancy of the European Left brought a readjustment and an altered presentation of those war aims, but modified them insufficiently for a compromise. The groping feelers via unofficial intermediaries failed to develop into serious negotiations. Wary now about open annexationism, the European Powers from Germany in the Baltic to France in the Rhineland and Britain in the Middle East fell back on buffer States and indirect control. Given the Provisional Government's refusal of a separate peace, and Wilson's waiting game, the new forces could not break the stalemate. Ribot and Lloyd George—but also Wilson—believed that only victory would make possible a lasting peace. Lloyd George argued afterwards that the justification for their actions rested on the durability of the 1919 settlement compared with the likely durability of one attained by compromise with the Imperial Germany of 1917, a Germany in which Ludendorff had acquired a veto over foreign policy and was already looking to the next round.[84] In 1918 the sacrifices of the Allied armies won at least the possibility of constructing a more stable settlement, even if that possibility was not successfully exploited. Until then, even at the height of German willingness for concession in September 1917, a true compromise was anyway not on offer. And after September, with the arrival of the Bolsheviks in power, the belligerents drifted further apart than ever and the hour of dictated settlements was at hand.

5

Resolution by Force

NOVEMBER 1917–NOVEMBER 1918

(i) *The Fourteen Points and Brest-Litovsk*

From its Balkan origins the war had grown into a world-wide conflagration that a triple military, diplomatic, and domestic political stalemate fuelled until the end of 1917. It kindled a multiplicity of successor conflicts, one of which—the Russian Civil War—claimed more lives than did the contest between the Allies and the Central Powers itself. As long as the central struggle continued, it and local wars across the globe were liable to intermesh. In 1918 intervention in Russia by both sides was the most dramatic case in point. But once the central struggle had been resolved, the peripheral ones could be fought out with largely local forces, and gradually brought to an end. This chapter will therefore concentrate on the suspension of hostilities in the war that had begun in 1914. It will examine the separate treaties concluded on the Eastern Front in the spring of 1918; the intervention in Russia, in spite of this, by the Central Powers and the Allies in the summer; the commitment by the Allies to dismember Austria-Hungary; and the Southern and Western European armistices at the end of the year. As in 1917, an underlying theme of these developments was the failure of conciliation. But all three elements of the previous deadlock were now crumbling, and political decisions acquired a new finality as the war of movement returned. The relationship between military and political developments was, as ever, intricate. But for statesmen at the time it was omnipresent.

The Bolsheviks seized power in Petrograd on 7–8 November 1917, and gained control of much of European and Asiatic Russia by the following spring. Lenin became Chairman of the Council of People's Commissars, which on 8 November published the Decree on Peace, proposing a three-month armistice and negotiations for a general settlement without annexations or indemnities. Soon afterwards the Bolsheviks published and simultaneously disavowed the secret inter-Allied agreements to which Russia had been a party. On 15 December they signed a separate ceasefire with the Central Powers at Brest-Litovsk, where peace negotiations began a week later. The Russians presented a six-point programme for peace without annexations or indemnities, which the Central Powers accepted with reservations on Christmas Day, on the condition that the Allies should do the same. But this the latter refused, instead restating their war aims in a series of declarations of which the most notable were Lloyd George's Caxton Hall speech and Wilson's Fourteen Points. When negotiations resumed, the Central Powers therefore considered their 'Christmas Declaration' void, and imposed on Russia the Treaty of Brest-Litovsk, followed by the Treaty of Bucharest with Rumania.

Lenin was no pacifist. An admirer of Clausewitz, he judged war as had Marx and Engels, by its political utility. In his 1916 tract on *Imperialism: The Highest Stage of Capitalism*, he had interpreted the First World War as a global struggle to redistribute spheres of influence between the predatory and monopolistic capitalist systems of the leading Powers, supported by the venal 'labour aristocracy' of the socialist Right. It could be ended only by insurrection and by its metamorphosis into an international civil war between proletariat and bourgeoisie. In his *Letters from Afar*, also written in exile, he had set the immediate duties for the revolutionary regime as being to publish the secret treaties, propose a ceasefire, and invoke a general revolutionary war against bourgeois Governments that refused a peace based on the liberation of colonies and oppressed nations. On the eve of the Bolshevik takeover he professed to see a 99 per cent chance that the capitalists would be unable to prevent peace, and he cited the favourable revolutionary auspices in Germany as a justification for seizing power. Trotsky, who became People's Commissar for Foreign Affairs, had by a different intellectual route also concluded that the new regime must foment revolution across Europe.[1]

The Bolsheviks' presuppositions inclined them neither towards peace in the abstract nor towards a separate agreement with the Central Powers. Ideologically they were bound to treat the imperialist Governments with impartial hostility, and Lenin had decried a separate peace as being an instrument of capitalist diplomacy. The belief—held widely in the West—that the Bolsheviks were German agents was unjustified. Lenin had returned to Russia by arrangement with Germany, and after the revolution his party continued to receive subsidies from Berlin.[2] His diplomacy, however, rested not on prior commitments to the enemy but on the requirements of maintaining power. In the light of these requirements his exegesis of international capitalism was continuously readjusted, and they necessitated a rapid change of course when the predicted international revolutionary inferno failed to ignite. The precondition for the Bolsheviks' success had been policy changes that identified them with the aspirations of the Russian urban workforce and important sections of the army and navy. Their appeal, as Lenin understood, was partly to the peasant in uniform, and it was as a party of peace rather than as one of revolutionary war. A Congress of delegates from the armed forces made clear to him on 30 December that the Government should end hostilities at any price. Not to do so would be to risk the fate suffered by the Provisional Government, and when no German revolution intervened to extricate Lenin from his dilemma he was driven inexorably towards a separate agreement.[3]

The exigencies of survival not only obliged the Bolsheviks to call for peace but also shaped the manner of their appeal. The Decree on Peace was Wilsonian rather than Leninist. It neither blamed the war on capitalism nor, except faintly, issued a general revolutionary summons. It promised open diplomacy, and called for a 'democratic' peace without annexations and indemnities—the old slogan of the Petrograd Soviet. Similarly, the six points presented by the Bolsheviks to the Brest-Litovsk peace conference on 22 December called for any region in Europe or overseas that had shown nationalist discontent since the later nineteenth century to be allowed to settle its future by free referendum. This was to take up self-determination in its most sweeping form, but it harmonized with the call for open diplomacy as part of a strategy of appealing to the more moderate and reformist elements in the belligerent labour movements. Even as the Soviet regime edged towards an understanding with the Germans, it tried to keep its bridges to the Allies open. The ceasefire of 15 December left both sides in their existing positions, but forbade the Central Powers to move troops away from the Eastern Front except where this had already begun at the time of signature. Admittedly, this reservation deprived the clause of much of its effect. The agreement also provided for immediate peace negotiations, which Trotsky warned the Allied agents in Petrograd might lead towards a separate treaty. None the less, the Allied boycott of the meetings at Brest-Litovsk continued. [4]

The Central Powers approached the peace negotiations with their war aims yet again in flux. At Kreuznach in May 1917 Czernin had agreed to renounce an Austro-German condominium over the future kingdom of Poland, in return for predominance in Rumania. He doubted the wisdom of this transaction, and made clear in September that he wanted the agreement revised. In the same month Wilhelm II visited Rumania, and was inspired by the spectacle of its oil and grain. Kühlmann, meanwhile, gave to the alliance with Vienna the highest priority it had received since the *Mitteleuropa* exchanges of 1915. On 22 October he agreed with Czernin on a new package deal: a German–Austrian mutual assistance pact, a military convention, and tariff negotiations; Poland to be under Austrian sovereignty but in military and customs union with Germany; and Habsburg acceptance of German predominance in Rumania. Hindenburg and Ludendorff, however, now viewed Austria-Hungary as a new potential enemy, and insisted on a set of preconditions for an Austrian Poland, including the annexation of a broad frontier strip by Germany. As the Austrians refused sovereignty over Poland on these terms, its future remained undecided throughout the Brest-Litovsk negotiations. [5]

In the midst of this continuing uncertainty the Central Powers formulated policy towards the Bolsheviks. In a seminal letter to the German Chancellor on 10 November, Czernin argued that a ceasefire would allow the Russian peasant soldiers to drift back and participate in the land redistribution in their villages, thus making peace irreversible even if Lenin were overthrown. Beyond this, although the Soviet Government would seek a general peace, it could be drawn into a separate one if the Central Powers repudiated annexations and indemnities. They should protect themselves, however, by stage-managing declarations of independence among the nationalities under their occupation in Russia's western borderlands. Czernin was still pursuing a general peace, but was more confident about the Habsburg Monarchy's position than earlier in the year. He hoped the Allies could be drawn into negotiations on the basis of no annexations and the pre-war status quo. If this failed, a Bolshevik separate peace would allow the Germans to reach Paris and force the West to treat in even less favourable circumstances. But rather than see the negotiations fail altogether because of excessive demands from OHL, he warned Kühlmann, if need be Austria-Hungary would make peace alone.[6]

In fact Czernin discovered at Brest-Litovsk that Kühlmann's thinking was very similar. Sensing the limits on German power, Kühlmann hoped that what was left of Russia might become an associate rather than a mortal enemy. The first task was to break the ties between the Bolsheviks and the Allies, so as to be able to deal with Lenin and Trotsky in bilateral negotiations. This made it necessary to go through the motions of renouncing annexation, but this was facilitated by the steps already taken to pre-empt the future of the Russian border regions. A Council of Regency with limited administrative powers had been set up in Poland in the autumn of 1917. In Courland a nominally representative body, in fact dominated by the province's German minority, appealed in September for the Kaiser's 'protection'. Local assemblies in Livonia, Lithuania, and Estonia issued independence resolutions. And the Finnish Diet also voted for independence, which Germany and Russia recognized in January 1918. With varying degrees of justification, Kühlmann and Czernin could now assert that a a belt of subsidiary States on the Central Powers' eastern frontiers would emerge from Lenin's own principle of self-determination. They could aspire to a version of imperialism by consent.[7]

This procedure was too subtle and uncertain to commend itself to OHL, and the Brest-Litovsk negotiations led to another classic confrontation between the German civilians and the High Command. An exasperated Kühlmann complained in January that OHL obstructed his policy towards Austria-Hungary and Russia, yet had no alternative of its own. This was largely justified. Ludendorff's 'dictatorship' was essentially a negative, veto power. He rejected the idea of himself becoming Chancellor. But he and Hindenburg felt a 'moral' responsibility for the negotiations with the Bolsheviks, and his energy and command of detail made him a relentless enemy in bureaucratic infighting, with whom no agreement was final. In the east as in the west he considered Germany strong enough to dictate terms and take the territory it needed for a favourable position in the next war. Kühlmann's anxiety to base the settlement on acquiescence, from Austria, the Reichstag, and even the Bolsheviks themselves, he dismissed as secondary; or rather he contended that acquiescence was most effectively obtained by overawing the antagonist with a display of force.[8]

Hindenburg and Ludendorff were more than usually in a hurry because of the decision at the Mons staff conference in November to seek victory in 1918 by a co-ordinated series of offensives on the Western Front. Hence in Russia they desired 'clarity': a treaty ratifying the territorial changes necessary for Germany's security, and assuring the food and raw materials needed to counter the Allied blockade. In proposals sent to Kühlmann on 3 December Ludendorff asked for deliveries of grain and oil; Russian evacuation of eastern Galicia, Armenia, Finland, Estonia, and Livonia; an independent Poland; and German annexation of Courland and Lithuania. This last demand, coupled with OHL's continuing insistence on a Polish frontier strip, conflicted radically with Kühlmann's strategy of renouncing annexations in order to separate the Bolsheviks from the Allies and win Austrian favour for his *Mitteleuropa* schemes.[9]

The first round in the ensuing conflict was the Kreuznach Crown Council on 18 December. Hindenburg demanded Courland and Lithuania as manœuvering ground for his left flank in the next war; Ludendorff wanted them for their food and manpower. Kühlmann preferred to leave their future open; and in the end the Council reached no agreement on the crucial issues and he went to Brest-Litovsk without a clear mandate. This was a free hand of sorts, and he used it, in the Christmas Declaration, to implement the strategy of appearing to accept the Soviet terms. His relations with Hindenburg and Ludendorff never recovered from this blow, but for the moment he enjoyed support from the Kaiser and from Count Hertling, who had replaced Michaelis as Chancellor in October 1917. As during the previous opening to the British, however, Germany's external negoiating posture rested on a precarious domestic equilibrium.[10]

Peace negotiations failed to spread to the west. The feelers earlier in 1917 had come from the neutrals or the Central Powers rather than the Allies, and Berlin and Vienna were now more confident they could settle their differences with their enemies by force. The British and French, for their part, had decided to gamble that they could eventually achieve their war aims with American aid. Although soundings between Vienna and the Western Powers continued during the winter, they were less important than the earlier initiatives. Instead, the main development of the period was a new round of public diplomacy and war-aims declarations.

This would have been necessary even without the Bolshevik challenge. Each year war weariness reached its peak as another winter in the trenches loomed and the cold made shortages of food and fuel more difficult to bear. In France, according to the local military surveys, civilian morale fell in November 1917 almost to its lowest ebb. In Britain, the *Daily Telegraph* on 29 November printed a letter from Lord Lansdowne, who called for the war to be ended 'in time to avert a worldwide catastrophe', for Britain to confine itself to minimum aims, and for a new joint definition of Allied objectives. The Labour Party's 'Memorandum on War Aims', approved a month later, on several points came closer to the Bolshevik than to the British official position. And by now the British and American press had printed the secret treaties published in Petrograd.

At the Paris Conference held from 29 November to 3 December 1917 the Allies tried unsuccessfully to agree on a joint response to the Soviet initiatives. At the same time the American administration made a first assault upon its partners' war aims, sending a delegation under Colonel

House. The Conference was most successful in establishing
new institutions to co-ordinate the coalition's war effort,
although these had no supranational powers and Wilson was
anxious to protect his diplomatic independence. He placed
American representatives on the Allied Maritime Transport
Council, set up to allocate shipping, and on the Inter-Allied
Council on War Purchases and Finance, whose purpose was to
centralize war purchases made in the USA. These agencies
joined the Supreme War Council, established at the Rapallo
Conference in November 1917, which consisted of a permanent
committee of military and naval representatives at Versailles
and of regular meetings between the British, French, and
Italian civilian leaders. Wilson allowed an American observer
to attend it, but not to take part in its discussions. [11]

In the diplomatic sphere, House proposed at Paris that the
coalition should deny that it was fighting for 'aggression or
indemnity'. Wilson telegraphed his support, adding that the
American people would not fight for the 'selfish aims' of any
belligerent, 'with the possible exception of Alsace-Lorraine'.
Wilson and the Colonel had kept themselves informed about
the drift of British radical opinion, and while he was in Europe
House conferred with Briand and Lansdowne as well as with
the politicians in office. He found the British tepidly in favour
of his draft, but the Italians firmly against it, and he was
unable to isolate Sonnino. All the Conference could agree on
was a statement of its willingness to discuss war aims when a
'stable Government' was restored in Petrograd. Unlike the
Central Powers, the Allies thus withheld even lip service from
the Bolsheviks' Peace Decree. Instead, they responded to the
Decree and to the Christmas Declaration through independent
national statements and a new round of contacts with
Vienna. [12]

For the Allies, as for Kühlmann, the fates of Russia,
Austria-Hungary, and Poland were interdependent, and a
commitment over any one of them would foreclose options on
the others. In the autumn of 1917 the French and British both
got wind of their enemies' renewed consideration of an
'Austrian solution' for Poland, but they drew radically
different conclusions from the news. The French authorities
were converging on the policy of an 'eastern barrier' of newly

independent States that would replace the Tsarist Empire as a counterbalance to Berlin. They wanted the Allies to outbid the Central Powers, and at the Paris Conference they pressed unavailingly for a public commitment to a 'united' and 'autonomous' Poland. Undeterred by this rebuff, Clemenceau's Foreign Minister, Pichon, went to the Chamber of Deputies anyway, and pledged his Government's support for a Poland that would be 'united, independent, indivisible, with all the guarantees of its free political, economic, and military development'. [13]

Lloyd George, by contrast, objected to the French proposal on the grounds that the Allies lacked the military strength to realize it and that it would obstruct a separate peace with the Habsburgs. News had reached the Foreign Office that Czernin wanted an Anglo-Austrian meeting, and at the Paris Conference Lloyd George won authority to go ahead, provided that the mission confined itself to ascertaining the conditions on which Austria-Hungary would separate itself from Germany. In a memorandum to the Cabinet before leaving, however, the British representative, Smuts, envisaged smashing the enemy *Mitteleuropa* plans and creating an Austro-Hungarian 'counterpoise' to Germany by concluding a separate peace that would give the Habsburgs sovereignty over Russian Poland. When he met Count Mensdorff in Switzerland on 18–19 December he duly held out this bait. So the British were still attempting to draw Vienna out of Germany's orbit: a policy the French were now abandoning in favour of the 'eastern barrier' scheme. But the Smuts–Mensdorff conversations foundered on the usual reef. Mensdorff had authority to discuss only a general, not a separate, peace. And Smuts refused his offer of Austrian mediation between Britain and Germany. [14]

Mensdorff did, however, impress Lloyd George and Smuts by his willingness to compromise, and his call for the Allies to limit and define their war aims. This became an additional motive for the Prime Minister's speech at Caxton Hall on 5 January 1918. Lloyd George wished to encourge the opposition in Austria-Hungary and Germany, and deliver a riposte to the Christmas Declaration. But he also needed to reply to the Lansdowne letter and the Labour Memorandum on War Aims, especially as he needed trade-union co-operation with his Government's plans to alleviate the critical manpower shortage by releasing more civilians for the front. It was, therefore, to an audience of trade unionists that the speech was made.

Cabinet discussion of the speech was overshadowed by the extremely sobering effect on Ministers of the Third Ypres campaign. For the second autumn running, the British army had suffered hundreds of thousands of casualties in appalling battle conditions for a maximum advance of six miles. Lloyd George still expected eventual victory in the west, if now only with the aid of an American military effort whose purposes he distrusted. In the east he and Smuts remained willing to consider peace at Russia's expense, although most of the Cabinet took a different view. But the 1917 campaign suggested Germany could be defeated militarily only at a cost that would reduce Britain to a second-rank Power. And the speech was drafted largely by Smuts and Cecil, both from the more pessimistic tendency in the Government, as well as by the Prime Minister himself. None the less, it received Cabinet approval, and was delivered after consultation with Asquith, the Labour leaders, and some of the Dominions. Lloyd George could therefore present it as an authoritative statement of war aims, even if in private he hardly felt bound by its terms. [15]

Caxton Hall contrasted sharply with the hubris of earlier British official thinking and the January 1917 Allied reply to Woodrow Wilson. Characteristically, it tended to intransigence over Britain's extra-European goals and to compromise at the expense of the European Allies. The Ottoman Empire would be reduced to the ethnically Turkish regions, but would keep Constantinople, thus acknowledging the Bolsheviks' repudiation of the Straits Agreement. The German colonies would be disposed of on a basis acceptable to their inhabitants—but the Government expected that this basis would be one of continuing British control. [16] Within Europe, by contrast, Belgium would be restored, but there would be merely a 'reconsideration' of Alsace-Lorraine: a purposely vague phrase that Lloyd George qualified two weeks later by stating that the Government felt bound to stand by the French in attaining 'what they regard as fair'. [17] In the south he promised only 'the satisfaction of the legitimate claims of the Italians for union with those of their own race and tongue'. Provided Austria-Hungary gave its nationalities autonomy and met Italy's and Rumania's demands, however, its 'break-up' was 'no part of our war aims'. And although an independent Poland was desirable, Lloyd George's language in no sense committed Britain to fight on until this was achieved. Finally, although deploring Russia's 'economic and political enslavement to Germany', he warned that if the Russians themselves would not resist, the Western Powers must leave them to their fate. In the Gospel according to Caxton Hall, Britain remained committed to its extra-European objectives and to expelling the enemy from Europe's western and south-eastern fringes, but displayed indifference to German domination of Eurasia, offset by the continuing hope of detaching Austria-Hungary from the Central Powers. Given the Cabinet's military predicament, this had the merit of realism. But it differed, even at this dismal moment, from the conceptions of the other Allies. Not only the Clemenceau Government, with its Polish declaration, refused to wash its hands of the former Russian Empire. The same was true of the USA.

On returning from the Paris Conference, House proposed a unilateral American declaration as a substitute for the abortive joint communiqué on war aims. Unlike the European leaders, Wilson was under little domestic pressure to speak out, and American opinion was becoming more bellicose rather than war-weary. A new statement might reassure his Progressive and trade-union support, but its main purpose was external. The Fourteen Points, unveiled to Congress on 8 January, were drafted by House and Wilson in the greatest secrecy, even Lansing being allowed to make only minor last-minute alterations. They were designed to answer the Bolsheviks and the Christmas Declaration, and help keep Russia in the war. They were also meant to encourage the liberal and socialist opposition in the Central Powers. Finally, they might bolster the radicals whom House and Wilson saw as their kindred spirits in Western Europe, and serve notice on the Allied Governments that the newly published secret treaties must be revised.[18]

The detailed similarities between the Fourteen Points and Caxton Hall immediately impressed contemporaries, but the speeches were drawn up independently and differed fundamentally in their approach to the events—at Brest-Litovsk—to which both were primarily responding. The sixth of Wilson's Points called for Russia to be evacuated and for 'an unhampered and unembarrassed opportunity for the independent determination of her own political development . . . under institutions of her choosing'. Russia's treatment by its sister nations in the months ahead would be 'the acid test' of their 'intelligent and unselfish sympathy'. There were also ambiguities, not least in the definition of 'Russian territory'. Wilson regarded the Bolsheviks as naïve, and their championing of unlimited national self-determination as dangerous. But his immediate concern was to forestall a separate peace by flattery, by reformulating Allied aims, and by calling for non-intervention on all sides.

Five of the remaining Points were general, and developed themes already traced in earlier speeches. Point XIV called for a League of Nations. Points I–IV called respectively for an end to secret diplomacy; for 'absolute freedom of navigation on the seas, outside territorial waters, alike in peace and war, except as the seas may be closed in whole or in part by international action for the enforcement of international covenants'; for 'the removal, as far as possible, of all economic barriers and the establishment of an equality of trade conditions'; and for guarantees that national armaments would be 'reduced to the lowest point consistent with domestic safety'. Wilson knew the freedom of the seas might antagonize the British, and hoped his qualifying clause would make it more acceptable. His third Point envisaged not free trade, but tariffs that were lower and non-discriminatory. It would apply only between States 'consenting to the peace and associating themselves for its maintenance', which left an opening for Clémentel's proposals for continuing controls on trade with the enemy after the war.

But the most novel feature of the Points was a qualified American commitment to Allied territorial goals. Point V promised a 'free, open-minded, and absolutely impartial adjustment of all colonial claims'. Unlike the Bolshevik programme (and the Labour Memorandum on War Aims) it applied only to the possessions of the Central Powers, and respected the Allied colonies. Similarly, Wilson deliberately used 'must' for the evacuation and restoration of Belgium in Point VII, but 'should' for his remaining territorial proposals. British objectives within and outside Europe therefore won stronger American backing than those of the other Allies. According to Point VIII the invaded areas of France should be evacuated and restored, and 'the wrong done to France by Prussia in 1871 in the matter of Alsace-Lorraine . . . should be righted'. Point IX, deliberately challenging the secret treaties, stipulated that Italy's frontiers should follow 'clearly recognizable lines of nationality'. Rumania, Serbia, and Montenegro should be evacuated, and Serbia gain access to the sea, but Point XI was otherwise vague about the Balkans. Although America had declared war on Austria-Hungary in December 1917, Point X, that 'the peoples of Austria-Hungary, whose place among the nations we wish to see safeguarded and assured, must be accorded the freest opportunity of autonomous development', confirmed that American policy favoured self-government rather than independence for the subject nationalities. Point XII similarly promised only 'autonomous development' to the Ottoman subject peoples, whereas Lloyd George had wanted Turkish sovereignty over them to end. Point XIII, finally, envisaged that in 'the territories inhabited by indisputably Polish populations' there should be an independent State under international guarantee, with 'free and secure' sea access. In short, Wilson promised respect for Russian integrity, and supported Allied territorial and economic aims only within strict limits. He would allow Germany, Austria-Hungary, and even the Ottoman Empire to survive, although with internal changes. His endorsement of national self-determination was less radical than Lenin's, and he offered a road to international harmony and justice through a reformed capitalism rather than through global revolution.[19]

The Fourteen Points became the basis on which the armistice with Germany was signed, and formed the initial terms of reference for the Peace Conference in the following year. But their long-term repercussions exceeded their immediate effects. Within the Allied camp their success was at the level of public opinion, and they failed to alter official policy. In the test case of the Italian claims, Sonnino continued to assert his country's right to strategic frontiers, and Lloyd

George assured Orlando that the Caxton Hall speech did not challenge the Treaty of London.[20] By contrast, Wilson's speech appeared for a time to be remarkably successful in undermining the German home front and the Austro-German alliance. Hertling's Reichstag speech on 24 January, made in answer to the American President, guardedly accepted Wilson's general Points, but refused to discuss Belgium or make any concessions in Alsace-Lorraine, and insisted that the future of Poland and the treaty with Russia were matters for the Central Powers. This disappointed the German Left, and the Socialist press became more radical. The end of January saw the greatest strike wave since the outbreak of war, and a peace without annexations was one of the strikers' demands. The SPD and trade-union leaders had been against the action, but felt obliged to associate themselves with it. Although the strike was quickly broken, Wilson saw a chance to exacerbate German divisions by a new speech that would challenge Hertling with the arguments used by the SPD themselves.[21]

There was another reason for the propaganda offensive to continue. In mid-January there had been an equally impressive strike wave in Austria-Hungary, also directed against an annexationist peace at Brest-Litovsk. There were acute food shortages in Vienna, and signs of unrest in the army. In these circumstances Czernin seized on Anglo-American reassurances about the Monarchy's integrity. In his own speech in reply to Wilson he accepted the general Points and the specific one on Poland. He refused concessions to Italy, Serbia, Rumania, and Montenegro, but was silent about German demands in the west, and appealed to Wilson to initiate general peace negotiations. In Switzerland on 3–4 February the American agent, Herron, met Lammasch, an envoy from the Austrian Emperor, who said that Karl was willing to concede autonomy to the subject nationalities and accept at least the non-territorial Fourteen Points. Although Karl appears to have been acting once again without Czernin's knowledge, Wilson took the feeler seriously.[22] Indeed, Austria was now in contact with all three Western Powers. In November Clemenceau had authorized a new conversation between Armand and Revertera, who met twice in Switzerland during February 1918. And in mid-January the British Legation in Berne reported that according to the Austrian Legation there Czernin was willing to meet Lloyd George in person: news that delighted the Prime Minister.[23]

Whereas the Fourteen Points had been inspired primarily by events in Russia, therefore, the main purpose of Wilson's 'Four Principles' speech on 11 February was to exploit the divisions in the enemy camp. Welcoming Czernin's reply to the Fourteen Points, Wilson condemned Hertling's as evasive, and contrary to the Reichstag Peace Resolution of July 1917. But the President also fired another shot across the Allies' bows, in the shape of the 'Four Principles' themselves. Essentially these provided that territorial settlements must be in the interests of the populations concerned rather than the balance of power; and that 'all well defined national aspirations' must be satisfied as far as was possible without generating international conflict. In short, this was a commitment to national self-determination, although a heavily qualified one.[24]

The Principles had less impact than the Fourteen Points. In Germany the unrest had passed its peak, and the home front was entering a new phase of cohesion. The conversations with the Austrians were also fruitless. The final round in the Armand–Revertera dialogue revealed that there was now no possibility of Austria-Hungary supporting France's claim to Alsace-Lorraine.[25] As for the approach to Britain, the War Cabinet decided to send Philip Kerr, of Lloyd George's private secretariat, who on 14 March met not Czernin but Skrzynski, the Counsellor of the Austrian Legation at Berne. The outcome was another dead end, the Austrians refusing to be drawn into a separate peace, and the British refusing conversations with Germany.[26] But the most high-level exchange was with the USA. On 18 February Karl dispatched a message to Wilson via the King of Spain. He accepted the Four Principles, called for a peace without 'conquests and annexations', and offered sea access for Serbia and the restoration of Belgium. But he promised nothing to the subject nationalities and refused all territory whatever to the Italians. This was less encouraging than the Lammasch–Herron meeting, but Wilson sent a reply asking for clarification. A further Austrian response reached Madrid, but apparently never arrived in Washington. Even if it had done, there was insufficient basis for an understanding. The Austrians' rejection of the Fourteen Points rendered meaningless their acceptance of the Four Principles.[27] Caporetto, the armistice with Russia, and the impending German offensive in the west had hardened attitudes in Vienna and made it less likely than ever that Austria-Hungary would lever Europe into a general peace. A sequence of events was opening that would show that neither Vienna nor the German Socialists could prevent the resolution by force desired by the German High Command. This was the decision by the Central Powers to dictate peace at Brest-Litovsk, and the decision by the Bolsheviks to submit.

The first round of peace negotiations at Brest-Litovsk had ended on 28 December 1917 with an invitation to the Allies to participate on the basis of the Bolshevik proposals and the Christmas Declaration. On 5 January the Central Powers informed the Soviet Government that as the Allies had not responded within the agreed delay the Christmas Declaration was no longer binding. When negotiations resumed four days later Trotsky in person led the Russian delegation and separate representatives were sent by the Rada, the independent Parliament of the Ukraine. On 9 February the Central Powers signed a separate treaty with the Rada, and on the following day Trotsky walked out of the conference, declaring unilaterally that hostilities were ended, but refusing to accept the enemy terms. The bluff inherent in this tactic of 'no war, no peace' was called when on 18 February German forces resumed their advance. The Bolsheviks now agreed to terms worse than those they had previously rejected, and on 3 March the Treaty of Brest-Litovsk was signed.

Down to the declaration of no war, no peace the Central Powers' negotiating strategy remained in Kühlmann's and Czernin's hands. For them the Christmas Declaration had been a blind: its leading purpose, apart from propaganda, being as a golden bridge to lead the Bolsheviks away from the Allies. By repudiating annexations, they would detach the non-Russian border areas from Petrograd's control and cripple Russia as a Great Power, but with the acceptance, they hoped, of the Russians themselves. Thus on 28 December they made clear that they expected the Bolsheviks to concede the demands for independence issued by the German-sponsored assemblies in Poland and the Baltic provinces. And on 18 January they tried to cut discussion short by requiring Russia simply to renounce sovereignty over everything west of a line from Brest-Litovsk to the Gulf of Riga.

The test case for this strategy of expansion under a cloak of self-determination came in the Ukraine. In the November 1917 elections to the Kiev Rada the Bolsheviks had been heavily out-polled by the Ukrainian nationalists, and in January the Rada declared its independence and its willingness to negotiate with the Central Powers. For both sides the fate of the Ukraine was crucial. Its grain reserves were desperately needed both in Austria-Hungary and in the Bolshevik zone; it was Russia's richest agricultural and industrial region, and to lose control of it would leave the country's southern frontier dangerously exposed. During the negotiations in January Czernin was bombarded with appeals from Vienna to make peace in order to relieve the food shortages at home, and this impeded his resistance to the Ukrainian demands. Of these the most embarrassing was the Rada's desire for Cholm, in the former Russian Poland. To agree to this might cause a Polish outcry and ruin Vienna's chances of winning acceptance in the rest of Poland for an 'Austrian' solution, as well as threatening the Habsburgs' authority over even their existing Polish subjects. But at a Crown Council on 27 January the Austro-Hungarian leaders agreed none the less on the absolute priority of winning access to Ukrainian supplies. Hence the separate peace of 9 February ceded Cholm to the Rada in return for the Ukraine placing its surplus food at the Central Powers' disposal. There were riots in Russian Poland and Galicia, and Polish units in the Habsburg armies attempted to defect. [28] And there remained a further obstacle to the coveted grain, in that by the time the treaty was signed much of the Ukraine had been overrun by the Bolsheviks. This gave a powerful argument to OHL in the decisive confrontation over German policy that was now looming.

Trotsky's walk-out from the peace conference after the Ukrainian treaty brought the conflict in Berlin to a head. At the crucial Bad Homburg Crown Council on 13 February

Kühlmann wished to rest content with the no war, no peace declaration. Advancing into Russia to compel the Bolsheviks to sign a treaty, he predicted, would suck German forces ever deeper into a vain pursuit of a receding quarry. It would destabilize Germany itself, distract resources from the Western Front, and poison relations with Austria-Hungary. It would probably bring the Bolsheviks down, to the advantage of some more reactionary, pro-Allied regime. And a permanent 'German bolt' across Russia's access to the Baltic would inhibit an eventual Russo-German *rapprochement*. He favoured doing nothing, and leaving the Russians to liberate themselves from Bolshevik rule, if at all, by their own efforts. But Hindenburg and Ludendorff insisted on an imposed peace. This, they held, would safeguard the Ukrainian treaty, encourage Rumania to negotiate, and unite rather than divide the German home front. A renewed advance would make it possible to help the Whites in Finland, where civil war had broken out in January, as well as the Rada and the Baltic Germans. It might overthrow Bolshevik rule. This last point excited the imagination of the Kaiser, who launched into a tirade against Bolshevik agitation, and called for 'police measures' to help the Baltic Germans against them. The Bolshevik regime must be 'struck dead'. Hertling, who until now had supported Kühlmann, accepted the formula of 'police measures' after Ludendorff assured him that initially this would entail only limited advances along the Baltic and into the Ukraine in order to protect the local anti-Bolsheviks and to gather food. In fact the outcome of Bad Homburg, as of so many of the German wartime conclaves, was ambiguous. Hindenburg and Ludendorff harnessed Wilhelm's enthusiasm for an anti-Bolshevik crusade, but they did not, at first, envisage a march on Petrograd, and they secured Hertling's backing by promising only restricted operations. But there was no doubt that Kühlmann was the loser. Like Bethmann after the submarine decision he remained in office, and attempted to offset Bad Homburg's consequences, but the Council was another milestone in the advance of military influence.[29]

After 18 February German forces advanced against negligible resistance. Peace terms communicated to the Russians on the 21st closely resembled a draft submitted to Hertling by Ludendorff, and became the basis of the treaty signed on 3 March. As previously demanded, Russia yielded sovereignty over territory west of a line from the Gulf of Riga to Brest-Litovsk, and therefore including Poland, Courland, and Lithuania. Germany and Austria-Hungary would decide the future of these areas 'in agreement with their population'. German forces east of the line would be withdrawn when general peace in Europe returned. Estonia and Livonia, however, would remain occupied until 'proper national institutions' and 'public order' had been established. In the south, Russia would evacuate the districts of Kars, Ardahan, and Batum, and allow the inhabitants to decide their future in agreement with Turkey: in other words, Turkey would regain the frontier it had held before the war of 1877–8. Russia would evacuate the Ukraine, and recognize the Ukrainian peace treaty, thus surrendering sovereignty to the Rada. It would also evacuate Finland, disarm its warships, and demobilize its army. Reparations for damage were renounced—a gesture to the principle of no indemnity—but each side would reimburse the other for maintaining prisoners of war, a provision that would benefit the victors far more than it would the Russians. Russian sovereignty was lost over 34 per cent of the former Empire's population (some 55 million people), 32 per cent of its agricultural land, much of its heavy industry, 73 per cent of its iron-ore output, and 89 per cent of its coal.[30]

A provisional treaty, dictated in haste with Ludendorff's western offensive impending, Brest-Litovsk left the fate of the huge areas ceded by the Bolsheviks unresolved. It took no territory inhabited by ethnic Great Russians, and it followed Kühlmann's original concept of using a pretence of self-determination to dismember the former Empire. But the Treaty's forcible dictation, and the provisions for Livonia and Estonia, showed that the Foreign Minister was losing control and that his hopes for a later *rapprochement* were diminished in priority. Moreover, the aftermath of Brest-Litovsk vindicated OHL's judgement rather than his own: terms *were* successfully imposed, without upheaval on the German home front. Erzberger announced that the treaty would comply with the 1917 Reichstag peace resolution if genuine self-determination were applied in the border areas.[31] Only the USPD voted against ratification; the SPD was divided and spoke against, but abstained, while still voting war credits; the other supporters of the 1917 resolution voted in favour. Wilson considered that for the moment his attempts to cultivate the German Left had failed, and as in the summer of 1917 he shifted the emphasis of his policy towards supporting and encouraging the Allies. In his 6 April Baltimore speech, after Brest-Litovsk and the opening of Ludendorff's attack in France, he concluded that 'there is . . . but one response possible from us: force, force to the utmost, force without stint or limit . . .'.[32]

The Bolsheviks' submission to the German terms came only after an acute political crisis. In an expanded meeting of the Party Central Committee on 21 January, three days after the Central Powers had presented their territorial demands, Lenin expounded his 'Twenty-One Theses'. To gamble on the 'romantic' gesture of a 'revolutionary war' of resistance, he contended, would be to stake the survival of the Russian Revolution on the hope of one in Germany. Such a revolution would come, but was still too remote for this to be a responsible course. The peasant majority in the army would prefer an annexationist peace to a revolutionary war, and such a war would end in speedy defeat, the downfall of the regime, and peace on worse terms. Both a separate peace and a revolutionary war would violate Bolshevik principles by objectively favouring one capitalist coalition against the other; it was necessary to choose. At least peace would win a breathing space to expand the Red Army and settle accounts with the bourgeoisie at home. But Lenin's advocacy won only fifteen votes for an immediate separate treaty, as against thirty-two for revolutionary war and sixteen for Trotsky's course of no war, no peace. Bukharin and the Party Left, who for motives of revolutionary principle and Russian patriotism advocated resistance to the Central Powers, commanded a majority of the leadership and probably a larger one of the rank and file. Of two hundred local Soviets consulted, only Petrograd and Sebastopol supported Lenin's line.

Lenin's only option was to try to win the party over by following Trotsky's middle road. Trotsky's main concern, apart from abhorrence of giving the legitimacy of signature to

Germany's demands, was apparently to demonstrate to the outside world and to the Allied working class that there was no complicity between the Bolsheviks and the Central Powers. But he accepted that revolutionary war was impracticable, and assured Lenin that if the Germans renewed their advance he would support acceptance of their conditions. Lenin, estimating that the upshot would be the loss of Livonia and Estonia and that this price was acceptable, gave tactical support to Trotsky, and on 24 January the Central Committee voted 9 : 7 in favour of no war, no peace.

Kühlmann's defeat at Bad Homburg therefore meant Trotsky's defeat in Petrograd. The suppression of the German strike wave early in February already seemed to bear out Lenin's assessment, but only after news of the German advance had been confirmed did he win a majority in the Central Committee to ask for terms. The Committee approved the final conditions by 7 : 4, Trotsky abstaining and subsequently resigning from the Commissarship for Foreign Affairs. The Seventh Party Congress and the All-Russian Congress of Soviets ratified the Treaty by comfortable majorities early in March. It was, said Lenin, a 'Tilsit Peace', a temporary expedient until Russian strength could recover, and preferable to a revolutionary war that would serve the class interest of the bourgeoisie; but he did not intend to honour its terms. Brest-Litovsk destroyed the Bolsheviks' alliance with the left wing of the Socialist Revolutionary Party, who went into opposition. But Lenin emerged from the Seventh Party Congress with many of his opponents on the Central Committee removed, and politically stronger than before.[33]

The final element in the Central Powers' Eastern European settlement was the treaty with Rumania. The descent of southern Russia into anarchy after the Bolshevik Revolution worsened the Rumanian Government's strategic position, and it signed the armistice of Foçsani on 9 December 1917. It did not at first intend that this should lead on to a separate peace, but it concluded from the Caxton Hall speech and the Fourteen Points that even if the Allies won it was unlikely to gain the territories they had promised it. It also faced ultimata from the Central Powers first to begin negotiations and then to accept

the preliminary Peace of Buftea on 5 March, on pain of the
reigning dynasty being deposed.

The negotiations were prolonged less by resistance from the
Rumanians than by delicate intra-coalition diplomacy among
their enemies. Bulgaria had been promised the southern
Dobrudja under the alliance treaty of 1915, but it now claimed
the whole of the province. The Turks maintained that if
Bulgaria got the entire Dobrudja they should regain the
Maritsa area they had ceded to Bulgaria in 1915. Both
Radoslavov and Talat Pasha hinted that their political survival
was at stake, as well as the adherence of their countries to
the Central Powers. Kühlmann and Czernin mediated a
compromise under which Bulgaria gained the southern
Dobrudja, but the north went provisionally under a Four-
Power condominium, thus shelving the threat to alliance unity.

Between March and the definitive Bucharest treaty on
7 May, the negotiations proceeded on a more equal footing.
Kühlmann and Czernin, united in wanting good relations with
the conservative Marghiloman Government in Rumania, cut
by a half the protective frontier strip demanded by the
Hungarian Government along the crest of the Carpathians.
Rumania eventually lost 800,000 inhabitants, mostly in the
Dobrudja, although it was allowed in consolation to annex
Bessarabia from Russia. More striking than the treaty itself,
however, were the accompanying economic conventions, and
these particularly reflected German aims. Rumania was
obliged to sell at favourable prices to the Central Powers its
entire agricultural surplus until 1926. Leases of up to ninety
years on its oilfields were offered to a production company
dominated by German interests. A second German company
would monopolize the sale and marketing of the entire oil
output. Rumania also had to bear the cost of an indefinite
German occupation. It therefore became an outstanding
instance of German indirect control. But this time the SPD
voted to ratify the treaty, leaving the USPD completely isolated
in its opposition. As for Czernin, he had agreed in October
1917 to extensive German influence in Rumania, yet was still
without the quid pro quo of an Austrian Poland. Finally, the
harsh economic conditions saved for the Rumanians a measure
of goodwill from the Allies, whose Governments declared their

intention to revise at least some of the Bucharest terms. It remained to be seen if they would have the power.[34]

(ii) *The Powers and the Russian Civil War*

Brest-Litovsk inaugurated an even more spectacular expansion of German influence into the former Tsarist Empire, to which the subsequent Allied intervention responded. There was a series of military initiatives between March and June, whose driving force was OHL; and then a *rapprochement* between the Bolsheviks and the German Foreign Ministry, sealed on 27 August by the signature in Berlin of the Brest-Litovsk supplementary treaties.

After the Bad Homburg Council the German civilians lost control over a military advance that pushed hundreds of miles into Russian territory. Kühlmann faced a succession of *faits accomplis*, which he no longer resisted with his former vigour.[35] In Finland, civil war had broken out between the Whites and Reds, to whom the Bolsheviks gave covert aid. After Bad Homburg the Whites were induced to ask for German help, and signed treaties on 7 March that forbade the country to make treaties without German permission, as well as requiring it to co-operate militarily, allow German naval bases, and admit German exports duty-free. German troops arrived in April, and contributed to the Reds' rapid defeat. Hertling had wanted to delay, and Kühlmann to commit smaller forces, but they were overborne by OHL and the Kaiser's anti-Bolshevik mood.[36]

Meanwhile, in furtherance of the Homburg decisions, German forces entered the Ukraine in search of food and to restore the Rada's authority. But in April 1918 the German commanders replaced the Rada by a more pliable Government, under the Hetman Skoropadsky, and they advanced far beyond the limits originally approved. They also invaded the Crimea on the pretext of pursuing the Russian Black Sea Fleet, and in May Germany recognized the peninsula's right to self-determination. On the eastern shores of the Black Sea the Turks were independently moving forward. In August they annexed the region south of the 1877 Russo-Turkish frontier, which Brest-Litovsk had re-established as the limit of Russian sovereignty. North of this line, the three independent republics of Georgia, Armenia, and Azerbaijan were too weak to resist the Turkish advance. Georgia appealed to Germany for aid, and German troops arrived in June. The Poti agreements in the same month gave Germany joint control of the railways, and made it sole recipient of Georgia's valuable exports of minerals. The German High Command was detaching more and more of Russia from Bolshevik control, and Kühlmann and Hertling were unable to prevent it from doing so. But during May Ludendorff decided the southern advance had gone far enough, and at last halted operations. The Bolsheviks signed armistices with Skoropadsky and the Finns, and the period of greatest danger to them from the Central Powers was over.[37]

This was partly because of a Soviet counter-move. Hoping to stop the piecemeal amputation of their territory, the Bolsheviks offered on 13–15 May a political agreement that would fix the borders and end the Central Powers' advance, but also an economic one that would bestow on Germany extensive privileges in the Soviet zone. This was a deliberate effort to restrain the military by seducing German business; and it did indeed strengthen the German civilians, if partly because of Ludendorff's own willingness to pause. Kühlmann and his successor, Hintze, pushed through the negotiations for a supplementary peace treaty, despite the outrage caused by an anti-German uprising in Moscow on 6 July, during which the German Ambassador was assassinated. Ludendorff now favoured military intervention to overthrow Lenin. OHL and the navy co-operated, with the Kaiser's approval, in planning Operation 'Keystone', under which German and Finnish forces would occupy Petrograd. But all such schemes suffered from the evidence that a Government of the Russian Whites would repudiate Brest-Litovsk. In a memorandum to Ludendorff and in a statement to the Reichstag party leaders, Hintze defended himself in the language of *Realpolitik*: 'It is our policy to use the Bolsheviks as long as there is something to be got out of them'. To turn them out because of ideological distaste would be an emotional indulgence. Their own policies were keeping Russia militarily paralysed. If Germany intervened at all he felt, it should be only against a less tractable successor regime.[38]

The 27 August supplementary treaties more or less bore out Hintze's assessment that the Bolsheviks would accept unlimited impositions in order to stay in power. This time, however, Lenin had little trouble in winning support. In any case he paid small attention to the details of the treaties, and had no intention of honouring them more than he was obliged to. Russia conceded sovereignty over Livonia and Estonia, and recognized Georgian independence. It agreed to pay 6,000 million marks in compensation for damage done to German property by war and nationalizations. It promised to deliver one quarter of the production of the Baku oilfield, and to expel the Allied forces that had landed on the Arctic coast, failing which German and Finnish troops would do so. The Germans promised troop withdrawals in the Baltic and the Ukraine, and to end support for separatist movements elsewhere. They agreed that in the Russo-Ukrainian peace treaty Russia should get most of the Donets coalfield, and promised aid against General Alekseyev's White Army in the south-east. Less favourable than the Bolsheviks had proposed in May, the agreements left Petrograd militarily even more exposed, and for the first time extracted an indemnity. Yet there were also concessions on the German side, and by permitting the Bolsheviks to stay in office the treaties gave the German civilians their first victory over OHL for many months. Lenin won another breathing space, but at the price of moving from neutrality into economic and military co-operation with the Central Powers. This mirrored the deterioration of Allied–Bolshevik relations by August 1918 into undeclared war.[39]

Allied 'intervention' in Russia in 1918 meant committing forces against the Bolsheviks' armed resistance, although not necessarily with the purpose of overthrowing them. In the context of a Russian civil war whose casualties are unnumbered but may have reached twenty-five million, the Allied deployments were minute. They were also very unequally distributed among the coalition's members, as a survey of events down to the Allied armistice with Germany makes clear. Between August 1918 and April 1919 a British Empire force of about 1,000 men operated north of the Persian border to assist a Menshevik and Socialist Revolutionary Government at Ashkabad. Major-General Dunsterville's detachment, which occupied Baku between August and September at the invitation of the local Soviet, was little bigger. In North Russia British forces landed at Murmansk, at first with Trotsky's connivance, in March 1918; British, French, and American troops occupied Archangel, after staging a coup against the local Bolshevik authority, in August. After the Armistice the Archangel garrison reached a peak of just over 13,000. But in Siberia at the same date British and Canadian troops numbered over 6,000 and the Americans nearly 9,000, while the Japanese had committed 70,000 and the Czech Legion, also to be included among the interventionist forces, numbered 42,000 in March 1918. And during the summer the Czechs and Japanese temporarily destroyed Bolshevik authority along the entire belt of territory from the west side of the Urals to Vladivostok. [40] Intervention therefore required a prior consensus between those Allies who most urgently desired it and those who were able to bring it about. It originated from insistent lobbying by Britain and France for the American consent that was a precondition for Japan's involvement. American resistance to this lobbying was broken after fighting broke out at the end of May between the Bolsheviks and the Czech Legion. Finally, a hesitant American invitation in Tokyo opened the floodgates to the Japanese occupation of eastern Siberia.

Anglo-French policy was dominated by the emergency created by Ludendorff's offensives on the Western Front. These terminated the long period of peace feelers and war-aims declarations since December 1916, and opened a new, and final, phase. From 21 March to 15 July Ludendorff launched five great attacks. On the Somme in March, the Yser in April, and the Chemin des Dames at the end of May his troops broke through to open country. Enormous losses were inflicted on the French and British at a moment when few American forces were combat-ready. Only in June–July did the Allies regain numerical superiority, and the French counterstroke on 18 July in the Second Battle of the Marne marked the turning of the tide. This long and desperately dangerous crisis resulted from the reinforcement of the German armies made possible by the

eastern ceasefire. Continuing German penetration of the
Russian Empire might also undermine the Allied blockade,
threaten British India, and establish a Eurasian mastery that
would enable the Central Powers to resist indefinitely. In
addition, by August 1918 a Russo-German quasi-alliance
appeared to be coming into being. As the Bolsheviks tacked
between the opposing coalitions their relations with the Allies
alternated between attempted reconciliation and antagonism.
During the run-up to the Christmas Declaration France and
Britain committed themselves to assisting the Bolsheviks'
opponents in southern Russia. But between the no war, no
peace declaration and the German armies' halt in May the
Soviet Government and the Allies discussed possible military
collaboration. After May a rapid growth in tension culminated
in Bolshevik and Allied forces coming to blows.

In the spring of 1918 huge areas of the former Tsarist Empire
were still outside Bolshevik control, and the new regime compromised its *de jure* claims by dissolving the newly elected
Constituent Assembly, for which the Bolsheviks had secured
only a quarter of the votes cast. These circumstances complicated Allied–Soviet relations from the start, and created the
pre-conditions for intervention. The Allies were agreed in withholding recognition from the new authorities, although London,
Paris, and Washington remained in contact with Trotsky via
unofficial agents. The British and French, however, coupled
this with indirect intervention—rather than troop commitments—in the areas outside Bolshevik rule. A memorandum
agreed in Paris on 23 December 1917 provided that the two
Governments would 'keep in touch' with the 'semi-autonomous'
Ukraine, Don Cossacks, Caucasus, Finland, and Siberia, and
provide loans and military advisers in the hope of denying
South Russian supplies to the enemy. The Ukraine was
designated as a French sphere of action, the Don and the areas
to the south-east as Britain's responsibility. The Bolsheviks
were to be informed that France and Britain were not promoting counter-revolution or seeking to interfere in Russian
internal affairs: an apparent disingenuousness that reflected a
real confusion in the British Cabinet's mind. The Bolshviks'
success in Russian internal politics rested very largely precisely
on their opposition to the war. Yet the Cabinet felt it was

pursuing an anti-German rather than an anti-Bolshevik policy, and that its relations with the Soviet regime would depend on the latter's attitude toward the Central Powers.[41] Clemenceau, although at first dismissing the Bolsheviks as 'agents of Germany', eventually took a similar view. In addition, he felt that France's long-term interest was in a reunified Russia, as the only possible counterweight to the Central Powers. Support for the South Russian separatists could therefore only be a temporary expedient. But, as with the British, his main immediate concern was to keep an eastern front in being in order to tie down German manpower, protect the Rumanians, and debar access to Russian raw materials and food.[42]

Both Britain and France were fully stretched elsewhere, and indirect intervention accomplished little. British subsidies probably never reached General Denikin's White Army in the Don region; French hopes were concentrated on the Rada, and were dashed when it made a separate peace. Whether more could be achieved depended on the United States and Japan. Wilson, however, deterred partly by the memory of his two interventions in Mexico during the neutrality period, feared that involvement in Russia would strengthen reactionary forces rather than the Russian democrats. His administration had decided in 1917 to concentrate its military efforts on the Western Front rather than to risk overextending American resources, and it was anxious not to antagonize Congress. For all these reasons it opposed what became the main plank of Anglo-French intervention policy: support for a primarily Japanese expedition to Siberia.[43]

Japanese intervention originated in the British War Office, as a project designed to relieve an ominous military situation by recreating an eastern front. The Japanese were needed to guard the Allied military stores that had accumulated at Vladivostok. If they could also establish control of the Trans-Siberian Railway, the Allies could supply the Whites in the Don region, who were still hostile to Germany. The Foreign Office, and Lloyd George himself, however, suspected that the Japanese would occupy only eastern Siberia, and ensconce themselves permanently there. For this reason, and to reassure the Russians, the Foreign Office hoped to give the project a more international veneer by securing American participation; but the Americans, more remote from Ludendorff and closer to the Pacific, were less able to suppress their doubts. Wilson himself appears at this stage not to have suspected the Japanese of political ambitions. But he accepted House's arguments that an invitation to them would disturb the unity of American opinion and place the Allies on a similar moral plane to Germany, for a 'nugatory' military advantage. The administration therefore refused not only participation in an expedition but also its diplomatic support for an approach to Tokyo. Repeated Anglo-French *démarches* elicited a note on 5 March that only reiterated the existing position: Japanese intervention would strengthen the extremists in Russia and further alienate the country from the West; and although the United States itself accepted Japan's good faith, no assurances of Japanese disinterest would satisfy Russian opinion. [44]

Parallel to the impasse between Americans and Western Europeans was one between liberals and interventionists in Tokyo. Until the October Revolution the Terauchi Government was united in opposing intervention, but the spread of Bolshevism into Asiatic Russia altered this, and by the end of 1917 some of the General Staff, Terauchi himself, and the Foreign Minister, Motono, were beginning to favour an expedition to the Amur Basin. By controlling the railways and supporting client Governments there they hoped to protect Japanese trade and investment on the mainland and to safeguard the home islands. As the British Foreign Office feared, in fact, the Japanese interventionists intended to establish a permanent presence in Eastern Siberia, and their military planning never envisaged going beyond Lake Baikal. Advancing farther west would require an enormous logistical effort for no commensurate political gain. Until this point the ministry had enjoyed support from both the major factions in the bureaucracy (the Choshu and Satsuma cliques) and from the Seiyukai and Kokominto parties in the Diet. But the Seiyukai representatives and the Satsuma clique opposed *any* intervention, on the grounds that it would draw Japan into a great war that exceeded its resources. The question also set the advocates of meeting Japanese economic and security needs through an alignment with the West against the advocates of a self-sufficient sphere of influence in East Asia. In the Advisory Council on Foreign Relations (or ACFR), which brought together representatives of the political parties and of Government Departments, Motono's plans for immediate intervention were defeated in March. On the 19th Japan made known that unless its security were threatened it would act only with prior approval from the Allies and the USA. Motono himself was replaced in April by Goto, also an interventionist, but one more concerned to build up consensus prior to action.[45]

American consent was therefore needed to end the stalemate. Under the impact of Ludendorff's offensives, House softened his position during March and April to the extent of suggesting that an inter-Allied expedition might be acceptable if it received Bolshevik consent. This possibility hung like a mirage before the French and British between the no war, no peace declaration and Lenin's *rapprochement* with Germany after May. On 17 February the French Government authorized its representatives to offer arms and money if the Bolsheviks resisted the Central Powers.[46] Balfour sent similar instructions. On the 22nd the Central Committee—against fierce opposition from left-wing advocates of undiluted revolutionary war—voted 6:5 in favour of a Trotsky resolution, supported by Lenin, to accept Allied aid. But this was a measure of desperation at a moment when the Bolsheviks feared the Germans would refuse peace and would attempt to overthrow them. When it became clear on the following day that the Central Powers were still offering terms, Lenin quickly carried a majority for acceptance. Peace with Germany, if obtainable, was preferred over collaboration with the Allies. But there was another moment of panic when it was misreported that the final session at Brest-Litovsk had ended in breakdown. Trotsky approved a request from the Murmansk Soviet to seek Allied aid, and on 6 March a detachment of Royal Marines landed. It became the nucleus of a much larger presence.[47]

Even after Brest-Litovsk the Central Powers continued their advance, and Trotsky and his successor as Foreign Commissar, Chicherin, held out the possibility of co-operation with the Western European Allies. But the latter made co-operation dependent on Bolshevik consent to a Japanese expedition; and to this Soviet opposition hardly wavered. French and British attitudes towards the developing Russian Civil War were anyway hardening. The Quai d'Orsay, more ideologically opposed than the French military to Bolshevism, led the opposition to the co-operation policy. In February the Bolsheviks had begun nationalizing industry and banking, and had repudiated the Tsarist State foreign debt. As the prospects of military collaboration faded at the end of March, Pichon instructed his Ambassador in Russia that French policy should be to protect French economic interests and favour the reconstruction of a State in which French economic and diplomatic influence could be re-established. The Ministry of War accepted the Quai d'Orsay's position that the Red Army should be given aid only if there were guarantees that this would not be used to wage class war. Given that neither the Bolsheviks nor the White Russians were likely soon to reconstitute an eastern front, and given Bolshevik opposition to the Japanese, French favour was shifting decisively against the Soviet regime.[48] There was a similar reassessment in London. In early May Lenin persuaded the Central Committee that it was better to risk a war with Japan than one with Germany, and the Bolsheviks began their *rapprochement* with the Central Powers.[49] The result was increasing tension at the two flashpoints of Soviet-Allied relations: in the Arctic and over the future of the Czech Legion.

The crises were inter-related. In May Lenin condemned the Allied presence at Murmansk, and sent a special Commissar to discipline the city Soviet. But the latter needed the Allies for food and to protect the local fishing fleet against U-Boats, and it stood by its agreement with them. Murmansk and Archangel had mattered at first to the Allies for the military stores there that they wished to deny to the enemy. But they took on additional significance as possible embarkation points for the Czechs. The Czech Legion had been recruited from Czech prisoners of war in Russia, and in its dealings with the Bolsheviks was represented by the exiled politicians of the Czechoslovak National Council, or CNC. In March the CNC negotiated an agreement with the Bolsheviks to transport the Legion to France via Siberia. But the Czech troops were still mostly scattered on the two sides of the Urals when in May British and

French representatives concluded a revised agreement to re-route some of them via Archangel. The bewildered Legionaries had not been consulted, were suspicious of the Bolsheviks, and feared they were being divided as a strategem to weaken them prior to their destruction. At Cheliabinsk on the 14th they clashed with Hungarian prisoners of war and then with local Soviet forces. The Bolshevik Government ordered them to be disarmed. The Czechs resisted this by force, and resolved to fight their way through to Vladivostok. Thus, from 25 May the Czech revolt began.[50]

The Czechs were the strongest armed force in Siberia, and within a month they helped to place almost the entire length of the Trans-Siberian Railway east of the Urals under anti-Bolshevik rule. Although there is no evidence that the French and British Governments instigated the Revolt, it providentially aided their purposes. It made a reconstructed eastern front appear a less fantastic proposition, and it made up Wilson's mind. It also drastically worsened Allied–Soviet relations. The Allied representatives informed Trotsky (now Commissar for War) that any attempt to disarm the Czechs would be deemed a hostile act, and German-inspired. Unable to tolerate the ambiguity at Murmansk, the Bolsheviks on 15 June issued a categorical demand for Allied withdrawal. At the end of the month British troops disarmed a Bolshevik expedition to the Arctic, though as yet without casualties. Murmansk and the Czechs, but Murmansk because of the Czechs, became the Fort Sumter of the Allied–Soviet war.

The Czech Revolt precipitated American and Japanese intervention. Wilson was eased towards this because in the Arctic he saw fewer objections than in Siberia: no Japanese factor, the appearance of at least local Russian consent, and the German threat in Finland to Allied military stores. In the summer of 1918 he also gave high priority to inter-Allied solidarity. A message from Balfour on 27 May described Murmansk as 'vital' and American aid there as 'essential'; Wilson and Lansing agreed on 1 June to send troops to the Arctic if Foch, the newly appointed Allied Generalissimo on the Western Front, approved. Foch promptly obliged, and the Supreme War Council approved plans not only for an inter-Allied force at Murmansk but also for intervention at Archangel, where French and British forces established themselves on 1–2

August after a preliminary coup removed the local Bolshevik authority. There was consternation in Moscow, where an appeal was issued to the 'toiling masses' of the West. A speech by Lenin on 24 July had already suggested that the Bolsheviks considered themselves in a state of 'war' with the Allies: Chicherin explained afterwards that this meant 'defence'. The equivocation was apposite.[51]

By the time American troops reached Archangel in September, the United States was also committed in Siberia. Russia was always a secondary issue for Wilson, and one over which he doubted his own judgement. Although the War Department still opposed involvement, he was under pressure from the State Department, the Democratic Party, and the Allies, who had worn down House into accepting the need for a 'humanitarian' expedition, which would need military protection. Wilson's attitude to the Bolsheviks had hardened since the spring, partly because of the forged 'Sisson documents', which purported to show that they were German agents. But the Czech Revolt was essential to his decision. It allowed him to launch a limited operation in the guise of humanitarian relief, in a way that was less likely to offend the Russians and yet also made a gesture to the Allies. A White House conference on 6 July agreed it was impossible to re-establish an eastern front, but that international aid was needed to help the Czechs at Vladivostok link up with those in the interior. The Japanese should be invited to join an expedition to guard the railway at Vladivostok, each Power contributing approximately 7,000 men. Both would disclaim any intention of interfering in Russian internal affairs or encroaching on Russian sovereignty. An *aide-mémoire* to the Allied Ambassadors on 17 July justified a military commitment to rescue the Czechs and 'to steady any efforts at self-government or self-defence in which the Russians themselves may be willing to accept assistance'.[52] American intervention was thus intended as a minimum response by a harassed and preoccupied President to a concatenation of pressures. Lloyd George called it 'preposterous', and likened it to General Gordon's mission to Khartoum.[53] But it broke the deadlock in Tokyo.

The American invitation removed the need for the Japanese to choose between their East Asian ambitions and Washington's goodwill. Although Wilson's proposal was much more limited than what the Japanese army had in mind, they and Terauchi won agreement from the Cabinet to accept it, and seized the opportunity to launch a much larger enterprise. Both the Americans and their liberal allies in the ACFR tried to limit the expedition's numbers and its geographical scope, but no agreement was reached and the Japanese went ahead unilaterally in August, building up their forces by November to 70,000. Japanese intervention, as had been feared, created a new sphere of influence on the Asian mainland, while contributing little to the re-establishment of an eastern front or to the survival of the Czechs. And it was delayed until the turn of the tide on the Western Front deprived it of its principal rationale.[54] The uneasy restoration of peace between the Bolsheviks and the Central Powers had therefore almost immediately been followed by an undeclared war between the Bolsheviks and the Allies. Only when the issue in the west was settled would the Russian Civil War be allowed, eventually, to pursue its murderous course without interference from outside.

(iii) *The Fate of Austria-Hungary*

The Central Powers' decision to stake all on Ludendorff's offensives hardened Allied attitudes towards the Habsburg Monarchy. In the peace contacts between Karl and Wilson, Kerr and Skrzynski, and Armand and Revertera, the Austrians had again refused a separate peace, and their opposition to French and Italian objectives had become more unyielding. The Monarchy added its signature to the eastern peace treaties, and for the first time sent contingents to the Western Front. Against this background the 'Czernin incident' brought Vienna and the Allies to the parting of the ways.

In a speech on 2 April Czernin alleged that before Ludendorff's offensive had begun Clemenceau had enquired on what basis Austria-Hungary would be willing to negotiate. Czernin had replied that France must renounce Alsace-Lorraine, which condition Clemenceau had refused. Clemenceau was stung by the Austrian Foreign Minister's insinuation that he had secretly requested peace while publicly exhorting France to fight on. Czernin, he retorted, had 'lied'. In fact a misunderstanding

had arisen from the last stage of the Armand–Revertera conversations, in which Clemenceau had ordered Armand to listen
and say nothing, but Armand had proceeded none the less to
hold out the possibility of a broader exchange of views. As a
result there now opened a series of competitive disclosures,
culminating on 11 April in Clemenceau's publication of
the 24 March 1917 letter to Sixte in which Karl had supported
France's claim to Alsace-Lorraine. Czernin, who had not known
about the document, resigned and was replaced by Burián. The
Germans had also been ignorant of the letter, and on 12 May
Karl made his journey to Canossa, in the shape of a visit to
Wilhelm at Spa. There he apparently promised not to contact
foreign Powers in future without first consulting Berlin. The
two Governments also agreed to negotiate a long-term political
alliance, a military alliance, and a gradual transition to a customs
and economic union. Vienna's independent role was fading,
and *Mitteleuropa* came closer to reality than at any earlier
time.[55]

Clemenceau and Pichon informed the parliamentary commission of inquiry on the Czernin incident that France must
now unequivocally support self-determination for the Austro-
Hungarian nationalities.[56] Wilson and Lloyd George regretted
Clemenceau's action, but both the British and American
Governments concluded that a separate peace with Vienna had
become impracticable. In the words of a circular sent out with
Lloyd George's approval to British Ambassadors on 21 May,
the nationalities should receive 'all possible support', in the
hope of reducing Austria-Hungary 'to a reasonable frame of
mind'.[57] Even now, the Western Governments were not necessarily committed to the Habsburg Monarchy's destruction.
This never became an absolute war aim that they would fight
on for unrelentingly until it had been achieved. But the Brest-
Litovsk and Bucharest Treaties created a swathe of nominally
independent States that were in practice satellites of the
Central Powers. If this could not be countered by detaching
Austria-Hungary, the alternative course of encouraging the
oppressed nationalities was the only card to play. Played it was,
at first largely as a short-term expedient to win the war rather
than because of a considered judgement that self-determination
was a suitable basis for the Eastern European settlement in the

longer term. Support for the nationalities became embodied in the 'Versailles Declaration' by the coalition as a whole, and in a series of separate announcements by its members.

The Versailles Declaration was issued by the Supreme War Council, with American approval, on 3 June. The Allied leaders proclaimed that 'the creation of a united and independent Polish State, with free access to the sea, constitutes one condition of a just and lasting peace', and expressed their 'warm sympathy' for the Czechoslovaks and the Yugoslavs in 'their struggle for liberty and the realization of their national aspirations'. The Poles, therefore, received the stronger support. After the February Revolution the Allies had associated themselves with the Russian Provisional Government's promise of an independent Poland; but the Bolshevik Revolution obliged them, if they were to continue to encourage the Poles, to pledge to do so by their own efforts. In both Paris and London there were fears that this was foolhardy. But the Poles could be useful to the Allies as a source of recruits, and the competition with the enemy for Polish sympathies continued. The French established a Polish army in France in June 1917. In August the Polish National Committee was set up, under Dmowski, to lobby for the Polish cause in the Western capitals. It represented only the more conservative Polish parties, and Dmowski wanted territorial gains at Russian expense. To recognize it as the 'official' Polish organization in France, as the French authorities did on 20 September, was therefore an implicitly anti-Russian move and a step towards an independent Western commitment. None the less, Britain and the USA quickly followed the French lead.[58]

After the Bolshevik revolution and the failure of the peace contacts with Vienna, Poland became the kingpin in the French design for an alliance of newly independent States in Eastern Europe that would be strengthened at the Central Powers' expense and form a new eastern counterbalance in succession to the Tsar. Hence the French, earlier than the British and Americans, came to perceive national self-determination as being in their long-term interest, and the Versailles Declaration crowned six months of lobbying by the Quai d'Orsay in liaison with the Polish National Committee. Neither for the French nor the British, however, did the Declaration's reference to 'free access to the sea' necessarily promise more than internationalization of the Vistula. Both the Caxton Hall speech and the Fourteen Points had envisaged an independent Poland confined to the ethnically Polish areas. The French Government alone, in a letter to the Polish National Committee on 5 September, went on to pledge support for Poland's 'historic limits': the 1772 frontiers that would incorporate vast territories from Russia and give Poland a corridor to the Baltic that would split Germany in two.[59]

Poland was a special case. It benefited from consistent American sympathy, and from exceptional rivalry with the Central Powers. The most analogous among the other nationalities were the Rumanians, who also figured in the Quai d'Orsay's 'eastern barrier'. The Yugoslavs, by contrast, were handicapped by their uneasy relations with Serbia and with Italy. The South Slav leadership was divided between the Serbian Government—after 1915 in exile at Corfu—and the Yugoslavs under Habsburg rule. The Yugoslav deputies in the Vienna Reichsrat committed themselves after Brest-Litovsk to an independent South Slav State. Their exiled compatriots in the Yugoslav Committee had in July 1917 agreed with the Serbian Government on a united constitutional monarchy in which the non-Serbs' religious and linguistic distinctiveness would be respected. But they correctly suspected that Pašić would settle for an all-Serb union if the greater goal of a federation with the Croats and Slovenes proved unobtainable.

The Italian Government was a more serious obstacle. It allowed only Serbs to be recruited from its Austro-Hungarian prisoners of war, and sent them to join the Serbian army at Salonika. Hence the Yugoslav Committee, unlike its Czech and Polish counterparts, had no independent military force that it could use as a bargaining counter with the Allies. After Caporetto, however, the Italian Government temporarily followed a dual policy, which gave misleading encouragement to the Yugoslavs. In April 1918 a 'Congress of Oppressed Nationalities' met in the Italian capital. It included Transylvanian, Polish, and Czechoslovak representatives, as well as Italian politicians and members of the Yugoslav Committee. The Congress appealed to the Allies to make the emancipation of the Austro-Hungarian nationalities a war aim. And under the 'Pact of Rome' the

Italians and Yugoslavs pledged support for each other's national unity, with the borders between them being settled on the basis of national self-determination. Orlando received the delegates warmly and appeared to associate himself with their resolutions, but the Italian Government was not officially pledged, and Sonnino insisted on a very cautious wording in the Allies' Versailles Declaration in June. In September Bissolati won a mealy-mouthed declaration of approval from the Cabinet for the 'independence and the constitution into a free state' of the Yugoslavs, but Sonnino still supposed that Austria-Hungary would survive after the war and that Italy's Adriatic frontier must be protected as the Treaty of London had specified.[60]

The critical question for the survival of the Habsburg Monarchy, however, remained that of the Czechs, and the Czechoslavak National Council had a much stronger diplomatic position. Its leaders were respected by the Allied Governments, and at the moment when the search for a separate peace with Austria-Hungary faltered the Czech Legion became critical for Allied strategy. After the Czernin incident and the Spa meeting Lansing urged on Wilson that the Habsburg Monarchy had become irrevocably an instrument of German domination in South-Eastern Europe and should be broken up. Wilson agreed to a statement on 29 May that 'the nationalistic aspirations of the Czecho-Slovaks and Jugo-Slavs for freedom have the earnest support of this Government': a deliberately guarded step that made possible the equally guarded Versailles Declaration. But it led on to something more dramatic. After the Declaration there was anxiety in London, Paris, and Washington that the other nationalities would be discouraged through having received less emphatic backing than the Poles. A further American statement on 28 June explained that that of 29 May had meant that 'all branches of the Slav race should be completely freed from German and Austrian rule'. Wilson, otherwise preoccupied, had submitted casually to Lansing's pressure for this clarification, and had not expected it to be published. But he now agreed that Austria-Hungary should be broken up, and the administration had effectively abandoned the commitment in the Fourteen Points to keep the Monarchy in being.

The Czechs also benefited from Franco-British rivalry in the summer of 1918 over the Czech Legion, which the French wanted to transport to the Western Front and the British to leave in Siberia. On 29 June a letter from Pichon to Beneš of the CNC promised to support an independent Czechoslovakia 'within the historic limits of your provinces', and therefore including the Germans of the Sudetenland. French recognition of the CNC came on the following day. In the USA the decision to send American forces to Siberia encouraged sympathy for the Czech cause. Neither the Americans nor the British, however, gave the CNC so strong a form of recognition as did the French; and both avoided commitment over the Czech territorial claims.[61] None the less, gestures to the oppressed nationalities that had begun as a war measure now reflected a desire for permanent political change. All the Allies flatly rejected a final Austrian appeal on 14 September for non-binding discussion of peace terms in a neutral capital, even though Burián issued this independently of Germany and to its displeasure.[62] The military significance of the Allies' altered rhetoric, however, was limited. It contributed something to the disintegration of the Habsburg Monarchy, but less than the continuing pressure of their armies and of the blockade. Although Austria-Hungary's break-up was no longer unwelcome to them, except perhaps to Italy, it was accomplished by forces largely outside their control and whose operation they could not, even if they wanted to, reverse.

(iv) *The Armistices*

The smallest Central power, Bulgaria, began the avalanche. Its decision to seek an armistice precipitated Germany's request for one on 4 October 1918, and Austria-Hungary and Turkey immediately followed suit. The German Government asked not simply for a ceasefire but also for a peace based on the Fourteen Points, and it approached not the Allies collectively but Wilson alone. Hence there followed a period of public negotiations between Wilson and the Central Powers, during which the President promised a peace based on the Fourteen Points to Berlin, but refused one to Vienna. His partners, thus far on the sidelines, now reached an agreement with him over the Fourteen Points and the armistices' military clauses. And in the final phase their enemies accepted this compromise.

Germany's armistice request resulted primarily from military developments. Under the cumulative impact of defeat OHL came down in favour of a ceasefire. This began a process that deprived it of its veto over policy and ended in a much less favourable armistice agreement than Ludendorff had originally envisaged. Yet in the high summer of 1918 German expansion and OHL's authority had reached their maximum extent. Kühlmann was forced to resign early in July, after suggesting in the Reichstag that military decisions alone, unaccompanied by diplomacy, could not end the war. His successor, Hintze, was a naval officer with less experience in diplomacy, although he turned out to be an unexpectedly effective operator on behalf of similar goals. The Spa Crown Council on 2 July endorsed Western European war aims similar to those of 1917, and jettisoned the Austrian solution in Poland in favour of OHL's preference, the 'candidate solution'. Poland would choose its own ruler, but incorporate only the former Russian zone, while Germany annexed a wide frontier strip, commanded the army, and controlled the railways.[63] The French counter-offensive on the Marne on 18 July, however, forced Ludendorff to shelve his plans for a culminating onslaught in Flanders before American troops could arrive in strength. His general order on 2 August envisaged a defensive, prior to limited attacks that would wear the Allies out and oblige them to negotiate. And on the 8th a surprise British tank attack in front of Amiens took 16,000 prisoners and advanced 6–8 miles in one day. Alarming reports came in of a collapse in the German soldiers' morale. Reducing his immediate plans to a simple defensive, Ludendorff resolved that the war 'must be ended'.[64]

But even Amiens was an insufficient blow. At another Spa conference on 13–14 August Ludendorff's confidence had partially recovered. It was agreed to take the initiative in seeking neutral mediation, but only after 'the next German offensive in the west'. Conversations did take place, however, in Switzerland on the 24th and 26th, between the Belgian Minister in Berne, Peltzer, and the Bavarian aristocrat, Törring. Hintze was unable to tell Törring that Germany would renounce its claims on Belgium altogether, but he did agree with Ludendorff to abandon Belgium if no other country had superior political and economic privileges there. On American advice, the Belgians discontinued the exchange. The Germans still refused concessions in Alsace-Lorraine or amendments to the eastern peace treaties, and continued to pursue a far stronger position than they had occupied in 1914. They also repeatedly secured postponements of Austria-Hungary's plan to ask for non-binding conversations in a neutral capital—until Burián went ahead in defiance of them with his appeal of 14 September. The change in German war aims remained barely perceptible, and Hintze's dilatory diplomacy had yielded negligible results.[65]

Between 28 September and 4 October this position was transformed. Military considerations determined the timing of Germany's armistice request; but political ones determined its form. On 15 September the Allies at Salonika advanced against Bulgaria, which signed an armistice fourteen days later. On the 19th the British in Palestine began an offensive that expelled the Turks from Syria. On 26–8 September three co-ordinated attacks were launched along the Western Front, and on the 29th British forces pierced the celebrated Hindenburg line. These events broke Ludendorff's nerve. On the evening of the 28th he and Hindenburg agreed an armistice must be sought at once, and an approach made to Wilson rather than the Allies. On the same day Hintze had his Foreign Ministry officials prepare the arguments for a 'revolution from above': a new ministry, probably including the SPD, should appeal to the President for a peace based on the Fourteen Points. Democratization could both forestall a revolution from below, in the shock of defeat, and facilitate the *démarche* in Washington. The Ludendorff and Hintze plans went forward to a third Spa Crown Council, on 29 September, at which all present rejected the alternative of a military dictatorship. Hertling resigned rather than agree to a parliamentary regime, but the Kaiser endorsed Hintze's proposals. Ludendorff, fearing an imminent Allied breakthrough, insisted on an armistice request accompanying the change of ministry and the appeal to the USA. A new Government, with Prince Max of Baden as Chancellor, therefore brought in the SPD while excluding the right-wing parties. It introduced limited constitutional reforms that stopped short of full democratization, and on the night of 4–5 October sent off the note to Wilson. Max had wanted to spell out Germany's interpretation of the Fourteen Points, but Hintze's successor, Solf, persuaded him that this would increase the danger of rejection. Hence the note simply and briefly asked Wilson to take in hand arrangements for an immediate armistice and for peace negotiations, in which Germany would accept as a basis the Fourteen Points and his subsequent statements.[66]

Similar notes followed from Vienna and Constantinople, also accompanied by democratic genuflexions. A manifesto on 16 October promised a 'federated State' for the Austrian (though not Hungarian) half of the Dual Monarchy. The Government in Constantinople resigned in favour of a new, non-CUP, ministry under Izzet Pasha, which took office on the 14th and decided almost immediately to seek a separate peace. It was willing to accept 'autonomy' and even French and British 'protection' in the Arab and Armenian provinces of the Ottoman Empire, as well as internationalization of the Straits, as long as the capital remained under Turkish sovereignty.[67]

Wilson now had to judge the sincerity of these manœuvres. Although OHL insisted on an immediate armistice, it was unconverted to a Wilsonian peace. Rather, Ludendorff hoped for a breathing space while the German army regrouped on more defensible lines, and that the broadening of the Government would saddle the Left with some of the responsibility for Germany's predicament. When the Allied advance slowed down at the beginning of October he again became more optimistic, and the High Command warned Max that it would cede only small portions of Alsace-Lorraine and nothing in the east.[68] Similarly, Hintze's conception of appealing to the American President was another in the long line of attempts to split the opposing coalition. But now for the first time there was a Government on the Allied side whose preponderance relative to its partners was approaching that enjoyed by Germany among the Central Powers. A bilateral deal was possible that would end the stalemate of coalition diplomacy and conclude the war. What actually happened was more complex. The United States won general approval for a peace on Wilson's principles, but the European Allies won conditions acceptable to themselves as well as to the Americans. And by the time they did so German bargaining power—more intact in late September than Ludendorff supposed—had collapsed. Hintze's revolution from above began to erode the position of the High Command; and the diplomatic and political as well as military impasses that had prolonged the war in the west could be surmounted at last.

The second stage in the making of the armistices was Wilson's public exchange of notes with the Central Powers from 4 to 23 October. Now that the Allies' military emergency had passed the President was already becoming more assertive in his dealings with his partners. Allied economic projects were especially suspect, and repeated French *démarches* during 1918 on behalf of Clémentel's proposals for controls on post-war international commodity trade met with no reply. Wilson also reacted sharply to a speech made by Lloyd George on 31 July, and warned the British that he might have to dissociate himself from any threats of 'punitive post-war measures' against German commerce. The British hurriedly denied any such intention. More generally, House was concerned by reports that the political Right in Western Europe was gaining ground. He advised Wilson that military success would make the Allies less amenable, and that it was time to commit them to American aims. This the President's New York speech on 27 September attempted to do. Its 'Five Particulars' called for impartial justice in the peace settlement, and opposed either exclusive alliances or 'special, selfish economic combinations' within the League of Nations. The League would be the sole international security arrangement, and the sole institution with the power of international economic boycott. Private invitations for Allied comments on the speech, however, produced only non-committal replies.[69]

At this point the German note arrived. After Berlin opened the dialogue Wilson sent messages on 8, 14, and 23 October; the Germans responded on the 12th, 20th, and 27th. In retrospect the President appeared to have seized on the German approach in order to manoeuvre both sides into a *fait accompli* based on his terms, but in reality, especially at the beginning, he was feeling his way. The mid-Term Congressional elections were approaching, and a bellicose Republican opposition was campaigning for unconditional surrender. Most of the Senate and the American press called on him to reject the enemy appeal. He decided, however, to pursue the contact and to suppress his qualms about dealing with the German autocracy. He also decided to reply without consulting his allies. Beyond this, he betrayed his uncertainty by casting his note of 8 October largely in the form of an enquiry. Did Germany accept the principles in his speeches? And who did Max's Government speak for? The only military condition he mentioned was enemy evacuation of Allied soil. Relieved, the Germans replied affirming their willingness to evacuate Allied territory in return for a peace based on Wilson's declarations. At this point the Berlin Government still hoped, indeed, that it could escape without ceding Alsace-Lorraine.[70]

Wilson's second note, sent on 14 October, shattered these illusions and opened the decisive stage. He was probably influenced by the intransigence of American opinion, and by a message from Lloyd George, Orlando, and Clemenceau that evacuation of occupied territory was insufficient and the Allies' military advisers must be consulted about the ceasefire terms. The experts approached by the State Department mostly judged Max's constitutional changes inadequate. And on 12 October the British liner *Leinster* was torpedoed, with the loss of some six hundred lives. Wilson concluded that enemy atrocities must be stopped and Germany prevented from renewing the war, but that the contact must still be maintained. In his new note he stipulated that the armistice conditions must be left to the Allied and American military advisers, and guarantee the coalition's 'present military supremacy'. The 'arbitrary power' that had governed Germany must be destroyed or rendered impotent, and unrestricted submarine warfare must end.[71]

In effect Wilson had raised his conditions, and made Ludendorff's original design unrealizable. A ceasefire now would destroy Germany's bargaining position, and leave it reliant on the enemy's good faith in implementing the Fourteen Points. Ludendorff, if with little justification, had become more sanguine about the military prospects, and told the Cabinet on the 17th that he no longer feared an enemy break-through and that Germany should fight on rather than accept the present terms. OHL also supported the navy's insistence that unrestricted submarine warfare should continue. In a sense, given that the enemy would no longer concede the military advantage Ludendorff had hoped for, his position was consistent. But the Cabinet suspected OHL of shifting its ground for political reasons, and decided the negotiation must go on. Max was receiving disquieting information about unrest and demoralization on the home front, and the Commander of the German forces in Belgium had advised him that resistance could not be maintained beyond the end of the year. By threatening to resign, Max won round the Kaiser, and the German note of 20 October announced the end of torpedo attacks on passenger ships. It insisted that future Governments would be responsible to the Reichstag, and accepted that the Allied military advisers should decide the ceasefire terms on the basis of 'the actual standard of power on both sides in the field'.[72]

One final round was needed to overcome all German resistance. Wilson's note of 23 October announced that he was referring to the Allies for an armistice, but still pressed, at the least, for a full constitutional monarchy and parliamentary control over the High Command. Hindenburg and Ludendorff issued a public communiqué that the note was unacceptable and the war must go on; and they came to Berlin in violation of Max's instructions. The Chancellor now had the open disobedience that he needed to insist on Ludendorff's resignation, which took place after a stormy interview with the Kaiser on the 26th. Hindenburg, though accused of treachery by his colleague, obeyed Wilhelm's orders to remain in post. By degrees the German Cabinet had submitted to an armistice that would reduce Germany to helplessness, and had surmounted the opposition of the Kaiser, the navy, and OHL. The way was clear, as far as Berlin was concerned, for a peace based on the American programme.

Simultaneously, the Fourteen Points were being abandoned as a basis for the settlement with the Habsburgs. After Austria-Hungary's armistice request Wilson decided that in the light of the declarations made during the summer he must rescind his earlier promise to respect the Dual Monarchy's integrity. On 18 October he replied that autonomy for the Yugoslavs and Czechoslovaks would no longer suffice, and they rather than he

must decide what would satisfy them. This mortified the
Vienna leaders, and hastened the collapse of their authority
over the provinces.[73] On 21 October the German representatives in the Reichsrat declared the independence of the
German-speaking region. Three days later the Italians launched
an offensive that reduced much of the Habsburg army to a
rabble. The Czechoslovaks and the Yugoslavs declared their
independence, and on 1 November the Austro-Hungarian union
was dissolved. Ten days later Karl went into exile. By this
stage, on 30 October, 3 and 11 November respectively, the
Turkish, Austrian, and German armistices had been signed.
The negotiation of these armistices with the victorious Allies
must now be examined.

The armistices were technical, military documents, setting out
the terms on which the victors agreed to suspend hostilities.
Turkey, Austria-Hungary, and Germany tried to link the
military with a political agreement by seeking a Wilsonian peace. But Wilson rejected Austria-Hungary's appeal,
and the Turks, who were not at war with the Americans, concluded a purely military ceasefire. Only with Germany was
a combined agreement reached. These two elements of the
negotiation—the military and the political—must be considered
in turn.

The armistice conditions were decided in two conferences in
Paris from 6 to 9 October and 29 October to 4 November 1918.
The first represented only the European Allies, but the second
included an American delegation under Colonel House. Among
the first Conference's actions was to draft an armistice with
Turkey, which it did on the basis of British proposals that were
harshened because of the concern of the French and Italians to
secure their own objectives in the Ottoman Empire. But it was
with the British that the new Turkish Government made
contact, and the British Admiral Calthorpe was instructed by
his Government to exclude the other Allies from the armistice
negotiations that took place from 27 to 30 October off the
Aegean island of Mudros. Although this infuriated Clemenceau,
Calthorpe secured most of the points agreed at Paris. The
Mudros Armistice opened the Straits to Allied warships and
allowed Allied occupation of the Straits forts. Most of the

Turkish army was to be demobilized and the navy surrendered. The Allies took control of the railways and the right to occupy 'any strategic points' if their security were threatened. This was far stiffer than the Turks had hoped for, but the Ottoman Government accepted in the hope of conciliating Britain, which it saw, largely mistakenly, as its last chance of salvation.[74]

The Austrians were even less well placed to haggle. The second Paris conference approved the terms of the armistice signed at the Villa Giusti, near Padua, on 3 November. A separate armistice with the Hungarian half of the former Habsburg Monarchy followed ten days later at Belgrade. The main significance of the Villa Giusti Armistice was for the future power balance between Italy and Yugoslavia. The Serbs, Croats, and Slovenes under Habsburg rule declared their independence on 29 October, and were aided by the Serbian army in a race for territory with the Italians, but their union with Serbia was proclaimed only on 1 December. The Armistice dealt the emergent kingdom two serious blows. Much of the Habsburg navy was handed over to Italy. And Allied (in practice, largely Italian) forces were to occupy Austrian territory up to a limit almost identical with the Treaty of London line. Lloyd George and Clemenceau had supported this at Paris, and House consented, or so he wrote to Wilson, under protest and 'upon the explicit promise that this territory should have the same status as the territory to be occupied under the German armistice'. On paper, this did not prejudge the Adriatic peace settlement, but the Italian Government certainly intended the occupation to create a political *fait accompli*, and at once began to use it towards this end.[75]

These developments in the Adriatic were mirrored on the Rhine. At the first Paris Conference the Allied Premiers were angered and alarmed that Wilson was negotiating publicly with the enemy without consulting them. Hence their demand, which the President conceded, for their military advisers to be consulted about the armistice conditions. When Wilson forwarded his correspondence with Germany to his partners on 23 October he asked if they were willing to link the ceasefire to a peace based on the Fourteen Points, but he suggested no armistice conditions of his own, and in this way lost the initiative over the military clauses. He was, indeed, in a dilemma. He accepted that the armistice must be able to prevent Germany from renewing hostilities. But he also advised House that the terms must be 'as moderate and reasonable as possible within these limits, because it is certain that too much success or security on the part of the Allies will make a genuine Peace settlement exceedingly difficult if not impossible'. Specifically, he favoured German evacuation of Allied territory, but no Allied occupation of Germany, even Alsace-Lorraine; and internment of the U-boats in neutral waters rather than their surrender.[76]

The actual terms were far more severe. The French and British respectively were largely responsible for the land and sea clauses, and House did little to moderate their impositions. Clemenceau and Pichon accepted Foch's advice that 'the only definitive territorial sacrifices will be those conceded by the enemy when the Armistice is signed', and they correctly judged after mid-October that Germany would accept practically whatever was demanded. The land clauses presented by the French to the second Paris conference therefore entailed the occupation of a maximum of enemy territory. The Germans would evacuate France, Belgium, Luxemburg, and Alsace-Lorraine (which received a special status). The Allies would occupy the left bank of the Rhine and bridgeheads on the right bank at Mainz, Coblentz, and Cologne; and a 30–40 kilometre wide demilitarized strip would run east of the river. This embraced all the territory that wartime French Governments had aspired to control, and Lloyd George, who overestimated the danger that Germany would reject an armistice, argued that by seeking to go beyond Alsace-Lorraine the French were risking prolonging the war for unavowed political ambitions. The terms also far exceeded what Wilson had envisaged; but House ceased to resist them after an agreement with Clemenceau on 30 October, and Lloyd George, isolated, unwillingly acquiesced. House's primary purpose at the conference was to win his partners' agreement to the Fourteen Points, and he was ready to humour them over the technical military clauses, in the hope, presumably, that American economic power and Wilson's hold over public opinion would nullify any political advantage that the European Allies thus gained. The Peace Conference would determine whether this hope was justified.[77]

The second Paris conference also dealt with Eastern Europe and the naval terms. It agreed that the Brest-Litovsk and Bucharest Treaties and the 27 August Russo-German supplementary agreements should be annulled, and the Bolsheviks themselves meanwhile repudiated these. German troops were to withdraw to the 1914 borders, except where the Allies thought the 'internal situation' counselled delay. The former Russian Poland was evacuated, and by the end of November had merged with Austrian Galicia to form an embryonic Polish State. The Germans were allowed to stay on in the Baltic provinces, but the rest of their eastern *imperium* was destroyed. As for the naval clauses, Lloyd George reluctantly supported his Admiralty's demands for all the U-boats and much of the German surface fleet to be surrendered. He reached a compromise with the American Admiral Benson that the submarines would be handed over, but the designated surface ships (including ten battleships) would be interned in a neutral port. In the end no such port was found, and they proceeded to Scapa Flow. The naval clauses also provided for the Allied blockade of Germany to continue during the Armistice period.[78]

After the second Paris conference the military and naval clauses underwent only minor changes. France and Britain had obtained substantially what they wanted, and were a step closer to a strategic frontier on the Rhine and Germany's elimination as a naval Power. After Wilson's success in beating down the Germans, this might appear a serious American setback. But House was well satisfied with the outcome of the conference, and the President approved his handiwork. This was because of the accompanying Allied–American political agreement.

The point at issue was Germany's acceptance 'as a basis' for the peace negotiations of the Fourteen Points and Wilson's subsequent speeches. When the President forwarded the correspondence with Germany to his partners he neither advised them to accept nor to reject this 'basis', but if they did reject it they would evidently be prolonging the war after Washington and Berlin had reached a public consensus. The second Paris conference resulted in the 'Lansing Note' to Germany on 5 November, announcing the Allies' readiness to make peace on the basis indicated, but with two qualifications.

They reserved their positions over the second Point—the freedom of the seas—and they specified that by 'restoration' of the invaded territories they understood that 'compensation will be made by Germany for all damage done to the civilian population of the Allies and their property by the aggression of Germany by land, by sea, and from the air'. It appeared that both coalitions had accepted almost all the American goals, and that the hour for sweeping reform of the international system was at hand.

The appearance was deceptive. The Armistice agreement was in large measure 'one big diversionary manoeuvre, in which all parties had deliberately evaded actual confrontation',[79] but which had the enormous merit of bringing the carnage to an end. Lloyd George had quickly seen the danger of being hustled into commitment to a programme over which the United States had never consulted its partners. He thought the Fourteen Points were 'very nebulous' and 'very dangerous', and the War Cabinet was unanimous in its opposition to Point II.[80] Point IX was equally objectionable in Rome, while the French considered the second Paris conference should simply draft the technical clauses, and ignore the question of Wilson's programme.[81] On the American side Wilson gave House no instructions, 'because I feel you will know what to do',[82] but in fact the Colonel was probably more willing than his superior to compromise. The American position also suffered from ambiguity over what the Fourteen Points actually meant. Privately, the Americans tried to place a reassuring gloss on them, thus exposing themselves to later charges that at the Armistice Germany and the Allies had agreed to different things. On 16 October Wilson told the British secret service agent, Wiseman, that France must regain Alsace-Lorraine and he would be happy to see Britain get the German colonies, although for domestic reasons he would prefer it if they were administered in trust for the League of Nations. The League should have the sole power of economic boycott, and the Royal Navy might be placed under it. But the international law of blockade must be revised.[83] When House reached Europe he turned to Walter Lippmann of the Inquiry and to the journalist Frank Cobb for further clarification. On 30 October Wilson approved the resulting 'Cobb–Lippmann memorandum' as an exposition of his general Points; on the specific ones its comments were acceptable as 'illustrative suggestions'. House made extensive use of it at Paris. The first Point, according to the memorandum, meant that all Treaties must be published, although they could be negotiated in secret; the second greatly restricted the right of blockade, except as exercised by the League. The less authoritative commentary on the specific Points upheld an ethnic line between Italy and the Yugoslavs, and opposed any French claim to the Saar.[84]

None of this lifted Wilson's bar on expansion in the Rhineland and the Adriatic, or the challenge to Britain's right of blockade. When the Paris conference opened on 29 October Lloyd George refused to entrust the latter to an untried League. House warned that deadlock might lead to an American separate peace; Lloyd George said Britain would fight on, and Clemenceau promised his support. That night House decided to threaten that Wilson would take the issue to Congress, and on the 30th he advised the President to begin reducing American loans and shipments of troops and supplies. But the Atlantic balance of power was difficult to assess. True, by 2 November there were 1.872 million Americans in France, and they outnumbered the British contingents on the Western Front. Yet the American industrial effort was slow to come on stream, and over two-thirds of the Expeditionary Force's aircraft, all its tanks, and most of its munitions were of French manufacture. American finance was indispensable to the Allies, but the loans had been tied to the purchase of American goods, and to cut them off would damage American producers. Nor was it evident that the bellicose Congress and American public of November 1918 would endorse a separate peace.[85] In short, to start a tit for tat with the European Allies would be a dangerous game. And both sides' perceptions converged in favour of a settlement. Wilson feared his influence over European opinion would diminish if the war went on; Clemenceau, at least, saw merit in halting before the Americans won even greater material primacy.

European disunity gave House a tactical advantage. On 30 October Lloyd George presented him with a memorandum setting out the position eventually incorporated in the Lansing Note: a reservation over the Freedom of the Seas, and a clarification of 'restoration'. When Clemenceau arrived House duly threatened that Wilson would go to Congress, and Clemenceau abandoned a French memorandum he was preparing and fell in with Lloyd George. That afternoon the Italians, receiving no support in their objections to Point IX, also accepted Lloyd George's draft. The Lansing Note therefore incorporated an Allied acceptance of the Fourteen Points that had been drawn up from the British standpoint. France and Italy were pacified by their satisfaction over the military provisions. Clemenceau also inserted into the text of the Armistice a general claim to reparation of damage, which the French later maintained had overridden the Lansing Note's limitations. But by accepting Lloyd George's document House had avoided opening the floodgates to Allied reservations across the whole range of the American programme. For a few days more Wilson objected to a complete reservation over the freedom of the seas, and the Anglo-American debate was pursued with considerable vehemence. But for practical purposes the British won the argument when House accepted a letter from Lloyd George of 3 November that agreed to discuss the freedom of the seas at the Peace Conference but refused to concede the principle. The European Allies and the Americans had reached agreement on their terms for ending the war.[86]

By the time the Lansing Note arrived Germany's situation had dramatically worsened. The Austrian collapse made possible an invasion from the south and perhaps a separate peace between the Allies and Bavaria. The retreat in the west continued. And revolution had begun on the home front. Wilson had not explicitly demanded Wilhelm's abdication, but at the end of October the Socialist press began to call for it as a way of gaining easier terms. From the 29th mutiny spread through the High Seas Fleet after news was circulated of a plan to make a desperate sortie into the North Sea. On 4 November sailors and munitions workers established a soviet in Kiel; and soldiers sent against it fraternized. As the revolution expanded across North Germany Ludendorff's successor, Gröner, demanded that a ceasefire must be sought at once, and when the Government received the Lansing Note it was preparing to offer unconditional surrender. House had won the Germans more favourable terms than they could now secure for themselves. Their armistice commissioners, however, gained a few last-minute alleviations by pleading the revolutionary threat: fewer deliveries of lorries and weapons, the neutral zone east of the Rhine to be narrowed to ten kilometres, Allied agreement to 'contemplate' provisioning Germany with food. On 9 November the revolution reached Berlin; fearing the movement would escape their control completely, the SPD leaders announced the Kaiser's abdication, and Wilhelm fled to Holland. Prince Max handed over to a Council of People's Commissars representing the SPD and USPD, headed by the SPD leader, Ebert. It confirmed that the armistice must be signed. And at 11 am on 11 November the guns at last fell silent.[87]

1918 had opened with a spate of public declarations, on one of which—the Fourteen Points—the ceasefire was ostensibly based. But in the interim there was a new resort to force, even bloodier than those that had gone before. The end of Russian resistance allowed Ludendorff to try his gamble on victory before the Americans arrived. By staking its own fate on that gamble the Habsburg Monarchy pushed the Allies into a commitment by implication to the oppressed nationalities. The military emergency also drew the Allies into a search for desperate expedients to revive the Eastern Front. The main result was to flood eastern Siberia with Japanese troops at the moment when the strategic justification for doing so had ended, and to draw the Allies and the Bolsheviks into an undeclared war. But the failure of Ludendorff's offensive, and the advance of American primacy, created the conditions in which the struggle in the West could end. The Germans' last attempt to split their enemies succeeded to the extent that they, though not the Austrians, salvaged from the wreckage a paper commitment to peace on the basis of the Fourteen Points. But the armistice agreement was an ambiguous contract, and the European Allies paid only lip-service to Wilson's intentions. It was clear that the future map of Europe would not follow the grandiose lines of the Central Powers' war-aims conferences. But it remained to be seen how the conflicting aspirations of the Western Europeans, the Americans, and the Bolsheviks could be reconciled, if indeed they could be reconciled at all.

6

The Fruits of Victory
NOVEMBER 1918–NOVEMBER 1920

(i) *The Peacemakers and the Bolsheviks*

The peace treaties emerged from a sequence of compromises between the victor Powers, and from their attempts to impose those compromises on their smaller partners and the defeated enemy. In much of Europe they had little capacity to implement their wishes, and as time passed they were defied with increasing success. But they dominated the Peace Conference itself, and its history is best understood as a process of inter-Allied bargaining in which the ascendancy gained by American diplomacy at the Armistice was gradually dissipated. Wilson had manifestly failed in his attempt to remould the international order even before the American Senate in its votes of November 1919 and March 1920 withheld ratification from the Treaty of Versailles.

The Conference opened in Paris on 18 January 1919. Its plenary sessions, which all the Allies could attend, were few and largely formal, and the real discussions took place among the leaders of the Great Powers in the Supreme Council. Initially this latter was known as the Council of Ten, and consisted of two members each from Britain, France, Italy, Japan, and the USA. Eight commissions, considering notably reparations and the League of Nations, were nominally responsible to the plenary Conference and included delegates from the smaller Allies. But the major territorial and economic questions were settled in the Supreme Council and in committees appointed by it, representing the Great Powers alone. The outstanding feature of the first phase of the Conference was an Anglo-American axis, though one largely confined to the discussions on the League of Nations. Subsequently, from 15 February to 14 March, Wilson was away on a visit to the United States; and between 8 February and 5 March Lloyd George, too, was absent in London. Clemenceau was temporarily disabled on 19 February by an assassination attempt. When this second, 'interregnum', period ended in mid-March most of the German Treaty had still to be worked out, and the crucial decisions on it were taken under acute pressure in the weeks before provisional terms were presented to the German delegates on 7 May. Simultaneously, the Conference underwent successive crises over the French, Italian, and Japanese claims. The Council of Ten was too unwieldly to meet this challenge, and after 24 March Orlando, Clemenceau, Lloyd George, and Wilson met alone, except for a secretary and interpreter, as the Council of Four. Lesser business went to the Foreign Ministers of the victor Powers, in the Council of Five. After a further crisis over Germany's resistance to the Allied conditions the Treaty of Versailles was signed on 28 June and the Heads of Government left Paris. The Five became the Council of the Heads of Delegations (or CHD), and replaced the Four as the supreme body. During this phase the Treaties of Saint-Germain-en-Laye and Neuilly were signed on 10 September and 27 November respectively with Austria and Bulgaria. After Germany ratified the Versailles Treaty the Conference officially closed on 21 January 1920, and the CHD bequeathed its functions to a Conference of Ambassadors, together with summit meetings in London in February–April and at San Remo in April–May. In this final period attention shifted from South-Eastern Europe to the Levant, and the treaties with Hungary at the Trianon on 4 June and with Turkey at Sèvres on 10 August 1920 brought the peacemaking process to an end. [1]

The Conference created a more fragile and unstable settlement than those established in 1814–15 and after 1945. This, however, resulted less from the Conference's procedural difficulties than from the intractability of the substantive dilemmas that it faced. Of these among the most crucial was the peacemakers' inability either to reach an understanding with the Bolshevik Revolution or to crush it. [2] Negotiation failed despite the time and energy that the Supreme Council gave to it; and suppression failed although the Allies' intervention continued and even increased after the Armistice with Germany. They maintained their blockade of the Bolshevik zone, and the British gave training and vast quantities of weaponry to the White armies of General Denikin in South Russia and Admiral Kolchak in Siberia. In November 1918 British Empire forces occupied the Baku–Batum railway, and detachments remained in Baku until July 1920. The Royal Navy helped the Baltic States win independence; a Franco-Greek expedition landed in Odessa and held much of the Black Sea coast between December 1918 and April 1919. Of the earlier interventions, that in the Arctic continued until September 1919, and the Japanese abandoned Vladivostok only in 1922.[3]

This policy remained in part an anti-German one. Until Berlin had ratified the peace treaty, an Eastern Front might still be needed, especially as the Kaiser's overthrow brought nearer Lenin's vision of a Russo-German revolutionary alliance. In practice the Republican authorities in Germany rejected military collaboration with the Bolsheviks, for fear of jeopardizing possible Western food relief and losing American goodwill.[4] But the possibility remained that the far Left, which staged repeated insurrections in the spring of 1919, would oust the SPD. After the Armistice, none the less, motives other than containing Germany grew in importance as reasons for intervention. The British Government felt its past co-operation with the Whites obliged it to give them a reasonable chance of victory in the Russian Civil War. Intervention might also secure the Indian frontiers and weaken a traditional rival through the creation of independent border States. The French, by contrast, hoped at least until March 1919 to reunite Russia under White leadership and reinstate the traditional counterbalance to Germany. In addition, they wanted to protect their Ukrainian investments, and feared the Bolsheviks would try to spread their ideology across Europe by force. But Allied war aims in Russia were confused and inconsistent, and intervention continued partly through inertia. It was difficult to extricate the troops after the rivers had frozen over and the 1918–19 winter had set in; and both Lloyd George and Clemenceau had to tread with caution because of the anti-Bolshevism of their parliamentary following.

The domestic pressures on the Allied leaders, however, were conflicting. Intervention was denounced by the expanding socialist and labour movements. It clashed with the needs of Treasuries for retrenchment and of Chiefs of the General Staff—such as Sir Henry Wilson in Britain—for the dwindling troops available to be deployed elsewhere. Demobilization was also the priority for the soldiers themselves. All the occupation forces suffered from unrest and poor morale, and the French precipitately evacuated Sebastopol in April 1919 because of mutiny in their fleet offshore. On 15 March a Senate resolution in favour of pulling out all American troops was defeated only by the Vice-President's casting vote. Hence Lloyd George and, eventually, the French leaders came to fear that expanded intervention might destabilize their own societies.[5] Foch in Paris and Churchill, as War Minister, in London wished to commit much larger forces, but they lacked Clemenceau's and Lloyd George's support. As a result, the Western Governments intervened sufficiently to reinforce the Bolsheviks' suspicion of their intentions, but insufficiently to drive them from power.

The two main attempts at compromise between the Allies and the Bolsheviks were the Prinkipo conference proposal and the Bullitt mission. Prinkipo originated as a British suggestion, although one that encountered much hostility in Lloyd George's own delegation. After Wilson gave his backing Clemenceau also consented—for the sake, he said, of Allied unity—and on 22 January the Ten approved the proposal. They called for a ceasefire, and for a conference on Prinkipo island in the Sea of Marmora between representatives of all the Russian factions and the Allied Powers. A Soviet reply on 4 February accepted the invitation, and offered in exchange for peace to recognize and pay interest on Russia's foreign debts, to grant the Allies mining and forestry concessions, possibly to cede territory under Allied occupation, and to refrain from interfering in Allied internal affairs. Twelve days later, however, the Russian Political Conference, representing the Whites, rejected the Prinkipo summons.

What lay behind this sequence of events? Wilson, like Lloyd George, professed to be 'repelled' by Bolshevism, but both men suspected that military intervention would consolidate rather than overthrow it, and they refused to finance intervention on a larger scale. They also had reason in advance to count on Bolshevik acceptance of the Prinkipo offer. The November Armistice had relieved the pressure on the Soviet authorities, who strengthened the Red Army for possible intervention in Germany and prepared for co-ordinated agitation in the West through the Communist International, or Comintern, founded in March 1919. But Lenin also sought a 'second Brest': to buy time before the showdown with 'international imperialism' by bribing the Allied capitalist interests through economic concessions. In December 1918 Litvinov, from the People's Commissariat for Foreign Affairs, had arrived in Stockholm, and in response to a personal appeal from the Soviet emissary Wilson had sent William Buckler for conversations on 14–16 January. Litvinov had offered Buckler conditions very similar to those contained in the Bolsheviks' subsequent reply to the Prinkipo appeal. Prinkipo therefore emerged both from the Anglo-Saxon leaders' assessment that intervention was not working and should be liquidated if reasonable terms were available, and from Lenin's anxiety for a breathing space, a course he could impose on his Party more easily than a year before. The convergence of interests was temporary. And it was significant, given that the Red Army was improving its position on the ground, that the Allies set the condition of a ceasefire along the present battle lines, but the Bolsheviks failed to mention this in their reply.

The Russian Political Conference rejected Prinkipo on behalf of the three main White authorities, in Siberia, North Russia, and the Ukraine. The Whites vehemently opposed a meeting with the Bolsheviks, but at this point the military balance was moving against them and they needed Allied support. Prinkipo foundered not only on the enmity between the Russian factions but also on the disunity of the Allies, and in particular on the equivocal behaviour of the French. With the Odessa expedition the French Government was involved in its most ambitious attempt to reconstruct its former influence in Russia, and Clemenceau felt—or said he felt—that his ministry would be endangered if it appeared to favour compromise.[6] Although he judged it necessary to humour Wilson within the Supreme Council, the Quai d'Orsay and the Paris press encouraged White opposition to Prinkipo outside. As a result, the Anglo-

American effort to disengage from Russia by negotiation was rendered fruitless, and Bolshevik sincerity over the armistice question remained untried.

The Bullitt mission never came even this close to success. Bullitt was a junior member of the American delegation, who travelled unofficially to Moscow and began discussions with the Bolshevik leaders on 10 March. They told him they would accept a two-week ceasefire and a peace conference if the Allies made such an offer within a month. The Allies should lift their blockade, withdraw their forces, and end assistance to the Whites. All *de facto* Governments in Russia would stay in control of their territory unless changed by the decision of the conference or by the local inhabitants. On regaining Paris, Bullitt pressed for acceptance of the Bolshevik terms, but was unable to see Wilson, and the Allies failed to reply before the time limit expired.

The mission was bedevilled by a confusion of authority. House was the driving force behind it, and he appears to have won support in principle from Wilson before the President's mid-Conference visit to Washington. But Wilson seems to have supposed that Bullitt would gather information rather than negotiate; and the French were told it was merely a fact-finding expedition. Before Bullitt's departure, however, House indicated to him that the United States was willing to grant an armistice and to press for joint Allied withdrawal if the Bolsheviks undertook not to retaliate against the Whites. Philip Kerr, of Lloyd George's secretariat, set out similar conditions on behalf of the Prime Minister and Balfour, although he stipulated that the *de facto* Governments in Russia should stay within their territories, and that the Allies would withdraw only after local Russian forces had been demobilized. The Bolsheviks therefore offered terms similar to those that Bullitt had brought with him, and were now prepared to accept a temporary partition of Russia along the existing battle lines while the Allies disentangled themselves. But their qualifications (that *de facto* Governments could be replaced by their citizens, and that all aid to the Whites must end) betrayed their intention to return later to the attack.

Once again, Bolshevik good faith was never put to the test. For by the time Bullitt came back to Paris Wilson was losing confidence in House, and was 'against taking up the question at present'. House and Bullitt were isolated within the American delegation, and the Colonel and Lloyd George decided not to press the matter further in the face of public opposition in Britain and America to dealings with the Soviet regime. The existence of an apparent alternative may have facilitated the decision. On 16 April the Council of Four approved a suggestion by Hoover, the Director of the American food relief programme, for a neutral commission under the Norwegian, Nansen, that would distribute food in Russia on the conditions of a ceasefire and of commission control over the railways. The Nansen Plan was a counter-revolutionary as well as a humanitarian proposal, which House hoped would maintain the existing boundaries and alleviate the famine conditions that contributed to Bolshevik support. On 7 May the Bolsheviks replied that they were willing to talk to Nansen, but objected to the political condition of a ceasefire. By the time the Council of Four discussed this the Whites were advancing, and the Plan received no further consideration.[7]

Each of the successive Allied projects had been less favourable to the Soviet regime. And now that the military pendulum was swinging back towards Lenin's opponents the Allied leaders abandoned negotiation in favour of a military solution that White armies, rather than their own, would impose. On 27 May the Four took a first step towards recognizing Admiral Kolchak's Government at Omsk. In return for undertakings to set up an elected regime and to acknowledge the independence of Poland and Finland as well, perhaps, as other border territories, they promised to send him volunteers and munitions and assist him in establishing an all-Russian Government. Allied policy therefore became to continue the blockade and to aid the Whites and border States, but avoid further direct intervention. By now the French Odessa expedition had ended in débâcle. Wilson withdrew his contingents from the Arctic as soon as the thaw permitted, and he continued to limit strictly the role of his forces in Siberia. During the autumn the British evacuated their forces from the Arctic, Siberia, and most of Transcaucasia, and stopped supplying Kolchak and Denikin, although they did so at a moment when Denikin's armies were advancing on Moscow

and White victory seemed near. When the tide turned, and
Denikin was thrown back, the British took the lead in a further
realignment of policy. They agreed with France and Italy in
December to continue aid to Poland and the other border
States but to give nothing to the Whites beyond the consign-
ments that had already been promised. Early in 1920 the same
three Powers decided in effect to end the blockade of the Soviet
zone, and the British reached an agreement on the exchange of
prisoners. The undeclared Allied–Soviet war was thus ended
by an undeclared peace.[8]

With the eventual Bolshevik triumph in the Russian Civil
War intervention had failed in almost all of its objectives.
True, there re-emerged a Russian State free from German
dominance, but this was made possible less by intervention
than by the Allied victory over Germany in the West. And the
severance of Russia's borderlands made it unlikely that the
Bolsheviks would take up the Tsar's old function as an eastern
ally against Berlin. Nor did the Allied leaders accomplish the
broader, less anti-German aims for which intervention was
continued after November 1918. They shrank from committing
the hundreds of thousands of their own troops that would be
needed to overthrow Lenin, and discovered no White forces
strong enough to carry out the task. Given this, however, it is
unlikely that they missed an opportunity to achieve through
negotiation what was unattainable through force. An agreement with the Bolsheviks in the spring of 1919 would have
secured limited economic concessions and a decent interval
before the Civil War was fought to a finish anyway. But the
absence of agreement greatly complicated the peacemakers'
broader task. The Treaty of Versailles abrogated Brest-
Litovsk, required German forces to evacuate Russia when the
Allies saw fit, and reserved Russia's right to claim reparations.
Otherwise the country's future remained opaque, and the
peacemakers were obliged to decide the fate of Germany in
ignorance of how the chaos in the east would be resolved. In
addition, in the absence of a compromise with Moscow, the
Conference became self-consciously a gathering of capitalist
Powers, aiming not only to impose their will on the defeated
enemy but also to repel a challenge to their economic and
social system. The problem of responding to that challenge,

however, exacerbated rather than reduced their own divisions.

(ii) *The United States, Britain, and the League*

On paper, both the general principles of the peace settlement and many of its specific provisions had been predetermined by the Lansing Note. In the event, both the Germans and disenchanted Allied critics were to accuse the Western leaders of violating the letter and the spirit of the Armistice agreement.[9] Several of the general passages in Wilson's speeches were indeed ignored or interpreted one-sidedly, and the treaties much exceeded his territorial proposals. This, however, was not only because of the demands of Wilson's partners but also because of the American delegation's own inconsistencies and limitations. The contractual basis was anyway shaky. America had never been at war with Turkey and Bulgaria, and Wilson himself admitted that the Lansing Note did not cover the Austrian Armistice.[10] With Germany the contractual position was clearer, but the ambiguities in the President's speeches remained unresolved. At Wilson's request the Inquiry (now renamed the Division of Territorial, Economic, and Political Intelligence) tried to clarify the situation by presenting detailed territorial recommendations on 21 January and 13 February 1919. This was the nearest approach to a comprehensive American programme, but it was never officially approved, and Wilson departed radically from some of its suggestions. Individual members of the Inquiry served on the relevant Conference committees, but as a group the American territorial experts increasingly felt ignored.[11]

This was partly because of the Conference's structure. The Great Powers' own territorial claims—those of Britain, France, Italy, and Japan—were handled by the Supreme Council itself or in temporary and *ad hoc* committees. Only lesser questions went to the more formal committees of territorial experts appointed by the Council in February. These latter committees' recommendations, if unanimous, were accepted by the Allied leaders over everything except the frontiers of Poland. But the British and American experts were inadequately briefed, and repeatedly lost the initiative to their French opposite numbers. Although all the delegations had difficulty in presenting a consistent front across the myriad of Conference institutions, the Americans probably grappled with the problem least successfully. Their delegation rarely convened as a body. Of the five commissioners, three—Lansing, General Bliss, and the token Republican, White—met regularly to lament their ignorance, but saw little of Wilson and House. The Colonel deputized for Wilson during the February–March interregnum, and while the President was ill from 2 to 5 April. But from mid-March, at the latest, Wilson's trust in House was undermined by the latter's greater willingness to compromise with the European Allies and his failure to consult his superior. After early April none of the other commissioners had much influence on the President. [12]

As a negotiator, however, Wilson had serious failings. He lacked the stamina of Clemenceau and Lloyd George; as the Conference went on his health deteriorated; and he was sometimes unfamiliar with crucial points of detail. Economic questions interested him little, and he allowed his commercial and financial experts to pursue a course of American economic nationalism that harmed his broader goals. There was also a conceptual problem. Wilson came to Paris with his attention focused on the League of Nations. Once it was an accomplished fact, he said to House, 'nearly all the serious difficulties will disappear'. [13] His task was to achieve this at the outset, and then await the Allied claims, in the hope that the League would create a feeling of security that would allow these to be whittled down. On points of detail the American position would remain undefined, and Wilson would act as an arbiter, working with his expert advisers for a 'scientific' peace, based on 'facts'. [14] But this would place the initiative in others' hands. And after the League had been established, the differing interpretations of the 'facts' persisted. Before he arrived, the President confessed on 25 April, 'the difficulties here would have been incredible to me'. [15]

In support of the American programme, if reassurance through the League proved insufficient, Wilson could draw on sympathy from elements of European public opinion, on economic leverage, and on America's value as a potential

future ally. The last of these was probably most effective, but
none were decisive. The European Allied leaders, Wilson told
his experts, did not represent their peoples, and the American
delegation must ensure that the latters' will prevailed. Yet in
practice he avoided gestures of solidarity with the French
Socialist opposition to Clemenceau.[16] And his one attempt
to use the weapon of opinion—an appeal in April over the
heads of the Italians—actually strengthened the Orlando
Government's domestic position. His natural constituency
of moderate socialists and liberals controlled only the
Governments of the Central Powers, and was everywhere
losing ground to the nationalist Right and the pro-Soviet Left.
In December 1918 it was further weakened by Bissolati's
resignation from the Italian Government and the victory of a
Unionist-dominated coalition under Lloyd George in the
'coupon' election in Britain. Similarly, Wilson and his advisers
were aware of their economic and financial power, and used it,
notably, in the 1918–19 food-relief programme that was
designed to prevent the spread of revolution into Central and
Western Europe.[17] Yet at the Peace Conference they generally
threatened economic sanctions only over economic issues, and
in particular against attempts to redistribute inter-Allied debt.
The new American naval strength, too, was used to support the
American negotiating position only in naval matters. With
Italy again a partial exception, these levers were applied in
furtherance of direct American interests rather than against
European territorial demands.[18]

Conversely, however, Wilson's partners failed to exploit his
own main source of vulnerability. In the November 1918 mid-
Term elections the wartime American foreign-policy consensus
broke down. Wilson warned that in Europe a Republican
victory would be seen as a repudiation of his leadership, but the
Republicans won majorities in both Houses of Congress, and
the chairmanship of the Senate Foreign Relations Committee
passed to an inveterate personal and political foe of the
President, Henry Cabot Lodge. Lloyd George and Clemenceau,
however, were even more cautious about meddling in American
domestic politics than was Wilson about meddling in theirs.
Lodge warned Balfour in December that the Peace Treaty
would have difficulty passing Congress if the League were

included in it, but the British and French assumed in practice that Wilson would be able to get the Treaty ratified, and refrained from liaison with the Republicans.[19] Even before the Conference opened the Lloyd George Cabinet decided to accede to Wilson's wish that the Treaty should incorporate the League Covenant. As the Senate had never yet refused to ratify a peace treaty the President hoped by this device to disarm the opposition to the League. That *neither* might be approved seemed at this stage too improbable to contemplate.[20]

Both the Americans and the British could approach the European settlement with a primary interest in the stability of the continent as a whole rather than in more direct territorial and economic demands. The United States faced only the remotest of security threats from Europe, and its reparations claims were small, although it did require repayment of the wartime loans made to its allies. It could remove the precipitant of its entry into war by depriving Germany of submarines. Beyond this, its interest lay in stabilizing Europe as a peaceful trading partner, free from the extremes of both xenophobic nationalism and Bolshevism. A peace settlement that eliminated the roots of international tension—irredentism, trade discrimination, exclusive alliances, arms races—could become self-regulating, and the reserve guarantee embodied in the League of Nations might never need to be invoked. Although Wilson had a vision of this kind, however, his thinking was not, at least consciously, a sophisticated justification of American self-interest. On the contrary, he told his experts that the Americans would be 'the only disinterested people' at the Conference;[21] or, as he put it to Congress on 2 December, the essential aim was a more peaceful world, and achieving this would depend on implementing the programme embodied in the Armistice agreement. Even if he believed that his proposals were in America's as well as humanity's interest, he spoke habitually of the latter, and set up the ideal of an altruistic policy of service as opposed to European egotism.

The British Government more calculatedly pursued European stabilization as an extension of national interest. A basic Foreign Office memorandum on 'The Settlement' defined British goals in Europe as peace, stability, trade, and avoiding entanglement in a future war. Once the balance of power and the security of the Low Countries were assured, 'our interest entirely coincides with the principle of nationality, and the doctrine of self-determination'.[22] The influence of the Foreign Office staff, like that of the American experts, was confined largely to the details of the Versailles treaty.[23] But the 'Fontainebleau memorandum' of 25 March 1919, produced at a special weekend meeting between Lloyd George and his closest advisers, also advanced a stabilization concept. To be lasting, it contended, the peace must seem 'just' to Germany, and not drive it into Bolshevism or an alignment with the Soviet Union. German commerce should be allowed to recover, and as few Germans as possible come under foreign rule.[24]

Significantly, Wilson sympathized with the general thesis of the Fontainebleau memorandum rather than its specific recommendations. Both the British and the Americans aspired to a settlement that would endure without the continuous exercise of Allied power, and would therefore allow their traditional avoidance of obligations on the Continent to continue. League of Nations membership seemed an abrupt departure from American traditions, yet the very universality of the organization was intended to heal the conditions from which future wars and crises involving the United States might otherwise arise. But there were crucial differences in the prior assumptions of British and American stabilization policy, and the two delegations failed, except over the League, to form a common front against the demands of the other Allies.[25] For Wilson, justice required that Germany should be penalized for its misdeeds, and at least temporarily, therefore, the settlement would include a punitive, coercive strand.[26] Lloyd George, however, as the French Government's rebuttal of the Fontaine-bleau memorandum commented, assumed that 'just' demands existed that could be severe yet also win the Germans' voluntary compliance. But the French doubted whether any terms were acceptable to Germany short of an abandonment of everything the Allies had fought for, and they noted that the memorandum proposed to conciliate the enemy mainly at the continental Allies' expense. Britain's own acquisitions—notably Germany's destruction as a naval and colonial rival—would remain unimpaired.[27] British stabilization policy, in other words, was one-sided, possible only because the Lloyd George Government's own objectives had been accomplished in the Peace Conference's early stages, or even before it met.

The Armistices had already confirmed British occupation of the German colonies, Palestine, and Mesopotamia, Germany's expulsion from Belgium, and British possession of much of the German fleet. The Lansing Note had confirmed American support for Belgian integrity and independence. All of the Allies could agree, moreover, on stripping Germany of most of its army and navy, and the German disarmament clauses of the Treaty were settled by early March. The Armistice agreement had also respected Britain's right of blockade, and although Wilson had reserved the right to discuss the Freedom of the Seas at the Peace Conference he did not, in the event, revive the issue. The questions remaining unresolved were Britain's claims on German territory outside Europe, Anglo-American naval rivalry, and British economic demands. All but the last of these were settled in conjunction with the Anglo-American diplomacy that created the League of Nations.

This was made possible by the policy reassessment conducted by the Imperial War Cabinet after Lloyd George first met Wilson at Buckingham Palace on Boxing Day 1918. The Prime Minister reported that Wilson would give way on the points of substance that mattered to Britain if he could obtain the League. After debating the merits of co-operation at the Peace Conference primarily with France or primarily with the USA the Cabinet decided, with some reservations, in favour of the second. When the Conference opened Balfour and Lloyd George therefore disregarded French objections, and supported Wilson's desire that the League should head the agenda. The Conference's League of Nations Commission, which deliberated from 3 February onwards, accepted with little alteration the Anglo-American 'Hurst–Miller draft' of the League Covenant, and alternative, chiefly French, proposals were voted down. On the 14th, a plenary session of the Conference endorsed the Commission's recommendations.[28]

Anglo-American co-operation thus enabled Wilson to incorporate the League into the peace treaties, and the Covenant developed from an Anglo-American compromise. House and

Wilson had begun detailed drafting work only in July and August 1918, and the President came to Europe with his thinking even on this aspect of the settlement inchoate, and with a willingness to borrow ideas. On the British side Lloyd George and most of his Ministers treated the League primarily as a gesture needed to maintain co-operation with the Americans and to reassure domestic opinion that the Government supported a reform of the international system in order to reduce the danger of war. The two main British pro-League pressure groups had merged in October–November 1918 to form the League of Nations Union. In the December general election all the main parties and most of the press supported the League idea. But Lloyd George treated the details of the organization's machinery as being of small importance, and although his preference was for a weak, purely consultative, body, he delegated the negotiations at the Conference to the principal League enthusiasts in his Government, Smuts and Cecil.

Cecil had resigned as a Minister in November 1918, but was placed in charge of the Foreign Office's League of Nations section, and his 'Cecil Plan' of 14 December drew heavily on the earlier proposals of the Phillimore Committee. Smuts's memorandum, 'The League of Nations: A Practical Suggestion', advocated the model of Council, Assembly, and Secretariat that became the basis of the League's structure, and suggested that the League could act as a 'mandatory' for the States arising from the wreckage of the Austrian, Russian, and Turkish Empires. Wilson's 'Paris drafts' of the Covenant were indebted to both sources. He abandoned his first idea of universal compulsory arbitration, and dropped all reference to the Freedom of the Seas, justifying this afterwards by arguing that the concept of neutral rights would be obsolete in future wars, which the League would make the concern of all. From Smuts he took the League's institutional structure, and the mandate idea. From Cecil and the Phillimore Committee he took the procedures, eventually becoming the Covenant's Articles XII–XVI, for the peaceful settlement of disputes. Under these Articles, members in dispute would accept a cooling-off period, submitting their differences to arbitration, judicial settlement, or consideration by the League Council, and would refrain from war until three months after the judgement or the conciliators' report was known. If the Council, on which Britain, France, Italy, the USA, and Japan had permanent seats, was unanimous, except for one or more parties to the dispute, members would not go to war with any State that accepted the Council's report. If it was not unanimous, war would still be possible, although only after a delaying period in which public opinion supposedly could restrain the contestants. If a Government defied an arbitrator's award, a court ruling, or a unanimous Council report, members would be obliged to sever economic relations with it, but the Council could only recommend, rather than require, them to use armed force. Essentially these Articles tried to remedy the weaknesses of the Concert of Europe and the Hague Conference machinery, by admitting America and Japan to the Great-Power circle and by placing legal restrictions on the right to go to war. In appearance moderate, by rendering impossible a rapid and secret resort to force they actually struck at the heart of national sovereignty.

Although most of the Covenant was British in inspiration, it also paid lip-service to the Fourteen Points. Treaties were to be binding only if registered with the League and published; the Council would advise on armaments reductions; and members would seek 'equitable treatment' for each other's commerce. But Wilson's essential contribution was the general guarantee of members' independence and integrity in the Covenant's Article X, which in the vain hope of assuaging French security fears he deliberately deprived of flexibility.[29] Cecil's Article XIX, which gave the Assembly only advisory power to review international treaties, was too weak to counteract this freezing of the new international status quo. Embedded in the Covenant, then, were the British conception of a reinforced Concert of Europe and Wilson's notion of a general guarantee that would diminish international insecurity and allow a more detached discussion of the details of the settlement. It was a compromise, rather than a consistent scheme. Wilson later disarmingly admitted that Article X was 'binding in conscience only, not law',[30] but the Covenant was weaker than he would have liked, and much weaker than the French desired. Lloyd George, conversely, thought it too

restrictive of national sovereignty, but he wanted to humour
Wilson and anyway believed the League was less important
than the settlement's more specific terms.[31]

Anglo-American harmony over the League faltered over the
American naval programme and the mandate issue. The latter
produced a confrontation in the Council of Ten from 27 to 30
January, which was resolved by what became the Covenant's
Article XXII. This provided for 'advanced nations' to become
League mandatories over the Central Powers' colonial possessions. The 'A' mandates in the Ottoman Empire would
receive only 'administrative advice and assistance' prior to
independence. Germany's African territories would become
'B' mandates under the mandatory's direct rule, although
military and naval bases and the conscription of the native
population for other than defensive purposes would be
forbidden, and other League members would have equal access
for their trade. Finally, 'C' mandates in the Pacific would be
governed as 'integral portions' of the mandatory's territory,
subject again to demilitarization and the Open Door. As
League supervision even of 'A' mandates was confined to
receipt of an annual report, the system was *de facto* one of
protectorates and colonies. And the assignment in May 1919 of
mandatories for Germany's possessions generally followed the
wartime agreements and military occupations. The North
Pacific islands went as 'C' mandates to Japan, the South
Pacific ones to Australia and New Zealand. South Africa took
German South-West Africa as a 'B' mandate; Britain and
Belgium partitioned German East Africa; and Britain and
France partitioned Togo and the Cameroons.

Article XXII was drawn up by the British Empire delegation,
and represented only a nominal victory for Wilson. But the
President, unlike Lenin, had never championed national self-
determination outside Europe, and he considered the African
colonies a secondary issue. Even before the Conference, he had
accepted that Germany should lose its overseas possessions.
Whereas Smuts's 'Practical Suggestion', however, had envisaged that Russian, Turkish, and Austro-Hungarian territory
would come under the mandate system, Wilson deleted Russia
and Austria-Hungary but added Germany. This brought him
into conflict with South Africa, Australia, and New Zealand,

all of which hoped to annex the territories they had occupied, and the British Government felt obliged to support them for reasons of imperial solidarity. Given the modesty of Wilson's challenge, however, and Lloyd George's willingness to accept the mandate principle, compromise was relatively easy. Clemenceau, once assured of special French rights of military recruiting in West Africa, also acquiesced. And the Japanese delegates, while preferring annexation, had instructions to keep in line with British policy. Indeed, the 'C' mandates device helped to mollify the Australian Government, as well as serving American strategic purposes, by preventing Japan from fortifying its Pacific acquisitions. The British had therefore successfully eliminated Germany as a colonial rival while avoiding a breach with the USA. [32]

The second clash between Washington and London followed Wilson's visit home during the Conference's interregnum. In the 'round robin' of 3 March thirty-nine Senators and Senators-elect declared the Covenant in its present form unacceptable: enough to deny the two-thirds majority needed for ratification. In his Metropolitan Opera House speech on the following day Wilson warned that he would bind the Covenant and the Treaty inextricably together, but he also returned to Europe seeking three amendments designed to ease the Covenant's passage through Congress, of which the most important was a stipulation that the League would respect the Monroe Doctrine. This prolonged his diplomatic dependence on the British, and Cecil warned him on 26 and 27 March that Lloyd George would neither support the Monroe Doctrine reservation nor include the Covenant in the Treaty unless America concluded a naval agreement with Britain. On 10 April however, an Anglo-American understanding concluded the so-called 'naval battle of Paris', and with British backing Wilson was able to override French objections in the League of Nations Commission and carry the amendments that he required. [33]

After the Armistice the Royal Navy had quickly been subjected to drastic retrenchment, while its American rival was poised for rapid growth. The building programme already approved in 1916 would give the United States rough numerical equality with Britain in capital ships, and qualitative superiority. And in 1918 the Navy Department, supported by

Wilson, asked Congress to finance an additional programme. The navy saw this as a means of diplomatic leverage and an insurance against war with Britain and Japan; Wilson also thought it 'necessary for the accomplishment of our objects' at Paris, but was willing to suspend it as part of a broader armaments compromise.[34] In fruitless Anglo-American conversations during March and April Lloyd George and the Admiralty held out for Britain's traditional naval superiority to be recognized, but the Treasury in London was anxious to reduce armaments spending, and the Prime Minister was warned that if necessary America could outbuild Britain.

The 10 April understanding negotiated between Cecil and House reflected this balance of strength. The Americans abandoned the 1918 programme, but this had anyway been unlikely to win Congressional approval. House denied any intention of 'building a fleet in competition with Great Britain', and offered annual consultations over building plans.[35] But he refused to curtail the 1916 programme, and in May the administration confirmed that it would implement it in full. Lloyd George therefore failed to secure American acknowledgement of British naval superiority, and Wilson's diplomatic dependence on him was now at an end. So, more generally, was the Anglo-American negotiating bloc, which never became a concerted front against the claims of other Powers. This was partly because of Britain's secret wartime treaties with Italy and Japan, as well as a clash of personality between the two leaders. But an Anglo-American front would anyway have violated Wilson's conception of his role as arbiter, and although he admired British culture and institutions he felt no sentimental bond. The Americans, he considered, were no longer 'brothers' of the British.[36] His vision of a just, and if necessary punitive, settlement was potentially in conflict with Lloyd George's desire for a cheap, self-enforcing one. And in economic questions there was a continuing and tangible division of interest, to which it is now necessary to turn.

(iii) *The Economic Settlement, France, and Japan*

The underlying question in the Conference economic debates was the cost of war and reconstruction and by whom it should be borne. Taxation had covered the cost of war in proportions varying from one third in Britain to one sixth in Germany and France.[37] The balance was met through inflation and internal and external borrowing. Debt service accounted for 30 per cent of spending in the first post-war British budget, and for even more in French ones.[38] To restore balance by domestic measures alone would mean savage retrenchment or tax increases at a time of acute social conflict. Given that these internal budget deficits were accompanied by equally alarming external balance-of-payments ones it was natural for the European Allies to seek redress abroad, but this did not necessarily mean from the Central Powers. At the beginning of the Peace Conference they hoped rather that American altruism could relieve their difficulties, through a continuation of the wartime inter-Allied controls on shipping and trade and through cancellation of the wartime US Treasury loans.

On neither count were their hopes fulfilled. In December 1918 Clémentel approached the British for undertakings that France would receive credit, shipping, and commodities to escape 'a situation of inferiority resulting from the war'. The British, who also wanted to avoid too fast a deregulation of international trade, sympathized in principle, but subject to the position of the United States, which made no response to a similar French appeal.[39] Wilson had accepted the advice of his officials that the wartime inter-Allied agencies must be dismantled as rapidly as possible, and after the Armistice American representation on them was diminished or withdrawn. The State Department approved a memorandum by Hoover that wished to withhold support from 'any programme that even looks like inter-Allied control of our economic resources after peace', although this was thought too blunt to be communicated to the Europeans. At the same time as the Americans disengaged from the wartime shipping and commodity arrangements, however, they were determined that Hoover's new food-relief programme should be under their control, and by December this, with concessions to the appearance of inter-Allied supervision, had been attained.[40]

In the financial sphere a similar pattern emerged. American Government loans to the Allies in 1917–18 totalled some $9,500 million, or one quarter of American war costs and

40 per cent of the American public debt. Most of it was owed, in ascending order, by Italy, France, and Britain.[41] And although Britain's debts to the Americans were offset by its own loans to the other Allies it behaved at the Conference as a debtor rather than a creditor Power. Hence, although the Americans tried to veto discussion of inter-Allied debts at Paris, the subject was repeatedly raised. In April Lloyd George recommended to Wilson the 'Keynes Plan', under which the former Central Powers and the Eastern European successor States would issue £1,445 million of bonds, interest payments on these being guaranteed by the principal Allied Powers, the Western European neutrals, and the USA. Most of the proceeds would be distributed among the Allies as a first reparation payment, although the defeated States would retain a portion to finance their import needs. The 'ultimate share of each country', according to British calculations, would be nothing for the USA, £200 million for Germany, £225 million for Britain, and £500 million for France.[42] The scheme would give some economic security to the former Central Powers, hasten reconstruction in France and Belgium, and allow 'the acute problem of inter-Allied indebtedness' to be 'sensibly ameliorated'. Given that in the circumstances of 1919 the main purchasers of the bonds were likely to be American private investors, the United States was being asked to guarantee arrangements whereby its own citizens would enable the Allies to repay their war debts and would become claimants on Germany for reparations.[43]

Wilson's experts correctly advised him that the Plan was a veiled attempt at inter-Allied debt redistribution, and he told Lloyd George that Congress was unlikely to approve. He feared that the Plan would overload the capital market and fuel inflation in the United States, and he objected that the Allies were intending in the reparation clauses of the peace treaty to strip Germany of the very working capital that Keynes proposed to restore at American expense. In general the American position was that European reconstruction must be financed as far as possible through private credit. In practice this would certainly entail lending by American banks and other investors, but the American Government would be involved only through a three-year moratorium on the servicing and amortization of Allied war debts. The American Treasury held the Europeans partly to blame for their predicament, because of their disorderly currencies, labour unrest, and protectionist barriers to trade. And although (as Lloyd George remonstrated) America's public finances were much healthier than those of its partners the Treasury was worried about its own ability to fund its debt and about its diminishing gold reserves. Probably also, given how recently the United States had been a net recipient of European capital, it was anxious to preserve the country's new-won financial independence. It became clear, therefore, that the Allies would neither be able to preserve the wartime pooling arrangements nor obtain cancellation of their debts to the USA. [44]

American economic nationalism was not alone responsible, however, for the reparation demands of the Treaty of Versailles. Britain and France—which had the largest claims on Germany and provided the joint driving force—had independent reasons for their policy. Both Clemenceau and Lloyd George faced greater domestic pressure over reparations than any other issue. Moral, punitive motives lay behind their actions, as well as a desire for reconstruction aid. And reparations could weaken Germany's trading competitiveness and war potential as well as, in the French case, justifying a prolonged occupation of the Rhineland. The fighting had left a trail of destruction in northern France, and a legacy of inflation that threatened the savings of hundreds of thousands of holders of Government bonds. Either France or Germany, according to the Parisian press, must be ruined. A 'manifesto' supported in April by over three hundred French Deputies demanded not just reparation for damage but repayment of the entire cost of the war. [45] Official policy, however, was more ambiguous. The Finance Ministry, under Klotz, also claimed war costs and reparation for damage, as well as reimbursement of disablement and widows' pensions and the repayment, with accumulated compound interest, of the indemnity paid by France to Germany after 1871. Clémentel and the Commerce Ministry, by contrast, feared that large cash payments would dislocate the French economy, and make Germany more competitive by depreciating the mark; and wished to demand them only if inter-Allied co-operation came to an end. Once it became clear that it would indeed come to an end, Clemenceau's Reconstruction Minister, Loucheur, replaced Clémentel as his chief economic adviser. But Loucheur was also moderate on the reparations issue, and France therefore seemed to be pursuing a dual policy until Clemenceau eventually gave a lead.[46]

British behaviour was even more complex.[47] At the time of the Armistice the Treasury and the Board of Trade maintained their relatively lenient wartime position, advising that Britain should pursue only reparation for damage rather than war costs. But the Australian Prime Minister, Hughes, led the opposition to this in the Imperial War Cabinet with the argument that to claim only for damage would mean that the Dominions got nothing. Hoping to restrain him, Lloyd George made Hughes chairman of a Cabinet Committee on reparations, which reported, however, in favour of a claim for both damages and war costs, totalling £24,000 million. In the xenophobic atmosphere of the December 1918 election campaign *The Times* leaked details of the Hughes report, and at Bristol on the 11th Lloyd George committed the Government to press for costs, although warning against exaggerated hopes over German capacity and stipulating that payment must not take a form that damaged Britain more than the enemy. A Cabinet resolution at the end of the month, reflecting Ministers' scepticism about Hughes, authorized the British delegation 'to endeavour to secure from Germany the greatest possible indemnity she can pay consistently with the well-being of the British Empire and the peace of the world and without involving an army of occupation in Germany for its collection'.[48] Even so, Lloyd George always felt insecure at home over reparations, and at the beginning of the Conference Britain, like France, formally demanded war costs, thus contravening the Lansing Note.[49] Lords Sumner and Cunliffe, the British representatives on the Commission for Reparation of Damage, pleaded for a high assessment of Germany's capacity to pay. But in March the focus of discussion became the Council of Four and the *ad hoc* committees of experts appointed by it. In these latter Montagu and Keynes, who represented Lloyd George, were more moderate, but were unable to count on the Prime Minister's full support. And in the Fontainebleau Memorandum Lloyd George similarly gave an appearance of reasonableness while avoiding tying himself down.

American policy was more straightforward, and its crucial element was the fixed sum: a German reparation liability that was moderate and was specified in the Peace Treaty, on the basis defined in the Lansing Note. Naturally it was easier for the USA, with its negligible material damage, to take such a stand. But the fixed sum would also end uncertainty about Germany's liability, and create more favourable conditions for a European reconstruction financed by American private loans. At the Conference the French and British successfully challenged this position in a series of reparations controversies that centred on the definition of Germany's debt, the size and duration of its repayments, and the enforcement machinery.

Only over the first of these did the Americans have much success. In the Commission on the Reparation of Damage during February they countered Franco-British demands for war costs by holding to a strict interpretation of the Lansing Note, confining Germany's reparation liability to damage inflicted on civilian property, and to the death, injury, and forced labour of non-combatants. In the face of this, Klotz eventually softened his position, possibly because the French had seen that a more restricted claim based on damage rather than on war costs would entitle them to a larger share of whatever was actually paid.[50] The compromise eventually accepted by the Council of Four on 5 April was embodied in Articles 231 and 232 of the Versailles Treaty. Article 231 asserted 'the responsibility of Germany and her allies for causing all the loss and damage to which the Allied and Associated Governments and their nationals have been subjected as a consequence of the war imposed on them by the aggression of Germany and her allies'; but Article 232 recognized that Germany's resources were inadequate to meet the whole of this, and required it to compensate for the damage to the Allies' civilian population and property as defined in an appended annex. Article 231, later notorious as the 'war guilt' clause, was not intended primarily to assert Germany's moral responsibility for the war, although the Allied leaders certainly took that responsibility for granted. Its main purpose was to reconcile Lloyd George's and Clemenceau's political exigencies over war costs with the language of the Lansing Note. In that it effectively interred the claim to costs, however, it constituted the principal American victory in the reparation discussions.

This victory was largely nullified by the remaining provisions. To start with, 'Annex I', defining the categories of Germany's liability, included not only damage to civilian property and welfare as a result of invasion and land and sea attack but also reimbursement of separation allowances and of invalidity, widows', and orphans' pensions. Including pensions approximately doubled Germany's liability, and was urged by Lloyd George, with French backing, at the end of March. A memorandum by Smuts persuaded Wilson that the claim was compatible with the Lansing Note, and on 1 April he overrode his experts and agreed to it. This was easier for the Americans to swallow because they expected there to be a time limit on Germany's payments and the effect therefore to be mainly a reapportionment of receipts in Britain's favour. But there is no evidence that the British saw it in this relatively innocuous light, and Lloyd George threatened to leave the Conference over the issue. [51]

The time limit itself would anyway not survive much longer. At the end of March the Council of Four abandoned its attempts to agree on a fixed sum. Article 233 of the Treaty specified no figure, and left it to an inter-Allied Reparation Commission to assess Germany's liability by 1 May 1921 and draw up a schedule for discharging it over thirty years, but gave the Commission discretion to prolong this if need be. The solution arose from a proposal by Clemenceau in the Four on 5 April, when House was deputizing for Wilson. House disregarded the insistence of the American experts that the thirty-year limit should be final, and Wilson abided by the decision. [52] Two days later the Four agreed that the Reparation Commission would need unanimous approval from its member Governments before it could write off any of Germany's debt. Britain and France could therefore veto any reduction in the figure to be fixed in 1921, and German payments could be prolonged indefinitely. These were the main lines of the reparation settlement, although Germany was also required to pay 20,000 million marks in cash and kind before May 1921. Included in its reparations liability were the loss of most of its merchant fleet, and coal deliveries over a period of ten years that would average more than thirty million tons annually.

The reparation clauses of the Versailles Treaty were among the first to be challenged successfully by Germany, partly because German voluntary compliance was needed to enforce them, and partly because they caused the severest inter-Allied discord. The settlement, though arguably compatible with the Lansing Note, was a signal defeat for the fixed sum and for American diplomacy. Wilson was generally isolated over reparations, and France and Britain generally aligned, although Lloyd George's ambiguous behaviour obscured this. When the issue came to a head, at the beginning of April, Wilson was vulnerable over the Monroe Doctrine reservation and at odds with Britain over naval building and with the French over their territorial claims. His health was inadequate to the strain, and House, standing in for him, was anxious to break the impasse. As for Lloyd George, he had advocated a time limit in the Fontainebleau Memorandum, but did not subsequently insist. Delaying the fixing of Germany's liability would relieve him from domestic pressure and keep his options open. There was also genuine difficulty in assessing Germany's capacity and in evaluating damage, and this seems to have influenced Clemenceau.[53] But the upshot was that the economic legacy of Paris was almost wholly negative: inter-Allied co-operation would end, without the conditions being created for a reconstruction based on private American loans. After the Second World War the threat of expanding Soviet influence eventually elicited the Marshall Aid that removed the need for French reparation claims. After the First, however, subversion in Central Europe was contained comparatively cheaply by American food relief. American economic nationalism therefore enjoyed a freer rein. But French and British pressure over reparations would not have been eliminated by greater altruism in Washington. And for France, by the time Clemenceau gave his delegates a lead at the beginning of April, reparations had become integrally linked into a broader security programme. This brings us to the central Peace Conference issue of the protection of Germany's neighbours against attack and the collision between Anglo-American stabilization policy and French strategic needs.

By the time that Wilson and Lloyd George departed in mid-February most of Britain's objectives were secure and Wilson had gained preliminary approval for the League. During the succeeding, interregnum period Clemenceau presented his maximum demands against Germany, and the 'French crisis' of the Conference began.[54] By the last week of April it had been overcome, and Italian, Japanese, and German crises followed. In the discussions of Germany's European frontiers the French representatives held the initiative, both in the consideration of France's own borders by the Council of Four and in the deliberations of the relevant territorial committees. Part III of the Versailles Treaty, the 'Political Clauses for Europe', incorporated numerous Anglo-American modifications, but derived essentially from the French conception of the settlement.

This conception was related only indirectly to the demands of unofficial French opinion.[55] The Parisian press and Parliament were less united over security questions than over reparations, and support existed for a wide range of choices. French heavy industry had less influence than in the period of war-aims formulation under Briand. At governmental level, the Quai d'Orsay, like the British Foreign Office, was by-passed in December 1918. Unlike in London, however, Clemenceau's Cabinet was also not consulted until it was presented with a virtual *fait accompli* in the following April. None the less, Poincaré, as President of the Republic, and Foch, whose prestige as the Allied Generalissimo on the Western Front gave him a position without parallel in Britain, broadly supported the Government's initial negotiating stance. It was only after Clemenceau made concessions that consensus among the governing élite broke down.

The French negotiating posture, then, was decided by the Prime Minister and his circle of intimates, among whom he owed most to Loucheur and to the former French High Commissioner in the United States, Tardieu. Germany's borders other than with France were considered by Tardieu in a series of meetings that brought together representatives of Foch and of the Quai d'Orsay with members of the *Comité d'études*, an academic study group on territorial questions set up in 1917. It was agreed to support the Polish frontier claimed by the Polish National Committee, including a broad corridor to the Baltic at Danzig, although the 'internationalization' of this latter area was held in reserve as a compromise position. Similarly, France would endorse the Czechoslovaks' claim to the Sudetenland and the Belgian Government's designs on the Dutch territories of South Limburg and the left bank of the Scheldt, for whose loss the Dutch would be 'compensated' in Germany. Finally, Luxemburg was a potential gap in French defences, and many French officials believed its population wanted association or union with France. But the relevant meeting was unable to decide on how to reconcile this with the need for good relations with the Belgians, who had their own aspirations in the Grand Duchy.

There remained the Franco-German frontier. Clemenceau eventually demanded not only the Alsace-Lorraine lost in 1871 but also the 1814 border of the two provinces, incorporating two salients round Saarbrücken and Landau. He wanted in addition a nominally independent republic under French occupation in the remaining portion of the Saar coalfield. French claims in the Saarland therefore rested partly on a need for coal (and the return of Alsace-Lorraine would intensify French dependence on imported energy), partly on Clemenceau's sentimental attachment to the 1814 frontier and his belief that the local population was still francophile. The larger French objective was defined in February as a permanent occupation of the Rhine as a military frontier and the cessation of German sovereignty west of the river. The inhabitants of the left bank, argued Tardieu, would accept this if they were placed in one or more nominally independent buffer states, exempted from conscription, brought into the 'Western European customs zone', and given preference over Germany in raw-material supplies. German disarmament, he contended, though also necessary, could be evaded: only the Rhine military frontier could prevent another surprise attack on Western Europe. Nor was the 1918 revolution and the establishment of the 'so-called German democracy' a sufficient guarantee.[56] The French leaders hoped the revolution would encourage separatism, but they acknowledged that Germany could not be forcibly broken up, and intended to secure their goals through a combination of disarmament, reparation, economic constraints, trimming Germany's borders, and an indefinite occupation of the Rhine.

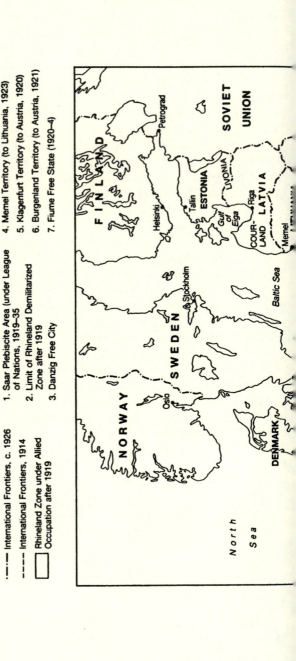

— · — International Frontiers, c. 1926

– – – International Frontiers, 1914

▭ Rhineland Zone under Allied
Occupation after 1919

1. Saar Plebiscite Area (under League
of Nations, 1919–35

2. Limit of Rhineland Demilitarized
Zone after 1919

3. Danzig Free City

4. Memel Territory (to Lithuania, 1923)

5. Klagenfurt Territory (to Austria, 1920)

6. Burgenland Territory (to Austria, 1921)

7. Fiume Free State (1920–4)

**North
Sea**

NORWAY

Oslo

DENMARK

SWEDEN

Stockholm

Baltic Sea

FINLAND

Helsinki

Petrograd

Tallin

ESTONIA

Gulf
of
Riga

LIVONIA

Riga

COUR-
LAND   LATVIA

Memel

SOVIET
UNION

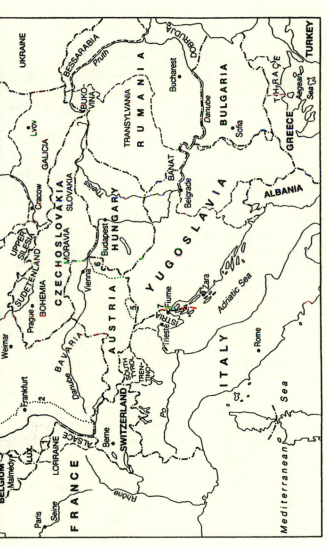

MAP 7. European Territorial Changes after the First World War

This must be seen in context. Clemenceau had warned the Chamber of Deputies that at the Conference the maintenance of Allied unity would be his 'directing thought'.[57] Just as Clémentel hoped that continuing inter-Allied economic co-operation might reduce the need for reparations, so Clemenceau was prepared to compromise on his security programme if the wartime alliance remained in being. But his interest was to avoid a choice. Independent action on the ground might create *faits accomplis* that would help towards this. Thus, military assistance was provided for the Czechoslovak occupation of the Sudetenland, and French trade was permitted with the occupied Rhineland as a signal to the separatist politicians there that they could campaign in public with French support. Clemenceau also attempted an advance understanding with Lloyd George. At the London Conference of 1–3 December 1918 he consented to a modification of the Sykes–Picot Agreement that would bring Palestine and Mosul under British control. Although nothing was written down, Tardieu asserted afterwards that the quid pro quo was British support over the Rhine, which when the time came was withheld.[58] Finally, there was an effort to humour the Americans. Clemenceau gave tactical support to the League of Nations, on the advice, probably from Tardieu, that it might cover a *de facto* American alliance. But the French representatives on the League of Nations Commission were excluded from the prior Anglo-American agreement. They proposed amendments that would perpetuate Germany's exclusion from the League, and give the League a military and naval planning staff as well as powers of surveillance over armaments.[59] When these amendments were voted down, Clemenceau's strategy was stalemated. *Faits accomplis* on the ground had been useful, but not decisive. The British evaded a diplomatic combination against Wilson. Nor had support for international organization elicited the American economic and security assistance that had been hoped for. During the February–March interregnum, in consequence, the French presented their maximum programme for their own frontier with Germany, and supported Germany's other neighbours in the Conference's territorial committees. When Wilson and Lloyd George returned to Paris, battle was joined.[60]

The President now confronted an unambiguous challenge to both the general principles and the specific provisions of his 1918 speeches and the Armistice agreement. He had hoped the League of Nations would give France sufficient security reassurance; he questioned whether Germany could be controlled permanently by military force; and he feared that a French garrison on the Rhine would encroach still deeper on Germany's independence and integrity. As for the Saar, to yield would violate national self-determination and set a precedent for Italy's claims.[61] At the height of the controversy over the coalfield he publicly summoned his ship, the *George Washington*, as a warning that he might leave the Conference. Whereas Wilson began from the Lansing Note, Lloyd George's starting-point was Britain's interest in a cheap, stable, and self-enforcing European settlement, now that its own maritime and colonial objectives had been attained. The Prime Minister wished, in consequence, to avoid creating reverse Alsace-Lorraines that would breed permanent German resentment. In contrast to Wilson, however, he objected most strongly and consistently not to French pretensions in the Saar but to a prolonged occupation of the Rhine; whereas Clemenceau always denied that Germany could be prevailed on to accept the settlement without the continuing exercise of military power.

The key to the compromise that emerged was limited sovereignty. Germany could keep the territory inhabited by Germans, but only with severe restrictions on its sovereign rights. This was already evident in the military and naval clauses agreed in March, about which there was little inter-Allied dispute. The preamble to the clauses justified them as a precondition for more general arms limitation, but in practice they constituted a drastic, permanent, and unilateral restriction on the independence of a major Power. A military commission under Foch recommended a small conscript army; Lloyd George won Clemenceau over to an even smaller one of no more than 100,000 long-service volunteers. The navy's battleships were reduced to six. Germany was allowed no General Staff, no military aviation, no poison gas, tanks, or submarines. All fortifications on the left bank of the Rhine and in a fifty-kilometre wide strip along the right bank must be destroyed. This was the first Anglo-American concession to French security needs.[62]

The second was the guarantee of France offered to Clemenceau by Wilson and Lloyd George on 14 March. Wilson seems not to have viewed it very seriously, disarmingly informing Clemenceau that it would amount 'to very little more than Article X of the Covenant'.[63] None the less the French accepted, and dropped their demands for buffer States and an indefinite occupation, but substituted the concept of one linked to the execution of the reparation clauses, with a right of reoccupation if Germany violated the demilitarized zone. After a month of deadlock Clemenceau and Wilson reached a compromise on 20 April while Lloyd George was away in London, which he grudgingly accepted on his return. The Allies would evacuate the Rhineland in three stages over fifteen years, provided that Germany faithfully executed the Treaty. If during or after this period it reneged on its reparations obligations, they would reoccupy the whole area. A later amendment gave France the right to prolong the occupation if after fifteen years the guarantees against German aggression were still deemed inadequate: a precaution apparently taken for fear that the Anglo-American guarantee would not be ratified. All of this supplemented the disarmament and demilitarization clauses, as well as the promise in the guarantee treaties signed conjointly with the Treaty of Versailles that Britain and America would immediately give assistance against 'any unprovoked movement of aggression by Germany'. In return for the deterrent of the guarantee, Clemenceau had abandoned his demand for buffer States, but had gained a permanently disarmed Germany and demilitarized Rhineland. Whether these gains could be enforced depended ultimately on France's right to occupy; but this, after the initial fifteen years, would depend on Germany's execution of the reparation clauses. Clemenceau's personal interest in reparations after April, and his resistance to a fixed sum, were therefore linked to his desire for a permanent security screen. 'Germany', he told his Ministers, 'will default and we shall stay where we are, with the alliance. Remember that, so that you can remind me of it on my tomb . . .'[64]

Limited sovereignty also offered a solution in the Saar. Just as Wilson and Lloyd George accepted a legitimate French security interest in the Rhineland, so both acknowledged France's right to compensation for the wartime devastation of its northern coalfield. Working on this chink in the opposing front, Clemenceau and Tardieu jettisoned the claim to the 1814 frontier, and asked for ownership of the Saar mines combined with a special administrative regime. For fifteen years, pending a plebiscite, France should occupy the region and have a veto over the local Parliament's decisions, thus gaining a continuing lever to win over the inhabitants. But in contrast to the Rhine dispute the French also continued to insist that Germany should lose *sovereignty* in the Saarland, at least during the transition period, and against this Wilson, without the backing of Lloyd George, held out. Under the compromise agreed on 9 April the Saar would indeed remain German until the plebiscite, but under the 'government' of a League of Nations commission. It would be in monetary and customs union with France, which would occupy it militarily and own the mines. The President's lonely stand had thus prevented a transfer of sovereignty in violation of national self-determination and the Armistice agreement, although at the price of stripping sovereignty of almost all its content.

In the discussion of Germany's southern and eastern borders the French won preliminary successes by championing in the relevant territorial committees the claims of Germany's neighbours. The British and American representatives on the committees had inadequate guidance and generally failed to take the lead, but anyway tended to sympathize with the new States' economic and strategic exigencies rather than a rigorous application of the national principle.[65] Thus the Commission on Polish Affairs recommended Polish annexation of the port of Danzig, which was overwhelmingly German, and of Marienwerder, which was a predominantly German district but one judged necessary to protect Polish railway communications in the corridor.[66] Lloyd George, with his usual fear of reverse Alsace-Lorraines, had recommended in the Fontaine-bleau Memorandum that the corridor should be drawn so as to include as few Germans as possible. He assailed the Danzig and Marienwerder recommendations. In spite of Clemenceau's misgivings, the Council of Four decided to hold a plebiscite in Marienwerder, which in 1920 duly confirmed Germany's continuing rule. Danzig, they agreed on 1-2 April, should be a free city under League of Nations guarantee and with a League

High Commissioner, but the Poles would control its railways, conduct its foreign relations, and incorporate it in their customs zone.

The Fourteen Points gave Wilson only ambiguous guidance over Danzig, and his sympathy for Polish aspirations induced him to accept an even greater breach of German sovereignty than in the Saar. Indeed, he would have conceded still more to the Poles had not Lloyd George's advocacy persuaded him that the French were simply trying to weaken Germany by giving Poland territory to which it had no just claim.[67] The conduct of the Polish representatives in Paris also diminished Anglo-American confidence in the Warsaw Government by making it appear more imperialistic and dependent on the French than was actually so. But even with the Danzig and Marienwerder provisions the compromise arrived at by the Four split Germany in two and deprived it of the major coalfield and industrial region of Upper Silesia, despite the latter's German majority. Given this, and given Clemenceau's broader desire for co-operation with the Anglo-Saxon Powers, his willingness to give way over the Baltic littoral is readily understood.

The future of the Germans previously under Habsburg rule, in the Sudetenland and Austria, occasioned much less debate.[68] The Commission on Czechoslovak Affairs agreed that the Czechs should have the Sudetenland, but disagreed over details, the French supporting the Czech claims for more than the 1914 frontier, and the Americans wishing to award them less. When House in the Council of Four on 4 April accepted a 'compromise' proposed by Clemenceau in favour simply of the 1914 line, the Czechs gained the substance of their demands. In Austria, the Provisional National Assembly voted unanimously in November 1918 in favour of *Anschluss*, or union, with Germany. Clemenceau, advised by Tardieu, wished to prevent it, on the grounds that the movement in support of it was artificial, that it would aggravate the Franco-German demographic imbalance, and that it would encircle Czechoslovakia. He proposed a German commitment to respect Austrian independence, and to this Lloyd George and Wilson agreed. In deference to the President, however, Article 80 of the Treaty made Austrian independence inalienable unless the League of Nations decided otherwise. This softened the challenge to the national principle and met Wilson's political requirements by ever more inextricably intertwining the League and the Treaty (as over Danzig and the Saar), while also leaving France with a right of veto. The British and Americans therefore showed comparative indifference to the two and a half million Sudeten Germans (and the seven million in Austria) as against the much smaller numbers in Danzig and the Saar. But here again Wilson had no clear commitment arising from the Armistice agreement, and the German Government itself gave lower priority to these areas than to losses from its own possessions.[69]

The remaining frontier questions lay in the north. In Schleswig, lost by Denmark in 1864, the French wanted a plebiscite in a larger area than was desired by the Danes themselves, who feared a permanent source of friction with their larger neighbour. Voting took place in two stages in a reduced zone in 1920, as a result of which the more southerly opted to remain within Germany.[70] In the Low Countries it was agreed that Belgium should regain its independence and integrity, and that Germany should cede it Eupen, Malmédy, and neutral Moresnet. Characteristically, the French successfully supported the Eupen claim on economic and strategic grounds, despite Anglo-American misgivings. The Belgians' territorial demands, however, were directed primarily against their neutral neighbours. Lloyd George and Wilson ruled out any compulsory transfer of territory by the Dutch, but the Treaty of Versailles left Luxemburg's future more open. The Grand Duchy lost its statutory neutrality, and withdrew from the German customs union. Ownership of its principal railway was transferred from Germany to France, and this gave the French a valuable asset in their efforts to trade concessions to Brussels over Luxemburg in exchange for Franco-Belgian economic and military co-operation. Finally, in the reparation clauses the Belgians, uniquely, won full reimbursement of the war costs, and priority over the other recipients in the payment of the first $500 million of their due. This they achieved by threatening in early May to withdraw from the Conference at a moment when the Italians had already done so and the Japanese were considering the same course. The 'Belgian crisis' at Paris, then, ended with remarkable success for the

Belgian financial demands, but much less for the territorial ones. [71]

The Four had now struck the compromises that determined the Versailles military and financial clauses and, with one major change in June, the future German frontiers. Wilson and Lloyd George, though lacking in co-ordination, had forced major French concessions over Danzig, the Rhineland, and the Saar. But over reparations Lloyd George had helped Clemenceau win arrangements that might justify a continuing Rhineland occupation far into the future. Even so, the Rhineland compromise was unacceptable to Foch, and the Marshal's press attaché engineered the introduction of a French Senate resolution, calling on the Government to insert in the treaty the 'military guarantees indicated by the Commander of the Allied Armies'. This was of dubious constitutionality, and Clemenceau and Pichon forced it to be withdrawn. At the crucial Cabinet meeting on 25 April Poincaré, though also disaffected, failed to intervene on Foch's behalf and the draft terms were approved. [72] Not only had Clemenceau reached agreement with Wilson and Lloyd George, but he could now be sure of carrying the agreement at home. The one remaining obstacle to inter-Allied agreement on the Versailles Treaty was Japan's Far Eastern demands.

Japanese claims were regional and limited, but advanced from a position of strength. [73] The Tokyo Government instructed its delegates to require the unconditional surrender of Germany's rights in Shantung and the North Pacific islands, but to try to keep in step with the other Allied Powers, especially Britain, and stay out of matters irrelevant to Japanese interests. [74] In the first phase the leading Japanese concern was to insert safeguards in the League of Nations Covenant against racial discrimination by member Governments against foreign citizens on their soil. But in the second round of discussions in the League of Nations Commission, after Wilson returned from the USA, every formula they proposed was rejected by Hughes of Australia. The British were unable or unwilling to override him, and Wilson and House, aware of the difficulties a racial equality clause would create in the Senate, offered Japan sympathy without effective support. At the crucial session, on 11 April, the Japanese asked for the Covenant to endorse 'the principle of equality of nations and just treatment of their nationals'. Eleven of the sixteen members of the Commission voted in favour; the British and Americans abstained; and Wilson, as chairman, declared that in the absence of unanimity the amendment was lost. The Japanese had taken up the issue for reasons of prestige and because of domestic opinion. In addition, it might facilitate Japanese emigration, and improve the treatment of Japanese-Americans.[75] But given this setback, and given that they received Germany's Pacific islands only under a 'C' mandate and therefore could not fortify them, they had reasons for dissatisfaction by the time Shantung came to the fore.

The ensuing dispute reached a climax between 21 and 30 April. Under the 1915 treaty, signed after the crisis over the Twenty-One Demands, China had agreed to accept whatever Japan agreed with Germany about Shantung, although the Japanese had indicated that when Germany's rights had been transferred to them they would, on conditions, restore the leased territory to Peking's control. At the Peace Conference the Chinese argued that this agreement had been extracted under duress and that their entry into the war had invalidated it: they demanded, in consequence, that China should regain all of Germany's rights. The Japanese, conversely, still intended to restore the leased area, but to negotiate this bilaterally, without outside interference, rather than as part of the general settlement.

Once again, the Fourteen Points gave Wilson little guidance. Aligning himself with the radical position of the Chinese delegation, he proposed that *all* the Powers should renounce their 'special rights' in China, but this Lloyd George refused.[76] The remaining options were to give way or to face a confrontation in highly unfavourable conditions. The Tokyo Government had instructed its delegates not to sign the Treaty unless they obtained satisfaction, and Wilson, unlike many of his subordinates in the American delegation, judged correctly that the Japanese 'are not bluffers, and they will go home unless we give them what they should not have'.[77] A creditor Power, with flourishing exports and a large mercantile marine, the Japanese could withstand financial and economic pressure.

They already occupied Shantung, and Wilson considered that American opinion would not support him to the point of war. He was also isolated. The Japanese had unambiguous backing for their claims in their 1917 agreements with the European Allies, and Lloyd George and Clemenceau made clear that they considered themselves bound. The Italian delegation walked out of the Conference on 24 April, and both the Americans and the Japanese were conscious of the similarities between the Italo-Yugoslav dispute—which had prompted this—and the Sino-Japanese one.[78] With Italy gone, and Belgium threatening to follow, Wilson feared that a split with Japan would break up not only the Conference but also the League. On the 30th he accepted a compromise mediated by Balfour. This confirmed that Japan would restore the German lease to China, but set no date for this, and the Treaty itself unconditionally transferred Germany's rights to Tokyo. The Chinese, therefore, refused to sign.

The compromise probably caused the President more distress than any other at Paris. But he saw the alternative as a possible Russian–German–Japanese alliance and a return to the old balance-of-power system he had hoped to destroy. If the Powers could be kept together and in the League, better might be achieved in future, including justice for the Chinese. It was a bitter irony that Shantung was a major reason for the subsequent defeat of the Treaty and the League in the American Senate. But for the moment the Allies were at last agreed amongst themselves on the Versailles terms. These had now to be imposed upon the former enemy.

(iv) *Versailles*

Until the Allies presented the draft treaty to the German delegation on 7 May the defeated Powers were excluded from the Conference. Even now, the Germans were permitted only to make written objections rather than enter round-the-table discussions. The Allies would accept only 'practical suggestions' rather than more fundamental challenges to the Treaty, and the exchange of notes was to conclude within a rigorous time limit.[79]

The Germans were caught off balance both by these restrictions and by the severity of the terms themselves. The Constituent Assembly of what was to become the Weimar Republic had been elected in January 1919. More than two-thirds of the seats were won by the SPD, the Centre Party, and the liberal DDP, who formed a coalition ministry under the Socialist, Scheidemann. A series of insurrections by the far Left, starting with the ill-fated Spartakist rising in Berlin in January, culminated at the end of April in a short-lived Communist Government in Bavaria. Because of their fear of the Revolution slipping out of their control, the Weimar leaders failed to purge the officer corps, and much of the Imperial civil service, including the officials of the Foreign Ministry, remained in place. The Foreign Minister from December 1918 to June 1919, Brockdorff-Rantzau, had been the wartime German representative in Copenhagen. He ruled out co-operation with Bolshevik Russia, and shared his colleagues' opposition to further radicalization of the revolution at home, despite his acknowledgement that this left Germany with few cards to play other than an appeal to British and American opinion on the basis of the Lansing Note. Even so, he was too optimistic in his predictions of the Allied terms.[80]

The immediate German reaction to the 7 May draft was that it was 'unfulfillable and unbearable', and contravened the Armistice agreement.[81] The main German reply, submitted on 29 May, was organized around this accusation. It accepted the disarmament clauses, though required in compensation immediate entry to the League. The reparation provisions it condemned as unjust and impossible to discharge, although it offered to pay 20,000 million gold marks by 1926 and up to 80,000 million more thereafter. But it concentrated its fire on the territorial issues. There should be a plebiscite in Alsace-Lorraine, and preferably also in Austria and the Sudetenland. The Poles could receive territory in Posen, but Germany should retain the Polish corridor, Danzig, Upper Silesia, and the Saar, and regain its colonies, although it might do this latter as a League of Nations mandatory. Finally, German democratization and League membership would better guarantee the execution of the Treaty than would a Rhineland occupation, and the Allies should therefore withdraw their forces within six months. [82]

Up until this point the Allied leaders had considered piecemeal aspects of the settlement rather than the treatment of Germany as a whole. They had decided at the outset against a fixed agenda, with the result that after initial delays the impatience of their public opinion and a new revolutionary upsurge in Central Europe had forced them to decide most of the German settlement in a scramble between mid-March and the beginning of May. Reparations and the Franco-German frontier were handled by the Four themselves; elsewhere they broadly adopted the recommendations of the territorial committees, except over Danzig and Marienwerder. Other Conference bodies drafted the commercial clauses and those demanding the delivery for trial of the Kaiser and of German war criminals. As late as March the Allied leaders appear to have supposed that the Conference was drafting a 'preliminary peace' that would then be discussed with the enemy at a broader 'Peace Congress', although their terminology was often inconsistent. Hence, the specialized committees could suppose the terms they were debating were provisional, and subject to later moderation. But in the event much of the Treaty had to be rushed into print at the last moment, and was available for scrutiny by the Allied delegations only hours before its presentation to the Germans. The terms shocked many in the British and American delegations when considered in their entirety, but the exhausting battles of the French crisis of the Conference had by this stage tested Allied solidarity to the limit, and it had become too dangerous to expose it to enemy probing. [83]

Yet despite these features of the Conference's organization the most contentious passages in the Treaty *had* been thoroughly discussed by the Council of Four, even if the intricacies of the lesser clauses had passed through unreviewed. Clemenceau, Wilson, and Lloyd George had no reason for surprise at the main provisions, and if they had insisted on carrying their delegations with them every inch of the way they would have reached no agreement at all. Broadly, Clemenceau's and Tardieu's conception of the settlement with Germany had triumphed, although with concessions to Britain's concern for continental stabilization and Wilson's preoccupations with the Armistice agreement and the League. The Allies had little heeded two points urged especially by the Weimar delegates: that Germany now had a democratic Government, and that it was threatened by Bolshevism. Article 231 explicitly made a moral connection between the new Germany and the war guilt of its predecessor, and although Wilson had earlier wanted Germany to be a founder member of the League, he changed his mind after the Armistice and considered democracy there was still too precarious.[84] As for the Bolshevik danger, by May it had passed its peak. Some junior members of the American delegation had been alarmed by it, but it seems to have influenced Wilson himself only over reparations. The American response to Bolshevism was to take executive measures, such as food relief, rather than to urge revision of the Treaty terms.[85] Nor did Bolshevism cause the French to compromise. Its strongest effect was probably on the British delegation, at the time of the Fontainebleau Memorandum, although even then it was only one of the considerations invoked by Lloyd George.

It is difficult to argue that the Conference's organization had made the German Treaty greatly harsher than the Four intended. But the organizational problem does help to explain the revolt that developed within the British delegation during May.[86] So does the German accusation that a solemn contract had been violated. Many British and American officials feared that the Germans would refuse to sign, thus forcing a choice between humiliating concessions and intervention with incalculable consequences. A final influence on the British came in the Rhineland, where General Mangin, the commander of the French Tenth Army, was in contact with a separatist movement headed by Dr Dorten. On 1 June Dorten launched a coup in Mangin's occupation zone, but got little support and had to abandon the attempt. Although Clemenceau was obliged to veto Mangin's activities, his Government had hitherto connived at them, thus feeding British suspicions that the French envisaged the Rhineland occupation as a political instrument.[87]

After the presentation of the final German note, the British Empire delegation deliberated on 1 and 2 June. The Rhineland occupation, the German–Polish frontier clauses, and—to a lesser extent—the reparation provisions came under the heaviest attack. Lloyd George was authorized to press for revision of the eastern border, for a promise to bring forward Germany's entry into the League if it met its treaty obligations, for a shorter Rhineland occupation with a smaller garrison, and for Germany to be allowed to offer a reparation fixed sum to be considered by the Allies. As he warned that persuasion alone would not suffice, he won agreement to refuse the use of the British army for an advance into Germany, and that of the navy for enforcing a blockade. [88] These proposals were still far short of what was needed to win Germany's voluntary compliance, and were open, like the Fontainebleau Memorandum, to the charge of being a one-sided programme of concessions at other people's expense. In the event, although Lloyd George duly delivered his threat in the Council of Four on 2 June, he ran into frontal opposition from Clemenceau, and the great majority of the Treaty terms remained unaltered in the final Allied reply to Germany on the 16th.

Wilson held the balance between his partners. The British initiative offered an opportunity to reconcile the Treaty more closely with the Armistice agreement. But over Poland and the Rhineland the President had always been closer to Clemenceau than was the British Prime Minister; and Lloyd George had decided against reconsidering the Saar. Wilson told the American delegation on 3 June that he was willing to remove stipulations that 'ought not to have been there', but not to make changes simply in order to get the Treaty signed. Certainly it was 'hard—but the Germans earned that. And I think it profitable that a nation should learn once and for all what an unjust war means in itself.' He could accept a plebiscite in Upper Silesia, and reconsider reparations if they were unworkable; but he could give no date for an early end to the occupation, as this would depend on Germany's entry into the League, and this in turn would depend on Germany's democratization proving 'genuine and permanent'. Finally, as over Shantung, he was anxious to hold the alliance together, and not to allow the Rhineland to push France and Britain apart. [89] American policy had completed another revolution in a recurrent cycle. Between August 1914 and February 1916, between

December 1916 and April 1917, and between January and April 1918 Wilson had three times shifted from relative impartiality towards Germanophobia. Now, once again, he had moved from a position of arbiter in November 1918 to one where he had accommodated the Allies' demands and was imposing terms unilaterally on Berlin. Probably, as before, breaking Germany's resistance had come to seem a precondition to the remoter goal of an international system reformed through the agency of the League. The imperative of diplomatic solidarity militated once again against negotiation and compromise. Wilson's attitude to Germany combined a punitive element with a desire to restore the prodigal to the family of nations; but in the short term (which might mean a generation) he placed chastisement first, and only later, after the Saar, reparation, and Rhineland clauses had ceased to operate, would reintegration follow.[90]

The President therefore refrained from exploiting Anglo-French dissension in order to bring forward new proposals of his own. His one initiative was to press again for a reparation fixed sum, but Lloyd George deliberately refrained from pursuing this, and instead joined Clemenceau in opposing it, citing as usual the constraints of British public opinion. Otherwise Wilson acted in his accustomed role of arbiter, and his attitude more or less determined the fate of the British proposals. Clemenceau argued that the more concessions were made to Germany the more would be demanded, and initially offered to reconsider only the cost of the Rhineland garrison. Wilson shared his view that it was too early for a commitment over German entry to the League, and the Allies promised only that political stability and fulfilment of international obligations would bring admission closer. But Clemenceau was isolated in his opposition to an Upper Silesian plebiscite, and was obliged to give way. This was the most important of the June concessions, although the eventual vote there in 1921 transferred most of the coalfield into Polish hands.[91] As over Danzig Lloyd George feared a new Alsace-Lorraine, Wilson accepted that national self-determination had been infringed, and Clemenceau yielded for the sake of the alliance and of more immediate interests elsewhere. Similarly, by satisfying Wilson's wishes for the Rhineland occupation to come under stronger civilian control, he sidestepped Lloyd George's more dangerous demand for a shorter time limit. The Rhineland Convention of 13 June made a civilian Inter-Allied Rhineland High Commission the Allies' 'Supreme Representative' in the region. But the Rhineland Declaration three days later contained only a hypothetical suggestion that if Germany gave satisfactory assurances the Allies might leave before the fifteen years expired. Essentially, Clemenceau had escaped unscathed. [92]

On 16 June a final memorandum, incorporating these painfully wrought accommodations, was handed to the German delegation with an ultimatum to sign. The Allied leaders agreed that force must be employed if necessary, and they refused a German appeal on the 22nd for a prolongation. They approved Foch's plans for an advance on Berlin from the south, and only the collapse of German resistance prevented these from being put into effect. The German delegates, in the meantime, had advised their Government that the changes made since 7 May were insignificant, or worse than what had gone before. They recommended rejection. [93] Thus far the German home front had been remarkably solid, and in a special session of the National Assembly on 12 May only the Independent Socialists had been reluctantly willing to sign. But now the cracks began to show. As in October 1918 this was fundamentally because resistance would inflict great damage on Germany without achieving better terms. But once again this unpalatable truth was accepted only by degrees, and after a ministerial crisis.

Erzberger, now Minister for Armistice Affairs, took the lead. In the Cabinet on 3–4 June he contended that at least signature would allow Germany to retain its unity and re-enter the world economy, and would diminish support for Bolshevism. The alternative was an Allied invasion that would cut off the southern part of the country and encourage Rhineland separatism, and culminate in 'Russian conditions', civil war in the cities, and an even harsher peace. At first only a small minority of the Cabinet supported this analysis, and decision was referred to the component parties. Most of the DDP were against signing, most of the Socialists (despite their leaders' opposition) were in favour, and the Centre once more held the balance. Erzberger manœuvred his party into accepting all but articles 227 (the trial of the Kaiser) and 231 (the war-guilt clause). When Brockdorff-Rantzau and his delegation returned from France therefore, they met strong opposition to their views. The Cabinet split 7 : 7, and on 19 June it resigned. The new Bauer Government, based on the Centre and the SPD, won authority from the National Assembly by 237 : 138 on the 22nd to accept everything except articles 227 and 231. The Allies refused to agree to this, and there was a new political crisis, during which it became clear that the opposition parties were unwilling to take the responsibility of forming a Government and Ludendorff's successor, Gröner, gave a qualified recommendation in favour of submission. On 23 June German resistance ended, and the way was open for the signing ceremony five days later in the Versailles Hall of Mirrors. [94]

At the last moment the German Government and the General Staff had recoiled from endangering the slow recovery of political stability by creating conditions that would benefit the extremists of Left and Right and the French military's separatist plans. Brockdorff-Rantzau's assertions that the Allies were bluffing—or that their unity would crumble once military operations resumed—remained unverified. The Germans' gamble in October 1918 that they could mitigate the consequences of defeat by accepting Wilson's programme had therefore yielded little, although Allied solidarity had been severely strained in April and June. In the end the British had fulfilled their naval and colonial goals, and the French, if less completely, their territorial and financial ones. The more specific of the Fourteen Points had been interpreted in the Allies' favour; the more general, except for such prospects for the future as resided in the League, largely set aside. But the settlement with Germany was only part, if the major part, of the settlement as a whole. The lesser treaties must now be considered before a conclusion is drawn.

(v) *The Settlement in South-Eastern Europe*

Against Germany the Allies were still strong enough to impose their will. In South-Eastern Europe their power was much less.

Italy had local military preponderance in the Adriatic, but only one battalion in the remainder of the region in August 1919, alongside 15,000 French troops and a mere forty British.[95] In practice, Poland and Rumania defied the rulings of the Conference with impunity. But for most of the time South-Eastern Europe was anyway a second-rank preoccupation for the peacemakers, and the treaties in the region had the appearance of assembly-line products, once the machinery had been devised in the struggle over Germany. The Treaties of Saint-Germain, Neuilly, and Trianon all contained the League of Nations Covenant and war-guilt and reparation clauses on the Versailles pattern, with the exception that the Bulgarian treaty, uniquely, contained a reparation fixed sum. Disarmament clauses, similarly, limited Austria's land forces to 30,000, Hungary's to 35,000, and Bulgaria's to 20,000 volunteers. As for the territorial settlement, its main outlines were decided by the revolutions and the movements of the local armies at the end of 1918. The Allies had little capacity to reverse these changes, even if they so desired. But the details of the new frontiers were mostly worked out in the Conference's territorial committees, and approved by the Council of Five or the Council of the Heads of Delegations. And the Council of Four itself approved in outline the new Austrian and Hungarian boundaries before the Heads of Government dispersed.

An incomplete summary of the Austrian treaty was handed to a delegation from Vienna on 2 June. The full text was presented on 20 July, and, after consideration of an Austrian counter-proposal, the Treaty was signed on 10 September. The Council of Four had already decided to prohibit *Anschluss*, and to include the Sudetenland in Czechoslovakia. In July the Council of the Heads of Delegations agreed to modify the previous border with Hungary in the Burgenland in Austria's favour: this was compatible with national self-determination and the need to protect Vienna against the Hungarian Bolshevik regime of Béla Kun.[96] Allied unity was tested more severely over the Klagenfurt basin, which was Slovene in the south and German in the north, and was occupied by the Yugoslavs after heavy fighting at the end of May and in early June. A compromise proposed by Wilson arranged for two plebiscite zones, the southern to vote first and, if it decided in

Austria's favour, the northern one to accompany it into Austria without a vote of its own. When the southern plebiscite took place in October 1920 this was indeed the outcome.[97]

In the Klagenfurt controversy the Italians supported Austria as part of a more general obstruction of Yugoslav claims. A reversal of alliances had taken place, and an Italo-Yugoslav antagonism had risen from the ashes of the Italo-Habsburg one. Yet Italian war aims had been realized to an extent that for the French, still facing a united Germany, was enviable. A Great Power of fifty million people had been replaced by the Austrian Republic of seven million and the fissiparous Yugoslav kingdom of twelve. Despite this, in the Italian crisis of the Conference at the end of April Orlando's Government not only reasserted the Treaty of London demands but went beyond them. The result was a bruising confrontation with Wilson that was still unresolved when the President returned home. Only after a long process of attrition did Italy gain the majority of its objectives in the November 1920 Italo-Yugoslav Treaty of Rapallo.[98]

The most striking feature of the Italian demands, apart from their extent, was the inconsistency of the arguments used to support them. In the north the Italians wanted essentially the Brenner frontier promised in 1915. In the north-east they wanted the 1915 line in Dalmatia and more than this in Istria, so as to include, in particular, the port of Fiume. Italy's African and Near Eastern aspirations had a much lower priority, and Orlando did not stress them in his basic statement of 19 April to the Council of Four. Nor did he dwell on the Treaty of London, asserting rather the arguments of a natural, geographical frontier in the Brenner and in Istria; Italy's historic ties with and strategic interests in Dalmatia; and national self-determination in Fiume.[99]

This combination of claims prevented the Italians from splitting their partners as had the Japanese, and was a grave tactical error. It resulted from a compromise between Sonnino and Orlando, and between two variants of Italian nationalism. Sonnino stood for goals inherited from the world of 1915, and for treating Yugoslavia as a reincarnation of the Habsburg peril. It was necessary, he maintained, to prepare for a new war in a few years' time, against the French and the South

Slavs. After the Armistice the Italians occupied Dalmatia up to the Treaty of London line, censored the local press, and purged the municipal councils. They continued to blockade the Yugoslav coast, and the Cabinet approved a secret General Staff plan to foment sectional conflict in the new Kingdom.[100] Sonnino and the naval Commander-in-Chief argued the strategic case for annexations in Dalmatia, in opposition to the Chief of the General Staff, Diaz, who thought they would be a liability. Presumably for reasons of negotiating tactics, and to maintain unity in his delegation, Orlando decided to support the Dalmatian claim.[101]

The Prime Minister himself, however, probably gave higher priority to Fiume. The city had not been promised in the Treaty of London, and constituted an Italian-speaking enclave. The 1910 Habsburg census suggested there was an Italian majority in Fiume proper, but a small Slav minority if the conurbation were taken to include the suburb of Sušak. But the claim had more of a national basis than that to Dalmatia, where there were 19,000 Italians and 611,000 Slavs.[102] On 30 October 1918 a National Council of the Fiume Italians proclaimed their annexation to Italy, and Orlando authorized an Italian landing in the following month. Sonnino appears to have had misgivings precisely out of fear that the operation would jeopardize a negotiating position based on Italy's treaty rights. But Orlando was now aligned with the extreme nationalist agitation led by Mussolini and d'Annunzio in demanding both Fiume and fulfilment of the promises made in 1915.

Opposition to Orlando in the Council of Four came primarily from Wilson. The ninth of the Fourteen Points had envisaged redrawing Italy's frontiers along 'clearly recognizable lines of nationality', but Wilson himself acknowledged that the armistice with Austria was a purely military agreement that was independent of the Lansing Note. He contended, however, that on grounds of equity the treatment of the enemy Powers should be consistent.[103] Yet much of the Italians' resentment stemmed from their belief that Wilson *had* departed from his principles to accommodate France and Britain, and that Italy had been picked on. Wilson, thought one member of the Italian delegation, 'wanted to retrieve his virginity at our expense'.[104]

Nor, in fact, was the President's an uncompromising stand on ethnic lines. In late December or in early January he agreed to an Italian northern frontier on the Brenner Pass. Later he regretted this and felt he had been badly informed, but he stood by the decision, and the Treaty of Saint-Germain placed some 230,000 Austrian Germans in the South Tyrol under Italian rule.[105] Elsewhere, however, Italy's claims were directed not against Germans, but against Slavs. When Wilson first met Orlando and Sonnino in December 1918 he accepted that Italy faced a continuing security risk in the Adriatic, and that Yugoslav naval strength must be kept limited. But he objected to a wholesale transfer of sovereignty in Dalmatia, and appears to have decided early on to make the Adriatic a test case. Having agreed a frontier with his experts in January, he defended it with little deviation from then on. The Adriatic became the classic instance of an American attempt to impose a 'scientific' solution derived from a disinterested academic assessment.[106]

In Istria the American experts proposed the 'Wilson line', which would give Italy the ports of Trieste and Pola and 370,000 of the 715,000 Slavs in the province. But in Dalmatia Italy should get nothing, although Yugoslavia should be allowed no coastal fortifications or naval bases. When the issue came to the Council of Four after 19 April Wilson proposed that Fiume should be a free port with considerable autonomy, but within Yugoslavia. Subsequently he agreed that it might be a 'free city', but Italian sovereignty he absolutely opposed, and if persuasion failed he was willing to apply pressure. In May the American Government took measures to obstruct private loans; and Bissolati had assured the President that Italian public opinion was 'waiting for the word' from him.[107] On 23 April, after five days of fencing in the Council of Four and unsuccessful Franco-British mediation, Wilson tested this by publicly appealing to the Italian people. On the following day the Italian leaders left for Rome.

As over Shantung, Clemenceau and Lloyd George occupied the middle ground. Both felt distaste for the Treaty of London, and preferred the Wilson line in Istria.[108] Both made clear, however, that if called upon to do so they would honour the 1915 undertakings. But these undertakings denied Italy Fiume, and Orlando would have to choose. Wilson declared that the Treaty of London contravened American principles, but the Italians failed to isolate him by abandoning Fiume and falling back on their 1915 demands. This was partly because of domestic pressure. A telegram on 14 April from 250 deputies demanded both Fiume and the Treaty of London gains.[109] Orlando predicted that the army would defy an order to evacuate Fiume, and that if Wilson got his way there would be revolution in Italy. In addition—although the Italians preferred not to admit it—annexing Fiume would assist the general strategy of weakening Yugoslavia, by depriving it of one of the best North Adriatic ports. All of this made Franco-British mediation unlikely to succeed. And the Italian leaders took with them on their return to Rome the 'Balfour Memorandum', in which Clemenceau and Lloyd George reiterated that they were bound by the 1915 agreement, but used very similar arguments to Wilson's against Italy's claims in Dalmatia, and opposed Italian annexation of Fiume. Even if there was no British–French–American front, there was no doubt that Italy was isolated in its stand.

The upshot of the crisis, however, was a stalemate that lasted more than a year. In Paris, the Fiume demand gave Lloyd George and Clemenceau the opportunity that they needed to avoid a breach with Wilson. But in Italy it was an issue on which strategic and self-determination nationalists could agree, and Orlando returned to a hero's welcome. Wilson had taken the plunge in the expectation that the Balfour Memorandum, or something like it, would be published, thus demonstrating that Italy stood alone. But although Clemenceau was willing to oblige, Lloyd George wished not to close all bridges to the Italians, and feared British opinion would not support him in a confrontation. He seems also to have feared that Orlando would be replaced by a Giolitti ministry that would presumably be a less reliable ally.[110] Hence Wilson's manifesto was ineffective; but the Italian leaders, conversely, left Rome on 5 May to return to Paris with nothing to show for their self-imposed exile. In their absence the Council of Four had distributed mandates for the German colonies on a basis that gave almost everything to Britain, France, and Japan. It had also allowed the Greeks to occupy a portion of the Turkish area allotted to Italy at Saint-Jean-de-Maurienne. Italian interests were therefore being compromised, and Lloyd George warned that if Italian representatives were absent when terms were presented to Germany on 7 May Britain and France would conclude that Italy was making a separate peace and the London Treaty had ceased to be binding.

Public gestures by both sides having thus failed, the Conference returned to secret discussion. Before Wilson left Paris the area of disagreement was considerably narrowed, and Orlando made most of the concessions. He agreed to abandon Dalmatia except for Zara, Sebenico, and the offshore islands, on condition that the Yugoslav coastline of the province was demilitarized. He accepted as a basis for negotiation the 'Tardieu Plan', whereby Fiume would become a free city under the League of Nations, pending a plebiscite in fifteen years. But Wilson wanted a plebiscite after five years at most, and wanted to enlarge the free city to include more Slavs, while reducing Italian influence on the governing commission. With this new failure to reach agreement the Conference abandoned its last attempt at compromise before Orlando's Government was defeated in the Italian Chamber on 14 June and Wilson and Lloyd George left Paris. None the less, the outlines of a settlement were becoming plain. Under the Austrian peace treaty the Italians gained the Brenner frontier and the Tarvis salient, with its strategic railways. They were willing to give up most of mainland Dalmatia, and they, the French, the British, and even the Yugoslavs were agreed in principle on a free State in Fiume. This left open the free State's boundaries and administrative arrangements, and the Istrian border.

The final stage of the negotiations proceeded within these confines. Lloyd George and Clemenceau were anxious for agreement, provided they could reconcile it with continuing co-operation with the USA. Orlando's successor, Nitti, wanted American reconstruction aid. In September 1919 a private army of Italian nationalists under d'Annunzio occupied Fiume, and Nitti considered his own armed forces too unreliable to eject them. Even so, France and Britain moved still closer to the Italian position in the 'Nitti compromise' of January 1920, and although Wilson's objections overthrew this arrangement, this was the last time he was able to prevail.

After the final defeat of the Versailles Treaty and the League of Nations in the American Senate in March, Britain and France no longer had much cause to antagonize Italy in the interests of humouring the President. The way was open for a solution through bilateral Italo-Yugoslav negotiations, which were driven to a conclusion by the Giolitti ministry that replaced Nitti in June.

The decisive conference took place in November 1920 at Santa Margherita Ligure. Giolitti was anxious to liquidate the expense and tension of the Adriatic conflict as part of a vain attempt to restore Italian political stability; his Foreign Minister, Sforza, hoped to include the Yugoslavs in a broader anti-Habsburg front of the Austro-Hungarian successor States. The Yugoslavs themselves were now willing to concede Italian sovereignty over Fiume, and the most serious issue was Istria, where Giolitti's Cabinet sought a strategic frontier, including Monte Nevoso, that was close to that of 1915. Before the November conference Sforza arranged for French and British warnings to Yugoslavia to settle now or accept a unilateral imposition of the London Treaty. After news arrived that the Democrats had been defeated in the American Presidential elections the Yugoslavs accepted virtually the entirety of Giolitti's terms, and the Treaty of Rapallo was signed on 12 November. Italy obtained the Monte Nevoso frontier, Zara, and four offshore islands, thus in effect renouncing the Treaty of London line in Dalmatia, but gaining it in Istria. Fiume, from which Italian troops had cleared d'Annunzio in September, became a small free State. Mussolini's Treaty of Rome in 1924 annexed the city to Italy and ceded the rest of the free State to the Yugoslavs, consolidating frontiers that survived for the next fifteen years.[111]

The Wilson line in Istria was therefore a casualty of the ebb of American power. The November 1920 free State was also much more favourable to Italy than the large, temporary, Slav-dominated entity that was the most to which Wilson had ever agreed. Dalmatia had been abandoned, but was of dubious value anyway. Eventually also the Italians received minor colonial compensations from Britain and France in Africa. Orlando's Fabian strategy, initiated after the confrontation of April–May 1919, had yielded fruit. There was little justification for the widespread Italian assessment, encouraged by the Orlando Government's own rhetoric, that only a 'mutilated victory' had been won. Whether it was worth the cost was another matter. The price of victory already included 600,000 dead and a shattering blow to Italian social and political stability. In the longer term, it included the eclipse of the liberal regime.

Elsewhere in South-Eastern Europe there was no comparable clash of Great-Power interests, and peacemaking was conducted at a lower level of decision. The Bulgarian Treaty, signed at Neuilly in November 1919, was drafted largely by the Allied Foreign Ministers and the territorial committees, in which the French and British were most hostile to the Bulgars, the Italians were willing to defend them as a counterbalance to Yugoslavia, and the Americans to do so on national self-determination grounds. Bulgaria ceded territory to Yugoslavia, although less than the latter wished. But the major difficulty lay in Thrace, which had hitherto given Bulgaria access to the Aegean. Its ethnic geography raised a characteristic Balkan difficulty, in that Western Thrace was in majority Turkish and Eastern Thrace in majority Greek. Athens claimed both, with French and British support; but in July Wilson proposed that the whole of Thrace should join a new internationalized State centred on Constantinople. The Treaty of Neuilly postponed decision on the issue, but the London Conference of February–April 1920, no longer having to heed American scruples, awarded the Greeks the whole of the province. As over Fiume, the American retreat from Europe made it possible to break the deadlock. In consequence, the settlement reflected British wishes to build up Greece and French ones to build up Yugoslavia and Rumania as reliable partners, and greatly weakened Bulgaria as a Balkan Power.[112]

The main decisions over Hungary's frontiers were taken in the first months of 1919 by the Conference's Committee on Czechoslovak Questions and its Committee on Rumanian and Yugoslav Affairs. The French representatives, seeking as usual to construct an 'eastern barrier' at the expense of the Central Powers, supported most strongly the claims of Hungary's neighbours. The Americans, once more devoid of guidance from the Fourteen Points, tended to give more weight to ethnic considerations. The British generally inclined to the French view; and the Italians were predictably hostile to Yugoslavia but sympathetic to Rumania, whose claims, based on the 1916 Bucharest Treaty, were analogous to their own. The Allies confirmed the transfer of Slovakia from Hungary to the new Czechoslovak State, and endorsed Czech claims to a southern frontier on the Danube. They also conceded most of Yugoslavia's wishes, although the main difficulty here was a Yugoslav–Rumanian dispute, over the Banat, which the 1916 treaty had promised entirely to Rumania but was now partitioned. In Transylvania also the Rumanians demanded what had been promised in 1916. The Committee on Rumanian and Yugoslav Affairs decided to award them a less favourable, more easterly line, but one that was still based on strategic rather than ethnic considerations and therefore gave rise to fruitless American protests. With the cession of the Burgenland to Austria, decided in July 1919, Hungary's frontiers had substantially been settled, and on the basis that the territorial committees had proposed. The defeated State lost two-thirds of its former area and population, and although most of this territory did not contain a Magyar majority, the border areas ceded to Czechoslovakia, Rumania, and Yugoslavia did. Under the June 1920 Trianon Treaty 3.3 million Magyars passed under foreign rule.[113]

The major problem presented to the Allies by the Hungarian settlement was not of agreement amongst themselves but of implementation. In the winter of 1918–19 there was a scramble to establish military occupation of disputed territories, and intermittent border clashes flared up between the Hungarians and the Rumanians and Czechs. Out of these events the Hungarian Revolution of March 1919 emerged. Budapest had already experienced a republican revolution in the aftermath of defeat; but unlike in Germany this led on to a Communist one, if of an initially moderate kind. In October 1918 Karl had appointed Michael Károlyi the last Prime Minister of the old monarchy. Károlyi, leading a coalition of his own Independence Party, of the Radicals, and of the Hungarian Social Democrats, hoped for good relations with the Western Powers. But the occupation lines established in the Belgrade

Convention between Károlyi and the Allies on 13 November were almost immediately violated by the Rumanians, and in Budapest, where a coal blockade paralysed the factories and railways, political opinion drifted towards the newly established Communist Party of Béla Kun. On 26 February the Council of Ten delivered the final blow, by approving a new demarcation line in Transylvania and a neutral zone between the Rumanian and Hungarian forces that pushed the latter back even behind the line promised to Rumania in 1916. By the time Vix, the head of the French military mission in Budapest, presented the Allied demands on 20 March, the Government faced a wave of strikes and land seizures as well as unrest in the army. Károlyi, now President of the Republic, considered his policy of co-operation with the West was bankrupt. He rejected Vix's ultimatum, and resigned. A new Government was formed under Béla Kun, based on a Socialist and Communist fusion. It announced that it would seek an alliance with Soviet Russia, and prepared to defend the frontiers by force. [114]

The events in Budapest coincided with a new revolutionary outbreak in Germany and with the crisis in Paris over the French claims. The risk of deepening anarchy in Europe caused foreboding in the American and British delegations and helped inspire Lloyd George's Fontainebleau Memorandum. But Hungary's borders with Czechoslovakia and Yugoslavia had already been virtually settled. The final Rumanian border, drawn in May, ran slightly to the west of the Rumanian occupation line contained in Vix's note, but most of the neutral zone remained under Hungarian sovereignty. This, and the later award of the Burgenland to Austria, suggest that Hungary was more harshly treated because of the Kun upheaval, but that the permanent losses inflicted on it as a result of the revolution were small. Instead, the Allied leaders' response to the Hungarian Revolution was primarily one of containment. The British and Americans were militarily powerless in the region, and at no stage were they willing to commit troops. Clemenceau did have forces available, but was extremely reluctant to use them. On 27 and 28 March the Four therefore rejected proposals from Foch for military intervention, opting instead to send additional supplies to

Rumania while keeping Hungary under blockade. They then received a note from Kun (who was anxious to win time in the hope that the revolution might spread), offering to negotiate. Wilson considered the Allies' own actions had contributed to Kun's rise. 'The only means to kill Bolshevism', he had said on 28 March, '. . . is to fix the frontiers and to open all avenues to commerce.'[115] But he agreed with the French that negotiations were impossible, and the Allied mission sent under Smuts to Budapest on 4–5 April was empowered only to listen to Kun and to present Allied demands. When Kun attempted to bargain, Smuts immediately withdrew.

As in Russia, then, the Four could bring themselves neither to intervene in strength nor to negotiate, and the situation was left to be resolved on the ground. On 13 June they made their strongest effort to assert control, sending notes to Hungary, Rumania, and Czechoslovakia to announce the definitive frontiers between them, and requiring their armies to retire behind these. Although Kun did indeed evacuate Slovakia, however, the Rumanians ignored the Allies' demands. Towards the end the Supreme Council hardened in its attitude, and on 26 July it in effect appealed to the Hungarian people to overthrow Kun if they wished for an end to blockade and foreign occupation and for peace to be signed. But it was still Rumanian troops, acting independently of the Allies, who early in the following month entered Budapest and terminated Kun's regime. They then repeatedly disregarded Allied requests that they should withdraw.[116] Only when they had at last done so was the way clear for the Hungarian delegates to come to Paris and for the Treaty of Trianon to be signed.

By the middle of 1920 the inter-war boundaries of the States of Eastern Europe, except those with the Soviet Union, had been resolved. Most of the frontiers in the region were decided with the participation of the American experts, but with little guidance, outside the Adriatic, from Wilson himself. Where the President did make a stand—over Fiume, Istria, and Thrace—domestic American developments undermined his position after the end of 1919. Italian efforts to moderate the treatment of the enemy States also largely failed. The broad lines of the settlement were determined by the local balance of power after the Habsburg Monarchy disintegrated, and this the Allied leaders had neither the capacity nor the will to rearrange. The details of the new frontiers, by contrast, were determined in large measure by the Conference territorial committees, in which the views of French and British experts predominated. These views, however, were generally acceptable to Czechoslovakia, Yugoslavia, Rumania, and Greece as the strongest local Powers. Perhaps for this reason, the Peace Conference was remarkably successful in its handling of the Balkan tinderbox, little though this compensated for its failures in the settlements with Germany, in Russia, and in the Levant.

(vi) *San Remo and Sèvres*

This leads on to the final and most evanescent of the Conference's products. American influence on peacemaking in the Near East was confined mainly to the period before Wilson left Paris in June 1919. Thereafter, the settlement with the Ottoman Empire emerged from Anglo-French discussions in September and December 1919 and from more formal sessions of the Supreme Council in London from February to April 1920 and at San Remo in April–May. This time France and Britain had more success in forming a prior diplomatic front and obtaining a settlement to their liking, although the outcome satisfied Paris less than London and the price paid for the combination was to forfeit Italian assistance in the task of enforcement and to necessitate reliance on Greece. In the non-Turkish outlands of the Empire, located in Europe and the Arab world, the Allies had the military strength to impose their will; but in the central promontory of Asia Minor, extending from Constantinople to Armenia and Kurdistan, their power was speedily confined to the coastal fringes. Their treatment of the periphery of the Empire and of its heart will therefore be considered in turn.

In Europe Thrace was awarded, in defiance of American wishes, to Greece. In the Arab lands American influence had two main results: the mandate system and the King–Crane Commission. Britain and France conceded from February 1919 that they would exercise authority as League of Nations mandatories. On 20 March, however, prompted by Anglo-

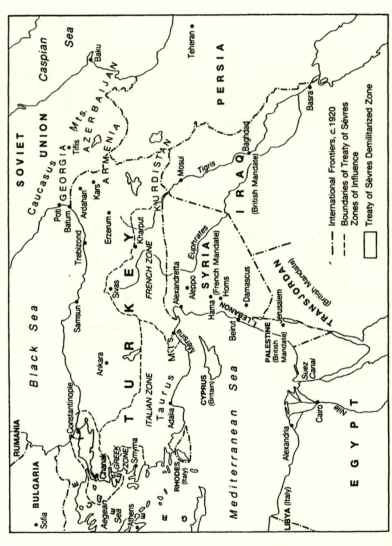

MAP 8. The Middle East after the First World War

French controversy over Syria, Wilson made the characteristic proposal that the Conference should send a commission 'to elucidate the state of opinion' there, and show 'that the Conference had tried to do all it could to find the most scientific basis for a settlement'.[117] Lloyd George and Clemenceau accepted rapidly and with subsequent reservations. Although the ambit of what became the King–Crane Commission was extended from Syria to the other Arab territories of the Ottoman Empire, the American Commissioners eventually went alone, without French or British companions.

Neither King nor Crane was a Middle Eastern expert, and they spent almost all their time in Syria. With all its limitations, however, their report, which was ready by the end of August, was some guide to the implications of self-determination in the Levant. Syria, they advised, should become with the Lebanon and Palestine a constitutional monarchy under Hussein's son, the Emir Feisal, with preferably the United States as mandatory or, failing this, Britain; but emphatically not France. Arab opinion strongly opposed Jewish immigration into Palestine, which should therefore be restricted. Mesopotamia should become another constitutional monarchy, with Britain as mandatory. Only this last point bore much resemblance to the distribution of mandates eventually agreed by the Allies at San Remo in 1920. France became the mandatory in Syria and the Lebanon, Britain in an area roughly corresponding to present-day Jordan and Iraq and pre-1967 Israel; and no limit was placed on Zionist settlement. Ironically, all these mandates, except Britain's in Palestine, were 'A' mandates under Article XXII of the League Covenant, with its stipulation that 'the wishes of these communities must be a principal consideration in the selection of the Mandatory'. But it is doubtful if Wilson ever read the King–Crane report, whose fate was another indication of the President's retreat into passivity after June 1919. And it became clear by the autumn that Congress was unlikely to sanction any American mandates, with the associated cost and responsibility. With the Unites States thus removed, the San Remo settlement emerged from a conflict between British, French, and Arab goals.[118]

The British had now to reckon with the consequences of the undertakings they had distributed in the Middle East during the war. The Bolshevik Revolution and the Fourteen Points had further complicated matters by causing France and Britain to modify the public presentation of their aims.[119] In June 1918 the British 'Declaration to the Seven' promised the Arabs 'complete and sovereign independence' in areas they emancipated from the Turks by their own efforts, although in practice the British allowed the Arab army to operate only in areas placed by Sykes–Picot under French control.[120] On 7 November Britain and France issued a joint declaration that they had fought for 'the complete and definite emancipation of the peoples so long oppressed by the Turks, and the establishment of national Governments and administrations deriving their authority from the initiative and free choice of the indigenous populations', although even this did not necessarily contradict the Sykes–Picot terms.[121] The most serious challenge to Sykes–Picot after the Armistice came not, in fact, from Arab nationalism, but from British revisionist aspirations. Once these aspirations had been modified and a new Anglo-French understanding had been reached the two Powers tacitly co-operated in imposing their will at the Arabs' expense.

In November 1918 the British had forces of over a million in the Middle East and enjoyed overwhelming military dominance. With limited Arab assistance, they had conquered Palestine and Mesopotamia, and penetrated deep into Syria. The occupation arrangements reflected this. The British High Command allowed Feisal's troops to take Damascus, which became the centre of a *de facto* Arab administration under the Emir. An Anglo-French agreement of 30 September had allowed the French to administer the southern part of the Sykes–Picot blue zone, but inland from the coast their influence was minimal. Lloyd George, meanwhile, considered that Britain had made the preponderant contribution to victory over Turkey, and should draw proportionate benefit. Sykes–Picot, he told the Cabinet, was 'altogether a most undesirable agreement from the British point of view'.[122] In December the Cabinet's Eastern Committee resolved to seek a British or American rather than an international administration in Palestine, and to expand the province's boundaries in order to incorporate territory from the French zone to the north. Britain should otherwise respect France's rights in the Lebanon, but must have exclusive influence over the emergent Arab State in Syria. In pursuing these ambitions the British benefited from the presence of a French Prime Minister who was willing, at least at first, to throw over the Quai d'Orsay's continuing attachment to the 1916 accord. In London early in December Clemenceau agreed with Lloyd George that a Palestine with redrawn frontiers should come under British control, and that Mosul with its oil should be transferred from the Sykes–Picot French ('A') area to the British ('B') one. But in return he probably expected not only British support in Europe but also an agreed share of the Mosul oil and British acknowledgement of French preponderance in the remainder of area 'A' and the blue zone.

This, at first, he failed to obtain. Although not seeking a Syrian mandate for themselves, the British endeavoured in the Conference's opening months to exclude the French from Syria either entirely or in all but name. They paid the expenses of Feisal's delegation, which pressed for independence for all the Arab peoples, and they pushed the French into discussions with him, warning that their forces would not leave Syria until British requirements were satisfied. The alternative, they feared, was a Franco-Arab war, and in consequence a more general nationalist upheaval that would endanger Britain's own position in the Middle East and the loyalty of the Indian Muslims. On the French side the sentimental and economic motives that had traditionally attracted the colonialist pressure group to Syria continued to apply, and Clemenceau himself was infuriated by Lloyd George's conduct and the sense of having been cheated in the December 1918 deal. From February 1919 the French position was redefined as being to seek a mandate over the whole of area 'A' and the blue zone, excluding Mosul only on condition of a guaranteed percentage of its oil. In May, after a series of explosive rows between the two Prime Ministers, discussions over Syria in the Council of Four and Anglo-French bilateral negotiations over Mosul and the Palestine frontiers reached an impasse. This continued until a change in Britain's position made possible an accord.

For practical purposes, British efforts to debar the French from Syria ended in September 1919. The colonialist agitation in the French Parliament and press helped persuade British Ministers that there was a danger of permanent damage to Anglo-French relations. The Cabinet was under pressure to retrench, and the Imperial General Staff wished to concentrate its forces on Ireland, India, Egypt, and Mesopotamia, and against civil unrest at home. The India Office, concerned lest pan-Arab agitation should spread into Mesopotamia, gave priority to the French entente. Lloyd George and Curzon, who replaced Balfour as Foreign Secretary in October, were determined to avoid a 'rupture with the French', whatever that phrase might mean. [123] Early in the month the Cabinet therefore authorized the Prime Minister to accept the replacement of British by French troops in the Syrian interior, and in Paris on 15 September Lloyd George confirmed this with Clemenceau. Feisal, not consulted, was urged to reach an understanding with the Paris Government, and in December he reluctantly agreed to a *de facto* French protectorate. But on his return to Syria he failed to win acceptance for these terms, and in March 1920 the Syrian General Congress in Damascus declared an independent kingdom with the Emir as its head. In July, after Syrian nationalists had launched attacks against the Lebanon, French forces moved in and quickly defeated Feisal, who went into exile. The British, who were suppressing a rising against their own authority in Mesopotamia, disapproved of the invasion but had been informed beforehand, and took no action.

Once the British had opted for Clemenceau rather than for Feisal the negotiation of the final disposition in the Arab lands was a matter of time. Under the San Remo oil agreement of April 1920 the French Government was promised 25 per cent at market prices of the output of the Mosul field if the British Government developed it; or a 25 per cent shareholding if the development was by private enterprise. France would allow two pipelines to run from the British oil concessions in Persia to the Mediterranean across its mandated area. The Syrian-Mesopotamian frontier was agreed in December 1919; that between Syria and Palestine at the end of the following year. At San Remo the French attempted to prevent the Balfour

Declaration from being incorporated into the British Palestine mandate, but an Anglo-Italian combination successfully opposed them. The outstanding issues were thus resolved, and French and British imperial requirements largely satisfied. The mandates system was a convenient artifice for placating Wilson and for genuflecting towards the McMahon–Hussein promises. The losers were the Syrian Arab Nationalists and Hussein's dynasty. The British supported Arab self-determination only until their perception of their interests changed; American support was more altruistic, but suffered from the weakness of America's position as a non-belligerent against the Ottomans, and from Wilson's preoccupations elsewhere. For the moment, an old-fashioned imperial bargain decided the fate of the Arab Middle East. What no one had to worry about was the former enemy.

This last was the outstanding point of contrast between the settlement in the Ottoman periphery and the settlement in the heartland. [124] For six months after the Mudros Armistice the disarmament of the Turkish forces proceeded smoothly, and there was little reason to foresee difficulty in implementing the eventual terms. During this period the leading problem for the Supreme Council was to adjudicate between Greek and Italian claims. But in doing so it took an action which meant that when treaty-making began in earnest the Turks were no longer behaving as a beaten race, and the enforcement problem had become very pertinent indeed.

    Italy claimed the Smyrna region on the basis of the Saint-Jean-de-Maurienne agreement, which Britain and France denounced in November 1918 on the ground that Russia had failed to ratify it. Italian pretensions to Smyrna were also challenged by a rival demand from the Greek Prime Minister, Venizelos. The Greek community in the region had been expanded by nineteenth-century immigration, and had suffered from deportations and atrocities during the war. In January 1915 Grey had offered Smyrna as the bait for Greek intervention, but this had not been taken up, and although Greece had eventually joined the Allies in 1917 no wartime pledges bound the latter over the city. At the end of January 1919, however, the British delegation decided to approve a

Greek zone in Asia Minor, and from now on the Lloyd George Government was Venizelos's strongest supporter: partly because it wished to keep him in office and exclude his more Germanophile enemies; partly because Greece appeared a reliable ally in the Eastern Mediterranean that could defend British interests without it being necessary to commit British forces; and partly because of Lloyd George's vigorous personal sponsorship. [125] In the Conference's Committee on Greek Affairs the British and French backed Venizelos's claims in Smyrna against Italian opposition; as did the Americans after Wilson returned to Paris in mid-March, and was swayed by his abhorrence of Ottoman atrocities and his growing antipathy towards Italy. And at this crucial moment Orlando and Sonnino absented themselves over the Adriatic issue. Intensely irritated by the Italians' behaviour, and fearing a pre-emptive Italian landing, Wilson, Lloyd George, and Clemenceau decided on 6 May to authorize the occupation of Smyrna by a nominally inter-Allied but in fact overwhelmingly Greek force. At the same time they denied that the city's eventual fate had been prejudged. But the Smyrna occupation set the spark to a Turkish resistance movement under Mustafa Kemal that made Greece indispensable to the Allied leaders if their designs for Asia Minor were to be realized.

Kemal was a regular officer with a distinguished wartime record, who had quarrelled with Enver and resented German as much as any other kind of foreign domination. After the Smyrna occupation a new nationalist movement, at first professedly loyal to Sultan Mehmet VI at Constantinople, began to coalesce around Kemal at Samsun. British officers in the interior noted the beginnings of opposition to demobilization and an erosion of the central Government's control. In January 1920 a newly elected Parliament approved the principles of Kemalist foreign policy laid down in the National Pact. The Bosphorus could be open to international shipping, provided that Constantinople's security was assured. The future of Western Thrace and of the Arab- and Kurdish-majority areas of the former Empire could be decided by plebiscite. Elsewhere, minority rights would be respected, but Turkey must enjoy complete political, financial, and judicial independence. This was a moderate programme of acceptance of the loss of the outlying areas but insistence on full sovereignty over what remained. And although prepared for limited co-operation with Soviet Russia, Kemal was a Western-orientated nationalist who from the beginning established contacts with the Allies that would later help him to undermine their fragile solidarity. [126]

By the time the Conference got down to serious discussion of the Turkish peace the Kemalists held much of the Anatolian interior. Preoccupation with the other treaties and with domestic questions was the main reason for delay, but there was also uncertainty over the future American role. A United States mandate over the Straits seemed to the British a cheap and attractive method of denying traditional rivals control over the waterway. House and Wilson expressed confidence at Paris that America would accept mandates in Constantinople and Armenia. But in November 1919, after the first defeat in the Senate of the Treaty of Versailles, Lansing warned that such acceptance had become extremely improbable. With American influence effectively at an end, the British accepted a French proposal for bilateral conversations before the Peace Conference turned formally to the Turkish issue.

Anglo-French discussion in London in December 1919 therefore preceded the more formal inter-Allied peacemaking at the London and San Remo Conferences in the following year. Most of the differences left outstanding from the first of these encounters were settled at the London Conference between February and April 1920, and the San Remo meeting was largely confined to ratifying previous decisions. By now Clemenceau wanted the Greeks to withdraw, and French preferences were in general for respecting Turkish territorial integrity while limiting Turkish sovereignty through disarmament and financial control. Lloyd George and the British Foreign Office, by contrast, although disagreeing with each other on several points, were less willing to adjust their policy to the rise of Kemal. In the events leading up to the Treaty of Sèvres in August 1920 Constantinople and the Straits, Armenia, and Allied spheres of influence in Asia Minor were the principal issues at stake. [127]

The French wanted continuing Turkish sovereignty over Constantinople; the British were divided amongst themselves.

Clemenceau believed a Turkish Government in the city would be more exposed to Western naval pressure than would one in the interior, and he feared unrest in Muslim French North Africa if the Sultan were dislodged. The British Government objected to the French proposal in part because French investors held most of the Turkish public debt, and it therefore expected France to have a powerful influence on the future Ottoman rulers. The status of the Straits was traditionally significant for British policy. It was made more sensitive now by the wartime closure of the waterway and the sacrifice of lives there during the Gallipoli campaign. Initially, as has been seen, Lloyd George favoured an American mandate over Constantinople and the Straits zone, but the elimination of this convenient possibility threw the question back into the melting pot. On 6 January 1920, the Cabinet rebelled against the Prime Minister and Curzon, and decided to allow continuing Turkish sovereignty over the city, relying on an international commission to control the waterway. The general unrest in the British Empire motivated this volte-face, much as it did the September 1919 change of line over Syria. The India Office feared Muslim disaffection in the Raj; the service departments shared the French opinion that a Constantinople Government would be more vulnerable, and advised that to go beyond a Straits Commission would overstretch military manpower. Finally—and this was reminiscent of the Fontainebleau Memorandum—the Cabinet feared a Kemalist–Bolshevik alliance. Acccordingly, the Treaty of Sèvres allowed the Turks to retain Constantinople after all, but the Straits and the Sea of Marmora were to be open in peace and war to merchant ships and naval vessels of all nations. A Commission of the Straits, representing the regional Governments and the Great Powers, would police and administer the waterway, and could call on Allied forces to maintain freedom of passage. [128]

Over Armenia there were similar signs of waning Allied confidence. Unlike the Arabs or the Smyrna Greeks, the Armenians lacked a contiguous area where they were numerically preponderant. Nor, after Tsarist Russia was defeated, did any external Power perceive an interest in taking responsibility for them that would justify the likely casualties and expense. An Armenian Republic was formed in 1918 on previously Russian territory, and in January 1919 the Council of Ten agreed that Turkish sovereignty over Armenia and Kurdistan must cease. But in August Britain began evacuating the garrison it had stationed in Turkish Armenia since the Armistice: the motives being cost, as usual, and fear of becoming through inertia a *de facto* mandatory. This, together with the rise of Kemal and the passing of hope for an American mandate, sealed the Armenians' fate. The London Conference agreed that a small Armenian State should be added to the existing Republic, but at San Remo the Allies decided they could neither guarantee the new entity, nor protect it beyond helping to officer and equip a defence force. By the end of 1920 the Bolsheviks had overrun the Armenian Republic, and the question had anyway become hypothetical. As for Kurdistan, the Sèvres Treaty provided for the Allies to draft a scheme for local autonomy there, and for a possible subsequent appeal to the League of Nations for independence. But essentially the nationalities lacking outside sponsors with the capacity or will to support them were abandoned when Turkish power revived. [129]

The Allies' own interests were to be protected by informal rather than formal control. The Sykes–Picot French and British zones in the Arab lands were sublimated at San Remo into mandates. But Sykes–Picot and the 1915 London Treaty had also envisaged French and Italian annexations in Asia Minor itself. In the Council of Four in May 1919 Lloyd George showed willingness to accept French and Italian mandates there; but then had to reverse himself because of a revolt from the War and India Offices, which feared that too naked a partition would be impossible to implement and would endanger Britain's authority elsewhere in its empire. From this point on the British consistently opposed mandates in the Anatolian interior, and in the December 1919 London conversations Clemenceau, needing British support to enforce the Treaty of Versailles, agreed to confine mandates to the Arab zones. The Italians were left isolated, and the original spheres of influence eventually survived in only vestigial form. Sèvres itself made no reference to them, but a British–French–Italian 'Tripartite Pact', signed concurrently, recognized Italy's 'special interests' in southern Anatolia and those of France in Cilicia and western

Kurdistan. In these areas they would have a right of first refusal on industrial and commercial concessions, responsibility for protecting minorities, and special claims to provide advisers for the local administration and police.

This compromise over spheres of influence appears less moderate in the context of the Sèvres provisions as a whole.[130] Turkish land forces were limited to 50,700 men, belonging mostly to a 'gendarmerie' that could be deployed outside its local districts only with Allied consent. The navy was even more drastically restricted; and conscription, military aviation, submarines, gas, and tanks were as usual banned. The Straits and the offshore Aegean islands would become a demilitarized zone, in which fortifications would be demolished and only forces under Allied command would be allowed to operate. Other clauses testified to the Allies' particular contempt for the Turks among their adversaries. The Constantinople Government must guarantee equal civil and political rights and protect minorities. The judicial aspects of the pre-war Capitulation system might be reformed, but the commercial ones would be restored. And a new Financial Commission, representing Britain, France, and Italy, received a veto power over the Turkish budget and over foreign and domestic borrowing, as well as authority to impose consumption taxes and raise or lower tariffs. Between them the new Commission and the pre-war Ottoman Debt Council, which remained in place, controlled all Turkish revenues.

The draft terms represented an accumulation of impositions that radically conflicted with the National Pact. Whether they could be enforced had still to be seen. In March 1920 an inter-Allied expedition occupied Constantinople and subsequently forced the Sultan to dissolve the Turkish Parliament and declare the Kemalists to be rebels. When the terms were presented to the Sultan in May, therefore, the Turkish nationalists no longer even nominally recognized his authority. Nitti warned that Italy would stay out of any hostilities that might ensue, and at the end of the month the French signed a ceasefire with the Kemalists in Cilicia. A new rebel offensive in June brought the Kemalists close to the Straits and the British positions. None the less, against War Office advice, Lloyd George stood by the terms agreed between February and April in London. One consideration still militated against compromise. Under the draft terms sovereignty over Western and Eastern Thrace, including most of the European coastline of the Sea of Marmora and the Dardanelles, would pass to Greece. In the Smyrna region Athens was made responsible for administration, public order, and defence, and Turkish sovereignty was limited to the right to fly one flag on a fort outside the city. Faced with the new Kemalist offensive, warned that French and Italian assistance would be unforthcoming, and reluctant to commit fresh British troops, Lloyd George at the Hythe Conference on 20 June won French agreement to authorize the Greeks to advance from Smyrna in order to force the Turks to submit. Venizelos's armies rapidly took over Thrace and cleared the Kemalists away from the Straits region. The Greco-Turkish war escalated up a further stage. But on 10 August the Treaty of Sèvres between the Allies and the Sultan's Government was signed. It was never ratified and neither in law nor in fact did it ever take effect.

Sèvres and its auxiliary arrangements were a thinly veiled system of imperialist control. In the former Ottoman Empire, as in China, the Allies repudiated annexation but infringed on sovereignty and the self-determination principle by less obtrusive means. In the settlements with Austria, Hungary, and Bulgaria, by contrast, national self-determination conformed more closely with the interests of the victor Powers and their local partners, although here also its application was selective. American influence on the lesser treaties was slight even before Congress repudiated the President, and only towards Germany were the Allies bound even formally by Wilson's principles. In the negotiation of the Versailles clauses themselves Wilson moderated aspects of the territorial and reparation provisions, but was handicapped by his preoccupation with the League and by a more fundamental imprecision of purpose that dated back to American entry into the war. His New Diplomacy failed to transform international relations, and the treaties served the traditional functions of registering a compromise between the victor Powers' interests, and their ability to impose their will on the defeated enemy.

The peacemakers could less afford than their predecessors at Vienna to show indifference to opinion at home. Domestic pressures probably inhibited Lloyd George over reparations,

Orlando over Fiume, and Wilson in that they obliged him to seek amendments to the Covenant in March–April 1919. The Supreme Council also faced a revolutionary upsurge that, as the Fontainebleau Memorandum pointed out, was still vigorous, rather than subsiding as a century before. Revolutions in Germany, Hungary, and Turkey all complicated the peacemakers' task, although only with Turkey did an appreciable modification of the peace terms result. Elsewhere the Allied leaders took executive action to contain the spread of Bolshevism, but largely ignored it in their legislative, treaty-making role. Finally, again in contrast to Vienna, the Conference had to minister to the needs of a Europe that was now industrialized and economically interdependent. Here American negative influence—against continuing the wartime system of co-operation and against remission of war debts—had major effects. No other Power could fill the gap. American economic policy, and the evident deficiencies of the League, ensured the domination of the Conference by Wilson's allies' drive to solve their economic and security problems independently, rather than through institutional co-operation.

Yet the victors also recognized that there were limits to their ability to reach their goals alone. Hence the British hoped to reconcile their other objectives with a lasting partnership with the USA; and Clemenceau attempted to consolidate the Versailles settlement by an alliance with the maritime Powers. There was a similar imperative to reach agreement for the fledgeling Eastern European successor States and even for the Italians, if less for the secure and isolated Japanese. In consequence a long and arduous process of inter-Allied bargaining became the Conference's central feature. Rather than repeat it, the victors imposed the results upon the enemy, and the exigencies of coalition politics not only helped prolong the war but now contributed to the unprecedented harshness of the peace. For the Versailles Treaty, even if justified, as Wilson thought, by the enormity of Germany's transgressions, rivalled Brest-Litovsk in being more exacting than any dictated since Napoleon's prime. And Saint-Germain, Trianon, and Sèvres were even more severe. The harshness of the settlement, however, fails to account for its impermanence. A war that had inflicted measureless sacrifice was now unable to redeem it with lasting stability. Instead, the treaties were revised with extraordinary speed, compromising first the war aims they incorporated and eventually peace itself. But this resulted less from the content of the treaties than from the failure to enforce them; and this leads back to coalition politics and the failure of the peacemakers to establish a consensus either between the victorious and the defeated Powers or among the victors themselves. This failure must now finally be set against its repercussions in the inter-war years.

Conclusion

BUT what good came of it at last? None even of the Governments of 1914–18, leaving aside the balance of profit and loss for their individual citizens, attained in full their wartime goals. Austria-Hungary was destroyed by the very combination of domestic uprising and foreign attack that its leaders had hoped by eliminating Serbia to hold at bay. Germany had more success in its objectives of weakening the encirclement by the Triple Entente and retarding the growth of Russian military might, but it failed to achieve the European domination that the war aims of the Berlin leaders envisaged as the necessary basis for survival as a world Power. And even the qualified success of its armistice appeal to Woodrow Wilson had only limited influence on the Versailles terms. For the defeated, the price of war was largely paid in vain.

Among the Allies, it was easiest for those outside Europe to fulfil their purposes at what, by the standards of the time, was an acceptable cost. Japan, indeed, although denied the League of Nations racial equality clause and Group V of the Twenty-One Demands, emerged with almost too complete success, and soon had to abandon many of its gains. By contrast, although American casualties were also comparatively light, Wilson won his League at Paris only to lose it in the Senate at home, and he was unable to ground it in a general reconstruction of the international system on the basis of his principles of open diplomacy, disarmament, self-determination, and the freedom of the seas. In the peace negotiations the President was trapped once more by the alliance logic that he had repeatedly attempted to transcend. The Covenant failed to moderate his partners' security demands, and became instead a guarantee of the embodiment of those demands in the new international status quo. Among the European Allies, Russia accomplished neither a Polish buffer State nor control of Constantinople, and a new regime had come to power for which Tsarist war aims, as yet, had little relevance. For the survivors from the imperial governing élite it was presumably little consolation to see Serbia enlarged and the hereditary Habsburg enemy brought down. Italy came closer to fulfilling its maximum ambitions, but did so in circumstances that left the leadership in Rome preoccupied with the incompleteness of what had been achieved. This left Britain and France, but especially Britain, as the Powers with the greatest vested interest in upholding the post-war settlement. The British had satisfied their naval and imperial concerns, while on the continent they had seen Belgium regain and France preserve its independence, and Germany so weakened as no longer to endanger the European equilibrium. Even Russia, the traditional competitor in Asia, had fortuitously been reduced to an ideological and propaganda threat, rather than a military one. As for the French, although compromising much more radically than the British on their initial Peace-Conference objectives, they too had made large colonial acquisitions and had won enough constraints on Germany to prevent it from again imperilling their security— for as long, at least, as those constraints could be upheld.

The Franco-British triumph was vitiated by its staggering cost in wealth and lives. For this the triple stalemate of 1914–17—in military operations, between the opposed home fronts, and between the two sides' diplomatic, territorial, and economic objectives—bore most of the blame. In 1918 the stalemate had been overcome: partly because of revolution in Berlin as well as Petrograd, and partly because of the displacement of coalition forces that permitted an approximation to a German–American deal. But the precondition for both Wilson's diplomatic triumph and the downfall of the Kaiser was the return to a more mobile pattern of campaigning and the defeat of Ludendorff's offensives by Haig's and Pétain's veterans on the Western Front. To that extent, although American aid was indispensable, France and Britain had made the victory, as well as emerging as its principal beneficiaries. They were to reap only a transient reward.

Earlier peace settlements had been modified in the defeated Powers' favour as the artificial preponderance bestowed by military success had ebbed. And all, eventually, had been engulfed by new hostilities. But much of the 1919–20 settlement had been revised within as little as five years of the treaty signatures, and the remainder was overturned within two decades. When war broke out again, moreover, it was substantially *the same* war—of Germany and South-Eastern Europe against France, Britain, Russia, and the USA—except that Italy and Japan were now on Germany's side and the Western European Allies fought at a greater disadvantage than in the first round. Yet whatever the deficiencies of the Treaty of Versailles, it had contained enough within it to make this outcome tragically unnecessary. When Hitler became Chancellor in 1933 Germany was still unable, as well he understood, even to threaten Poland convincingly, let alone attack a major Power. Versailles certainly failed to win legitimacy and German voluntary acceptance. But the failure of conciliation would have been manageable in its consequences had it not been for an accompanying failure of enforcement, and this second failure again stemmed in large measure from the functioning—or, more precisely, malfunctioning—of coalition diplomacy.

The non-enforcement of the German Treaty was foreshadowed in the non-enforcement of the Turkish one. The Treaty of Sèvres was the product of a Franco-British compromise in which the French, needing help in Europe, made the greater concessions. The United States had little part in the negotiations and the Italians felt they had little stake in the result. Implementation, given that Paris and London had other and more pressing military commitments, rested essentially on the Greeks, and proved beyond their strength. France effectively made a separate peace with the Kemalists at the end of 1920; in the next two years the Greeks suffered a military débâcle, culminating in their evacuation from a Smyrna left in flames. The 1923 Lausanne Treaty, negotiated on an equal footing between the Turks and their former conquerors, maintained the demilitarization of the Straits, but restored full fiscal sovereignty to Turkey, and lifted the restrictions on its right to arm. Given the country's limited strength, and Kemal's moderate goals in foreign policy, this first breach in the postwar settlement had few long-term repercussions.

But inter-Allied disunity also undermined the efforts of France—which had an analogous role to Greece as an enforcing agent—to uphold the Treaty of Versailles. Except at Brest-Litovsk, Germany had failed in its successive attempts to divide its enemies not only before and during the war but also at the Peace Conference. Yet in the next two decades Italy and Japan were lost to the revisionist camp; the Soviet Union and the USA oscillated between solidarity with the Western European Powers and isolationism; and Britain hampered French enforcement policy not only against the relatively innocuous Weimar Republic but also against a Nazi dictatorship whose expansionist ambition and whose creed of struggle as the natural law of international politics made even Ludendorff seem tame. The division of the victors enabled Germany to regain the military capability to launch a European war, and impeded the formation of a convincing deterrent alliance. In these circumstances, given Hitler's virtually limitless objectives and his incapacity for self-restraint, war would follow at the moment when the other Powers felt their vital interests no longer allowed them to stand by. With the demolition of the Versailles system of controls on Germany, the question became one less of whether than of when.[1]

Germany's recovery was the crucial step in the formation of a revisionist coalition against the victors of 1918. After the Fascist March on Rome in 1922 Italian policy was directed by a disillusioned interventionist who combined a Social Darwinist conception of the purifying role of bloodshed with a vestigial socialist resentment against the established, plutocratic, Western Powers and a determination to win Italian dominance of the Mediterranean and its shores. Only the re-emergence of a German counterbalance to France and Britain, however, allowed Mussolini to engage in more than piecemeal assaults upon the status quo. In 1935–6, after three years of hesitation, he threw in his lot with the revisionist forces, conniving at Hitler's remilitarization of the Rhineland and ceasing to resist the growth of Nazi influence in Austria. But by this time Hitler's crucial *fait accompli*—rearmament—was already substantially achieved. This made possible the Italian challenge to the victor Powers, rather than the other way round.

Japanese aggrandizement in Asia, similarly, directly threatened Western interests only after Hitler's European conquests in the summer of 1940 created a power vacuum in Indochina and the Dutch East Indies. True, the Washington Conference of November 1921–February 1922 had weakened the contractual Japanese connection with the West by replacing the Anglo-Japanese alliance with the looser Four-Power Treaty: an agreement by London, Paris, Washington, and Tokyo to consult if their Pacific interests were threatened. During the Conference the Japanese also negotiated an arrangement that restored to China most of their rights in Shantung, and soon afterwards they withdrew their forces from Siberia. In addition, under the threat of naval competition and possible war with the United States, they accepted in the Five-Power Treaty a statutory inferiority to Britain and America in capital ships.[2] Yet in practice, given the geographical dispersion of the Anglo-Saxon navies and the Treaty's offsetting provision that Britain would not fortify its possessions east of Singapore or the Americans theirs west of Hawaii, Japanese naval dominance of the Western Pacific was assured. The Conference opened a half-decade of ascendancy in Tokyo for the politicians who favoured peaceful, primarily commercial, expansion on the Asian mainland and satisfying Japanese economic and security needs through co-operation with the Western Powers. But at the end of the 1920s the military and industrial recovery of the Soviet Union and the restoration of an effective Chinese central Government under Chiang Kai-shek coincided with the collapse of Japanese exports to Western markets under the impact of protective tariffs and the Great Depression. With the onset of the Manchurian crisis in 1931 and the subsequent eclipse of parliamentary government the Japanese factions committed to the forcible subjection of an East Asian sphere, if necessary at the price of confrontation with the West, gained the upper hand. Even so it remained a British and American guiding principle, through the upheavals of the First World War, the Washington Conference, and the 1930s, not to risk war over Japanese expansion in China. It required Germany's destruction of the balance of power in Europe to produce the crisis over Japanese inroads into South-East Asia that precipitated the Pacific War.

The contribution of the new aggressiveness in Rome and Tokyo was therefore to accelerate French and British decline

once Hitler's breakout from the Versailles system had begun.
But a more deadly vulnerability of the post-war settlement was
Russia's conversion into a potentially revisionist Power. By the
end of 1920 Lenin had overcome the Whites and triumphed in
the Russian Civil War. But in Finland the Reds had been
defeated; Latvia, Lithuania, and Estonia had succeeded, with
Allied help, in winning independence; and in 1920 the Peace
Conference's Supreme Council confirmed the Central Powers'
earlier award of Bessarabia to Rumania. Above all, in the
Polish–Soviet War of 1919–20 the Soviet Government lost
not only pre-1914 Congress Poland but also a broad belt
of territory to the east inhabited by White Russians and
Ukrainians. As Poland had similarly won territory from
Germany in the west, there was now a permanent danger,
unless the new State became a satellite of Moscow or Berlin,
that a Russo-German combination would be formed to strip it
of its gains. But even if the two Great Powers remained mutual
enemies Russian troops could no longer threaten Germany
directly except by crossing the territory of a Polish Republic
that was unlikely to admit the Red Army voluntarily. In these
circumstances the survival of the settlement in Eastern Europe
rested in large measure on the network of alliances built up
there by the French in the 1920s and on French ability to
threaten Germany on the Rhine.

Soviet policy, however, cannot be analysed simply in these
terms. The loss of the western borderlands not only affronted
the Moscow leaders' residual Russian patriotism; it also
further dimmed their chances of exporting revolution. The new
regime found itself on the defensive at home—its natural
constituency in the cities outnumbered and surrounded by a
hostile countryside on which it depended for its food—and
isolated in an ideologically hostile world. During the 1920s the
Soviet leaders therefore tried to forestall another intervention
by exploiting capitalist divisions, and aligned themselves with
Weimar Germany against its Anglo-French enemies. They
withheld support from Western efforts to enforce the Versailles
reparation clauses, and helped the Germans to evade the
disarmament provisions. Once Hitler came to power, and
began rearming with the avowed intention of seizing living
space in the Ukraine, the Soviet Union attempted to restore the

Tsarist security alignment with the Western European capitals. But this was a more hesitant, ideologically divided, conflict-ridden grouping than the Triple Entente, and by 1939 Stalin appears to have concluded that France and Britain would tolerate German expansion eastwards, and give him little assistance in the event of war. Nor, this time, would alliance with the democracies relieve the Russians from anxiety in Asia, where in 1938–9 they fought a border war against the Japanese. Hence, at the crucial moment Stalin opted for a pact with Hitler that at least postponed a showdown with the Nazis and permitted him in 1939–40 to establish a security screen by absorbing eastern Poland and the Baltic States and by taking territory from Rumania and Finland. Hence also, when Hitler invaded Poland in September 1939 he could stage a local war, unlike Bethmann Hollweg twenty-five years previously, in the knowledge that even if it escalated he risked Great-Power hostilities only on one front. Nor did Stalin return to an alignment with the capitalist West until forced to by the Nazi invasion of the Soviet Fatherland.

America, too, wavered between an independent, isolationist policy and alignment with its former allies. Its most damaging isolationist impulse, however, came in the 1930s rather than with the rejection of the League of Nations a decade before. In itself, the League's defeat probably little altered American policy, and the issues of substance in Wilson's contest with the Senate are difficult to make out. The Shantung settlement, agreed to with extreme reluctance by the President himself, was unacceptable to Congress. But the Republican Senators generally supported the arrangements made for Germany in Europe, and most of them approved even so radical a departure from American tradition as the French treaty of guarantee.[3] Their differences with Wilson centred on the League Covenant, and especially on Article X, which he had elevated into what appeared to be a generalized guarantee of the international status quo and an unlimited commitment to intervention that alarmed even the more conciliatory Republican leaders. Yet Wilson reassured the Senate in August 1919 that in each specific instance of aggression Congress would retain its constitutional right to decide on whether to commit American troops, and that Article X was binding in 'conscience' rather than 'law'.[4] And Lodge, as the Republican leader in the Senate, proposed not changes in the treaty text itself but 'reservations', voted by the Senate as part of the instrument of ratification. The President, however, insisting (contrary to the Republicans' own assertions) that this would necessitate renegotiation with the Allies, would tolerate only 'interpretations', approved completely separately from both the Treaty and the ratification document. The result, shown in the voting of November 1919 and March 1920, was deadlock: no two-thirds majority for ratification either with the Lodge reservations or without them. In the Presidential election at the end of 1920 the Republican candidate, Harding, was swept to office. Although vaguely committed in his campaign to an 'association of nations', once in the White House he made no attempt to bring America back into the League.

This was much less harmful to the prospects of maintaining peace than it appeared at the time. Even within the League a United States with the Senate's prerogatives intact would presumably still have used its influence on behalf of caution, and the League was of only minor importance to international security anyway. More serious was that the League débâcle also prevented American ratification of the rest of the Versailles Treaty, as well as of the French guarantee, and this aggravated the European instability of the early post-war years. None the less, the Americans remained more interventionist in European politics than in any previous period. This was not intervention in the form adopted after 1945: there was no Government-to-Government aid on Marshall lines, no alliance treaty, and the last American troops left Germany in 1923. But during the 1920s, when Europe absorbed a small and diminishing proportion of American exports and no totalitarian State appeared capable of continental dominance, such measures seemed uncalled for. Instead, the primary instrument of American policy was the country's sudden emergence as the largest international lender. The Republican administrations of 1921–33 used the power of granting or denying access to the New York capital market in order to starve the Soviet Union of funds, to press the Western European Allies to repay their war debts, to encourage France and Germany to sign the 1925 Locarno Treaties, and to assist the 1924 and 1929

Dawes and Young Plan compromises over reparations. But the Great Depression stemmed the outflow of American private capital, and left Franklin Roosevelt after 1933 with no middle course between mere exhortation and the alternative of Government-to-Government economic assistance, military commitments, and guarantees. Simultaneously, the evident growth of danger both in Europe and in Asia pushed Congress and the American public into a much deeper isolationist mood. The Neutrality Acts of 1935–7 tried to bolt the stable door by requiring the President in the event of a foreign war to ban loans and arms sales to the belligerents and passage by American citizens on their ships, as well as giving him discretionary power to stipulate that American strategic raw materials could be purchased only in return for cash and if transported in the belligerents' own merchant vessels. British and French strategic planners—who assumed that a long war was the only war with Germany that they could win—now had to reckon with the likelihood that such a war would lead to bankruptcy with little prospect of another providential American intervention over the U-boat issue. Only after the Fall of France did Roosevelt feel able to make large inroads into the Neutrality Acts in order to keep Britain in the war. And by this stage Franco-British inherent strength had so diminished that it proved far easier to commit American power to uphold the European balance than to extricate it again.

During the 1920s both American and Soviet policy in Europe therefore aided moderate treaty revision. During the 1930s, as revision gathered momentum, both Powers chose crucial moments to retreat to isolation, and seek safety through an independent foreign policy rather than co-operation with Paris and London. In so doing they permitted Hitler, like Bismarck three-quarters of a century previously, to advance towards hegemony by piecemeal diplomatic coups and limited wars. By comparison with the pre-1914 period, and with the First World War itself, the fissiparousness of Germany's potential antagonists had become the outstanding feature of the international scene. This was also true of the central Franco-British combination, on which, if by default, the immediate burden of containment fell.

Not only were the French and British isolated; they were also, from the outset, divided between themselves. During the peace negotiations Lloyd George twice attempted to extract concessions to Germany at the expense of the French and their Eastern European protégés. After Versailles was signed J. M. Keynes's best-selling philippic, *The Economic Consequences of the Peace*, reinforced the view of British liberal opinion that the Treaty was unworkable and unjust. The arrival at the end of 1920 of mass unemployment in Britain's traditional export trades drove Lloyd George into a quest to re-establish commercial contact with Germany and Russia, and in this scheme of things reparations became an unwelcome hindrance to the Weimar Republic's economic recovery. More generally, postwar British Cabinets and public opinion were isolationist, francophobe, and hostile to commitments that might again embroil the nation in horrific sacrifice for very questionable returns. Even the guarantee of Belgium, the justification for British intervention in 1914, was allowed to lapse. And when the Americans failed to ratify the French guarantee the British Government also deemed itself no longer bound.

Following the demise of Clémentel's hopes for an international solution to France's economic problems, Clemenceau's international security solution—in return for which he had lessened his requirements in the Rhineland—had now also fallen through. For much of the inter-war period the French became seekers after a security commitment that neither Anglo-Saxon Power would give. Nor were France's continental security arrangements—a military convention with Belgium in 1920, and defensive pacts with Poland in 1921, Czechoslovakia in 1924, Rumania in 1926, and Yugoslavia in 1927—an effective substitute. These were not attachments to Great Powers, and if Soviet or German strength revived they might become liabilities rather than assets. Their value depended on France's own capacity to retain the margin of superiority over Germany incorporated in the Versailles terms.

This, it became evident, the French were unable to do.[5] Between 1919 and 1924 a cold war set a Paris Government bent on implementation (and even reinforcement) of the treaty clauses against a German one committed, as far as possible, to evasion. French policy was driven by a triple crisis. In the absence of Great Power guarantees, national security against an inherently stronger rival was inadequately assured. Second, the ratio of industrial strength, long unfavourable, was only temporarily modified by the Versailles provisions. The French steel industry remained dependent on German coal, and Germany's deliveries fell short of the quantities that the reparation clauses had specified. But the transfer of Alsace-Lorraine created no countervailing German dependence on French iron ore. The German steel industry successfully diversified its sources of supply, making greater use of scrap iron and of Spanish and Swedish imports. Aided by the depreciation of their outstanding debts as a result of the post-war rise in prices, the German steel firms compensated for the loss of their Lorraine mills by investing in new plant elsewhere. Conversely, on the eve of France's occupation of the Ruhr in January 1923, French steel production was only two-thirds of the pre-war level, and capacity lay idle for lack of coal. But the primary motive for the Ruhr occupation was the third aspect of France's post-war predicament: the desperate need for reparations to pay for reconstruction and to alleviate the deficits in the State budget and the balance of trade. After Germany's reparation liability was determined, as required by the Treaty, in the May 1921 London Schedule of Payments, the Weimar authorities within months pleaded inability to comply. During the 1920s reparations became the principal issue over which the battle to enforce the Treaty was fought, in large measure because it was the issue over which the victors were the most divided and because over it Germany could present them with acute dilemmas simply by suspending co-operation. When the French, after long inter-Allied wrangling, obtained resolutions by the Reparation Commission that Germany was in default on coal and timber deliveries, they went into the Ruhr with Belgian but without British support. They successfully overcame the German response of 'passive resistance'—a Government-financed general strike—and supplied themselves with coal from the region, but the more fundamental, financial, problem was one they could not solve by unilateral methods. The outcome of the crisis, negotiated at the London Conference of July–August 1924, was a French withdrawal from the Ruhr in exchange for German acceptance of the Dawes Plan: a new, easier payments schedule that was assisted by an initial German Government bond issue floated primarily in the USA. For the J. P. Morgan banking house to be willing to arrange the issue, however, the French had to reduce the uncertainty for potential American purchasers by accepting limits on the Reparation Commission's powers. For practical purposes they lost their ability to intervene unilaterally if Germany defaulted again.

This was only the beginning of a series of restrictions on the French enforcement role. Under the 1925 Locarno Treaties France, Germany, and Belgium mutually acknowledged their Versailles frontiers, including the Rhineland demilitarized zone, and Britain and Italy added their guarantee. Locarno at long last gave France the appearance of a British commitment, but one that was far from automatic in its wording, and did not extend to Germany's borders with France's Eastern European allies. Furthermore, the commitment simultaneously protected Germany against another *French* invasion; and during the Franco-German honeymoon period that followed Locarno the dismantling of the Versailles enforcement machinery continued. In 1927 the Inter-Allied Military Control Commission, charged with verifying Germany's observance of the disarmament clauses, was withdrawn. In 1930, five years before the expiry date envisaged in the 1919 Treaty, the last French troops evacuated the Rhineland.

For a time these concessions appeared justified by their contribution towards a more stable structure of peace. The late 1920s saw a return to prosperity in much of the capitalist world, an easing of domestic political conflict, and a short-lived international détente. After seven years of trial and error a suitable basis for world settlement seemed at last to have been found. Versailles was still the foundation, but it had been modified in the Far East by the Washington Treaties and in Europe by the Dawes Plan and Locarno. Franco-German economic rivalry was moderated by an inter-industry agreement on production quotas in the International Steel Cartel of 1926, and by a trade treaty in the following year. The United States reached agreement with its former allies on repayment of war debt, the Dawes loan inaugurated the long-awaited flow to Europe of American investment capital, and the currencies of the major industrial nations were stabilized and restored to convertibility on the basis of the gold-exchange standard. The potential revisionist Powers—Germany, Italy, the Soviet

Union, Japan—for their different reasons preferred limited co-operation with the West rather than an onslaught against it. And in this context of Great-Power harmony the League of Nations could resolve disputes between the smaller States with moderate success.

The equilibrium of the later 1920s rested on limited Anglo-American commitment in Western Europe and the Far East. More than anything else the threat of American naval strength had prompted the Japanese concessions at the Washington Conference; and Franco-German tension was alleviated by the primarily American Dawes loan and by the British Locarno guarantee. After 1929 this edifice disintegrated with terrifying speed, and dramatically exposed the limitations of both the American economic and the British political commitments. Even before the Wall Street crash new American loans to Europe dwindled, and existing ones began to be recalled. In 1930 an already highly protectionist American tariff was raised further at the same time as the Depression contracted American demand for foreign goods. These developments not only contributed to the exceptional severity of the German slump that was a precondition for Hitler's rise to power; they were also partly responsible for the snuffing out of Japanese democracy and Tokyo's return to the forcible pursuit of an East Asian sphere. The Depression, as has been seen, deprived the Americans of a convenient tool of policy and helped push them into isolationism at the very moment when their stabiliz-ing influence was most needed. But the international economic breakdown was paralleled in 1933–6 by the crucial Franco-British failure to intervene directly against Hitler's establish-ment of a dictatorship, his launching of rearmament, and his remilitarization of the Rhineland. A moment of opportunity, if a brief one, existed to curtail the Nazis before they could offer serious military resistance and before much harder choices were presented later on. But the British reaction to the new regime in Germany was to continue to seek agreement by negotiation, while beginning, cautiously and belatedly, to rearm. France also, after its 1923 experience, shrank back from unilateral intervention and tried instead to construct an en-circling alliance. This bore fruit in the Franco-Italian Rome Agreements and the Franco-Soviet Pact of 1935, and the conversion of Locarno after the March 1936 Rhineland crisis into a one-sided British guarantee of France against Germany. But Hitler detached Mussolini from this incipient coalition in 1935-6, and three years later Stalin, too, went his own way. Even the British fought shy of joint military planning on pre-1914 lines, and continued, with scant regard for French susceptibilities, their pursuit of an accommodation with Berlin. Only in March 1939, when Hitler tore up the Munich Agreement by occupying Prague, did it become unequivocally clear in London that his ambitions were not confined to incorporating Germans in the Reich, and potentially had no bounds. By guaranteeing Poland on 31 March, and by fighting five months later to honour the guarantee, Neville Chamberlain's Cabinet concluded as had the majority of Lloyd George's in 1917-18 that Britain could not tolerate the overthrow of the Eastern European balance of power.

Once Germany had begun rearming and had remilitarized the Rhineland the fragility of Western European preponderance became glaringly apparent. During the 1920s, when the revisionist Powers had been relatively weak and cautious, and economic rather than strategic issues had dominated European diplomacy, disunity among the victors had mattered little. But now the sudden emergence of a triple threat—from Germany, Italy, and Japan—left France overextended within Europe and Britain overextended world-wide. Hence the dismaying history of the 1930s was played out in a Europe insulated, for the last time, from the presence of the future Superpowers. Indeed, many of the long-term, seemingly inexorable, tendencies underlying the nineteenth-century international system were suspended in their operation in the inter-war years. The evolution from a single European into a global balance of power was halted; so was international economic integration. Not until 1924 did the volume of world trade recover to the pre-war figure, and throughout the 1930s it remained below the level of 1929. The emerging pattern was of regional blocs, protected by tariff and quota barriers and exchange controls, and of chronic unemployment in the export trades. Nor could the inter-war experiments in institutional co-operation check the deterioration after 1929. The League of Nations, though more ambitious than the Concert of Europe, altered the behaviour, if of anyone at all, only of the status quo Powers. It began and ended as a creature of the Western States, and its strength and effectiveness ebbed with theirs. Finally, the revelations of 1914–18 about the destructive power of modern warfare were ambiguous in their effects. In France and Britain, again as status quo Powers, it seemed obvious that major wars were all but redundant as an instrument of policy and that another must be avoided at almost any cost. Yet the trench stalemate *had* eventually been broken; and for others, including Hitler, a further revolution in weapons technology after 1918 promised a return to sharp, decisive, Bismarckian blows. Once the demolition of the 1920s equilibrium began, therefore, the underlying tendencies of international politics were no more able than before 1914 to arrest the slide to war.

After 1945, by contrast, the long-term nineteenth-century tendencies were reasserted with commanding force. Soviet and American armies met each other in the middle of Europe, and there they stayed. Economic integration between the capitalist States, including West Germany and France, reached unprecedented levels. And about the uncontrollability of warfare with the yet more powerful armaments that now became available there could be little room for doubt. At first sight also the 1940s brought about a diplomatic revolution, in which Italy, Japan, and most of Germany took up alignment with France, Britain, and the USA. A new era appeared to have begun, in which the anti-German combination formed in 1904–7 had finally been superseded and the most serious threat to peace arose from the divisions of Germany's former enemies. And yet, embedded in and indispensable to the more enduring settlement constructed after 1945, the containment of Germany lingered. The Soviet Union succeeded where France had failed, as a durable enforcing agent. Together with its allies it annexed one quarter of Germany's 1937 territory, and in a second quarter it set up a satellite regime. With Soviet tanks and missiles on the Elbe, any renewal of hostilities would lead immediately to the loss of West Berlin and to the devastation of West German soil. Only on this bedrock of a permanent and fundamental weakening in Germany's international status could the integration of the Federal Republic into the Western camp (itself conditional on the renunciation of independent nuclear weapons) successfully proceed. After the Berlin Wall was built in 1961 both major parties in West Germany acknowledged that the Democratic Republic would not speedily collapse from its own shortcomings, and by this stage the Social Democrats had followed Adenauer's Christian Democrats in conceding that detachment from the Western alliance in exchange for reunification would be too high a price to pay. Germany's containment had come to be accepted, at least provisionally, by most of the Germans themselves.

For the settlement after 1945 to last, however, it needed to command acceptance not only in the Federal Republic but also in France. Yet in 1944–6 French Governments had pursued even more draconian territorial and economic demands on Germany than in 1919. As in 1924–5 an Anglo-American commitment was required to transcend the Franco-German divide. Marshall Aid removed the necessity to pursue West German reparations; and the 1948 Brussels Pact, the 1949 North Atlantic Treaty, and the 1954 Paris Agreements on West German rearmament assured France of a continuing British and American commitment to safeguard its own security against Germany as well as that of Western Europe as a whole against the Soviet threat. The Cold War between East and West elicited the American and British undertakings that had been absent or deficient in the inter-war years, and which otherwise would probably have been so again. Only on this basis could France and Germany move on to economic *rapprochement*, with the 1950 Schuman Plan and the subsequent formation of the European Coal and Steel Community and the EEC. The Soviet–American confrontation produced the circumstances that made it possible to lay to rest the older—and perhaps inherently less manageable—Franco-German one.[6] It follows that if the Soviet Union and the United States should ever again withdraw from Europe as in the 1930s, or as did Britain and Russia during Bismarck's triumphs in the 1860s, not all the ghosts of World War I diplomacy may yet prove to be exorcized.

We approach the limits of explanation. At one level the First World War, like all wars, can be considered as a product of the international system. It is on this level—and especially on the dynamics of coalition diplomacy—that this analysis has concentrated. But at a second level the war resulted from the triumph within each belligerent of those who accepted over those who challenged the cost in blood and treasure of fighting on. And at a third, and deeper, level both the international and the domestic politics of the conflict were outgrowths of the mental universe and moral priorities of individual statesmen and citizens. This is not to consign political history to the role of spindrift: the decisions of the Cabinets mattered. Nor is it to go so far as Tolstoy's paradox that 'the higher a man's position in the social scale, the more connections he has with others, and the more power he has over them, the more conspicuous is the inevitability and predestination of every act he commits'.[7] But Governments could initiate and prolong the war only because of a great given: the mute, sad willingness of the 1914 generation to submit to squalor and indignity, to kill and to be killed, for purposes whose bearing on their own and on their families' welfare was tenuous, if discernible at all. To seek what lay behind the carnage at the battlefronts is in the end to shift the task of understanding to the little Peterkins of Europe, and to the motives that impelled them to their fate. An age of innocence perished with the dead, and they went to an unquiet grave.

NOTES

Notes to Preface

1. C. von Clausewitz, *On War*, ed. M. E. Howard and P. Paret (Princeton, 1984), 87.

Notes to Introduction

1. On the Concert, see F. H. Hinsley, *Power and the Pursuit of Peace* (Cambridge, 1963); R. T. B. Langhorne, *The Collapse of The Concert of Europe: International Politics, 1890-1914* (London, 1981); R. J. Crampton, 'The Decline of the Concert of Europe in the Balkans, 1913-14', *Sl.EER* 52/128 (1974), 393-419.
2. On the peace movement and arbitration, see F. S. L. Lyons, *Internationalism in Europe, 1815-1914* (Leiden, 1963), pt. v; J. Düffer, *Regeln gegen den Krieg? Die Haager Friedenskonferenz-von 1899 und 1907 in der internationalen Politik* (Berlin, 1981).
3. See E. H. Carr, *The Twenty Years' Crisis, 1919-1939* (pb. rep., London, 1981), ch. 4.
4. A. G. Kenwood and A. L. Lougheed, *The Growth of the International Economy, 1820-1960* (London, 1971), 40, 91, 93; G. Hardach, *The First World War, 1914-1918* (London, 1977), 109.
5. M. de Cecco, *Money and Empire: The International Gold Standard, 1890-1914* (Oxford, 1974), 124.
6. A. Offer, 'The Working Classes, British Naval Plans, and the Coming of the Great War', *P & P* 107 (1985), 204-26.
7. G. Ritter, *The Schlieffen Plan: Critique of a Myth* (London, 1958), 47.
8. On the military revolution, H. F. A. Strachan, *European Armies and the Conduct of War* (London, 1983), chs. 7-8; W. H. McNeill, *The Pursuit of Power: Technology, Armed Force, and Society since AD 1000* (Oxford, 1983), chs. 7-8. On General Staffs, P. M. Kennedy (ed.), *The War Plans of the Great Powers, 1880-1914* (London, 1979) and E. R. May (ed.), *Knowing One's Enemies: Intelligence Assessment before the Two World Wars* (Princeton, 1984).
9. G. A. Craig, *The Politics of the Prussian Army, 1640-1945* (pb. rep., London, 1973), 229.
10. N. Hart, *The Office of Foreign Secretary* (London, forthcoming). Z. S. Steiner, *The Foreign Office and Foreign Policy, 1898-1914* (Cambridge, 1969).
11. The paradox is well analysed in K. N. Waltz, *Man, the State, and War: A Theoretical Analysis* (New York, 1959), chs. 6-7. On the general problem of rationality in foreign-policy decision-making see also G. T. Allison, *Essence of Decision: Explaining the Cuban Missile Crisis* (Boston, 1971).

Notes to Chapter 1

1. The standard account of the origins of the war is L. Albertini, *The Origins of the War of 1914* (3 vols., London, 1957). For shorter introductions see J. Joll, *The Origins of the First World War* (London, 1984); L. C. F. Turner, *Origins of the First World War* (London, 1970); and the documents edited by I. Geiss, *July 1914: The Outbreak of the First World War* (London, 1967).
2. V. Dedijer, *The Road to Sarajevo* (New York, 1966), ch. xvii; Joll, *Origins*, 74.
3. Geiss, *July 1914*, doc. 9. For surveys of Austro-Hungarian policy see F. R. Bridge, *From Sadowa to Sarajevo: The Foreign Policy of Austria-Hungary, 1866–1914* (London, 1972); N. Stone, 'Hungary and the Crisis of July 1914', *JCH* 1/3 (1966), 153–70; and the essays by S. R. Williamson and W. Janner, in S. R. Williamson and P. Pastor (eds.), *Essays on World War I: Origins and Prisoners of War* (New York, 1983).
4. For the domino theory, Bridge, *Sadowa*, p. 9.
5. K. Hitchens, 'The Nationality Problem in Hungary: István Tisza and the Rumanian National Party, 1910–1914', *JMH* 53/4 (1981), 644.
6. The Russian capital was renamed Petrograd in 1914; Moscow replaced it as the seat of Government in March 1918.
7. D. C. B. Lieven, *Russia and the Origins of the First World War* (London, 1983), 39–43.
8. Bridge, *Sadowa*, docs. 37, 38; Albertini, *Origins*, i. 491.
9. R. J. Crampton, *The Hollow Détente: Anglo-German Relations in the Balkans, 1911–1914* (London, 1980) 117.
10. Crampton, 'Decline', pp. 399, 402; Bridge, *Sadowa*, pp. 341, 368, doc. 38; Albertini, *Origins*, i. 498; S. R. Williamson, 'Vienna and July 1914: The Origins of the Great War Once More', in Williamson and Pastor (eds.), *Essays*, pp. 17–18.
11. S. R. Williamson, 'Influence, Power, and the Policy Process: The Case of Franz Ferdinand, 1906–1914', *HJ* 17/2 (1974), 417–34.
12. N. Stone, 'Army and Society in the Habsburg Monarchy, 1900–1914', *P & P* 33 (1966), 110 (for Conrad); Stone, 'Hungary', p. 160; Albertini, *Origins*, i. 126–36; Bridge, *Sadowa*, pp. 368–70, doc. 37.
13. Geiss, *July 1914*, docs. 6, 8.
14. Ibid., docs. 9, 35.
15. W. Janner, 'The Austro-Hungarian Decision for War in July 1914', in Williamson and Pastor (eds.), *Essays*, pp. 55–72.
16. Geiss, *July 1914*, docs. 17, 71, 88, 95. On German policy generally in 1914 see especially V. R. Berghahn, *Germany and the Approach of War in 1914* (London, 1973); F. Fischer, *War of Illusions: German Policies from 1911 to 1914* (London, 1975); I. Geiss, *German Foreign Policy, 1871–1914* (London, 1976); K. H. Jarausch, 'The Illusion of Limited War: Bethmann Hollweg's Calculated Risk in July 1914', *CEH* 2/1 (1969), 48–76; D. E. Kaiser, 'Germany and the Origins of the First World War', *JMH* 55/3 (1983), 442–74.

17. Geiss, *July 1914*, doc. 173.
18. Kaiser, 'Germany', pp. 458, 461-2; K. H. Jarausch, *The Enigmatic Chancellor: Bethmann Hollweg and the Hubris of Imperial Germany* (New Haven, 1973), 106-7.
19. D. Groh, 'The "Unpatriotic Socialists" and the State', *JCH* 1/4 (1966), 171.
20. Good discussion in G. F. Kennan, *The Decline of Bismarck's European Order: Franco-Russian Relations, 1875-1890* (Princeton, 1979).
21. P. Winzen, 'Prince Bülow's *Weltmachtpolitik*', *AJPH* 22/2 (1976), 227-42; J. Steinberg, 'Germany and the Russo-Japanese War', *AHR* 75/7 (1970), 1965-86.
22. B. J. Williams, 'The Strategic Background to the Anglo-Russian Entente of August 1907', *HJ* 9/3 (1966), 360-73; P. M. Kennedy, *The Rise of the Anglo-German Antagonism, 1860-1914* (London, 1982); S. R. Williamson, *The Politics of Grand Strategy: Britain and France Prepare for War, 1904-1914* (Cambridge, Mass., 1969).
23. Fischer, *Illusions*, p. 63.
24. On Anglo-German détente, see Crampton, *Hollow Détente;* F. H. Hinsley (ed.), *British Foreign Policy under Sir Edward Grey* (Cambridge, 1977), ch. 15; Z. S. Steiner, *Britain and the Origins of the First World War* (London, 1977), chs. 5, 6.
25. M. Kent (ed.), *The Great Powers and the End of the Ottoman Empire* (London, 1984), ch. 4 by A. Bodger, is excellent on this subject.
26. On the consolidation of the Triple Entente, J. F. V. Keiger, *France and the Origins of the First World War* (London, 1983); D. N. Collins, 'The Franco-Russian Alliance and Russian Railways, 1891-1914', *HJ* 16/4 (1973), 777-88; R. Girault, *Emprunts russes et investissements français en Russie, 1887-1914* (Paris, 1973), ch. xi; Williamson, *Strategy*, chs. 9, 11-14.
27. E. Spears, *Liaison 1914: A Narrative of the Great Retreat* (2nd edn., London, 1968), 32. In general on the role of General Staffs and war plans in the July Crisis, see Kennedy (ed.), *War Plans*; May (ed.), *Knowing*; Ritter, *Schlieffen Plan*; L. C. F. Turner, 'The Role of the General Staffs in July 1914', *AJPH* 11/3 (1965), 305-23; essays on 'The Great War and the Nuclear Age' in special issue of *International Security* 9/1 (Summer 1984); J. Snyder, *The Ideology of the Offensive: Military Decision Making and the Disasters of 1914* (Ithaca, NY, 1984).
28. Albertini, *Origins*, i. 268-72; N. Stone, 'Moltke and Conrad: Relations between the Austro-Hungarian and German General Staffs, 1909-1914', in Kennedy (ed.), *War Plans*, ch. 10.
29. H. C. Meyer, *Mitteleuropa in German Thought and Action, 1815-1945* (The Hague, 1955), 50; Geiss, *German Foreign Policy*, p. 12.
30. On which, see I. V. Hull, *The Entourage of Kaiser Wilhelm II, 1888-1918* (Cambridge, 1982), ch. 9.
31. On Tirpitz in 1914, Albertini, *Origins*, iii. 250-1. On the War Council, see further below and discussion in Fischer, *Illusions*, ch. 9; J. C. G. Röhl, 'Admiral von Müller and the Approach of War, 1911-1914', *HJ* 12/4 (1969), 651-73; J. C. G. Röhl, 'An der Schwelle zum Weltkrieg:

Eine Dokumentation über den "Kriegsrat" vom 8 Dezember 1912 in Berlin', *Historisches Jahrbuch* 102 (1982), 183–97.

32. Turner, 'General Staffs', pp. 310–12; J. C. G. Röhl (ed.), *1914: Delusion or Design: The Testimony of Two German Diplomats* (London, 1973), 31–2.
33. W. J. Mommsen, 'The Topos of Inevitable War in Germany in the Decade before 1914', in V. R. Berghahn and M. Kitchen (eds.), *Germany in the Age of Total War* (London, 1981), 38; Fischer, *Illusions*, p. 471.
34. Ibid., pp. 395, 418; Albertini, *Origins*, i. 488–90. On the War Council, see n. 31 above.
35. Geiss, *July 1914*, doc. 6.
36. Ibid., docs. 112, 115.
37. In the Reichstag on 2 Dec. 1912. Röhl, 'Müller', p. 660.
38. Fischer, *Illusions*, p. 206.
39. This is a much disputed question. For evidence that the Germans did not expect British intervention, see H. F. Young, 'The Misunderstanding of August 1, 1914', *JMH* 48/4 (1976), 646–7; for a contrary view, W. J. Mommsen, 'Domestic factors in German Foreign Policy before 1914', *CEH* 6/1 (1973), 37–9.
40. Albertini, *Origins*, i. 577; Mommsen, 'Topos', p. 36.
41. For Jagow and the Foreign Ministry, Geiss, *July 1914*, docs. 15, 18, 20, 33, 35; for Bethmann, see K. Riezler, *Tagebücher, Aufsätze, Dokumente*, ed. K.-D. Erdmann (Göttingen, 1972), 183–5, 187, 190–2. It is often difficult in the Riezler diaries to disentangle Bethmann's views from those of his secretary. The diary entries also seem to have been edited later. The discussion of recent research on this subject by W. J. Mommsen in the *German Historical Institute Bulletin*, 14 (autumn 1983) 28–33, however, concludes that 'there is little doubt that they [Riezler's notes] reflect certain lines of thought of Bethmann Hollweg and his entourage, though perhaps seen from a distance'.
42. Groh, '"Unpatriotic Socialists"', pp. 172–3.
43. Young, 'Misunderstanding', p. 647.
44. Geiss, *July 1914*, docs. 130, 133, 139; Albertini, *Origins*, iii. 22–3.
45. Albertini, *Origins*, iii, ch. 5; Turner, 'General Staffs', pp. 314–16; U. Trumpener, 'War Premeditated? German Intelligence Operations in July 1914', *CEH* 9/1 (1976), 58–85.
46. Generally on Russian policy, see Lieven, *Origins*; also S. D. Sazonov, *Fateful Years, 1909–1916* (London, 1928); I. V. Bestuzhev, 'Russian Foreign Policy, February–June 1914', *JCH* 1/3 (1966), 92–112; L. C. F. Turner, 'The Russian Mobilization in 1914', in Kennedy (ed), *War Plans*, 252–66.
47. For Sazonov's preoccupation with the Balkan balance of power, Geiss, *July 1914*, docs. 77, 83, 123.
48. Lieven, *Origins*, 141–4; Albertini, *Origins*, ii. 352–62.
49. Fischer, *Illusions*, pp. 338–50; Turner, 'Russian Mobilization', pp. 254–5, 258–9. May (ed.), *Knowing*, pp. 18–24 gives a different view.
50. Geiss, *July 1914*, docs. 118, 123; Albertini, *Origins*, ii. 540–8.

51. Geiss, *July 1914*, docs. 103, 110, 125, 138.
52. May (ed.), *Knowing*, p. 22; Trumpener, 'War Premeditated?', pp. 68-80; Albertini, *Origins*, ii. 292-4; Lieven, *Origins*, pp. 149-50.
53. Geiss, *July 1914*, docs. 136, 137.
54. H. Rogger, 'Russia in 1914', *JCH* 1/4 (1966), 109.
55. A. J. Mayer, 'Domestic Causes of the First World War' in L. Krieger and F. Stern (eds.), *The Responsibility of Power* (New York, 1967), 294.
56. Lieven, *Origins*, pp. 108-18, 143; see also Snyder, *Offensive*, ch. 7.
57. Generally on French policy, see Keiger, *Origins*; and R. Poidevin and J. Bariéty, *Les Relations franco-allemandes, 1815-1975* (Paris, 1977).
58. Keiger, *Origins*, pp. 150-2; Geiss, *July 1914*, doc. 83; Albertini, *Origins*, ii. 188-97, 294-5, 582-626.
59. Geiss, *July 1914*, doc. 176.
60. Albertini, *Origins*, ii. 605.
61. Turner, *Origins*, p. 36; May (ed.), *Knowing*, p. 145; on Plan XVII see Snyder, *Ideology*, chs. 2-3; Williamson, *Strategy*, ch. 8.
62. On French public opinion see J.-J. Becker, *1914: Comment les Français sont entrés dans la guerre* (Paris, 1977); J. Howorth, 'French Workers and German Workers: The Impossibility of Internationalism, 1900-1914', *EHQ* 15/1 (1985), 71-97.
63. Geiss, *July 1914*, doc. 177. Generally on British policy, see Steiner, *Origins*, Hinsley (ed.), *Grey*; C. Hazlehurst, *Politicians at War, July 1914 to May 1915: A Prologue to the Triumph of Lloyd George* (London, 1971); K. M. Wilson, *The Policy of the Entente: Essays on the Determinants of British Foreign Policy, 1904-1914* (Cambridge, 1985).
64. Williamson, *Strategy*, chs. 12-15; T. Wilson, 'Britain's "Moral Commitment" to France in August 1914', *H* 64/212 (1979) 80-90.
65. D. H. Thomas, *The Guarantee of Belgian Independence and Neutrality in European Diplomacy, 1830s-1930s* (Kingston, Rhode Island, 1983), 511-13.
66. H. H. Asquith, *Memories and Reflections, 1852-1927* (2 vols., London, 1928), ii. 9.
67. Steiner, *Origins*, ch. 9; Hazlehurst, *Politicians*, chs. 4-9; K. M. Wilson, 'The British Cabinet's Decision for War, 2 August 1914', *BJIS* 1/2 (1975), 148-59; B. B. Gilbert, 'Pacifist to Interventionist: David Lloyd George in 1911 and 1914. Was Belgium an Issue?', *HJ* 28/4 (1985), 863-85.
68. Geiss, *July 1914*, doc. 83. See K. M. Wilson, 'Imperial Interests in the British Decision for War, 1914: The Defence of India in Central Asia', *RIS* 10/3 (1984), 189-203.
69. D. French, 'The Edwardian Crisis and the origins of the First World War', *IHR* 4/2 (1982), 207-21; Hazlehurst, *Politicians*, ch. 1.
70. Ibid., pp. 87-9; Offer, 'Naval Plans', pp. 222-4.
71. On the Second International, see especially, J. Joll, *The Second International, 1889-1914* (London, 1955); G. Haupt, *Socialism and the Great War: The Collapse of the Second International* (Oxford, 1972).

Notes to Chapter 2

1. For general accounts of the war see A. J. P. Taylor, *The First World War: An Illustrated History* (London, 1963); M. Ferro, *The Great War, 1914-1918* (London, 1973); K. Robbins, *The First World War* (Oxford, 1984); and, for economic and social aspects, G. Hardach, *The First World War, 1914-1918* (London, 1977). On military operations see C. R. M. F. Cruttwell, *A History of the Great War, 1914-1918* (2nd edn., Oxford, 1936); B. H. Liddell Hart, *History of the First World War* (London, 1970); and H. F. A. Strachan, *European Armies and the Conduct of War* (London, 1983). Dr Strachan is preparing a new general history of the conflict.
2. In general on Japanese war entry see I. H. Nish, *Alliance in Decline: A Study in Anglo-Japanese Relations, 1908-1923* (London, 1972); P. Lowe, *Great Britain and Japan, 1911-1915: A Study of British Far Eastern Policy* (London, 1969); M. Kajima, *The Diplomacy of Japan, 1894-1922*, iii (Tokyo, 1980).
3. See, in addition to the above sources, E. R. May, 'American Policy and Japan's Entrance into World War I', *MVHR* 40/2 (1953), 279-90.
4. Nish, *Alliance*, ch. vii; I. H. Nish, *Japanese Foreign Policy, 1869-1942: Kasumigaseki to Miyakezaku* (London, 1977), 93-6; P. S. Dull, 'Count Kato Komei and the Twenty-One Demands', *PHR* 19/2 (1950), 151-61. On the Twenty-One Demands, see ch. 3 below.
5. On Ottoman war entry, see generally W. W. Gottlieb, *Studies in Secret Diplomacy during the First World War* (London, 1957); Y. T. Kurat, 'How Turkey Drifted into World War I', in K. Bourne and D. C. Watt (eds.), *Studies in International History* (London, 1967), 291-315; U. Trumpener, *Germany and the Ottoman Empire, 1914-1918* (Princeton, 1968), ch. ii; G. E. Silberstein, *The Troubled Alliance: German-Austrian Relations, 1914 to 1917* (Lexington, Ky., 1970), chs. 2, 4. Kent, (ed.), *Ottoman Empire* contains excellent background material.
6. W. Corrigan, 'German-Turkish Relations and the Outbreak of War in 1914: A Reassessment', *P & P* 36 (1967), 144-52; U. Trumpener, 'Liman von Sanders and the German-Ottoman Alliance', *JCH* 1/4 (1966), 179-92; Trumpener, *Germany and the Ottoman Empire*, ch. 1; Kurat, 'Turkey', p. 295.
7. Ibid., pp. 297-301; Silberstein, *Alliance*, ch. 1; Djemal Pasha, *Memoirs of a Turkish Statesman, 1913-1919* (London, 1922), 107-15.
8. Gottlieb, *Diplomacy*, ch. ii; C. J. Smith, *The Russian Struggle for Power, 1914-1917: A Study of Russian Foreign Policy during the First World War* (New York, 1956), 69-76; E. Grey, *Twenty-Five Years, 1892-1916* (2 vols., London, 1925), ii, ch. xxv.
9. With the conclusion of the Pact of London in September 1914 the Triple Entente became a formal alliance. See ch. 3 below.
10. Kurat, 'Turkey', pp. 302-15; Trumpener, *Germany and the Ottoman Empire*, pp. 27-62; Silberstein, *Alliance*, ch. 4.
11. On Italy and the July Crisis, see Albertini, *Origins*; R. J. B. Bosworth,

Italy, the Least of the Great Powers: Italian Foreign Policy before the First World War (London, 1979); and the same author's *Italy and the Approach of the First World War* (London, 1983); C. Seton-Watson, *Italy from Liberalism to Fascism* (London, 1967); A. Salandra, *Italy and the Great War* (London, 1932); W. A. Renzi, 'Italy's Neutrality and Entrance into the Great War: A Re-examination', *AHR* 73/5 (1968), 1414–32; B. E. Schmitt, 'The Italian Documents for July 1914', *JMH* 37/4 (1965), 469–72.

12. Bosworth, *Approach*, p. 124; Salandra, *Italy*, pp. 54–8.
13. C. J. Lowe and F. Marzari, *Italian Foreign Policy, 1870–1940* (London, 1975), doc. 26.
14. L. Valiani, 'Italo-Austro-Hungarian Negotiations, 1914–1915', *JCH* 1/3 (1966), 114. For the background, W. C. Askew, 'The Austro-Italian Antagonism, 1896–1914', in L. P. Wallace and W. C. Askew (eds.), *Power, Public Opinion, and Diplomacy* (Durham, North Carolina, 1959), 172–221; Seton-Watson, *Italy*, pp. 396–410; May (ed.), *Knowing*, ch. 8.
15. Lowe and Marzari, *Italian Foreign Policy*, doc. 27; Salandra, *Italy*, pp. 62–5.
16. Ibid., p. 79; J. Whittam, *The Politics of the Italian Army, 1861–1918* (London, 1977), 178–83.
17. Salandra, *Italy*, pp. 222, 268–71; Gottlieb, *Diplomacy*, pp. 325–9.
18. Salandra, *Italy*, pp. 275–6, 292–3; Lowe and Marzari, *Italian Foreign Policy*, p. 436 (n. 62); C. J. Lowe, 'Britain and Italian Intervention, 1914–1915', *HJ* 12/3 (1969), 543.
19. Salandra, *Italy*, pp. 94–7; Gottlieb, *Diplomacy*, pp. 308, 319; Lowe, 'Britain and Italian Intervention', pp. 540–1.
20. C. J. Lowe and M. L. Dockrill, *The Mirage of Power: British Foreign Policy, 1914–1922* (3 vols., London, 1972), iii, doc. 81; Grey, *Twenty-Five Years*, ii. 207; Gottlieb, *Diplomacy*, p. 323.
21. On the Italo-Allied negotiations, see Smith, *Struggle*, pp. 243–71; Gottlieb, *Diplomacy*, ch. xxii; A. Dallin, *et al, Russian Diplomacy and Eastern Europe, 1914–1917* (New York, 1963), 179–93; K. J. Calder, *Britain and the Origins of the New Europe, 1914–1918* (Cambridge, 1976), 32–8; Lowe, 'Britain and Italian Intervention', pp. 541–8.
22. On the Italo-Austrian negotiations see Valiani, 'Negotiations'; L. Valiani, *The End of Austria-Hungary* (London, 1973), ch. ii; Gottlieb, *Diplomacy*, chs. xxi, xxiii; Salandra, *Italy*, ch. x; S. Burián, *Austria in Dissolution* (London, 1925), ch. ii. Also revealing is M. Komjáthy (ed.), *Protokolle des Gemeinsamen Ministerrates der Österreichischen-Ungarischen Monarchie (1914–1918)* (Budapest, 1966), e.g. pp. 160–1, 215–18, 221–3, 229–31.
23. Seton-Watson, *Italy*, pp. 443–4; Lowe and Marzari, *Italian Foreign Policy*, doc. 30; Valiani, *End*, pp. 71–2.
24. For military and naval opinions, Seton-Watson, *Italy*, p. 436; on decision-making generally see A. J. Thayer, *Italy and the Great War: Politics and Culture, 1870–1915* (Madison, Wisconsin, 1964), 359–69. See also Salandra, *Italy*, p. 218.
25. Whittam, *Italian Army*, p. 187.
26. A. Monticone, 'Salandra e Sonnino verso la decisione dell 'intervento', *Rivista di Studi Politici Internazionali* 24/1 (1957), 72–88.

27. S. Jones, 'Antonio Salandra and the Politics of Italian Intervention in the First World War', *EHQ* 15/2 (1985), 157–73.

28. G. Giolitti, *Memoirs of My Life* (London, 1923), 390–2. On public opinion, see Bosworth, *Approach*, ch. 6; Seton-Watson *Italy*, pp. 436–41.

29. On 'Radiant May', Thayer, *Italy*, ch. 11; Salandra, *Italy*, chs. xii-xiii; Giolitti, *Memoirs*, pp. 396–400; B. Vigezzi, 'Le "Radiose giornate" del maggio 1915 nei rapporti dei prefetti', *Nuova Rivista Storica* 42/3 (1959), 313–44.

30. J. Whittam, 'War and Italian Society, 1914–1916', in B. Bond and I. Roy (eds.), *War and Society: A Yearbook of Military History* (London, 1975), 152–4; Salandra, *Italy*, pp. 288–9; Jones, 'Salandra', p. 165.

31. In general on Bulgarian intervention see Silberstein, *Alliance*, ch. 7; Dallin, *Russian Diplomacy*, pp. 194–234; and Smith, *Struggle*, esp. pp. 309–35.

32. On Allied diplomacy, apart from the sources in n. 31, see C. J. Lowe, 'The Failure of British Diplomacy in the Balkans, 1914–1916', *CJH* 4/1 (1969), 73–100; and K. Robbins, 'British Diplomacy and Bulgaria, 1914–1915', *Sl.EER* 49/117 (1971), 560–85.

33. On Allied commitments to the Serbs, Calder, *New Europe*, pp. 40–6.

34. On Rumanian intervention see Silberstein, *Alliance*, chs. 8–10; G. E. Torrey, 'Rumania and the Belligerents, 1914–1916', *JCH* 1/3 (1966), 171–91; Smith, *Struggle*, esp. pp. 23–9, 287–309, 394–9, 411–18; Dallin, *Russian Diplomacy*, pp. 235–75; and S. D. Spector, *Rumania at the Paris Peace Conference: A Study in the Diplomacy of Ion I. C. Bratianu* (New York, 1962), 15–39.

35. G. Fotino, 'La Neutralité roumaine: Une séance historique au Conseil de la Couronne (3 aout 1914)', *Revue des Deux Mondes* (1 Aug. 1930), 529–41.

36. Torrey, 'Rumania', pp. 189–90.

37. Spector, *Rumania*, p. 35; M. S. Anderson, *The Eastern Question, 1774–1923: A Study in International Relations* (London, 1966), 332 n.

38. Greece's path to war was quite different from that of the other Balkan neutrals, and was much less the result of independent decision. The country became deeply divided between the advocates of intervention on the side of the Allies, led by Venizelos, head of the Liberal Party and Prime Minister at the outbreak of war, and the more conservative neutralist forces behind King Constantine. In October 1915 Anglo-French forces landed at Salonika, at the invitation of Venizelos, who intended to enter the war in order to assist the Serbs. After Constantine dismissed him, and insisted on remaining neutral, the Allies intervened more and more overtly in Greek internal affairs. In October 1916 Venizelos set up a Provisional Government at Salonika, which the Allies recognized in December. In June 1917 Constantine was forced to abdicate after an Allied ultimatum; he was replaced by his second son, Alexander, and in the following month a new Venizelos ministry brought Greece into the war alongside the Allies. For fuller accounts of these events see G. B. Leon, *Greece and the Great Powers, 1914–1917*

(Thessaloniki, 1974); and A. Mitrakos, *France in Greece during World War I: A Study in the Politics of Power* (New York, 1982).

39. On the strategic background, see J. A. S. Grenville and G. B. Young, *Politics, Strategy, and American Diplomacy: Studies in Foreign Policy, 1873–1917* (New Haven and London, 1966). On pre-war American public opinion, see E. R. May, 'American Imperialism: A Reinterpretation', *Perspectives in American History*, 1 (1967), 123–283, esp. chs. ii-iv, vi; and R. E. Osgood, *Ideals and Self-Interest in American Foreign Relations: The Great Transformation of the Twentieth Century* (Chicago, 1953), pt. I.

40. On the neutrality period and American entry into the war see generally D. M. Smith, *The Great Departure: The United States and World War I, 1914–1920* (New York, 1965); E. R. May, *The World War and American Isolation, 1914–1917* (Cambridge, Mass., 1959); P. A. Devlin, *Too Proud to Fight: Woodrow Wilson's Neutrality* (London, 1974); R. Gregory, *The Origins of American Intervention in the First World War* (New York, 1971); and A. S. Link, *Wilson* (Princeton, 1960–5) iii-v.

41. J. M. Cooper, jun., *The Vanity of Power: American Isolationism and the First World War, 1914–1917* (Westport, Conn., 1969), 28–9; May, *Isolation*, pp. 47–50.

42. J. M. Cooper, jun., 'The Command of Gold Reversed: American Loans to Britain, 1915–1917', *PHR* 45/2 (1976), 215; see also Devlin, *Too Proud*, pp. 176, 355–6.

43. Gregory, *Origins*, p. 43.

44. On the United States and the Allied blockade see May, *Isolation*, chs. i, iii, xv; Devlin, *Too Proud*, chs. v-vii, xvi; and especially J. W. Coogan, *The End of Neutrality: The United States, Britain, and Maritime Rights, 1899–1915* (Ithaca, NY, and London, 1981), which makes important corrections to previous accounts.

45. May, *Isolation*, p. 335.

46. C. M. Seymour (ed.), *The Intimate Papers of Colonel House* (4 vols., London, 1926–8), i. 309–10; Coogan, *Neutrality*, p. 180.

47. G. A. Ritter, *The Sword and the Sceptre: The Problem of Militarism in Germany* (4 vols., London, 1969–73), iii. 120–7.

48. D. F. Houston, *Eight Years with Wilson's Cabinet, 1913–1920* (2 vols., London, 1926), i. 132–7.

49. On the *Lusitania* crisis, May, *Isolation*, chs. vii-viii; Devlin, *Too Proud*, ch. x; Link, *Wilson*, iii, chs. xii-xiii.

50. S. Gwynn (ed.), *The Letters and Friendships of Sir Cecil Spring Rice* (2 vols., London, 1929), ii. 268–9.

51. Wilson to Bryan, 14 and 20 May, 2 and 7 June 1915, *FRUS: The Lansing Papers, 1914–1920* (2 vols., Washington, 1939), i. 406–39; May, *Isolation*, p. 153; Seymour (ed.), *House*, i. 437.

52. On the Congressional revolt see Cooper, *Vanity*, pp. 106–117.

53. On the *Sussex* crisis, May, *Isolation*, ch. ix; Devlin, *Too Proud*, ch. xv; Link, *Wilson*, iv. chs. viii-ix; Seymour (ed.), *House*, i. 225–45.

54. T. von Bethmann Hollweg, *Betrachtungen zum Weltkriege* (2 vols., Berlin, 1919), ii. 109. On German policy, see especially K. E. Birnbaum, *Peace*

Moves and U-Boat Warfare: A Study of Imperial Germany's Policy towards the United States, April 18, 1916–January 9, 1917 (Uppsala, 1958).

55. On which, see ch. 3 below.
56. Birnbaum, *Peace Moves*, pp. 4, 36; May *Isolation*, p. 209.
57. Birnbaum, *Peace Moves*, ch. III; Bethmann memorandum, 29 Feb. 1916, printed in Bethmann, *Betrachtungen*, ii, app. 2.
58. Ibid., pp. 126–8; Birnbaum, *Peace Moves*, ch. V; May, *Isolation*, chs. XII-XIII; P. W. E. von Ludendorff, *My War Memories, 1914–1918* (2 vols., London, 1919), i. 312–16.
59. Wilson's peace note is discussed further below; the note of the Central Powers is considered more fully in ch. 3. On this German–American diplomacy see Birnbaum, *Peace Moves*, chs. VI-IX; Ritter, *Sword*, iii. ch. 8; and S & G, i, docs. 285, 309, 320–1, 324, 330, 339, 390.
60. Birnbaum, *Peace Moves*, chs. X-XI; Ritter, *Sword*, iii. 300–34; Bethmann, *Betrachtungen*, ii. 129–38; S & G, i, docs. 450, 463, 474–6.
61. Devlin, *Too Proud*, p. 630.
62. Ibid., p. 631.
63. Bethmann, *Betrachtungen*, ii. 135.
64. Devlin, *Too Proud*, ch. XX; Cooper, *Vanity*, pp. 168–87; Houston, *Eight Years*, ch. XV (esp. p. 243).
65. Text of the War Message in *FRUS, 1917 Supplement I: The World War* (Washington, 1931), 195–201.
66. Houston, *Eight Years*, p. 229; Seymour (ed.), *House*, i. 444; R. Lansing, *War Memoirs of Robert Lansing* (Indianapolis and New York, 1935), 212–13.
67. For House, e.g. Seymour (ed.), *House*, i. 444, for Lansing see, e.g. Lansing to Wilson, 19 Mar. 1917, *FRUS: Lansing Papers*, i. 626–8.
68. Osgood, *Ideals*, chs. IX. X; Devlin, *Too Proud*, p. 518.
69. Ibid., pp. 585–6; Cooper, 'Command', pp. 221–5.
70. Link, *Wilson*, v. 410–11, 414.
71. Seymour (ed.), *House*, i. 249, 271, 437; Osgood, *Ideals*, p. 180; Devlin, *Too Proud*, chs. VIII-IX.
72. *FRUS: Lansing Papers*, i. 470–1.
73. On which, see Devlin, *Too Proud*, chs. XII-XV; Link, *Wilson*, iv. ch. IV; J. M. Cooper, jun., 'The British Response to the House–Grey Memorandum: New Evidence and New Questions', *JAH* 59/4 (1973), 958–71.
74. Text of the note in J. B. Scott (ed.), *Official Statements of War Aims and Peace Proposals, December 1916–November 1918* (Washington, 1921), 12–15. For the background, Devlin, *Too Proud*, ch. XVIII; Link, *Wilson*, v, ch. V; Seymour (ed.), *House*, i, ch. XIII; Lansing, *War Memoirs*, pp. 174 ff.
75. On this, see ch. 3 below.
76. Devlin, *Too Proud*, ch. XIX; text of the speech in *FRUS, 1917 Supplement I: The World War* (Washington, 1931), 24–9.
77. *FRUS: Lansing Papers*, i. 626–9.
78. Cooper, *Vanity*, p. 190; Seymour (ed.), *House*, i. 467.
79. For this analysis see Cooper, *Vanity*, ch. 5.
80. Houston, *Eight Years*, pp. 246–50.

Notes to Chapter 3

1. F. Fischer, *Germany's Aims in the First World War* (English edn., London, 1967), 103–5. Fischer's book is the fundamental source on German war aims, although not all of his interpretations are followed here. H. W. Gatzke, *Germany's Drive to the West: A Study of Western War Aims during the First World War* (Baltimore, 1950); Ritter, *Sword*, iii; and L. L. Farrar, *Divide and Conquer: German Efforts to Conclude a Separate Peace, 1914–1918* (New York, 1978) are important. I have drawn heavily on the documents edited by A. Scherer and J. Grünewald, abbreviated as S & G.

2. On the drafting of the Programme, Fischer, *Aims*, pp. 98–106; Fischer, *Illusions*, ch. 23; K. Riezler, *Tagebücher*, pp. 201–5; W. Rathenau, *Tagebuch, 1907–1922*, ed. H. Pogge von Strandmann (Düsseldorf, 1967), 185–6; E. Zechlin, 'Cabinet versus Economic Warfare in Germany: Policy and Strategy during the Early Months of the First World War', in H. W. Koch (ed.), *The Origins of the First World War: Great Power Rivalry and German War Aims* (London, 1972), 215–21; W. C. Thompson, 'The September Program: Reflections on the Evidence', *CEH* 11/4 (1978), 348–54.

3. P. R. Sweet, 'Leaders and Policies: Germany in the Winter of 1914–15', *JCEA* 16/3 (1956), 229–52; L. L. Farrar, *The Short-War Illusion: German Policy, Strategy, and Domestic Affairs, August–December 1914* (Santa Barbara, 1973), ch. 9; S & G, i, docs. 13, 14, 16, 20, 21.

4. Sweet, 'Leaders', pp. 244–7.

5. Rathenau, *Tagebuch*, p. 169; Zechlin in Koch (ed.), *Origins*, p. 204.

6. Geiss, *German Foreign Policy*, pp. 178, 191; Fischer, *Illusions*, p. 3.

7. Geiss, *July 1914*, doc. 139.

8. E. von Falkenhayn, *General Headquarters, 1914–1916, and its Critical Decisions* (London, 1919), 217–18.

9. Fischer, *Aims*, ch. 8; S & G, i, docs. 23, 35, 159: F. Petri, 'Zur Flamenpolitik des I. Weltkrieges', in R. Vierhaus and M. Botzenhart (eds.), *Dauer und Wandel der Geschichte: Aspekte Europäischer Vergangenheit* (Münster, 1966), 513–36.

10. S & G, i, docs. 264, 268, 302.

11. Fischer, *Aims*, pp. 215–24; S & G, i, docs. 172, 183, 206.

12. S & G, i, docs. 52, 75.

13. Ibid., docs. 119–21. On the frontier strip see I. Geiss, *Der Polnische Grenzstreifen, 1914–1918: Ein Beitrag zur Deutschen Kriegszielpolitik im Ersten Weltkrieg* (Lübeck and Hamburg, 1960), esp. 71–97.

14. S & G, i, docs. 131, 140.

15. Fischer, *Aims*, pp. 247–54. Zechlin in Koch (ed.), *Origins*, pp. 233 ff., 245.

16. S & G, i, docs. 134–5, 137, 139, 141. Meyer, *Mitteleuropa*, chs. vi–ix.

17. S & G, i, docs. 165, 167. Fischer, *Aims*, pp. 206–12.

18. Rathenau, *Tagebuch*, p. 186; Fischer, *Aims*, p. 250.

19. Meyer, *Mitteleuropa*, pp. 183–6, ch. xi; S & G, i, doc. 168; R. W. Kapp,

'Divided Loyalties: The German Reich and Austria-Hungary in Austro-German Discussions of War Aims, 1914-1916', *CEH* 17/2, 3 (1984), 120-39.

20. Ritter, *Sword*, iii. 111-16, 214-17. S & G, i, docs. 221, 227, 261, 296, 303-5. S. Burián, *Austria in Dissolution* (London, 1925), ch. 4.
21. Fischer, *Aims*, pp. 205, 238. S & G, i, docs. 104, 140.
22. Ibid., docs. 243, 255, 350, 384; Fischer, *Aims*, pp. 228-30; Farrar, *Divide*, ch. v.
23. Bethmann to Hertling, 26 Jan. 1918, in G. D. Feldman, *German Imperialism, 1914-1918: The Development of a Historical Debate* (New York, 1972), doc. 28; Ritter, *Sword*, iii. 220-30.
24. See discussion above in ch. 2, sect. ii.
25. Trumpener, *Germany and the Ottoman Empire*, chs. IV, X, XII.
26. Komjáthy (ed.), *Protokolle*, pp. 352-72; S & G, i, docs. 86, 144, 151, 162, 164; Ritter, *Sword*, iii. 83-9.
27. C. A. Macartney, *The Habsburg Empire, 1790-1918* (London, 1969), 810-13; Burián, *Austria*, chs. X, XIV.
28. Gatzke, *Drive* is strong on German public opinion. See also Fischer, *Aims*, ch. v; and (for Erzberger), K. Epstein, *Matthias Erzberger and the Dilemma of German Democracy* (Princeton, 1959), 95-117.
29. Fischer, *Aims*, p. 177.
30. Good short discussion in A. J. Ryder, *The German Revolution of 1918: A Study of German Socialism in War and Revolt* (Cambridge, 1967), chs. 3-4.
31. G. A. Craig, *Germany, 1866-1945* (Oxford, 1978), 364.
32. Bethmann, *Betrachtungen*, ii. 35.
33. Ritter, *Sword*, iii. 188, 199.
34. Bethmann, *Betrachtungen*, ii. 146-8, 154; S & G, i, docs. 306, 309, 311.
35. Ibid., docs. 347, 353-4, 357, 370, 374, 380, 396; Fischer, *Aims*, pp. 311-13; Ritter, *Sword*, iii. 282-5.
36. S & G, i, docs. 361, 365, 367, 369; Ritter, *Sword*, iii. 277, 283-4.
37. Text of the note in Scott (ed.), *War Aims*, pp. 2-3. Bethmann, *Betrachtungen*, ii. 154; S & G, i, docs. 396, 416, 422; Ritter, *Sword*, p. 289.
38. S & G, i, docs. 435, 437, 455, 457, 476; Fischer, *Aims*, pp. 316-22.
39. W. R. Louis, *Great Britain and Germany's Lost Colonies, 1914-1919* (Oxford, 1967), p. x. The essential work on British war aims is V. H. Rothwell, *British War Aims and Peace Diplomacy 1914-1918* (Oxford, 1971). But it should be supplemented by Louis; by R. E. Bunselmeyer, *The Cost of the War, 1914-1919: British Economic War Aims and the Origins of Reparation* (Hamden, Conn., 1975); and by K. J. Calder, *Britain and the Origins of the New Europe, 1914-1918* (Cambridge, 1976).
40. Rothwell, *War Aims*, pp. 32, 51-2.
41. Louis, *Great Britain*, ch. ii. On the Anglo-Japanese Agreement, ibid., pp. 79-80; Nish, *Alliance*, ch. XI. In the history of the British Dominions the war has long been recognized as a critical turning point in the growth of national awareness and a sense of separate identity. In 1914 the Dominions were automatically placed at war with Germany by virtue of Britain's declaration. But they had more control over their contribution

to the war effort, and the conscription issue became a fiercely contested one. Partly in the hope of alleviating the manpower shortage, the Lloyd George Government introduced in 1917–18 the system of Imperial War Conferences and the Imperial War Cabinet, which made consultation of the Dominions over foreign policy rather less perfunctory than hitherto. Subsequently, the Dominions obtained separate representation at the 1919 Peace Conference and in the League of Nations. For Canada, which lacked the colonial concerns of the other Dominions, this change in status was of particular importance. On these developments, see generally E. A. Benians, J. Butler, and C. E. Carrington (eds.), *The Cambridge History of the British Empire*, iii (Cambridge, 1959), and in more detail see *inter alia* W. K. Hancock, *Smuts: The Sanguine Years, 1870–1919* (Cambridge, 1962), L. F. Fitzhardinge, *William Morris Hughes: A Political Biography*, ii (Sydney, 1979), and C. P. Stacey, *Canada and the Age of Conflict: A History of Canadian External Policies*, i (Toronto, 1977).

42. Bunselmeyer, *Cost*, chs. 2–5; Rothwell, *War Aims*, pp. 266–71.

43. Ibid., p. 19.

44. On the Belgian issue, see D. Stevenson, 'Belgium, Luxemburg, and the Defence of Western Europe, 1914–1920', *IHR* 4/4 (1982), 504–23; S. Marks, *Innocent Abroad: Belgium at the Paris Peace Conference of 1919* (Chapel Hill, 1981), ch. 1; J. E. Helmreich, *Belgium and Europe: A Study in Small Power Diplomacy* (The Hague, 1976), ch. 7.

45. J. Gooch, 'Soldiers, Strategy, and War Aims in Britain, 1914–1918', in B. Hunt and A. Preston (eds.), *War Aims and Strategic Policy in the Great War, 1914–1918* (London, 1977), 21–40; P. Guinn, *British Strategy and Politics, 1914–1918* (Oxford, 1965), 178–87.

46. D. Stevenson, *French War Aims against Germany, 1914–1919* (Oxford, 1982), 12.

47. Grey, *Twenty-Five Years*, ii. 160–1.

48. The Lansdowne memorandum is in Asquith, *Memories and Reflections*, ii. 138–47. See discussion in C. J. Lowe and M. L. Dockrill, *The Mirage of Power: British Foreign Policy, 1914–1922* (3 vols., London, 1972), ii. 244–5; D. Lloyd George, *War Memoirs* (6 vols., London, 1933–6), 862–77.

49. Rothwell, *War Aims*, pp. 38–52; Calder, *New Europe*, pp. 93–101; Lloyd George, *War Memoirs*, ii. 833–41, 877–91; D. Lloyd George, *The Truth about the Peace Treaties* (2 vols., London, 1938), i. 31–50.

50. This note is discussed at the end of this chapter.

51. Rothwell, *War Aims*, pp. 70–5; Louis, *Great Britain*, pp. 80–4; Lloyd George, *War Memoirs*, iv. 1749 ff.

52. Ibid., p. 1773.

53. On French public opinion see above all Becker, *1914*; and its sequel J.-J. Becker, *The Great War and the French People* (English edn., Leamington Spa, 1985). On French war aims generally see Stevenson, *War Aims*; C. M. Andrew and A. S. Kanya-Forstner, *France Overseas: The Great War and the Climax of French Imperial Expansion* (London, 1981); P. Renouvin, 'Les Buts de guerre du gouvernement français, 1914–1918', *Revue historique* 235 (1966), 1–38; G. Soutou, 'La France et les marches de l'est, 1914–1919', *Revue historique* 528 (1978), 341–88; M. Trachtenberg,

Reparation in World Politics: France and European Economic Diplomacy 1916-1923 (New York, 1980).

54. As demonstrated in J. C. King, *Generals and Politicians: Conflict between France's High Command, Parliament, and Government, 1914-1918* (Berkeley and Los Angeles, 1951). R. A. Prete, 'French Military War Aims, 1914-1916', *HJ* 28/4 (1985), 887-99 has some new information.

55. Stevenson, *War Aims*, p. 13.

56. Ibid., pp. 12, 23, 38, 216-18.

57. Stevenson, 'Belgium', pp. 509-10.

58. Stevenson, *War Aims*, pp. 32-5; Trachtenberg, *Reparation*, pp. 1-6.

59. For this paragraph, Stevenson, *War Aims*, pp. 23, 26-7, 38-9.

60. For the origins of the Cambon letter and Doumergue Agreement, ibid., pp. 36-44, 48-56.

61. Smith, p. 7. On Tsarist war aims generally see, apart from Smith, Dallin, *Russian Diplomacy*.

62. On Russian refusal of a separate peace, S & G, i, docs. 59, 119, 350; Smith, *Struggle*, pp. 409-11.

63. Dallin, *Russian Diplomacy*, p. 7. In 1914 Poland was still partitioned: the former Congress Kingdom of Poland was under Russian sovereignty, Galicia under Austrian, and there were large numbers of Poles under German rule in East and West Prussia, Posen, and Upper Silesia.

64. Smith, *Struggle*, pp. 45-50, 97-108; W. A. Renzi, 'Who Composed "Sazonov's Thirteen Points"? A Re-examination of Russia's War Aims of 1914', *AHR* 88/2 (1983), 347-57.

65. Stevenson, *War Aims*, p. 31.

66. G. Buchanan, *My Mission to Russia, and other Diplomatic Memories* (2 vols., London, 1923), ii. 26; Dallin, *Russian Diplomacy*, p. 157.

67. Dallin, *Russian Diplomacy*, ch. 1; Calder, *New Europe*, pp. 87-8.

68. Stevenson, *War Aims*, pp. 31-2, 51-2; Dallin, *Russian Diplomacy*, pp. 43-69; Sazonov, *Fateful Years*, chs. XIII-XIV.

69. See ch. 2, sect. ii above. Calder, *New Europe* is the best introduction to Allied policy towards Austria-Hungary; see also Dallin, *Russian Diplomacy*, ch. 2.

70. Stevenson, *War Aims*, p. 28; W. Fest, *Peace or Partition: The Habsburg Monarchy and British Policy, 1914-1918* (London, 1978), 25; Dallin, *Russian Diplomacy*, p. 89; Paléologue to Delcassé, 28 Mar. 1915, French Foreign Ministry Archives, Papiers d'Agents: Maurice Paléologue, Correspondance politique: II: 1915.

71. Smith, *Struggle*, p. 18.

72. Dallin, *Russian Diplomacy*, ch. 2; D. Perman, *The Shaping of the Czechoslovak State: Diplomatic History of the Boundaries of Czechoslovakia, 1914-1920* (Leiden, 1962), ch. 1.

73. J. Whittam, 'War Aims and Strategy: The Italian Government and High Command, 1914-1919', in Hunt and Preston (eds.), *War Aims*, pp. 94-6; Calder, *New Europe*, p. 82.

74. Ibid., ch. 4; Stevenson, *War Aims*, pp. 41, 48, 57-8.

75. Kent (ed.), *Ottoman Empire* and I. Friedman, *The Question of Palestine, 1914-1918: British-Jewish-Arab Relations* (London, 1973), ch. 1, give the

background. The partition of the Ottoman Empire needs a new general account. Kent; Friedman; Smith, *Struggle*; and Andrew and Kanya-Forstner, *France Overseas*, all contain important material. On Ibn Saud see G. Troeller, 'Ibn Sa'ud and Sharif Husain: A Comparison in Influence in the Early Years of the First World War', *HJ* 14/3 (1971), 627–33; D. Silverfarb, 'The Anglo-Najd Treaty of December 1915', *MES* 16/3 (1980), 167–77; J. Goldberg, 'The Origins of British–Saudi Relations: The 1915 Anglo-Saudi Treaty Revisited', *HJ* 28/3 (1985), 693–703.

76. Hinsley (ed.), *Grey*, p. 429.

77. On Britain and the Straits Agreement, ibid., ch. 25; Smith, *Struggle*, pp. 82–116, 185–243; R. J. Kerner, 'Russia, the Straits and Constantinople, 1914–1915', *JMH* 1/3 (1929), 400–15; C. J. Smith, 'Great Britain and the 1914–1915 Straits Agreement with Russia: The British Promise of November 1914', *AHR* 70/4 (1965), 1015–34; W. A. Renzi, 'Great Britain, Russia, and the Straits, 1914–1915', *JMH* 42/1 (1970), 1–20; Gottlieb, *Diplomacy*, chs. IV-VI.

78. Sazonov, *Fateful Years*, p. 252; M. de Taube, *La Politique russe d'avant-guerre et la fin de l'Empire des Tsars (1904–17)* (Paris, 1928), 396–8; Smith, *Struggle*, pp. 185–222.

79. Ibid., pp. 225–32; Grey, *Twenty-Five Years*, pp. 179–82.

80. R. Poincaré, *Au Service de la France: Neuf années de souvenirs* (10 vols., Paris, 1926–33), vi. 92–6; Paléologue to Delcassé, 6 Mar. 1915, French Foreign Ministry Archives, Papiers d'Agents: Maurice Paléologue, Correspondance politique: II: 1915; Smith, *Struggle*, pp. 222–4, 232–8.

81. On the McMahon–Hussein correspondence, see E. Kedourie, *In the Anglo-Arab Labyrinth: The McMahon–Husayn Correspondence and its Interpretations, 1914–1939* (Cambridge, 1976); Friedman, *Palestine*, ch. 5; I. Friedman, 'The McMahon–Hussein Correspondence and the Question of Palestine', *JCH* 5/2, (1970), 83–122; discussion between Friedman and A. Toynbee in *JCH* 5/4 (1970), 185–201; Hinsley (ed.), *Grey*, ch. 26; Lowe and Dockrill, *Mirage*, ii. 208–18.

82. Kedourie, *Labyrinth*, p. 94. An expeditionary force sent by the Government of India occupied Basra in November 1914, and subsequently moved into the interior. See generally, V. H. Rothwell, 'Mesopotamia in British War Aims, 1914–1918', *HJ* 13/2 (1970), 273–94.

83. Kedourie, *Labyrinth*, p. 120. The main letters in the correspondence are printed in J. C. Hurewitz (ed.), *Diplomacy in the Near and Middle East: A Documentary Record, 1914–1956* (Princeton, 1956), ii, doc. 8.

84. Andrew and Kanya-Forstner, *France Overseas*, ch. 4; and the same authors' 'The French Colonial Party and French Colonial War Aims, 1914–1918', *HJ* 17/1 (1974), 79–106.

85. On the negotiations, apart from Andrew and Kanya-Forstner, see Friedman, *Palestine*, ch. 7; Lowe and Dockrill, *Mirage*, ii. 219–22; J. Nevakivi, *Britain, France, and the Arab Middle East, 1914–1920* (London, 1969), 36–44; Hinsley (ed.), *Grey*, pp. 447–51.

86. Ibid., p. 450; Friedman, *Palestine*, pp. 67–8, 81–96, 117–18.

87. Smith, *Struggle*, pp. 363–82, 418–24.

88. Lowe and Dockrill, *Mirage*, ii. 223-7; C. Seton-Watson, *Italy from Liberalism to Fascism, 1870-1925* (London, 1967), 462-7.
89. T. E. La Fargue, *China and the World War* (Stanford, 1937), ch. 2.
90. On the drafting of the Twenty-One Demands, see Lowe, *Great Britain and Japan*, ch. VIII (text of the Demands in ibid., pp. 258-65); P. S. Dull, 'Count Kato Komei and the Twenty-One Demands', *PHR* 19/2 (1950), 151-61; M. B. Jansen, 'Yawata, Hanyehping, and the Twenty-One Demands', *PHR* 23/1 (1954), 31-48; M. B. Jansen, *The Japanese and Sun Yat-sen* (Cambridge, Mass., 1954), ch. 8; La Fargue, *China*, chs. II-III; and Nish, *Japanese Foreign Policy*, ch. 5.
91. Lowe, *Great Britain and Japan*, ch. VIII; La Fargue, *China*, ch. 2; R. J. Gowen, 'Great Britain and the Twenty-One Demands of 1915: Cooperation versus Effacement', *JMH* 43/1 (1971), 76-106.
92. Nish, *Japanese Foreign Policy*, pp. 105-10; Nish, *Alliance*, p. 198.
93. Scott (ed.), *War Aims*, pp. 26-9; S. J. Kernek, 'The British Government's Reactions to President Wilson's "Peace" Note of December. 1916', *HJ* 13/4 (1970), 721-66; Stevenson, *War Aims*, pp. 45-6.
94. Scott (ed.), *War Aims*, pp. 35-8; Kernek, loc. cit.; Stevenson, *War Aims*, pp. 45-7; Lowe and Dockrill, *Mirage*, pp. 245-51.
95. Above, p. 120.
96. Calder, *New Europe*, pp. 104-8.

Notes to Chapter 4

1. The conventional usage will be followed of referring to the revolution of 17 Mar. 1917 (when Russia became a Republic) as the February Revolution; that of 7-8 Nov. 1917 (when the Bolsheviks seized power in Petrograd) as the October Revolution.
2. Ritter, *Sword*, iii. 373-7.
3. Ibid., pp. 384-6; Lloyd George, *War Memoirs*, iv. 1987-8; W. B. Fest, 'British War Aims and German Peace Feelers during the First World War (December 1916-November 1918)', *HJ* 15/2 (1972), 292.
4. *FRUS: 1917* Supplement I, 40-44, 55-65; Lansing, *War Memoirs* pp. 245-9.
5. In general on the Sixte affair see Prince Sixte de Bourbon, *L'Offre de paix séparée de l'Autriche (5 décembre 1916-12 octobre 1917)* (Paris, 1920); R. A. Kann, *Die Sixtusaffäre und die geheimen Friedensverhandlungen Österreich-Ungarns im ersten Weltkrieg* (Vienna, 1966); G. Pedroncini, *Les Négociations secrètes pendant la Grande guerre* (Paris, 1969), 58-67.
6. Sixte, *L'Offre*, pp. 35-105; A. Ribot (ed.), *Journal d'Alexandre Ribot et correspondances inédites, 1914-1922* (Paris, 1936), 62 n.
7. Ibid., pp. 63-72, 103-25; Sixte, *L'Offre*, pp. 114-262; Lloyd George, *War Memoirs*, iv, ch. LXI.
8. Calder, *New Europe*, pp. 116-19.
9. S & G, ii, docs. 20, 33; Ritter, *Sword*, iii. 386-95; K. Epstein, 'The Development of German-Austrian War Aims in the Spring of 1917',

JCEA 17/1 (1957), 24-47 is a very useful survey. See also W. Steglich, *Die Friedenspolitik der Mittelmächte, 1917-18,* (Wiesbaden, 1964).

10. Ritter, *Sword,* iii. 392-3, 396-7; Bethmann, *Betrachtungen,* ii. 200-3; S & G, ii, doc. 45.

11. Ibid., docs. 42, 78; Macartney, *Habsburg Empire,* pp. 822-4.

12. S & G, ii, doc. 68; R. F. Hopwood, 'Czernin and the Fall of Bethmann Hollweg', *CJH* 2/2 (1967), 49-61; Epstein, *Erzberger,* pp. 173-4.

13. S & G, ii, docs. 49, 71, 76, 82, 87, 129; Fischer, *Aims,* pp. 346-51.

14. S & G, ii, docs. 87, 115; Feldman, *German Imperialism,* doc. 10.

15. S & G, ii, docs. 104, 113.

16. Ibid., docs. 123, 127; Hopwood, 'Czernin', p. 55; Ritter, *Sword,* iii. 440-1.

17. O. Czernin, *In the World War* (London, 1919), 19-39 for general discussion of Czernin's attitude towards a separate peace.

18. I. Sinanoglou, 'Frenchmen, their Revolutionary Heritage, and the Russian Revolution', *IHR* 2/4 (1980), 566-84. For the more pessimistic British assessments, K. E. Neilson, 'The Break-up of the Anglo-Russian Alliance: The Question of Supply in 1917', *IHR* 3/1 (1981), 62-75.

19. R. P. Browder and A. F. Kerensky (eds.), *The Russian Provisional Government, 1917* (3 vols., Stanford, 1961), ii, doc. 948; see generally R. A. Wade, 'Why October? The Search for Peace in 1917', *SS* 20/1 (1968), 36-45; R. A. Wade, 'Iraki Tseretelli and Siberian Zimmerwaldianism', *JMH* 39/4 (1967), 425-31; and R. A. Wade, *The Russian Search for Peace, February-October 1917* (Stanford, 1969).

20. Browder and Kerensky (eds.), *Provisional Government,* ii, docs. 905, 908, 909, 922, 963-4, 966-7; Buchanan, *Mission,* ii. 108, 119, 122-3, 126-7.

21. Ibid., pp. 117-18.

22. Calder, *New Europe,* p. 152; T. Komarnicki, *Rebirth of the Polish Republic: A Study in the Diplomatic History of Europe, 1914-1920* (London, 1957), 152-66.

23. Bethmann, *Betrachtungen,* ii. 197-9; Epstein, *Erzberger,* p. 168; Ritter, *Sword,* iii. 407-9.

24. Epstein, *Erzberger,* pp. 166-78; S & G, ii, docs. 40, 85, 88, 90, 93, 98.

25. Ibid., docs. 107-8, 110, 114, 119, 134; Browder and Kerensky (eds.), *Provisional Government,* ii, docs. 936-8, 1006-7; Epstein, *Erzberger,* pp. 178-9.

26. G. D. Feldman, *Army, Industry, and Labour in Germany, 1914-1918* (Princeton, 1966), chs. v-vi; Ryder, *German Revolution,* ch. 5.

27. Jarausch, *Chancellor,* pp. 329-38; P. W. E. Ludendorff, *My War Memories, 1914-1918* (2 vols., London, 1919), ii. 447.

28. Epstein, *Erzberger,* pp. 182-92.

29. Ibid., pp. 202-4; S & G, ii, doc. 169; text of the Resolution in Feldman, *German Imperialism,* doc. 12.

30. M. Kitchen, *The Silent Dictatorship: The Politics of the German High Command under Hindenburg and Ludendorff, 1916-1918* (London, 1976), ch. 6; Epstein, *Erzberger,* pp. 193-201.

31. Ibid., p. 206.

32. Browder and Kerensky (eds.), *Provisional Government,* ii, docs. 964, 972-5, 986, 989; Wade, 'Why October?', pp. 41-3.

33. Neilson, 'Break-up', p. 68; Stevenson, *War Aims*, pp. 66-7, 71.
34. On international socialism and the Stockholm Conference, see M. Fainsod, *International Socialism and the World War* (repr., New York, 1973), chs. IV-V; H. Meynell, 'The Stockholm Conference of 1917', *IRSH* 5 (1960), 1-25, 202-25; D. Kirby, 'International Socialism and the Question of Peace: The Stockholm Conference of 1917', *HJ* 25/3 (1982), 709-16; D. Kirby, *War, Peace, and Revolution: International Socialism at the Crossroads, 1914-1918* (London, 1986). In general on the connections between international and domestic politics in 1917, A. J. Mayer, *Political Origins of the New Diplomacy, 1917-1918* (New Haven, 1959) is fundamental.
35. Czernin, *World War*, p. 168; S & G, ii, docs. 95, 102, 215.
36. *FRUS: Lansing Papers*, ii. 17; Fainsod, *International Socialism*, pp. 113, 140.
37. Discussed below in section iii of this chapter.
38. This is based mainly on Seton-Watson, *Italy*, pp. 468-92.
39. Becker, *French People*, chs. 13-16; J.-B. Duroselle, *La France et les Français, 1914-1920* (Paris, 1972), ch. 4 give surveys of the French crisis.
40. Stevenson, *War Aims*, pp. 68-71.
41. A. J. P. Taylor, *English History, 1914-1945* (Harmondsworth, 1970), 128; D. Gill and G. Dallas, 'Mutiny at Étaples Base in 1917', *P & P*, 64 (1975), 88-112. M. Swartz, *The Union of Democratic Control in British Politics during the First World War* (Oxford, 1971), chs. 8-9, however, shows that some ministers were concerned about the growth of opposition to official policy.
42. Lloyd George, *War Memoirs*, iv. 1881-1934; Meynell, 'Stockholm Conference', pp. 203-9; Buchanan, *Mission*, ii. 163-4; PRO, Cabinet Papers, CAB/23/2-3: meetings of 21 May, 1, 8, 10 August 1917.
43. Mayer, *Origins*, p. 317; Swartz, *Union of Democratic Control*, pp. 161 ff; J. M. Winter, 'Arthur Henderson, the Russian Revolution, and the Reconstruction of the Labour Party', *HJ* 15/4 (1972), 753-73.
44. D. Živojinović, 'Robert Lansing's Comments on the Pontifical Peace Note of August 1, 1917', *JAH* 56/3 (1969), 562.
45. Bethmann, *Betrachtungen*, ii. 210-14; S & G, ii, docs. 157, 175.
46. Text of the note (dated 1 August) in Scott (ed.), *War Aims*, pp. 129-31. For the background, and on the 1917 secret negotiations generally, see P. Renouvin, *La Crise européenne et la Première Guerre Mondiale (1904-1918)* (Paris, 1969), 474-506; P. Renouvin, 'Le Gouvernement français et les tentatives de paix en 1917', *La Revue des deux mondes* (15 Oct. 1964), 492-513; Pedroncini, *Négociations*, ch. 4; Farrar, *Divide*, chs. VI-VII; Rothwell, *War Aims*, pp. 102-9.
47. S & G, ii, docs. 181, 207, 211, 216, 221, 225; Epstein 'Development', p. 46; Ritter, *Sword*, iv. 28-37, 42.
48. Stevenson, *War Aims*, pp. 72-5; S & G, ii, docs. 231, 233, 235.
49. Seymour (ed.), *House*, iii, 159; Stevenson, *War Aims*, p. 80.
50. PRO, Cabinet Papers, CAB/23/3; Foreign Office Papers, FO/371/3083, Balfour to de Salis, 21 Aug. 1917, with note by 'C. H. S.', 22 Aug. 1917; Ribot (ed.), *Journal*, p. 188.
51. Scott (ed.), *War Aims*, pp. 133-5 for Wilson's reply. S & G, ii, doc. 230.

52. Ibid., doc. 235; W. Michaelis, 'Der Reichskanzler Michaelis und die Päpstliche Friedensaktion, 1917: Neue Dokumente', *GWU* 12/7 (1961), 432; Ritter, *Sword*, iv. 45.
53. S & G, ii, docs. 236, 247, 251, 275; Michaelis, 'Der Reichskanzler Michaelis' pp. 17–19; Ritter, *Sword*, iv. 51–5; L. G. Farrar, 'Opening to the West: German Efforts to Conclude a Separate Peace with England, July 1917–March 1918', *CJH* 10/1 (1975), 73–90.
54. D. R. Woodward, 'David Lloyd George, a Negotiated Peace with Germany, and the Kühlmann Peace Kite of September 1917', *CJH* 6/1 (1971), 75–93; Lloyd George, *War Memoirs*, iv. 2083–99; Lowe and Dockrill, *Mirage*, iii, doc. 121.
55. Pedroncini, *Négociations*, pp. 68–73; Stevenson, *War Aims*, pp. 88–90.
56. S & G, ii, docs. 236, 259.
57. Ibid., docs. 189, 235.
58. Woodward, 'Lloyd George', pp. 88–92; Farrar, 'Opening', p. 85; Stevenson, *War Aims*, pp. 75, 91.
59. For stark expressions of Ludendorff's world-view, Ludendorff, *War Memories*, ii. 523–4; S & G, ii, docs. 251 and (for Hindenburg) 112.
60. Ibid., docs. 236, 251.
61. A. Kaspi, *Le Temps des Américains: Le concours américain à la France en 1917–1918* (Paris, 1976), 75.
62. Ibid., pp. 51–63; K. Burk, 'Great Britain in the United States, 1917–1918: The Turning Point', *IHR* 1/2 (1979), 228–45; K. Burk, *Britain, America, and the Sinews of War, 1914–1918* (Boston and London, 1985); E. B. Parsons, *Wilsonian Diplomacy: Allied–American Rivalries in War and Peace* (St Louis, 1978), p. viii.
63. Lloyd George, *War Memoirs*, iv. p. 2104; Stevenson, *War Aims*, p. 80.
64. Seymour (ed.), *House*, iii. 32 ff, 167–72; L. W. Martin, *Peace without Victory: Woodrow Wilson and the British Liberals* (New Haven, 1958), 140–1; L. E. Gelfand, *The Inquiry: American Preparations for Peace, 1917–1919* (New Haven, 1963), 26.
65. W. B. Fowler, *British–American Relations, 1917–1918: The Role of Sir William Wiseman* (Princeton, 1969), 43–4; Seymour (ed.), *House*, iii. 39–51, 63–4; PRO, FO Papers FO/371/3081, docket note by C. H. S., 3 May 1917; Browder and Kerensky (eds.), *Provisional Government*, ii, doc. 975.
66. V. Mamatey, *The United States and East Central Europe, 1914–1918: A Study in Wilsonian Diplomacy and Propaganda* (Princeton, 1957), 114, 119; Seymour (ed.), *House*, iii. 52–3.
67. Stevenson, *War Aims*, pp. 75–86.
68. T. E. La Fargue, 'The Entrance of China into the World War', *PHR* 5/3 (1936), 222–33; La Fargue, *China*, ch. iv.
69. Lansing, *War Memoirs*, pp. 287–9; *FRUS: Lansing Papers*, ii, 431; R. W. Curry, *Woodrow Wilson and Far Eastern Policy, 1913–1921* (repr., New York, 1968), ch. 6.
70. J. J. Safford, *Wilsonian Maritime Diplomacy, 1913–1921* (New Brunswick, 1978), 127–40 (on the embargo); Curry, *Wilson*, p. 173 (for Wilson's views), Seymour (ed.), *House*, iii. 25–6; M. Chi, *China Diplomacy,*

1914-1918 (Cambridge, Mass., 1970), 105; B. F. Beers, *Vain Endeavour: Robert Lansing's Attempts to End the American-Japanese Rivalry* (Durham, North Carolina, 1962), 41, 44, 48-9, 94-5.

71. For the Lansing-Ishii negotiations, Kajima (ed.), *Diplomacy*, iii, ch. vii; Lansing, *War Memoirs*, ch. xx; K. Ishii, *Diplomatic Commentaries* (US edn., Baltimore, 1936), ch. vi; *FRUS: Lansing Papers*, ii. 432 ff., Chi, *China Diplomacy* pp. 111-13; in addition to the sources so far cited.

72. Kajima (ed.), *Diplomacy*, iii. 308; Curry, *Wilson*, pp. 171-3; Nish, *Alliance*, pp. 216-19.

73. G. W. Egerton, *Great Britain and the Creation of the League of Nations: Strategy, Politics, and International Organization, 1914-1919* (Chapel Hill, 1978), pp. 42, 45-8, 64-72.

74. PRO, Cabinet Papers, CAB/23/2-4: meetings of 3 April, 20 Aug., 27 Nov. 1917; Rothwell, *War Aims*, pp. 272 ff.

75. In general on the Balfour Declaration, see L. Stein, *The Balfour Declaration* (London, 1961); Friedman, *Palestine*; D. Z. Gillon, 'The Antecedents of the Balfour Declaration', *MES* 5/2 (1969), 131-50; M. Vereté, 'The Balfour Declaration and its Makers', *MES* 6/1 (1970), 48-76.

76. Friedman, *Palestine*, chs. 2, 8.

77. Stein, *Balfour Declaration*, pp. 62-81. J. Kimche, *The Unromantics: The Great Powers and the Balfour Declaration* (London, 1968), ch. 2.

78. Stein, *Balfour Declaration*, pp. 459-60; Friedman, *Palestine*, chs. 8, 14.

79. Ibid., ch. 11; Andrew and Kanya-Forstner, *France Overseas*, pp. 129-30; R. N. Lebow, 'Woodrow Wilson and the Balfour Declaration', *JMH* 40/4 (1968), 501-23.

80. Ibid., pp. 509-23; Friedman, *Palestine*, ch. 16; Lowe and Dockrill, *Mirage*, iii, docs. 104-6.

81. Friedman, *Palestine*, ch. 18.

82. Kedourie, *Labyrinth*, chs. 5-6.

83. Rothwell, *War Aims*, pp. 123-38; Friedman, *Palestine*, ch. 13; Trumpener, *Germany and the Ottoman Empire*, ch. v.

84. Lloyd George, *War Memoirs*, iv. 2107-9.

Notes to Chapter 5

1. See the discussions in E. H. Carr, *The Bolshevik Revolutions, 1917-1923* (3 vols., Harmondsworth, 1966), iii. 541-60; and R. K. Debo, *Revolution and Survival: The Foreign Policy of Soviet Russia, 1917-1918* (Toronto, 1979), ch. 1.

2. P. W. Dyer, 'German Support of Lenin during World War I', *AJPH* 30/1 (1984), 46-55. For Allied views, see J. Bradley, 'France, Lenin, and the Bolsheviks in 1917-1918', *EHR* 86 (1971), 783-9; G. F. Kennan, 'The Sisson Documents', *JMH* 28/2 (1956), 130-54.

3. Carr, *Revolution*, iii. 21; Debo, *Survival*, p. 59.

4. J. Degras (ed.), *Soviet Documents on Foreign Policy* (3 vols., London, 1951-3), i. 1-3; Carr, *Revolution*, iii. 21-3; J. W. Wheeler-Bennett, *Brest-*

Litovsk: The Forgotten Peace, March 1918 (London, 1938), 83-94.

5. Ritter, *Sword*, iv. 145-59; S & G, ii, docs. 266, 269, 280, 299, 302.

6. Z. A. B. Zeman (ed.), *Germany and the Revolution in Russia, 1915-1918: Documents from the Archives of the German Foreign Ministry* (London, 1958), doc. 77; Czernin, *World War*, pp. 217-18.

7. R. von Kühlmann, *Erinnerungen* (Heidelberg, 1948), 522-5; Fischer, *Aims*, ch. 17, and pp. 492-3.

8. S & G, iii, doc. 151; Ludendorff, *War Memories*, ii. 530.

9. S & G, iii, doc. 45.

10. Wheeler-Bennett, *Brest-Litovsk*, pp. 107-10.

11. Kaspi, *Temps*, ch. vii; D. F. Trask, *The United States in the Supreme War Council: American War Aims and Inter-Allied Strategy, 1917-1918* (Westport, Conn., 1961), 47.

12. Seymour (ed.), *House*, iii. 284-91; Lloyd George, War Memoirs, v. 2570-1.

13. Stevenson, *War Aims*, pp. 87-8, 98-9; K. Hovi, *Cordon sanitaire or Barrière de l'Est? The Emergence of the New French Eastern European Alliance Policy, 1917-1919* (Turku, 1975), 71-5.

14. Calder, *New Europe*, pp. 171-4; Rothwell, *War Aims*, pp. 158-61; Lloyd George, *War Memoirs*, v. 2461-79.

15. On the background to the speech, ibid., pp. 2483-6; Rothwell, *War Aims*, pp. 145-53, 162; G. A. Riddell, *Lord Riddell's War Diary, 1914-1918* (London, 1932), 304-5.

16. Louis, *Great Britain*, pp. 93-102. Text of the speech in Scott (ed.), *War Aims*, pp. 225-33.

17. Ibid., pp. 244-5.

18. On the background to the Fourteen Points, Mayer, *Origins*, pp. 329-67; Seymour (ed.), *House*, iii. ch. xi; Gelfand, *Inquiry*, ch. 5; Mamatey, *East Central Europe*, pp. 171-3, 184. Text of the Points in Scott (ed.), *War Aims*, pp. 234-9.

19. Mamatey, *East Central Europe*, pp. 171, 174; general discussion in N. G. Levin, jun., *Woodrow Wilson and World Politics: America's Response to War and Revolution* (New York, 1968), ch. ii.

20. Mamatey, *East Central Europe*, pp. 197-202; I. J. Lederer, *Yugoslavia at the Paris Peace Conference: A Study in Frontiermaking* (New Haven and London, 1963), 27.

21. Text of the speech in Scott (ed.), *War Aims*, pp. 246-54; for the strike wave, Feldman, *Army, Industry, and Labour*, pp. 442-57; Kirby, *Crossroads*, pp. 215-17. See generally J. L. Snell, 'Wilson's Peace Programme and German Socialism, January-March 1918', *MVHR* 38/2 (1951), 187-214.

22. Mamatey, *East Central Europe*, pp. 219-22; text of Czernin's speech in Scott (ed.), *War Aims*, pp. 255-61.

23. Pedroncini, *Négociations*, p. 77; H. Hanak, 'The Government, the Foreign Office, and Austria-Hungary, 1914-1918', *Sl.EER*, 47/108 (1969), 184.

24. Text of the speech in Scott (ed.), *War Aims*, pp. 265-71.

25. Article on the Armand-Revertera conversations in *L'Opinion* (31 July 1920), 115-20.

26. Lloyd George, *War Memoirs*, v. 2498-502.
27. Pedroncini, *Négociations*, pp. 83-91; Mamatey, *East Central Europe*, pp. 226-32; Seymour (ed.), *House*, iii. 383-95.
28. On the Ukrainian Treaty, Wheeler-Bennett, *Brest-Litovsk* ch. v and app. IV; Czernin, *World War*, pp. 231-53.
29. Ritter, *Sword*, iv. 106-9; W. Baumgart, *Deutsche Ostpolitik, 1918: Von Brest-Litovsk bis zum Ende des Ersten Weltkrieges* (Vienna and Munich, 1966), 24-6; S & G, iii, docs. 192, 228, 232, 241, 250; Ludendorff, *War Memories*, ii. 557-60.
30. S & G, iii, docs. 274, 275; Debo, *Survival*, p. 158; text of the Treaty in Wheeler-Bennett, *Brest-Litovsk*, app. v.
31. Epstein, *Erzberger*, p. 234.
32. Scott (ed.), *War Aims*, pp. 309-12; Seymour (ed.), *House*, iii. 437-8.
33. Wheeler-Bennett, *Brest-Litovsk*, chs. v and vii, apps. iii, vi; Debo, *Survival*, chs. 4-6; L. Trotsky, *My Life: The Rise and Fall of a Dictator* (London, 1930), ch. xxxii.
34. On the Treaty of Bucharest, Spector, *Rumania*, pp. 45-56; Kitchen, *Dictatorship*, ch. 8; Ritter, *Sword*, iv. 171-85; Czernin, *World War*, ch. xi; Burián, *Austria*, pp. 320-2; Kühlmann, *Erinerrungen*, pp. 550-67; Fischer, *Aims*, pp. 515-23; Foreign Office Political Intelligence Department 'Memorandum on the Meaning and Effect of the Bucharest "Peace Treaty" ', PRO FO/800/11021*. Text of the Treaty in *FRUS: 1918. Supplement I. The World War*, i. 771-7.
35. Baumgart, *Ostpolitik*, p. 374.
36. Kitchen, *Dictatorship*, ch. 9; Ritter, *Sword*, iv. 270-2; Fischer, *Aims*, pp. 510-15.
37. Debo, *Survival*, ch. 9; Kitchen, *Dictatorship*, ch. 10; Trumpener, *Germany and the Ottoman Empire*, ch. vi.
38. For Hintze see Fischer, *Aims*, pp. 571-3; Ritter, *Sword*, iv. 263-5; for the Bolshevik initiative, Debo, *Survival*, ch. 9; for 'Keystone', H. H. Herwig, 'German Policy in the Eastern Baltic Sea in 1918: Expansion or Anti-Bolshevik Crusade?', *SR* 32/2 (1973), 339-57.
39. Debo, *Survival*, ch. 12; text of the treaties in Wheeler-Bennett, *Brest-Litovsk*, apps. vii-ix.
40. R. H. Ullman, *Anglo-Soviet Relations, 1917-1921* (3 vols., Princeton, 1961-72), i. 152, 309, 320, 332; ii. 20, 28.
41. Ibid., pp. 42-55; Lloyd George, *War Memoirs*, v. ch. lxxi; Lowe and Dockrill, *Mirage*, ii. 304-12; iii, docs. 150-3. J. Bradley, *Allied Intervention in Russia* (London, 1968) is the most recent general history of intervention, but must be supplemented by reading on the individual Powers.
42. I. Sinanoglou, 'France looks Eastward: Policies and Perspectives in Russia, 1914-1918' (Columbia Ph.D, 1974), ch. viii; M. J. Carley, *Revolution and Intervention: The French Government and the Russian Civil War, 1917-1919* (Kingston, Ontario, and Montreal, 1983), ch. 2.
43. For general discussions, G. F. Kennan, *Soviet-American Relations, 1917-1920* (2 vols., London, 1956-8), i; E. P. Trani, 'Woodrow Wilson and the Decision to Intervene in Russia: A Reconsideration', *JMH* 48/3

(1976), 440-61; Fowler, *Wiseman*, ch. 7; Trask, *Supreme War Council*, ch. 6.

44. Seymour (ed.), *House*, iii. 398-408; B. M. Unterberger, 'President Wilson and the Decision to send American Troops to Siberia', *PHR* 24 (1955), 63-74; C. Lasch, 'American Intervention in Siberia: A Reinterpretation', *PSQ* 77 (1962), 205-23; on the British side see especially, D. R. Woodward, 'The British Government and Japanese Intervention in Russia during World War I', *JMH* 46/4 (1974), 663-85.

45. J. W. Morley, *The Japanese Thrust into Siberia, 1918* (New York, 1957), is the essential source on Japanese policy.

46. Sinanoglou, 'France looks Eastward', p. 286.

47. Debo, *Survival*, pp. 135-43; 154-5.

48. M. J. Carley, 'The Origins of French Intervention in the Russian Civil War, January-May 1918: A Reappraisal', *JMH* 48/3 (1976), 413-39.

49. Debo, *Survival*, p. 259.

50. Ibid., ch. 11; Bradley, *Allied Intervention*, ch. 4.

51. J. W. Long, 'American Intervention in Russia: The North Russian Expedition, 1918-1919', *DH* 6/1 (1982), 45-67; Debo, *Survival*, pp. 295-9.

52. For the White House conference and the *aide-mémoire FRUS: 1918 Russia*, ii. 262-3, 287-90.

53. Ullman, *Anglo-Soviet Relations*, i. 217.

54. Morley, *Thrust*, pp. 260-89.

55. Scott (ed.), *War Aims*, pp. 298-322. Ritter, *Sword*, iv. 237-40.

56. Hearings of Clemenceau and Pichon by the Chamber Commission on External Affairs, 3 and 7 May 1918, French National Archives, Box C. 7491.

57. Mamatey, *East Central Europe*, pp. 237, 256-8; Calder, *New Europe*, pp. 176, 182.

58. Stevenson, *War Aims*, pp. 107, 86-7.

59. Ibid., pp. 106-8, 112; Hovi, *Cordon sanitaire*, pp. 71-4, 106-8, 125-8.

60. On the Yugoslav question, Lederer, *Yugoslavia*, pp. 25-40; Calder, *New Europe*, pp. 190-1, 201-3; Mamatey, *East Central Europe*, pp. 239-45, 273-4, 314-315; D. Sepić, 'The Question of Yugoslav Union in 1918', *JCH* 3/4 (1968), 29-43.

61. On the Czechs, Perman, *Shaping*, ch. 2; Mamatey, *East Central Europe*, pp. 252-73, 300-11; Calder, *New Europe*, pp. 191-4, 204-11.

62. Burián, *Austria*, chs. xx-xxi; Scott, (ed.), *War Aims*, pp. 386-9.

63. Fischer, *Aims*, pp. 532, 622-3; Ritter, *Sword*, iv. 242.

64. Ludendorff, *War Memories*, ii. 684. P. Renouvin, *L'Armistice de Rethondes, 11 novembre 1918* (Paris, 1968), and H. Rudin, *Armistice 1918* (New Haven, 1944) are the best accounts of the German Armistice.

65. Ritter, *Sword*, iv. 323-4, 336-9.

66. Ibid., pp. 341, 344-8; Kitchen, *Dictatorship*, ch. 11; Ludendorff, *War Memories*, ii. 717-33; Max of Baden, *Memoirs* (2 vols., London, 1928), ii. 4-42. The German-American armistice correspondence is in Scott (ed.), *War Aims*, pp. 115 ff.

67. On Turkey, see G. Dyer, 'The Turkish Armistice of 1918', *MES* 8 (1972), 143-78, 313-47.

68. Max of Baden, *Memoirs*, p. 20.
69. Scott (ed.), *War Aims*, pp. 399-405; Seymour (ed.), *House*, iv. 62-73; Martin, *Peace without Victory*, pp. 171-82.
70. Renouvin, *Rethondes*, pp. 115-16, 121-2, 145. I. Floto, *Colonel House in Paris: A Study of American Policy at the Paris Peace Conference, 1919* (Aarhus, 1973), ch. 1 is important on American policy.
71. Ibid., pp. 36-8; Seymour (ed.) *House*, iv. 81-4; Ritter, *Sword*, iv. 350, 353.
72. Max of Baden, *Memoirs*, pp. 89-161.
73. Mamatey, *East Central Europe*, pp. 322, 333-4.
74. Dyer, 'Turkish Armistice'; Lloyd George, *War Memoirs*, vi. 3264-8, 3309-15; Rothwell, *War Aims*, pp. 236-44.
75. Sepić, 'Yugoslav Union'; Floto, *House*, p. 45; Lederer, *Yugoslavia*, pp. 59, 62-3.
76. Floto, *House*, pp. 41-2; B. Lowry, 'Pershing and the Armistice', *JAH* 55 (1968-9), 283-5.
77. Stevenson, *War Aims*, pp. 122-7; Rudin, *Armistice*, ch. xii.
78. On the naval clauses, Seymour (ed.), *House*, iv. 129-38; Rothwell, *War Aims*, pp. 258-63; Rudin, *Armistice*, ch. xii pp. 426-32.
79. Floto, *House*, p. 60.
80. Riddell, *War Diary*, pp. 371, 374; Rothwell, *War Aims*, p. 260.
81. Stevenson, *War Aims*, p. 124.
82. Seymour (ed.), *House*, iv. 88.
83. J. L. Snell, 'Wilson on Germany and the Fourteen Points', *JMH* 26/4 (1954), 364-9.
84. Seymour (ed.), *House*, iv. 156-8, 198-209.
85. For a discussion of these points, Kaspi, *Temps*, ch. xi; D. M. Kennedy, *Over Here: The First World War and American Society* (New York and Oxford, 1980), ch. 6; Burk, 'Great Britain in the United States', pp. 228-45.
86. Floto, *House*, pp. 49-60; M. G. Fry, 'The Imperial War Cabinet, the United States and the Freedom of the Seas', *Journal of the Royal United Services Institution* 110/640 (1965), 353-62.
87. Rudin, *Armistice*, chs. ix. x. xiii-xv; Renouvin, *Rethondes*, ch. xii.

Notes to Chapter 6

1. There is no satisfactory account of the Peace Conference as a whole. Of the more specialized studies M. L. Dockrill and J. D. Goold, *Peace without Promise: Britain and the Peace Conferences, 1919-1923* (London, 1981) is the best introductory survey. F. S. Marston, *The Peace Conference of 1919: Organization and Procedure* (Oxford, 1944) deals with the mechanics of peacemaking.
2. On Bolshevism and the Peace Conference generally see A. J. Mayer, *Politics and Diplomacy of Peacemaking: Containment and Counter-revolution at Versailles, 1918-1919* (London, 1968) and, especially, J. M. Thompson, *Russia, Bolshevism, and the Versailles Peace* (Princeton, 1966).

3. On French intervention, see Carley, *Revolution and Intervention*; on British see Ullman, *Anglo-Soviet Relations*, ii; M. G. Fry, 'Britain, the Allies, and the Problem of Russia, 1918-1919', *CJH* 2/2 (1967), 62-84; J. D. Rose, 'Batum as Domino, 1919-1920: The Defence of India in Caucasia', *IHR* 11/2 (1980), 266-87.
4. Mayer, *Peacemaking*, ch. 8.
5. See for example Lloyd George to Churchill, 16 Feb. 1919, LG Papers, HLRO, F/8/3/18.
6. On French reaction to the Prinkipo initiative, see P. Miquel, *La Paix de Versailles et l'opinion publique française* (Paris, 1972), 113-17, 153-66.
7. Generally on the Prinkipo, Bullitt, and Nansen affairs, see Thompson, *Versailles Peace*, chs. 4, 5, 7; Mayer, *Peacemaking*, chs. 10, 13-14; Levin, *Wilson*, ch. vi; D. Lloyd George, *The Truth about the Peace Treaties* (2 vols., London, 1938), i, ch. vii; Floto, *House*, ch. 3.
8. On these developments see Thompson, *Versailles Peace*, ch. 10; Ullman, *Anglo-Soviet Relations*, ii. esp. 194, 207, 215; R. K. Debo, 'Lloyd George and the Copenhagen Conference of 1919-1920: The Initiation of Anglo-Soviet Negotiations', *HJ* 24/2 (1981), 429-41.
9. For example, H. Nicolson, *Peacemaking 1919* (new edn., London, 1937), 44.
10. R. Albrecht-Carrié, *Italy at the Paris Peace Conference* (New York, 1938), 134.
11. Gelfand, *Inquiry*, chs. 7, 8, 11.
12. Floto, *House*, is the best discussion of American decision-making at the Conference.
13. Seymour (ed.), *House*, iv. 263.
14. R. S. Baker, *Woodrow Wilson and World Settlement* (3 vols., London, 1923), i. 184-5.
15. R. H. Fifield, *Woodrow Wilson and the Far East: The Diplomacy of the Shantung Question* (New York, 1952), 261.
16. Seymour (ed.), *House*, iv. 291; Mayer, *Peacemaking*, pp. 172-6.
17. Ibid., ch. 9.
18. These points are discussed more fully below.
19. Floto, *House*, app. 2.
20. On Wilson and the Senate see generally T. A. Bailey, *Woodrow Wilson and the Great Betrayal* (New York, 1945); J. E. Hewes, jun., 'Henry Cabot Lodge and the League of Nations', *PAPS* 114 (1970), 245-55; D. Mervin, 'Henry Cabot Lodge and the League of Nations', *JAS* 4/2 (1970), 201-14.
21. Seymour (ed.), *House*, iv. 291.
22. H. I. Nelson, *Land and Power: British and Allied Policy on Germany's Frontiers, 1916-1919* (London and Toronto, 1963), 93-7.
23. M. L. Dockrill and Z. Steiner, 'The Foreign Office at the Paris Peace Conference in 1919', *IHR* 2/1 (1980), 55-86.
24. Printed in Lloyd George, *Truth*, i. 404-16.
25. See S. P. Tillman, *Anglo-American Relations at the Paris Peace Conference of 1919* (Princeton, 1961), for a general account.
26. Levin, *Wilson*, pp. 154-61.

27. A. Tardieu, *La Paix* (Paris, 1921), 129-32.
28. Egerton, *Creation*, chs. 5, 6. This is the best source on the origins of the League; but see also G. B. Egerton, 'The Lloyd George Government and the Creation of the League of Nations', *AHR* 79/2 (1974), 419-44; P. Raffo, 'The Anglo-American Preliminary Negotiations for a League of Nations', *JCH* 9/4 (1974), 153-76; Tillman, *Anglo-American Relations*, ch. 4; Seymour (ed.), *House*, iv, ch. ix; R. Cecil, *A Great Experiment* (London, 1941), ch. ii; Lloyd George, *Truth*, i, ch. xiv; D. H. Miller, · *The Drafting of the Covenant* (2 vols., New York, 1928).
29. F. Costigliola, *Awkward Dominion: American Political, Economic, and Cultural Relations with Europe, 1919-1933* (Ithaca, NY, 1984), 29.
30. Tillman, *Anglo-American Relations*, p. 131.
31. Lloyd George considered the Covenant 'a bundle of assignats': in contrast with his own 'sovereigns' of the German colonies and Mesopotamia. G. A. Riddell, *Lord Riddell's Intimate Diary of the Peace Conference and After, 1918-1923* (London, 1933), 24.
32. On the mandates issue, see Tillman, *Anglo-American Relations*, ch. 3; Louis, *Great Britain*, ch. iv; W. R. Louis, 'The United States and the African Peace Settlement of 1919: The Pilgrimage of George Louis Beer', *J. Afr. H* 4/3 (1963), 413-33; G. Curry, 'Woodrow Wilson, Jan Smuts, and the Versailles Settlement', *AHR* 66/4 (1961), 968-86; H. D. Hall, 'The British Commonwealth and the Founding of the League Mandate System', in Bourne and Watt (eds.), *Studies*, 345-68.
33. On the naval dispute: Tillman, *Anglo-American Relations*, ch. 11; A. J. Marder, *From the Dreadnought to Scapa Flow: The Royal Navy in the Fisher Era, 1904-1919*, (London, 1970), v, chs. ix, x; Egerton, *Creation*, ch. 7; Floto, *House*, pp. 209-11; J. K. MacDonald, 'Lloyd George and the Search for a Postwar Naval Policy, 1919', in A. J. P. Taylor (ed.), *Lloyd George: Twelve Essays* (London, 1971), 189-222.
34. Tillman, *Anglo-American Relations*, p. 288.
35. Floto, *House*, p. 211.
36. Tillman, *Anglo-American Relations*, p. 66.
37. Hardach, *The First World War*, p. 155.
38. D. P. Silverman, *Reconstructing Europe after the Great War* (Cambridge, Mass., and London, 1982), 15.
39. Stevenson, *War Aims*, p. 149.
40. Tillman, *Anglo-American Relations*, ch. 10; A. Walworth, *America's Moment, 1918: American Diplomacy at the End of World War I* (New York, 1977), chs. xiii-xiv (the Hoover quotation is on p. 216); M. J. Hogan, 'The United States and the Problem of International Economic Control: American Attitudes towards European Reconstruction, 1918-1920', *PHR* 44/1 (1975), 84-103.
41. D. Artaud, 'Le Gouvernement américain et la question des dettes de guerre au lendemain de l'armistice de Rethondes (1919-1920)', *RHMC* 20 (1973), 203.
42. Austen Chamberlain to Lloyd George, 17 Apr. 1919, LG Papers, HLRO, F/7/2/27.
43. Lloyd George to Wilson, 23 Apr. 1919, Baker, *Wilson*, iii, doc. 48.

44. Wilson to Lloyd George, 5 May 1919; Lamont and Davis to Wilson, 15 May 1919, Baker, *Wilson*, iii, docs. 49, 51; see Artaud, 'Dettes de guerre' for an excellent discussion; also Hogan, 'International Economic Control', pp. 47–8; and P. P. Abrahams, 'American Bankers and the Economic Tactics of Peace: 1919', *JAH* 56/3 (1969), 572–83.

45. For French public opinion, Miquel, *Paix de Versailles*, pp. 419–542.

46. Trachtenberg, *Reparation*, pp. 29–65; Stevenson, *War Aims*, pp. 152–4, 165–9.

47. Bunselmeyer, *Cost*, chs. 5–10, traces British policy on the eve of the Peace Conference.

48. Lloyd George, *Truth*, i. 475–83.

49. P. M. Burnett, *Reparation at the Paris Peace Conference (from the Standpoint of the American Delegation)* (2 vols., New York, 1940), ii, doc. 470, Annex VIII. Burnett's book is the best general account of the reparation issue at the Conference, and what follows is based mainly on it. See also Trachtenberg, *Reparation*, ch. 2; E. Weill-Raynal, *Les Réparations allemandes et la France* (3 vols., Paris, 1947), i; and the conflicting assessments by J. M. Keynes, *The Economic Consequences of the Peace* (London, 1920); and E. Mantoux, *The Carthaginian Peace, or the Economic Consequences of Mr Keynes* (London, 1946); and the articles in *JMH* 51/1 (1979), 4–85.

50. Tardieu, *La Paix*, p. 321.

51. M. Trachtenberg, 'Reparation at the Paris Peace Conference', *JMH* 51/1 (1979), 46.

52. Floto, *House*, p. 202.

53. Lloyd George, *Truth*, i. 507.

54. Baker, *Wilson*, ii, p. xiii.

55. For French unofficial opinion see generally Miquel, *Paix de Versailles*; for the formulation of French negotiating aims, Stevenson, *War Aims*, ch. vi.

56. Ibid., p. 157.

57. Ibid., p. 148.

58. Andrew and Kanya-Forstner, 'Colonial Party', p. 104.

59. Stevenson, *War Aims*, p. 165.

60. On French frontier questions at the Conference see generally ibid., ch. vii; Nelson, *Land and Power*, pp. 198–281; W. A. McDougall, *France's Rhineland Diplomacy, 1914–1924: The Last Bid for a Balance of Power in Europe* (Princeton, 1978), ch. 2; K. L. Nelson, *Victors Divided: America and the Allies in Germany, 1918–1923* (Berkeley, Los Angeles, and London, 1975), chs. 4–5; D. R. Watson, *Georges Clemenceau: A Political Biography* (London, 1974), 344–59; J. C. King, *Foch versus Clemenceau: France and German Dismemberment, 1918–1919* (Cambridge, Mass., 1960); J. R. McCrum, 'French Rhineland Policy at the Paris Peace Conference, 1919', *HJ* 21/3 (1978), 623–48.

61. Baker, *Wilson*, i. 220–1; ii. 10–11, 73.

62. See generally L. S. Jaffe, *The Decision to Disarm Germany. British Policy towards Postwar German Disarmament, 1914–1919* (London, 1985).

63. Floto, *House*, p. 181.

64. J. Bariéty, 'De l'exécution à la négociation: L'évolution des relations

franco-allemandes après la Première Guerre Mondiale (11 novembre 1918-10 janvier 1925): Forces profondes et actions politiques', (University of Paris I thesis, 1975), 83.

65. Marston, *Peace Conference*, pp. 117-18; Perman, *Shaping*, pp. 123-5, 138-42. See for example the recommendations agreed informally between British and American experts on 21 Feb. 1919, in Foreign Office Archives, PRO, FO/608/141. 477/1/3.

66. On the Polish question at the Conference see generally K. Lundgreen-Nielsen, *The Polish Problem at the Paris Peace Conference: A Study of the Great Powers and the Poles, 1918-1919* (Odense, 1979); the same author's 'The Mayer Thesis Reconsidered: The Poles and the Paris Peace Conference, 1919', *IHR* 7/1 (1985), 68-102; Nelson, *Land and Power*, pp. 145-97; P. S. Wandycz, *France and her Eastern Allies, 1919-1925; French-Czechoslovak-Polish Relations from the Paris Peace Conference to Locarno* (Minneapolis, 1962), chs. 1, 4; Komarnicki, *Rebirth*, pp. 273 ff.

67. Baker, *Wilson*, ii. 60.

68. On Czechoslovakia and Austria see Nelson, *Land and Power*, pp. 282-311; Perman, *Shaping*, chs. VI-VII; Wandycz, *Eastern Allies*, ch. 2; Stevenson, *War Aims*, pp. 182-3.

69. Perman, *Shaping*, pp. 176-80; D. P. Myers, 'Berlin versus Vienna: Disagreement about *Anschluss* in the Winter of 1918-1919', *CEH* 5/2 (1972), 150-75.

70. On this question see A. Tardieu, *Le Slesvig et la paix, janvier 1919-janvier 1920* (Paris, 1928).

71. On the Low Countries, see Nelson, *Land and Power*, pp. 312-20; Stevenson, 'Belgium', pp. 512 ff.; Helmreich, *Belgium*, pp. 199 ff.; but especially Marks, *Innocent*, pp. 103 ff.

72. Miquel, *Paix de Versailles*, pp. 376-90; King, *Foch versus Clemenceau*, pp. 60-64.

73. On Japan at the Conference and the Shantung question see especially Fifield, *Far East*; also R. H. Fifield, 'Disposal of the Carolines, Marshalls, and Marianas at the Paris Peace Conference', *AHR* 51/3 (1946), 472-9; and the same author's 'Japanese Policy towards the Shantung Question at the Paris Peace Conference', *JMH* 23/3 (1951), 265-72. On the Japanese side see also Nish, *Japanese Foreign Policy*, pp. 118 ff.; Nish, *Alliance*, ch. xv; Kajima (ed.), *Diplomacy*, iii, pt. II. Baker, *Wilson*, ii, pt. VII is important for Wilson's motives.

74. Kajima, (ed.), *Diplomacy*, iii. 343-52.

75. Ibid., iii. 395-418; Fifield, *Far East*, pp. 158-72; Nish, *Alliance*, pp. 269-71.

76. Baker, *Wilson*, ii. 254, 260.

77. Ibid., ii. 258.

78. For the Italo-Yugoslav dispute see section (v) below.

79. A. Luckau, *The German Delegation at the Paris Peace Conference* (New York, 1941), 62. This is the best account in English of German policy; in German see K. Schwabe, *Deutsche Revolution und Wilson-Frieden: Die Amerikanische und Deutsche Friedensstrategie zwischen Ideologie und Machtpolitik, 1918-19* (Düsseldorf, 1971); L. Haupts, *Deutsche Friedenspolitik, 1918-19:*

Eine Alternative zur Machtpolitik des Ersten Weltkrieges (Düsseldorf, 1976); P. Krüger, *Deutschland und die Reparationen, 1918-19: Die Genesis des Reparationsproblem zwischen Waffenstillstand und Versailler Friedensschluss* (Stuttgart, 1973).

80. O.-E. Schüddekopf, 'German Foreign Policy between Compiègne and Versailles', *JCH* 4/2 (1969), 181-97; Schwabe, *Deutsche Revolution*, pp. 659-60; Luckau, *German Delegation*, pp. 43-5.

81. Ibid., p. 94.

82. Ibid., doc. 57.

83. See Marston, *Peace Conference*, for a general discussion of these problems; also Nicolson, *Peacemaking*, pp. 95-103, 112-31.

84. K. Schwabe, 'Woodrow Wilson and Germany's Membership in the League of Nations, 1918-1919', *CEH* 8/1 (1975), 3-22.

85. Schwabe, *Deutsche Revolution*, p. 654.

86. On this revolt see for example Lloyd George, *Truth*, i, ch. xvi; J. Headlam-Morley, *A Memoir of the Paris Peace Conference, 1919*, eds: A. Headlam-Morley, R. Bryant and A. Cienciala (London, 1972), 103-4, 118.

87. King, *Foch versus Clemenceau*, pp. 73-104; McCrum, 'French Rhineland Policy', pp. 644-6.

88. Nelson, *Land and Power*, pp. 321-38; Lloyd George, *Truth*, i. 688 ff.

89. Baker, *Wilson*, iii. 494-504.

90. Levin, *Wilson*, ch. v; Schwabe, *Deutsche Revolution*, pp. 655-6.

91. F. G. Campbell, 'The Struggle for Upper Silesia, 1919-1922', *JMH* 42/3 (1970), 385.

92. Generally on the June crisis, see Tillman, *Anglo-American Relations*, ch. 13; Nelson, *Land and Power*, pp. 338-62; P. Mantoux, *Les Délibérations du Conseil des Quatre (24 mars-28 juin 1919)* (2 vols., Paris, 1955), ii. 265-427.

93. Luckau, *German Delegation*, p. 89.

94. For these developments generally see ibid., ch. iv; Epstein, *Erzberger*, pp. 301-23.

95. Spector, *Rumania*, p. 168.

96. A. D. Low, 'The Soviet Hungarian Republic and the Paris Peace Conference', *TAPS* ns, 53/10 (1963), 38-9. On Béla Kun see further below.

97. Lederer, *Yugoslavia*, pp. 219-27, 294-7; Tillman, *Anglo-American Relations*, pp. 215-17.

98. The principal sources in English on the Adriatic dispute are Albrecht-Carrié, *Italy*; Lederer, *Yugoslavia*; and D. R. Zivojinović, *America, Italy, and the Birth of Yugoslavia (1917-1919)* (New York, 1972). A new account is needed.

99. Mantoux, *Délibérations*, i. 277-81.

100. Seton-Watson, *Italy*, p. 506; Lederer, *Yugoslavia*, pp. 71-5.

101. Seton-Watson, *Italy*, p. 528; Lowe and Marzari, *Italian Foreign Policy*, pp. 160-66.

102. Ibid., p. 160; Albrecht-Carrié, *Italy*, p. 100.

103. Mantoux, *Délibérations*, i. 295-6.

104. Seton-Watson, *Italy*, p. 528 n.
105. Ibid., p. 527; Baker, *Wilson*, ii. 146.
106. Floto, *House*, pp. 90–4.
107. Albrecht-Carrié, *Italy*, p. 170; Floto, *House*, p. 93.
108. Albrecht-Carrié, *Italy*, p. 116.
109. Mayer, *Peacemaking*, p. 688.
110. Lloyd George, *Truth*, ii. 859, 863–8.
111. On the Rapallo Treaty see Seton-Watson, *Italy*, pp. 577–9; Lederer, *Yugoslavia*, pp. 301–7; Albrecht-Carrié, *Italy*, ch. xi.
112. On Bulgaria and Thrace, see Dockrill and Goold, *Peace*, pp. 93–101; P. C. Helmreich, *From Paris to Sèvres: The Partition of the Ottoman Empire at the Paris Peace Conference of 1919–1920* (Columbus, Ohio, 1974), 39–40, 153–8, 265.
113. I. Déak, *Hungary at the Paris Peace Conference: The Diplomatic History of the Treaty of Trianon* (New York, 1942), pt. II; Low, 'Hungarian Republic', pp. 31–9; see also generally Spector, *Rumania*.
114. Low, 'Hungarian Republic' is the best account of the Conference and the Hungarian Problem. See also Thompson, *Versailles Peace*, ch. 6; Mayer, *Peacemaking*, chs. 16, 17, 21, 24; P. Pastor, 'The Vix Mission in Hungary, 1918–1919: A Re-examination', *SR* 29/1 (1970), 481–98; J. Smallwood, 'Banquo's Ghost at the Paris Peace Conference: The United States and the Hungarian Question', *EEQ* 12/3 (1978), 289–307.
115. Low, 'Hungarian Republic', p. 47.
116. Spector, *Rumania*, pp. 168 ff.
117. Lloyd George, *Truth*, ii. 1072.
118. On the King–Crane Commission see H. N. Howard, *The King–Crane Commission: An American Inquiry in the Middle East* (Beirut, 1963).
119. Andrew and Kanya-Forstner, *France Overseas*, pp. 156–7.
120. E. Kedourie, *England and the Middle East: The Destruction of the Ottoman Empire, 1914–1921* (repr., Hassocks, 1978), 113–17.
121. Dockrill and Goold, *Peace*, p. 139; Nevakivi, *Arab Middle East*, p. 81; Andrew and Kanya-Forstner, *France Overseas*, pp. 161–2. On Anglo-French relations and the Arab Middle East, these are the most useful works. But see also Helmreich, *Paris to Sèvres*, for the best general account of the Ottoman settlement.
122. Andrew and Kanya-Forstner, *France Overseas*, p. 162; cf. Lloyd George, *Truth*, ii. 1022–6.
123. Kedourie, *England*, p. 135.
124. For this see generally Helmreich, *Paris to Sèvres*; Goold and Dockrill, *Peace*, ch. 5.
125. On the background to Anglo-Greek relations and the Smyrna dispute see M. L. Smith, *Ionian Vision: Greece in Asia Minor, 1919–1922* (London, 1973), chs. 1–3; A. E. Montgomery, 'Lloyd George and the Greek Question, 1918–1922', in Taylor (ed.), *Lloyd George*, pp. 255–84. Also helpful is J. G. Darwin, 'The Chanak Crisis and the British Cabinet', *H* 65/213 (1980), 32–48.
126. R. H. Davison, 'Turkish Diplomacy from Mudros to Lausanne', in G. A. Craig and F. Gilbert (eds.), *The Diplomats, 1919–1939* (Princeton, 1953), ch. 6; S. R. Sonyel, *Turkish Diplomacy, 1918–1923:*

Mustafa Kemal and the Turkish National Movement (London and Beverly Hills, 1975).

127. On peacemaking see, apart from Helmreich, *Paris to Sèvres* and Goold and Dockrill, *Peace*, the article by A. E. Montgomery, 'The Making of the Treaty of Sèvres of 10 August 1920', *HJ* 15/4 (1972), 775–87.

128. See A. L. MacFie, 'The British Decision Regarding the Future of Constantinople, November 1918–January 1920', *HJ* 18/2 (1975), 391–400.

129. For a discussion of the Armenian issue, A. Nassibian, *Britain and the Armenian Question, 1915–1923* (London, 1984).

130. For the text of the Sèvres treaty, L. W. Martin (ed.), *The Treaties of Peace, 1919–1923* (2 vols., New York, 1924), ii. 789–941.

Notes to Conclusion

1. No attempt will be made to indicate the reading available on all the topics touched on in this conclusion. But see P. M. H. Bell, *The Origins of the Second World War in Europe* (London, 1986) for a good, up-to-date account of its theme. On the battle in the American Senate over the League of Nations see the sources referred to in ch. 6, n. 20; on the Washington Conference see T. H. Buckley, *The United States and the Washington Conference, 1921–1922* (Knoxville, Tenn., 1970), R. Dingman, *Power in the Pacific: The Origin of Naval Arms Limitation, 1914–1922* (Chicago, 1976), Nish, *Alliance*, and Nish, *Japanese Foreign Policy*; and on the Polish–Soviet War see N. Davies, *White Eagle, Red Star: The Polish–Soviet War, 1919–20* (London, 1972).

2. The Treaty provided for a freeze on new construction of battleships and battlecruisers, and set tonnage limits of 525,000 each for Britain and the USA, 175,000 each for Italy and France, and 315,000 for Japan.

3. L. E. Ambrosius, 'Wilson, the Republicans, and French Security after World War I', *JAH* 59/2 (1972), 341–52.

4. Hewes, 'Cabot Lodge', p. 249.

5. An impressive new literature on Franco-German relations in the 1920s has appeared since the opening of the French archives. For an introduction to it, see J. Jacobson, 'Strategies of French Foreign Policy after World War I', *JMH* 55/1 (1983), 78–95; and the same author's 'Is There a New International History of the 1920s?', *AHR* 86/3 (1983), 617–45. See also the important article by S. A. Schuker, 'France and the Remilitarization of the Rhineland, 1936', *French Historical Studies* 14/3 (1986), 299–338.

6. For the stabilizing factors in Soviet-American relations, see J. L. Gaddis, 'The Long Peace: Elements of Stability in the Postwar International System', *International Security* 10/4 (1986), 99–142.

7. L. Tolstoy, *War and Peace* (Pan books edn., London, 1972), 655–6. For two fine discussions of the motivation of the combatants, see J. Keegan, *The Face of Battle* (London, 1976) and D. Winter, *Death's Men: Soldiers of the Great War* (Harmondsworth, 1978).

BIBLIOGRAPHY

Parts of this book are based on research in the British, French, and Belgian archives. For the sources there consulted see the author's *French War Aims against Germany, 1914-1919* (Oxford, 1982), 224-5; and 'Belgium, Luxemburg, and the Defence of Western Europe, 1914-1920', *IHR* 4/4 (1982), 504 n. Other sources used are listed here under four headings:

    I. Published Documentary Material;
    II. Memoirs and Other Primary Accounts;
    III. Secondary Works: Books and Theses;
    IV. Secondary Works: Articles.

I. *Published Documentary Material*

BROWDER, R. P., and KERENSKY, A. F. (eds.), *The Russian Provisional Government, 1917* (3 vols., Stanford, 1961).

DEGRAS, J. (ed.), *Soviet Documents on Foreign Policy* (3 vols., London, 1951-3).

FELDMAN, G. D., *German Imperialism, 1914-1918: The Development of a Historical Debate* (New York, 1972).

FRUS: Papers Relating to the Foreign Relations of the United States, 1914, 1915, 1916, 1917, 1918, 1919 (Washington, 1928-33); *Papers Relating to the Foreign Relations of the United States: The Lansing Papers, 1914-1920* (2 vols., Washington, 1939); *Papers Relating to the Foreign Relations of the United States: The Paris Peace Conference, 1919* (13 vols., Washington, 1942-7).

GEISS, I. (ed.), *July 1914: The Outbreak of the First World War* (London, 1967).

GWYNN, S. (ed.), *The Letters and Friendships of Sir Cecil Spring Rice* (2 vols., London, 1929).

HUREWITZ, J. C. (ed.), *Diplomacy in the Near and Middle East: A Documentary Record* (2 vols., Princeton, 1956).

KAJIMA, M., *The Diplomacy of Japan, 1894-1922* (vol. iii, Tokyo, 1980).

KOMJÁTHY, M. (ed.), *Protokolle des Gemeinsamen Ministerrates der Österreichischen-Ungarischen Monarchie (1914-1918)* (Budapest, 1966).

MANTOUX, P., *Les Délibérations du Conseil des Quatre (24 mars-28 juin 1919): Notes de l'officier interprète Paul Mantoux* (2 vols., Paris, 1955).

MARTIN, L. W. (ed.), *The Treaties of Peace, 1919-1923* (2 vols., New York, 1924).

L'Opinion, 10, 24, 31 July 1920. Three articles on the Armand-Revertera conversations.

SCHERER, A., and GRÜNEWALD, J. (eds.), *L'Allemagne et les problèmes de la paix pendant la Première Guerre Mondiale* (4 vols., Paris, 1966-78).

SCOTT, J. B. (ed.), *Official Statements of War Aims and Peace Proposals, December 1916-November 1918* (Washington, 1921).

STEVENSON, D. (ed.), *The First World War, 1914-1918* (12 vols., Frederick, Maryland, forthcoming), in Bourne, K., and Cameron Watt, D. (eds.), *British Documents on Foreign Affairs: Reports and Papers from the Foreign Office Confidential Print*.

ZEMAN, Z. A. B. (ed.), *Germany and the Revolution in Russia, 1915-1918: Documents from the Archives of the German Foreign Ministry* (London, 1958).

II. *Memoirs and Other Primary Accounts*

ASQUITH, H. H., *Memories and Reflections, 1852-1927* (2 vols., London, 1928).

BAKER, R. S., *Woodrow Wilson and World Settlement* (3 vols., London, 1923).

BETHMANN HOLLWEG, T. von, *Betrachtungen zum Weltkriege* (2 vols., Berlin, 1919).

BRUCE LOCKHART, R. B., *Memoirs of a British Agent: Being an Account of the Author's Early Life in Many Lands and of his Official Mission to Moscow in 1918* (repr., London, 1974).

BUCHANAN, G., *My Mission to Russia, and other Diplomatic Memories* (2 vols., London, 1923).

BURIÁN, S., *Austria in Dissolution* (London, 1925).

CECIL, R., *A Great Experiment* (London, 1941).

CLEMENCEAU, G., *Grandeurs et misères d'une victoire* (Paris, 1930).

CZERNIN, O., *In the World War* (London, 1919).

DJEMAL Pasha, *Memoirs of a Turkish Statesman, 1913-1919* (London, 1922).

FALKENHAYN, E. von, *General Headquarters, 1914-1916, and its Critical Decisions* (London, 1919).

GIOLITTI, G., *Memoirs of My Life* (London, 1923).

GREY, E., *Twenty-Five Years, 1892-1916* (2 vols., London, 1925).

HANKEY, M., *The Supreme Command, 1914-1918* (2 vols., London, 1961).

—— *The Supreme Control at the Paris Peace Conference: A Commentary* (London, 1963).

HEADLAM-MORLEY, J., *A Memoir of the Paris Peace Conference, 1919*, eds.

A. Headlam-Morley, R. Bryant, and A. Cienciala (London, 1972).

HINDENBURG, P. von, *Out of My Life* (London, 1920).

HOUSTON, D. F., *Eight Years with Wilson's Cabinet, 1913–1920* (2 vols., London, 1926).

ISHII, K., *Diplomatic Commentaries* (Baltimore, 1936).

KEYNES, J. M., *The Economic Consequences of the Peace* (London, 1920).

KÜHLMANN, R. von, *Erinnerungen* (Heidelberg, 1948).

LANSING, R., *War Memoirs of Robert Lansing* (Indianapolis and New York, 1935).

LLOYD GEORGE, D., *War Memoirs* (6 vols., London, 1933–6).

—— *The Truth about the Peace Treaties* (2 vols., London, 1938).

LUDENDORFF, P. W. E., *My War Memories, 1914–1918* (2 vols., London, 1919).

MAX OF BADEN, Prince, *Memoirs* (2 vols., London, 1928).

MILLER, D. H., *The Drafting of the Covenant* (2 vols., New York, 1928).

NICOLSON, H., *Peacemaking, 1919* (new edn., London, 1937).

PALÉOLOGUE, M., *La Russie des Tsars pendant la Grande Guerre* (3 vols., Paris, 1921–2).

POINCARÉ, R., *Au service de la France: Neuf années de souvenirs* (10 vols., Paris, 1926–33).

—— *A la recherche de la paix, 1919*, ed. J. Bariéty and P. Miquel (Paris, 1974).

RATHENAU, W., *Tagebuch, 1907–1922*, ed. H. Pogge von Strandmann, (Düsseldorf, 1967).

RIBOT, A., *Journal d'Alexandre Ribot et correspondances inédites, 1914–1922*, ed. A. Ribot (Paris, 1936).

RIDDELL, G. A., *Lord Riddell's War Diary, 1914–1918* (London, 1932).

—— *Lord Riddell's Intimate Diary of the Peace Conference and After, 1918–1923* (London, 1933).

RIEZLER, K., *Tagebücher, Aufsätze, Dokumente*, ed. K.-D. Erdmann (Göttingen, 1972).

SALANDRA, A., *Italy and the Great War* (London, 1932).

SAZONOV, S. D., *Fateful Years, 1909–1916* (London, 1928).

SEYMOUR, C. M. (ed.), *The Intimate Papers of Colonel House* (4 vols., London, 1926–8).

SIXTE DE BOURBON, Prince, *L'Offre de paix séparée de l'Autriche (5 décembre 1916–12 octobre 1917)* (Paris, 1920).

SPEARS, E., *Liaison 1914: A Narrative of the Great Retreat* (2nd edn., London, 1968).

TARDIEU, A., *La Paix* (Paris, 1921).

—— *Le Slesvig et la Paix, janvier 1919–janvier 1920* (Paris, 1928).

TAUBE, M. de, *La Politique russe d'avant-guerre et la fin de l'Empire des Tsars (1904–17)* (Paris, 1928).

TROTSKY, L., *My Life: The Rise and Fall of a Dictator* (London, 1930).

III. Secondary Works: Books and Theses

ALBERTINI, L., *The Origins of the War of 1914* (3 vols., London, 1957).

ALBRECHT-CARRIÉ, R., *Italy at the Paris Peace Conference* (New York, 1938).

ANDERSON, M. S., *The Eastern Question, 1774–1923: A Study in International Relations* (London, 1966).

ANDREW, C. M., and Kanya-Forstner, A. S., *France Overseas: The Great War and the Climax of French Imperial Expansion* (London, 1981).

BAILEY, T. A., *Woodrow Wilson and the Lost Peace* (New York, 1944).

—— *Woodrow Wilson and the Great Betrayal* (New York, 1945).

BARIÉTY, J., 'De l'exécution à la négociation: L'évolution des relations franco-allemandes après la Première Guerre Mondiale (11 novembre 1918–10 janvier 1925): Forces profondes et actions politiques', (University of Paris I thesis, 1975).

—— *Les Relations franco-allemandes après la Première Guerre Mondiale, 11 novembre 1918–10 janvier 1925: De l'exécution à la négociation* (Paris, 1977).

BAUMGART, W., *Deutsche Ostpolitik, 1918: Von Brest-Litovsk bis zum Ende des Ersten Weltkrieges* (Vienna and Munich, 1966).

BECKER, J.-J., *1914: Comment les Français sont entrés dans la guerre* (Paris, 1977).

—— *The Great War and the French People* (Leamington Spa, 1985).

BEERS, B. F., *Vain Endeavour: Robert Lansing's Attempts to End the American-Japanese Rivalry* (Durham, North Carolina, 1962).

BERGHAHN, V. R., *Germany and the Approach of War in 1914* (London, 1973).

—— and KITCHEN, M. (eds.), *Germany in the Age of Total War* (London, 1981).

BIRNBAUM, K. E., *Peace Moves and U-Boat Warfare: A Study of Imperial Germany's Policy towards the United States, April 18, 1916–January 9, 1917* (Uppsala, 1958).

BOND, B., and ROY, I. (eds.), *War and Society: A Yearbook of Military History* (London, 1975).

BOSWORTH, R. J. B., *Italy, the Least of the Great Powers: Italian Foreign Policy before the First World War* (London, 1979).

—— *Italy and the Approach of the First World War* (London, 1983).

BOURNE, K., and WATT, D. C. (eds.), *Studies in International History* (London, 1967).

BRADLEY, J., *Allied Intervention in Russia* (London, 1968).

BRIDGE, F. R., *From Sadowa to Sarajevo: The Foreign Policy of Austria-Hungary, 1866–1914* (London, 1972).

BUNSELMEYER, R. E., *The Cost of the War, 1914–1919: British Economic War Aims and the Origins of Reparation* (Hamden, Conn., 1975).

BURK, K., *Britain, America, and the Sinews of War, 1914–1918* (Boston and London, 1985).

BURNETT, P. M., *Reparation at the Paris Peace Conference (from the Standpoint of the American Delegation)* (2 vols., New York, 1940).

BUSCH, B. C., *Britain, India, and the Arabs, 1914–1921* (Berkeley, 1971).

—— *Mudros to Lausanne: Britain's Frontier in West Asia, 1918–1923* (Albany, NY, 1976).

CALDER, K. J., *Britain and the Origins of the New Europe, 1914–1918* (Cambridge, 1976).

CARLEY, M. J., *Revolution and Intervention: The French Government and the Russian Civil War, 1917–1919* (Kingston, Ontario, and Montreal, 1983).

CARR, E. H., *The Bolshevik Revolution, 1917–1923* (3 vols., Harmondsworth, 1966).

CHAMBERS, F. P., *The War behind the War, 1914–1918: A History of the Political and Civilian Fronts* (London, 1939).

CHI, M., *China Diplomacy, 1914–1918* (Cambridge, Mass., 1970).

COOGAN, J. W., *The End of Neutrality: The United States, Britain, and Maritime Rights, 1899–1915* (Ithaca, NY, and London, 1981).

COOPER, J. M., jun., *The Vanity of Power: American Isolationism and the First World War, 1914–1917* (Westport, Conn., 1969).

COSTIGLIOLA, F., *Awkward Dominion: American Political, Economic, and Cultural Relations with Europe, 1919–1933* (Ithaca, NY, 1984).

CRAIG, G. A., *The Politics of the Prussian Army, 1640–1945* (London, 1955).

—— *Germany, 1866–1945* (Oxford, 1978).

—— and GILBERT, F. (eds.), *The Diplomats, 1919–1939* (Princeton, 1953).

CRAMPTON, R. J., *The Hollow Détente: Anglo-German Relations in the Balkans, 1911–1914* (London, 1980).

CRUTTWELL, C. R. M. F., *A History of the Great War, 1914–1918* (2nd edn., Oxford, 1936).

CURRY, R. W., *Woodrow Wilson and Far Eastern Policy, 1913–1921* (repr., New York, 1968).

DAKIN, D., *The Unification of Greece, 1770–1923* (New York, 1972).

DALLIN, A., et al., *Russian Diplomacy and Eastern Europe, 1914–1917* (New York, 1963).

DÉAK, F., *Hungary at the Paris Peace Conference: The Diplomatic History of the Treaty of Trianon* (New York, 1942).

DEBO, R. K., *Revolution and Survival: The Foreign Policy of Soviet Russia, 1917–1918* (Toronto, 1979).

DEDIJER, V., *The Road to Sarajevo* (New York, 1966).

DEVLIN, P. A., *Too Proud to Fight: Woodrow Wilson's Neutrality* (London, 1974).

362 BIBLIOGRAPHY

DOCKRILL, M. L., and GOOLD, J. D., *Peace without Promise: Britain and the Peace Conferences, 1919–1923* (London, 1981).

DUROSELLE, J. -B., *La France et les Français, 1914–1920* (Paris, 1972).

EGERTON, G. W., *Great Britain and the Creation of the League of Nations: Strategy, Politics, and International Organization, 1914–1919* (Chapel Hill, 1978).

ELCOCK, H., *Portrait of a Decision: The Council of Four and the Treaty of Versailles* (London, 1972).

EPSTEIN, K., *Matthias Erzberger and the Dilemma of German Democracy* (Princeton, 1959).

FAINSOD, M., *International Socialism and the World War* (repr., New York, 1973).

FARRAR, L. L., *The Short-War Illusion: German Policy, Strategy, and Domestic Affairs, August–December 1914* (Santa Barbara, 1973).

—— *Divide and Conquer: German Efforts to Conclude a Separate Peace, 1914–1918* (New York, 1978).

FELDMAN, G. D., *Army, Industry, and Labour in Germany, 1914–1918* (Princeton, 1966).

FERRO, M., *The Great War, 1914–1918* (London, 1973).

FEST, W. B., *Peace or Partition: The Habsburg Monarchy and British Policy, 1914–1918* (London, 1978).

FIFIELD, R. H., *Woodrow Wilson and the Far East: The Diplomacy of the Shantung Question* (New York, 1952).

FISCHER, F., *Germany's Aims in the First World War* (London, 1967).

—— *War of Illusions: German Policies from 1911 to 1914* (London, 1975).

FLOTO, I., *Colonel House in Paris: A Study of American Policy at the Paris Peace Conference, 1919* (Aarhus, 1973).

FOWLER, W. B., *British–American Relations, 1914–1918: The Role of Sir William Wiseman* (Princeton, 1969).

FRIEDMAN, I., *The Question of Palestine, 1914–1918: British–Jewish–Arab Relations* (London, 1973).

GARRATY, J. A., *Henry Cabot Lodge: A Biography* (New York, 1953).

GATZKE, H. W., *Germany's Drive to the West: a Study of Western War Aims during the First World War* (Baltimore, 1950).

GEISS, I., *Der Polnische Grenzstreifen, 1914–1918: Ein Beitrag zur Deutschen Kriegszielpolitik im Ersten Weltkrieg* (Lübeck and Hamburg, 1960).

—— *German Foreign Policy, 1871–1914* (London, 1976).

GELFAND, L. E., *The Inquiry: American Preparations for Peace, 1917–1919* (New Haven, 1963).

GIRAULT, R., *Emprunts russes et investissements français en Russie, 1887–1914* (Paris, 1973).

GOTTLIEB, W. W., *Studies in Secret Diplomacy during the First World War* (London, 1957).

GREGORY, R., *The Origins of American Intervention in the First World War* (New York, 1971).

GRENVILLE, J. A. S., and Young, G., *Politics, Strategy, and American Diplomacy: Studies in Foreign Policy, 1873-1917* (New Haven and London, 1966).

GUINN, P., *British Strategy and Politics, 1914-1918* (Oxford, 1965).

HANAK, H., *Great Britain and Austria-Hungary during the First World War: A Study in the Formation of Public Opinion* (London, 1962).

HARDACH, G., *The First World War, 1914-1918* (London, 1977).

HAUPT, G., *Socialism and the Great War: The Collapse of the Second International* (Oxford, 1972).

HAUPTS, L., *Deutsche Friedenspolitik, 1918-1919: Eine Alternative zur Machtpolitik des Ersten Weltkrieges* (Düsseldorf, 1976).

HAZLEHURST, C., *Politicians at War, July 1914 to May 1915: A Prologue to the Triumph of Lloyd George* (London, 1971).

HELMREICH, J. E., *Belgium and Europe: A Study in Small Power Diplomacy* (The Hague, 1976).

HELMREICH, P. C., *From Paris to Sèvres: The Partition of the Ottoman Empire at the Peace Conference of 1919-1920* (Columbus, Ohio, 1974).

HINSLEY, F. H. (ed.), *British Foreign Policy under Sir Edward Grey* (Cambridge, 1977).

HÖLZLE, E., *Die Selbstentmachtung Europas: Das Experiment des Friedens vor und im Ersten Weltkrieg* (Frankfurt and Zürich, 1975).

HOVI, K., *Cordon sanitaire or barrière de l'est? The Emergence of the New French Eastern European Alliance Policy 1917-1919* (Turku, 1975).

HOWARD, H. N., *The Partition of Turkey: A Diplomatic History, 1913-1923* (Norman, Oklahoma, 1931).

—— *The King-Crane Commission: An American Inquiry in the Middle East* (Beirut, 1963).

HULL, I. V., *The Entourage of Kaiser Wilhelm II, 1888-1918* (Cambridge, 1982).

HUNT, B., and PRESTON, A. (eds.) *War Aims and Strategic Policy in the Great War, 1914-1918* (London, 1977).

JAFFE, L. S., *The Decision to Disarm Germany: British Policy towards Postwar German Disarmament, 1914-1919* (London, 1985).

JANSEN, M. B., *The Japanese and Sun Yat-sen* (Cambridge, Mass., 1954).

JARAUSCH, K. H., *The Enigmatic Chancellor: Bethmann Hollweg and the Hubris of Imperial Germany* (New Haven, 1973).

JOLL, J., *The Second International, 1889-1914* (London, 1955).

—— *The Origins of the First World War* (London, 1984).

KANN, R. A., *Die Sixtusaffäre und die geheimen Friedensverhandlungen Österreich-Ungarns im ersten Weltkrieg* (Vienna, 1966).

KASPI, A., *Le Temps des Américains: Le concours américain à la France en 1917-1918* (Paris, 1976).

KEDOURIE, E., *England and the Middle East: The Destruction of the Ottoman Empire, 1914–1921* (repr., Hassocks, 1978).

—— *In the Anglo-Arab Labyrinth: The McMahon–Husayn Correspondence and its Interpretations 1914–1939* (Cambridge, 1976).

KEEGAN, J., *The Face of Battle* (London, 1976).

KEIGER, J. F. V., *France and the Origins of the First World War* (London, 1983).

KENNAN, G. F., *Soviet–American Relations, 1917–1920* (2 vols., London, 1956–8).

KENNEDY, D. M., *Over Here: The First World War and American Society* (New York and Oxford, 1980).

KENNEDY, P. M., *The Rise of the Anglo-German Antagonism, 1860–1914* (London, 1982).

—— (ed.), *The War Plans of the Great Powers, 1880–1914* (London, 1979).

KENT, M. (ed.), *The Great Powers and the End of the Ottoman Empire* (London, 1984).

KIMCHE, J., *The Unromantics: The Great Powers and the Balfour Declaration* (London, 1968).

KING, J. C., *Generals and Politicians: Conflict between France's High Command, Parliament, and Government, 1914–1918* (Berkeley and Los Angeles, 1951).

—— *Foch versus Clemenceau: France and German Dismemberment, 1918–1919* (Cambridge, Mass., 1960).

KIRBY, D., *War, Peace, and Revolution: International Socialism at the Crossroads, 1914–1918* (London, 1986).

KITCHEN, M., *The Silent Dictatorship: The Politics of the German High Command under Hindenburg and Ludendorff, 1916–1918* (London, 1976).

KOCH, H. W. (ed.), *The Origins of the First World War: Great Power Rivalry and German War Aims* (London, 1972).

KOMARNICKI, T., *Rebirth of the Polish Republic: A Study in the Diplomatic History of Europe, 1914–1920* (London, 1957).

KRIEGER, L., and Stern, F. (eds.), *The Responsibility of Power* (New York, 1967).

KRÜGER, P., *Deutschland und die Reparationen, 1918–1919: Die Genesis des Reparationsproblems in Deutschland zwischen Waffenstillstand und Versailler Friedensschluss* (Stuttgart, 1973).

LA FARGUE, T. E., *China and the World War* (Stanford, 1937).

LANGHORNE, R. T. B., *The Collapse of the Concert of Europe: International Politics, 1890–1914* (London, 1981).

LEDERER, I. J., *Yugoslavia at the Paris Peace Conference: A Study in Frontier-making* (New Haven and London, 1963).

LEON, G. B., *Greece and the Great Powers, 1914–1917* (Thessaloniki, 1974).

LEVIN, N. G., jun., *Woodrow Wilson and World Politics: America's Response to War and Revolution* (New York, 1968).

LIDDELL HART, B. H., *History of the First World War* (London, 1970).

LIEVEN, D. C. B., *Russia and the origins of the First World War* (London, 1983).

LINK, A. S., *Wilson* (5 vols., Princeton, 1947–65).

LOUIS, W. R., *Great Britain and Germany's Lost Colonies, 1914–1919* (Oxford, 1967).

LOWE, C. J., and Dockrill, M. L., *The Mirage of Power: British Foreign Policy, 1914–1922* (3 vols., London, 1972).

LOWE, C. J., and Marzari, F., *Italian Foreign Policy, 1870–1940* (London, 1975).

LOWE, P., *Great Britain and Japan, 1911–1915: a Study of British Far Eastern Policy* (London, 1969).

LUCKAU, A., *The German Delegation at the Paris Peace Conference* (New York, 1941).

LUNDGREEN-NIELSEN, K., *The Polish Problem at the Paris Peace Conference: A Study of the Great Powers and the Poles, 1918–1919* (Odense, 1979).

MACARTNEY, C. A., *The Habsburg Empire, 1790–1918* (London, 1969).

McDOUGALL, W. A., *France's Rhineland Diplomacy, 1914–1924: The Last Bid for a Balance of Power in Europe* (Princeton, 1978).

McNEILL, W. H., *The Pursuit of Power: Technology, Armed Force, and Society since A.D. 1000* (Oxford, 1983).

MAMATEY, V., *The United States and East Central Europe, 1914–1918: A Study in Wilsonian Diplomacy and Propaganda* (Princeton, 1957).

MARDER, A. J., *From the Dreadnought to Scapa Flow: The Royal Navy in the Fisher Era, 1904–1919* (5 vols., London, 1961–70).

MARKS, S., *The Illusion of Peace: International Relations in Europe, 1918–1933* (London, 1976).

—— *Innocent Abroad: Belgium at the Paris Peace Conference of 1919* (Chapel Hill, 1981).

MARSTON, F. S., *The Peace Conference of 1919: Organization and Procedure* (Oxford, 1944).

MARTIN, L. W., *Peace Without Victory: Woodrow Wilson and the British Liberals* (New Haven, 1958).

MAY, E. R., *The World War and American Isolation, 1914–1917* (Cambridge, Mass., 1959).

—— (ed.), *Knowing One's Enemies: Intelligence Assessment before the Two World Wars* (Princeton, 1984).

MAYER, A. J., *Political Origins of the New Diplomacy, 1917–1918* (New Haven, 1959).

—— *Politics and Diplomacy of Peacemaking: Containment and Counter-Revolution at Versailles, 1918–1919* (London, 1968).

MEYER, H. C., *Mitteleuropa in German Thought and Action, 1815–1945* (The Hague, 1955).

MIQUEL, P., *La Paix de Versailles et l'opinion publique française* (Paris, 1972).

MITRAKOS, A., *France in Greece during World War I: A Study in the Politics of Power* (New York, 1982).

MORLEY, J. W., *The Japanese Thrust into Siberia, 1918* (New York, 1957).

NÀSSIBIAN, A., *Britain and the Armenian Question, 1915–1923* (London, 1984).

NELSON, H. I., *Land and Power: British and Allied Policy on Germany's Frontiers, 1916–1919* (London, 1963).

NELSON, K. L., *Victors Divided: America and the Allies in Germany, 1918–1923* (Berkeley, Los Angeles, and London, 1975).

NEVAKIVI, J., *Britain, France, and the Arab Middle East, 1914–1920* (London, 1969).

NISH, I. H., *Alliance in Decline: A Study in Anglo-Japanese Relations, 1908–1923* (London, 1972).

—— *Japanese Foreign Policy, 1869–1942: Kasumigaseki to Miyakezaku* (London, 1977).

NORTHEDGE, F. S., *The Troubled Giant: Britain among the Great Powers, 1916–1939* (London, 1966).

OSGOOD, R. E., *Ideals and Self-Interest in American Foreign Relations: The Great Transformation of the Twentieth Century* (Chicago, 1953).

PARSONS, E. B., *Wilsonian Diplomacy: Allied–American Rivalries in War and Peace* (St Louis, 1978).

PEDRONCINI, G., *Les Négociations secrètes pendant la Grande guerre* (Paris, 1969).

PERMAN, D., *The Shaping of the Czechoslovak State: Diplomatic History of the Boundaries of Czechoslovakia, 1914–1920* (Leiden, 1962).

POIDEVIN, R., and Bariéty, J., *Les Relations franco-allemandes, 1815–1975* (Paris, 1977).

RENOUVIN, P., *L'Armistice de Rethondes, 11 novembre 1918* (Paris, 1968).

—— *La Crise européenne et la Première Guerre Mondiale (1904–1918)* (5th edn., Paris, 1969).

RITTER, G., *The Schlieffen Plan: Critique of a Myth* (London, 1958).

—— *The Sword and the Sceptre: The Problem of Militarism in Germany* (4 vols., London, 1969–73).

ROBBINS, K., *The First World War* (Oxford, 1984).

RÖHL, J. C. G. (ed.), *1914: Delusion or Design: The Testimony of Two German Diplomats* (London, 1973).

ROTHWELL, V. H., *British War Aims and Peace Diplomacy, 1914–1918* (Oxford, 1971).

RUDIN, H., *Armistice 1918* (New Haven, 1944).

RYDER, A. J., *The German Revolution of 1918: A Study of German Socialism in War and Revolt* (Cambridge, 1967).

SAFFORD, J. J., *Wilsonian Maritime Diplomacy, 1913-1921* (New Brunswick, 1978).

SCHULZ, G., *Revolutions and Peace Treaties, 1917-1920* (London, 1972).

SCHWABE, K., *Deutsche Revolution und Wilson-Frieden: Die Amerikanische und Deutsche Friedensstrategie zwischen Ideologie und Machtpolitik, 1918-1919* (Düsseldorf, 1971).

SETON-WATSON, C., *Italy from Liberalism to Fascism* (London, 1967).

SILBERSTEIN, G. E., *The Troubled Alliance: German–Austrian Relations, 1914 to 1917* (Lexington, Ky., 1970).

SILVERMAN, D. P., *Reconstructing Europe after the Great War* (Cambridge, Mass., and London, 1982).

SINANOGLOU, I., 'France looks Eastward: Policies and Perspectives in Russia, 1914-1918' (Columbia University PhD thesis, 1974).

SMITH, C. J., *The Russian Struggle for Power, 1914-1917: A Study of Russian Foreign Policy during the First World War* (New York, 1956).

SMITH, D. M., *The Great Departure: The United States and World War I, 1914-1920* (New York, 1965).

SMITH, M. L., *Ionian Vision: Greece in Asia Minor, 1919-1922* (London, 1973).

SNYDER, J., *The Ideology of the Offensive: Military Decision Making and the Disasters of 1914* (Ithaca, NY, 1984).

SONYEL, S. R., *Turkish Diplomacy, 1918-1923: Mustafa Kemal and the Turkish National Movement* (London and Beverley Hills, 1975).

SPECTOR, S. D., *Rumania at the Paris Peace Conference: A Study in the Diplomacy of Ion I. C. Bratianu* (New York, 1962).

STEGLICH, W., *Die Friedenspolitik der Mittelmächte, 1917-1918*, vol. i (Wiesbaden, 1964).

STEIN, L., *The Balfour Declaration* (London, 1961).

STEINER, Z. S., *Britain and the Origins of the First World War* (London, 1977).

STEVENSON, D., *French War Aims against Germany, 1914-1919* (Oxford, 1982).

STONE, N., *The Eastern Front, 1914-1917* (London, 1975).

STRACHAN, H. F. A., *European Armies and the Conduct of War* (London, 1983).

SWARTZ, M., *The Union of Democratic Control in British Politics during the First World War* (Oxford, 1971).

TAYLOR, A. J. P., *The First World War: An Illustrated History* (London, 1963).

—— *War by Timetable: How the First World War Began* (London, 1969).

—— *English History, 1914-1945* (Harmondsworth, 1970).

TAYLOR, A. J. P., *The Struggle for Mastery in Europe, 1848–1918* (pb. edn., Oxford, 1971).
—— and Pares, R. (eds.), *Essays Presented to Sir Lewis Namier* (London, 1956).
—— (ed.), *Lloyd George: Twelve Essays* (London, 1971).
TEMPERLEY, H. W. V. (ed.), *A History of the Peace Conference of Paris* (6 vols., London, 1920–24).
THAYER, A. J., *Italy and the Great War: Politics and Culture, 1870–1915* (Madison, Wisconsin, 1964).
THOMAS, D. H., *The Guarantee of Belgian Independence and Neutrality in European Diplomacy, 1830s–1930s* (Kingston, Rhode Island, 1983).
THOMPSON, J. M., *Russia, Bolshevism, and the Versailles Peace* (Princeton, 1966).
TILLMAN, S. P., *Anglo-American Relations at the Paris Peace Conference of 1919* (Princeton, 1961).
TRACHTENBERG, M., *Reparation in World Politics: France and European Economic Diplomacy, 1916–1923* (New York, 1980).
TRASK, D. F., *The United States in the Supreme War Council: American War Aims and Inter-Allied Strategy, 1917–1918* (Westport, Conn., 1961).
TRUMPENER, U., *Germany and the Ottoman Empire, 1914–1918* (Princeton, 1968).
TURNER, L. C. F., *Origins of the First World War* (London, 1970).
ULLMAN, R. H., *Anglo-Soviet Relations, 1917–1921* (3 vols., Princeton, 1961–72).
VALIANI, L., *The End of Austria-Hungary* (London, 1973).
VIERHAUS, R., and BOTZENHART, M. (eds.), *Dauer und Wandel der Geschichte: Aspekte Europäischer Vergangenheit* (Münster, 1966).
WADE, R. A., *The Russian Search for Peace, February–October 1917* (Stanford, 1969).
WALLACE, L. P., and ASKEW, W. C. (eds.), *Power, Public Opinion, and Diplomacy* (Durham, North Carolina, 1959).
WALTERS, F. P., *A History of the League of Nations* (2 vols., London, 1952).
WALWORTH, A., *America's Moment, 1918: American Diplomacy at the End of World War I* (New York, 1977).
WANDYCZ, P. S., *France and her Eastern Allies, 1919–1925: French–Czechoslovak–Polish Relations from the Paris Peace Conference to Locarno* (Minneapolis, 1962).
WATSON, D. R., *Georges Clemenceau: A Political Biography* (London, 1974).
WEILL-RAYNAL, E., *Les Réparations allemandes et la France* (3 vols., Paris, 1947).
WHEELER-BENNETT, J. W., *Brest-Litovsk: The Forgotten Peace, March 1918* (London, 1938).

W<small>HITTAM</small>, J., *The Politics of the Italian Army, 1861-1918* (London, 1977).
W<small>ILLIAMSON</small>, S. R., *The Politics of Grand Strategy: Britain and France Prepare for War, 1904-1914* (Cambridge, Mass., 1969).
—— and Pastor, P. (eds.), *Essays on World War I: Origins and Prisoners of War* (New York, 1983).
W<small>ILSON</small>, K. M., *The Policy of the Entente: Essays on the Determinants of British Foreign Policy, 1904-1914* (Cambridge, 1985).
W<small>INTER</small>, D., *Death's Men: Soldiers of the Great War* (Harmondsworth, 1978).
W<small>OODWARD</small>, E. L., *Great Britain and the War of 1914-1918* (London, 1967).
Y<small>OUNG</small>, H. F., *Prince Lichnowsky and the Great War* (Athens, Georgia, 1977).
Z<small>EMAN</small>, Z. A. B., *A Diplomatic History of the First World War* (London, 1971).
Z<small>IVOJINOVIĆ</small>, D. R., *America, Italy, and the Birth of Yugoslavia (1917-1919)* (New York, 1972).

IV. Secondary Works: Articles

A<small>BRAHAMS</small>, P. P., 'American Bankers and the Economic Tactics of Peace, 1919', *JAH* 56/3 (1969), 572-83.
A<small>MBROSIUS</small>, L. E., 'Wilson, the Republicans, and French Security after World War I', *JAH* 59/2 (1972), 341-52.
A<small>NDREW</small>, C. M., and K<small>ANYA-FORSTNER</small>, A. S., 'The French Colonial Party and French Colonial War Aims, 1914-1918', *HJ* 17/1 (1974), 79-106.
A<small>RTAUD</small>, D., 'Le Gouvernment américain et la question des dettes de guerre au lendemain de l'armistice de Rethondes (1919-1920)', *RHMC* 20 (1973), 201-29.
B<small>ESTUZHEV</small>, I. V., 'Russian Foreign Policy, February-June 1914', *JCH* 1/3 (1966), 92-112.
B<small>RADLEY</small>, J., 'France, Lenin, and the Bolsheviks in 1917-1918', *EHR* 86 (1971), 783-9.
B<small>URK</small>, K., 'Great Britain in the United States, 1917-1918: The Turning Point', *IHR* 1/2 (1979), 228-45.
C<small>AMPBELL</small>, F. G., 'The Struggle for Upper Silesia, 1919-1922', *JMH* 42/3 (1970), 361-85.
C<small>ARLEY</small>, M. J., 'The Origins of French Intervention in the Russian Civil War: A Reappraisal', *JMH* 48/3 (1976), 413-39.
C<small>OLLINS</small>, D. N., 'The Franco-Russian Alliance and Russian Railways, 1891-1914', *HJ* 16/4 (1973), 777-88.

COOPER, J. M., jun., 'The Command of Gold Reversed: American Loans to Britain, 1915-1917', *PHR* 45/2 (1976), 209-30.

—— 'The British Response to the House-Grey Memorandum: New Evidence and New Questions', *JAH* 59/4 (1973), 958-71.

CORRIGAN, W., 'German-Turkish Relations and the Outbreak of War in 1914: A Reassessment', *P & P* 36 (1967), 144-52.

CRAMPTON, R. J., 'The Decline of the Concert of Europe in the Balkans, 1913-14', *Sl. EER* 52/128 (1974), 393-419.

CURRY, G., 'Woodrow Wilson, Jan Smuts, and the Versailles Settlement', *AHR* 66/4 (1961), 968-86.

DARWIN, J. G., 'The Chanak Crisis and the British Cabinet', *H* 65/213 (1980), 32-48.

DAVIES, N., 'Lloyd George and Poland, 1919-1920', *JCH* 6/3 (1971), 132-54.

DEBO, R. K., 'Lloyd George and the Copenhagen Conference of 1919-1920: The Initiation of Anglo-Soviet Negotiations', *HJ* 24/2 (1981), 429-41.

—— 'The Maniulskii Mission: An Early Soviet Effort to Negotiate with France, August 1918-April 1919', *IHR* 8/2 (1986), 214-35.

DOCKRILL, M. L., and Steiner, Z. S., 'The Foreign Office at the Paris Peace Conference in 1919', *IHR* 2/1 (1980), 55-86.

DULL, P. S., 'Count Kato Komei and the Twenty-One Demands', *PHR* 19/2 (1950), 151-61.

DUTTON, D., 'The Deposition of King Constantine of Greece, June 1917: An Episode in Anglo-French Diplomacy', *CJH* 12/3 (1978) 325-45.

DYER, G., 'The Turkish Armistice of 1918', *MES* 8 (1972), 143-78, 313-47.

DYER, P. W., 'German Support of Lenin during World War I', *AJPH* 30/1 (1984), 46-55.

EGERTON, G. W., 'The Lloyd George Government and the Creation of the League of Nations', *AHR* 79/2 (1974), 419-44.

—— 'Britain and the "Great Betrayal": Anglo-American Relations and the Struggle for United States Ratification of the Treaty of Versailles, 1919-1920', *HJ* 21/4 (1978), 885-911.

ELCOCK, H. J., 'Britain and the Russo-Polish Frontier, 1919-1921', *HJ* 12/1 (1969), 137-54.

EPSTEIN, K., 'The Development of German-Austrian War Aims in the Spring of 1917', *JCEA* 17/1 (1957), 24-47.

FARRAR, L. L., 'Opening to the West: German Efforts to Conclude a Separate Peace with England, July 1917-March 1918', *CJH* 10/1 (1975), 73-90.

FEST, W. B., 'British War Aims and German Peace Feelers during the First World War (December 1916-November 1918)', *HJ* 15/2 (1972), 285-308.

FIFIELD, R. H., 'Disposal of the Carolines, Marshalls, and Marianas at the Paris Peace Conference', *AHR* 51/3 (1946), 472–9;

—— 'Japanese Policy towards the Shantung Question at the Paris Peace Conference', *JMH* 23/3 (1951), 265–72.

FOTINO, G., 'La Neutralité roumaine: Une Séance historique au Conseil de la Couronne (3 août 1914)', *Revue des Deux Mondes* (1 Aug. 1930), 529–41.

FRENCH, D., 'The Edwardian Crisis and the Origins of the First World War', *IHR* 4/2 (1982), 207–21.

FRIEDMAN, I., 'The McMahon–Hussein Correspondence and the Question of Palestine', *JCH* 5/2 (1970), 83–122.

FRY, M. G., 'The Imperial War Cabinet, the United States, and the Freedom of the Seas', *Journal of the Royal United Services Institution* 110/640 (1965), 353–62.

—— 'Britain, the Allies, and the Problem of Russia, 1918–1919', *CJH* 2/2 (1967), 62–84.

GILBERT, B. B., 'Pacifist to Interventionist: David Lloyd George in 1911 and 1914. Was Belgium an Issue?', *HJ* 28/4 (1985), 863–85.

GILLON, D. Z., 'The Antecedents of the Balfour Declaration', *MES* 5/2 (1969), 131–50.

GOWEN, R. J., 'Great Britain and the Twenty-One Demands of 1915: Co-operation versus Effacement', *JMH* 43/1 (1971), 76–106.

GROH, D., 'The "Unpatriotic Socialists" and the State', *JCH* 1/4 (1966), 151–77.

HANAK, H., 'The Government, the Foreign Office, and Austria-Hungary, 1914–1918', *Sl.EER* 47/108 (1969), 161–97.

HERWIG, H. H., 'Admirals versus Generals: The War Aims of the Imperial German Navy, 1914–1918', *CEH* 5/1 (1972), 208–33.

—— 'German Policy in the Eastern Baltic Sea in 1918: Expansion or Anti-Bolshevik Crusade?', *SR* 32/2 (1973), 339–57.

HEWES, J. E., jun., 'Henry Cabot Lodge and the League of Nations', *PAPS* 114 (1970), 245–55.

HITCHENS, K., 'The Nationality Problem in Hungary: István Tisza and the Rumanian National Party, 1910–1914', *JMH* 53/4 (1981), 619–51.

HOGAN, M. J., 'The United States and the Problem of International Economic Control: American Attitudes towards European Reconstruction, 1918–1920', *PHR* 44/1 (1975), 84–103.

HOPWOOD, R. F., 'Czernin and the Fall of Bethmann Hollweg', *CJH* 2/2 (1967), 49–61.

HOWORTH, J., 'French Workers and German Workers: The Impossibility of Internationalism, 1900–1914', *EHQ* 15/1 (1985), 71–97.

International Security 9/1 (1984): Special Issue on 'The Great War and the Nuclear Age'.

JANSEN, M. B., 'Yawata, Hanyehping, and the Twenty-One Demands', *PHR* 23/1 (1954), 31–48.

JARAUSCH, K. H., 'The Illusion of Limited War: Bethmann Hollweg's Calculated Risk in July 1914', *CEH* 2/1 (1969), 48–76.

JONES, S., 'Antonio Salandra and the Politics of Italian Intervention in the First World War', *EHQ* 15/2 (1985), 157–73.

KAISER, D. E., 'Germany and the Origins of the First World War', *JMH* 55/3 (1983), 442–74.

KAPP, R. W., 'Divided Loyalties: The German Reich and Austria-Hungary in Austro-German Discussions of War Aims, 1914–1916', *CEH* 17/2, 3 (1984), 120–39.

KEDOURIE, E., 'Cairo and Khartoum on the Arab Question, 1915–1918', *HJ* 7/2 (1964), 280–97.

KENNAN, G. F., 'The Sisson Documents', *JMH* 28/2 (1956), 130–54.

KERNEK, S. J., 'The British Government's Reaction to President Wilson's "Peace" Note of December 1916', *HJ* 13/4 (1970), 721–66.

KERNER, R. J., 'Russia, the Straits, and Constantinople, 1914–1915', *JMH* 1/3 (1929), 400–15.

KIRBY, D., 'International Socialism and the Question of Peace: The Stockholm Conference of 1917', *HJ* 25/3 (1982), 709–16.

LA FARGUE, T. E., 'The Entrance of China into the World War', *PHR* 5/3 (1936), 222–33.

LASCH, C., 'American Intervention in Siberia: A Reinterpretation', *PSQ* 77 (1962), 205–23.

LEBOW, R. N., 'Woodrow Wilson and the Balfour Declaration', *JMH* 40/4 (1968), 501–23.

LONG, J. W., 'American Intervention in Russia: The North Russian Expedition, 1918–1919', *DH* 6/1 (1982), 45–67.

LOUIS, W. R., 'The United States and the African Peace Settlement of 1919: The Pilgrimage of George Louis Beer', *JAfr.H* 4/3 (1963), 413–33.

LOW, A. D., 'The Soviet Hungarian Republic and the Paris Peace Conference', *TAPS*, NS 53/10 (1963), 3–89.

LOWE, C. J., 'The Failure of British Diplomacy in the Balkans, 1914–1916', *CJH* 4/1 (1969), 73–100.

—— 'Britain and Italian Intervention, 1914–1915', *HJ* 12/3 (1969), 533–48.

LOWRY, B., 'Pershing and the Armistice', *JAH* 55 (1968–9), 281–91.

LUNDGREEN-NEILSEN, K., 'The Mayer Thesis Reconsidered: The Poles and the Paris Peace Conference, 1919', *IHR* 7/1 (1985), 68–102.

McCRUM, J. R., 'French Rhineland Policy at the Paris Peace Conference, 1919', *HJ* 21/3 (1978), 623–48.

McDougall, W. A., 'Political Economy versus National Sovereignty: French Structures for German Economic Integration after Versailles', *JMH* 51/1 (1979), 4–23.

MacFie, A. L., 'The British Decision Regarding the Future of Constantinople, November 1918–January 1920', *HJ* 18/2 (1975), 391–400.

May, E. R., 'American Policy and Japan's Entrance into World War I', *MVHR* 40/2 (1953), 279–90.

Mervin, D., 'Henry Cabot Lodge and the League of Nations', *JAS* 4/2 (1970), 201–14.

Meynell, H., 'The Stockholm Conference of 1917', *IRSH* 5 (1960), 1–25, 202–25.

Michaelis, W., 'Der Reichskanzler Michaelis und die Päpstliche Friedensaktion von 1917', *GWU* 7/1 (1956), 14–24.

—— 'Der Reichskanzler Michaelis und die Päpstliche Friedensaktion von 1917: Neue Dokumente', *GWU* 12/7 (1961), 418–34.

Mommsen, W. J., 'Domestic Factors in German Foreign Policy before 1914', *CEH* 6/1 (1973), 3–43.

Montgomery, A. E., 'The Making of the Treaty of Sèvres of 10 August 1920', *HJ* 15/4 (1972), 775–87.

Monticone, A., 'Salandra e Sonnino verso la decisione dell 'intervento', *Rivista di Studi Politici Internazionali* 24/1 (1957), 72–88.

Myers, D. P., 'Berlin versus Vienna: Disagreement about *Anschluss* in the Winter of 1918–1919', *CEH* 5/2 (1972), 150–75.

Neilson, K. E., 'The Break-up of the Anglo-Russian Alliance: The Question of Supply in 1917', *IHR* 3/1 (1981), 62–75.

Offer, A., 'The Working Classes, British Naval Plans, and the Coming of the Great War', *P & P* 107 (1985), 204–26.

Parsons, E. B., 'Why the British Reduced the Flow of American Troops to Europe in August–October 1918', *CJH* 12/2 (1977) 173–91.

Pastor, P., 'The Vix Mission in Hungary, 1918–1919: A Re-examination', *SR* 29/1 (1970), 481–98.

Prete, R. A., 'French Military War Aims, 1914–1916', *HJ* 28/4 (1985), 887–99.

Raffo, P., 'The Anglo-American Preliminary Negotiations for a League of Nations', *JCH* 9/4 (1974), 153–76.

Renouvin, P., 'Le Gouvernement français et les tentatives de paix en 1917', *La Revue des deux mondes* (15 Oct. 1964), 492–513.

—— 'Les Buts de guerre du gouvernement français, 1914–1918', *Revue historique* 235 (1966), 1–38.

Renzi, W. A., 'Italy's Neutrality and Entry into the Great War: A Re-examination', *AHR* 73/5 (1968), 1414–32.

RENZI, W. A., 'Great Britain, Russia, and the Straits, 1914–1915', *JMH* 42/1 (1970), 1–20.

—— 'Who Composed "Sazonov's Thirteen Points"? A Re-examination of Russia's War Aims of 1914', *AHR* 88/2 (1983), 347–57.

ROBBINS, K., 'British Diplomacy and Bulgaria, 1914–1915', *Sl.EER* 49/117 (1971), 560–85.

ROGGER, H., 'Russia in 1914', *JCH* 1/4 (1966), 95–119.

RÖHL, J. C. G., 'Admiral von Müller and the Approach of War, 1911–1914', *HJ* 12/4 (1969), 651–73.

—— 'An der Schwelle zum Weltkrieg: Eine Dokumentation über den "Kriegsrat" vom 8 Dezember 1912', *Militärgeschichtliche Mitteilungen* 1 (1977), 77–134.

ROSE, J. D., 'Batum as Domino, 1919–1920: The Defence of India in Caucasia', *IHR* 11/2 (1980), 266–87.

ROTHWELL, V. H., 'Mesopotamia in British War Aims, 1914–1918', *HJ* 13/2 (1970), 273–94.

SCHMITT, B. E., 'The Italian Documents for July 1914', *JMH* 37/4 (1965), 469–72.

SCHÜDDEKOPF, O.-E., 'German Foreign Policy between Compiègne and Versailles', *JCH* 4/2 (1969), 181–97.

SCHULTE, B. F., 'Zu der Krisenkonferenz vom 8 Dezember 1912 in Berlin', *Historisches Jahrbuch* 102 (1982), 183–97.

SCHWABE, K., 'Woodrow Wilson and Germany's Membership in the League of Nations, 1918–1919', *CEH* 8/1 (1975), 3–22.

SEPIĆ, D., 'The Question of Yugoslav Union in 1918', *JCH* 3/4 (1968), 29–43.

SINANOGLOU, I., 'Frenchmen, their Revolutionary Heritage, and the Russian Revolution', *IHR* 2/4 (1980), 566–84.

SMALLWOOD, J., 'Banquo's Ghost at the Paris Peace Conference: The United States and the Hungarian Question', *EEQ* 12/3 (1978), 289–307.

SMITH, C. J., 'Great Britain and the 1914–1915 Straits Agreement with Russia: The British Promise of November 1914', *AHR* 70/4 (1965), 1015–34.

SNELL, J. L., 'Wilson's Peace Programme and German Socialism, January–March 1918', *MVHR* 38/2 (1951), 187–214.

—— 'Wilson on Germany and the Fourteen Points', *JMH* 26/4 (1954), 364–9.

SOUTOU, G., 'La France et les marches de l'est, 1914–1919', *Revue Historique* 528 (1978), 341–88.

STEVENSON, D., 'French War Aims and the American Challenge, 1914–1918', *HJ* 22/4 (1979), 877–94.

—— 'Belgium, Luxemburg, and the Defence of Western Europe, 1914–1920', *IHR* 4/4 (1982), 504–23.

STONE, N., 'Army and Society in the Habsburg Monarchy, 1900-1914', *P & P* 33 (1966), 95-111.

—— 'Hungary and the Crisis of July 1914', *JCH* 1/3 (1966), 153-70.

SWEET, P. R., 'Leaders and Policies: Germany in the Winter of 1914-15', *JCEA* 16/3 (1956), 229-52.

THOMPSON, W. C., 'The September Program: Reflections on the Evidence', *CEH* 11/4 (1978), 348-54.

TORREY, G. E., 'Rumania and the Belligerents, 1914-1916', *JCH* 1/3 (1966), 171-91.

TRACHTENBERG, M., ' "A New Economic Order": Étienne Clémentel and French Economic Diplomacy during the First World War', *French Historical Studies* 10/2 (1977), 315-41.

—— 'Reparation at the Paris Peace Conference', *JMH* 51/1 (1979), 24-55.

TRANI, E. P., 'Woodrow Wilson and the Decision to Intervene in Russia: A Reconsideration', *JMH* 48/3 (1976), 440-61.

TRUMPENER, U., 'Liman von Sanders and the German-Ottoman Alliance', *JCH* 1/4 (1966), 179-92.

—— 'War Premeditated? German Intelligence Operations in July 1914', *CEH* 9/1 (1976), 58-85.

TURNER, L. C. F. 'The Role of the General Staffs in July 1914', *AJPH* 11/3 (1965), 305-23.

UNTERBERGER, B. M., 'President Wilson and the Decision to Send American Troops to Siberia', *PHR* 24 (1955), 63-74.

VALIANI, L., 'Italo-Austrian Negotiations, 1914-1915', *JCH* 1/3 (1966), 113-36.

VERETÉ, M., 'The Balfour Declaration and its Makers', *MES* 6/1 (1970), 48-76.

VIGEZZI, B., 'Le "Radiose giornate" del maggio 1915 nei rapporti dei prefetti', *Nuova Rivista Storica* 42/3 (1959), 313-44.

WADE, R. A., 'Iraki Tseretelli and Siberian Zimmerwaldianism', *JMH* 39/4 (1967), 425-31.

—— 'Why October? The Search for Peace in 1917', *SS* 20/1 (1968), 36-45.

WARMAN, R. M., 'The Erosion of Foreign Office Influence in the Making of Foreign Policy, 1916-1918', *HJ* 15/1 (1972), 133-59.

WILLIAMSON, S. R., 'Influence, Power, and the Policy Process: The Case of Franz Ferdinand, 1906-1914', *HJ* 17/2 (1974), 417-34.

WILSON, K. M., 'The British Cabinet's Decision for War, 2 August 1914', *BJIS* 1/2 (1975), 148-59.

—— 'Imperial Interests in the British Decision for War, 1914: The Defence of India in Central Asia', *RIS* 10/3 (1984), 189-203.

WILSON, T., 'Britain's "Moral Commitment" to France in August 1914', *H* 64/212 (1979), 80-90.

WINTER, J. M., 'Arthur Henderson, the Russian Revolution, and the Reconstruction of the Labour Party', *HJ* 15/4 (1972), 753-73.

WOODWARD, D. R., 'David Lloyd George, a Negotiated Peace with Germany, and the Kühlmann Peace Kite of September 1917', *CJH* 6/1 (1971), 75-93.

—— 'The British Government and Japanese Intervention in Russia during World War I', *JMH* 46/4 (1974), 663-85.

YOUNG, H. F., 'The Misunderstanding of August 1, 1914', *JMH* 48/4 (1976), 644-65.

ZIVOJINOVIĆ, D., 'Robert Lansing's Comments on the Pontifical Peace Note of August 1, 1917', *JAH* 56/3 (1969), 556-71.

INDEX

Page numbers in bold type refer to major references. Sub-entries are in chronological order where significant.

Printed in the United States
5356